Health Economics

Research in health economics has developed into a separate discipline during the last 25 years. All this intense research activity has come about through the teaching of courses on health economics, mostly at graduate level. However, the Industrial Organization aspects of the health care market do not occupy a central place in those courses. The authors propose a textbook of health economics whose distinguishing feature is the analysis of the health care market from an Industrial Organization perspective. This textbook will provide teachers and students with a reference to study the market structure aspects of the health care sector.

The book is structured in three parts. Part I presents the basic principles of economics. It will bring readers to the required level of knowledge to follow subsequent parts. Part II reviews the main concepts of health economics. Part III contains the core of the book. It presents the Industrial Organization analysis of the health care market, based on the authors' own research.

The book is aimed at graduate students of different backgrounds following courses on health economics, and managers with responsibilities in the governance of health care centers and in policy design. It will also appeal to anyone interested in a proper understanding of the interactions among the agents in the health care market.

Pedro Luis de Oliveira Martins Pita Barros is Professor of Economics at the Universidade Nova de Lisboa, Portugal.

Xavier Martinez-Giralt is Professor of Economics in the Department of Economics and Economic History at the Universitat Autònoma de Barcelona, Spain.

Health Economics

An Industrial Organization perspective

Pedro Pita Barros and
Xavier Martinez-Gira

Routledge
Taylor & Francis Group

LONDON AND NEW YORK

Simultaneously published in the USA and Canada
by Routledge
711 Third Avenue, New York, NY 10017

Routledge is an imprint of the Taylor & Francis Group, an Informa business

British Library Cataloguing in Publication Data
A catalogue record for this book is available from the British Library

Library of Congress Cataloging in Publication Data
Health economics: an industrial organization perspective/by Xavier Martinez-Giralt and Pedro Barros.
    p. cm.
    1. Medical economics. 2. Medical care–Marketing.
    I. Barros, Pedro Pita II. Title.
RA410.5.M38 2011
338.4'73621–dc23   2011017182

ISBN: 978-0-415-55988-1 (hbk)
ISBN: 978-0-415-55989-8 (pbk)
ISBN: 978-0-203-35742-2 (ebk)

Typeset in Times Roman
by Sunrise Setting Ltd, Torquay, UK

Printed and bound in Great Britain by
TJ International Ltd, Padstow, Cornwall

To *Sofia, Henrique, and Carolina*
To *Montse, Ivette, and William*

Contents

x   *Contents*

List of figures

List of tables

Preface

Research in health economics has developed into a separate discipline during the last 25 years. The *Journal of Economics and Management Strategy* devoted two special issues to this in 1998 and 2005. The *Handbook of Health Economics* has two volumes, and recently Elgar published the *Elgar Companion to Health Economics*. The *Journal of Health Economics* and *Health Economics* rank among the most cited journals, and several others are included in the different rankings (ISI, JCR). All this intense research activity has resulted in the inclusion of courses on health economics, mostly at graduate level. However, the Industrial Organizations aspects of the health care market do not occupy a central place in those courses. This book will provide readers with a reference to study the market structure aspects of the health care sector.

Our proposal aims at standardizing the Industrial Organization perspective in the study of health economics. We intend to offer a book to a wide audience ranging from graduate students (with different backgrounds including doctors, nurses, administrators, economists, and managers) to managers in health care institutions worldwide. Also, we intend to capture a wider audience of readers without particular training in economics and/or health economics, interested in better understanding the functioning of the health care sector. Our approach is not an encyclopedic one. Instead, we choose to illustrate the main points with a selected number of works. As in any selection, it is a personal choice and reflects our views for presentation purposes.

To achieve this objective the book is structured in three parts. Part I is addressed to the readers without a specific training in economics. It contains the basic principles of economics that will be used in the other two parts. Part II reviews the main concepts of health economics. Part III contains the core of the book. It presents the Industrial Organization analysis of the health care market.

Wherever technical analysis becomes unavoidable, we use formal analysis, so that the reader can follow the arguments and profit from the reading. Nevertheless, to take full advantage of the book, the reader should have knowledge of basic calculus. We have sacrificed the use of more elaborate settings in favor of simpler models as long as the essential reasoning is present.

In terms of teaching, a full general course of health economics could include Chapters 8, 9, 10, 11, 12, 13, and 17. Also, Chapters 5 and 7 provide some necessary background. A shorter, more focused course in the analysis of competition in the health care market could include Chapter 11 and Part III.

Pedro Pita Barros and Xavier Martinez-Giralt
Lisbon and Barcelona, April 2011

Notations

Symbol	Description
C	Total cost function
c	Marginal cost function
$\bar{c}$	Average cost function
D	Demand function
e	Effort exerted by an agent
F	Production function
H	Health status of the individual
$\mathcal{I}$	Set of consumers
i	Index of consumer $i \in \mathcal{I}$
k	Index of a commodity
$\mathcal{L}_i$	Lerner index of monopoly power
m_j	[Quantity of] input j
p	Price system
p_k	Price of good k
P	Insurance premium
$\mathcal{P}$	Set of preferences
q_k	[Quantity of] good k
q_i	Consumption plan of consumer i
q_{ik}	Consumption of good k by individual i
Q	Set of production possibilities
$\mathbb{R}$	Set of real numbers
$\mathbb{R}^l_+$	Set of non-negative real numbers in the l-dimensional space
R	Revenue function
r	Marginal revenue
S	Supply function
T	Transformation function
U	Utility function
V	Indirect utility function
w_j	Price of input j
W	Welfare function
x_i	Location of provider i
X	Consumption set
y	Income
ϕ	Cost of quality

η_k	Income elasticity of demand of good k
ε_k	Own-price elasticity of demand of good k
ε_{kj}	Cross-price elasticity of demand of good k
λ	Lagrange multiplier
π	Probability
Π	Profit function
σ	Elasticity of substitution between two inputs

Acknowledgments

Our research has greatly benefited from interaction with many colleagues over the years. They always provided stimulating comments and remarks, as well as their own research. We were influenced on our views of health economics by numerous friends and researchers, in academia and in practice. Thank you to all.

Special gratitude by PPB goes to Thomas G. McGuire for bringing his attention to health economics, a fascinating field, many years ago. Also, XMG's particular thanks goes to the Institute of Economic Analysis (CSIC) for its hospitality during the academic year 2009–2010, and in particular to Clara Ponsatí, Ramon Caminal, and Roberto Burguet. They provided the optimal environment in which to make this book a reality. Also, our colleagues at CODE and our respective departments deserve a particular mention for offering a great environment in which to work.

We are particularly indebted to our families and dedicate this book to them, acknowledging their support and understanding during the course of writing which took away time that would otherwise have been spent with them.

Last but not least, all comments from our readers to improve the text will be warmly welcome.

Part I

Principles of economics

1   Introduction

This chapter introduces the main elements of an economic system: its agents, their decision making, and the limited availability of resources. It also argues that the use of models allows the capture of fundamental relationships among those agents in a simplified but meaningful way.

Economics is the study of the way in which economic agents make their decisions regarding the use (allocation) of scarce resources. This definition contains three concepts that must be defined to fully capture the meaning of economics. These include economic agents, scarce resources, and the decision-making mechanism.

Economic agents are the decision makers in the economy. These are individuals, households, enterprises, and the state. They make decisions on the use of the available resources by answering the following questions: (i) what to produce/consume; (ii) how much to produce/consume; (iii) how to produce/consume; and (iv) who produces/consumes.

The resources available in an economy are those goods and services used and transformed in other goods and services allocated among the agents participating in that economy. An economics problem arises only when resources are scarce, so that decisions on how to allocate them need to be taken.

A traditional taxonomy of resources classifies them in three types: land (physical resources of the planet), labor (human resources), and capital (resources created by humans to aid in production: tools, machinery, factories, etc.). Sometimes a fourth element is added under the label of enterprise. It refers to the organization of resources to produce goods and services.

The answers to the questions above depend on the organization of the economy. An economy can be centrally planned. In this case the state owns all the resources and allocates them. At the other extreme we find pure free market economies, where the allocation of resources is determined by the forces operating in the markets for goods and services without any state intervention. Most economies though combine elements of market allocation together with some state intervention. These are called mixed systems.

Real economies are far too complex to be studied as such. Therefore, we have to limit ourselves to use economic models (theories). An economic model is a set of assumptions providing a simplified representation of reality capturing the fundamental relationships among economic agents. To illustrate, the relation between an economic model and a real economy can be compared to the relation between a road map and the actual road network. There are two fundamental types of models according to the aim of the study. On the one hand, we find models built to describe the decision-making process and the allocation of resources. The solution to these types of models is called the equilibrium allocation of that economy. This approach avoids economic value judgments and is known as positive economics. Once

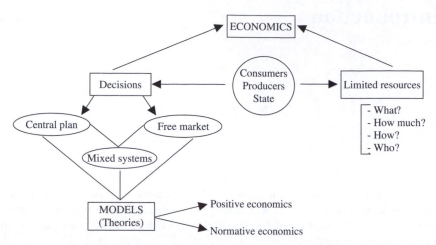

Figure 1.1 The meaning of economics.

an equilibrium allocation has been characterized, further questions can be brought forward. These incorporate value judgments about the equity and efficiency properties of the equilibrium allocation, and the particular policy actions that ought to be followed to achieve a desirable goal. This is the realm of normative economics, also known as welfare analysis. Figure 1.1 summarizes this.

This first part of the book is thus devoted to presenting the content of economics. Chapters 2 and 3 contain the analysis of consumers and producers. Chapter 4 studies the interaction of consumers and producers in the market. Next, we introduce the state as an actor both intervening in the functioning of the markets in Chapter 5 and also looking at concentration of producers (Chapter 6). Finally, and with the perspective of the health care sector, Chapter 7 is devoted to the study of the (differential) behavior between for-profit and nonprofit organizations.

2   Demand

In this chapter we address the decision making of a consumer in the market. From the primitive concept of preferences over consumption goods and the budget constraint, we derive the demand system, study its properties, and aggregate the individual demands into the market demand.

In this chapter we will study the behavior of consumers. A consumer is an agent making decisions on consumption. It may be an individual, a household, a community of apartment owners in a building, etc. as long as they share a common objective. The problem of deciding what to consume and how much arises because resources are scarce. This means that the consumer faces restrictions when taking the consumption decision. We summarize these restrictions into a single one described by the income available to the consumer.

The selection of goods to consume is made among all goods that (potentially) can be found in the economy. This is the so-called *consumption set*. A particular combination of these goods (i.e. a point in the consumption set) is labeled as a *consumption plan*. To be able to select, the consumer has to be endowed with a criterion allowing for comparison of all the possible consumption plans. The capacity to compare is described by the *preferences*. Figure 2.1 illustrates these elements. On the left-hand side we have the set of consumers, each one endowed with preferences and submitted to restrictions. The right-hand side of the figure illustrates an example of an economy with two goods (q_1 and q_2),[1] the consumption set (the space $q_1 - q_2$), and the restriction. This is the straight line crossing the consumption set diagonally. It represents how a certain level of income y is spent between two goods that are sold at prices p_1 and p_2. All points in the shaded area are feasible consumption plans, that is, bundles of goods affordable to the consumer. This is called the *feasible consumption set*. Formally, it is the subset of the consumption set defined by those affordable consumption plans given the consumer's income and the prices of the commodities. The particular consumption bundle chosen (given the income and prices) defines the demand of the consumer. To complete the description of the elements involved in the decision problem of the consumer it remains to introduce the utility. We will argue below that we do not have the mathematical tools to deal with preferences. Therefore, we "translate" with the tools of calculus the information given by the preferences into an index of satisfaction called *utility function* analytically tractable.

To summarize, the consumer must identify the consumption plan in the feasible consumption set yielding the highest possible level of satisfaction (i.e. utility). As such optimal consumption plans will be contingent on income and prices, the outcome of this decision-making process will be a function specifying for every level of income and every system of prices the utility maximizing consumption plan. This is the so-called *demand function*.

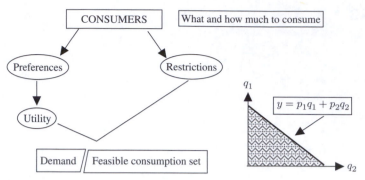

Figure 2.1 The consumer problem.

Before proceeding with the detailed analysis of the consumer behavior, some notation should be introduced.

In the economy the set of consumers is denoted by $\mathcal{I}$. A particular consumer is identified by $i \in \mathcal{I}$. A consumer i is characterized by a vector $(y_i, \succsim_i, X_i)$ where $y_i \in \mathbb{R}^l_+$ represents consumer i's initial income (wealth), $X_i \subset \mathbb{R}^l_+$ denotes the consumption set, and $\succsim_i \in \mathcal{P}$ denotes the preferences of $i \in \mathcal{I}$ on X_i. A consumption plan is denoted as $q_i = (q_{i1}, q_{i2}) \in X_i$. Let $X_i = X$, $\forall i \in \mathcal{I}$. Finally, we assume that in the economy there are l goods indexed as $k = 1, 2, \dots, l$.

2.1   The elements of the consumer problem

To guarantee that the problem of the consumer is properly defined, we need to introduce some assumptions regarding its elements. Regarding the consumption set X, we will assume that it is non-empty, closed, and convex. Non-emptiness is required so that the consumer may select a consumption plan. The other assumptions are technical. They are needed to derive the demand functions. However, they also have an economic content. A closed set means that the points in its frontier belong to the set. Therefore, those consumption plans in the boundary of X can also be compared with consumption plans in the interior of X. Convexity of X implies that we assume that goods are perfectly divisible. That is, the individual may consume those goods in any required amounts. Technically, convexity means that given any two consumption plans $(q_i^1, q_i^2) \in X$, any third consumption plan q_i^3 defined by a weighted average of the former two, is also an element of X.

Formally,

DEFINITION 2.1   (CONVEX SET).   Let $X \subset \mathbb{R}^l_+$. We say that the set X is convex if

$$\forall (q_i^1, q_i^2) \in X \quad \text{and} \quad \lambda \in [0, 1], \quad q_i^3 = \lambda q_i^1 + (1 - \lambda) q_i^2 \in X$$

Figure 2.2 illustrates this definition showing an example of a convex set in panel (a), and an example of a non-convex set in panel (b).

2.1.1   Preferences

To be able to select a consumption plan, the consumer needs a criterion to compare the elements $q_i \in X$. This criterion is represented by the preferences $\succsim_i \in \mathcal{P}$, where $\mathcal{P}$ denotes the

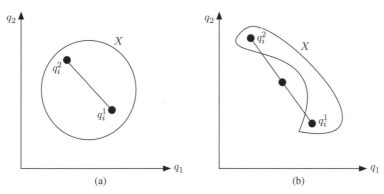

Figure 2.2 Convex and non-convex sets.

space of preferences. As we can only compare consumption bundles by pairs, the preference of consumer i is a binary relation $\succsim_i$ defined on X with the following interpretation. When comparing two arbitrary consumption plans $(q_i^1, q_i^2) \in X$ we assume that one and only one of these three alternatives holds:

(i)   (Strict preference) $q_i^1 \succ_i q_i^2$ meaning that alternative q_i^1 is preferred to (better than) alternative q_i^2,

(ii) (Indifference) $q_i^2 \sim_i q_i^2$ meaning that the consumer is indifferent to both alternatives,

(iii) (Weak preference) $q_i^1 \succsim_i q_i^2$ meaning that alternative q_i^1 is at least as preferred to (not worse than) alternative q_i^2.

As we have already mentioned, preferences are a binary relation. However, to be able to compare all bundles in the consumption set, we need to extend the capacity to compare to a third alternative. We therefore need to add a further assumption. This is the *transitivity of preferences*.

ASSUMPTION 2.1 (TRANSITIVITY OF PREFERENCES). $\forall (q_i^1, q_i^2, q_i^3) \in X_i$, *if* $q_i^1 \succsim_i q_i^2$ *and* $q_i^2 \succsim_i q_i^3$, *then* $q_i^1 \succsim_i q_i^3$.

This assumption extends the comparison two by two to a third alternative in a way to avoid circular preferences, thus ensuring the coherence of the decision-making process of the consumer. To illustrate, consider an economy with three goods: coffee, tea, and milk. A certain consumer prefers coffee to tea, tea to milk, and milk to coffee. As a consequence, there appears to be a circularity in these preferences so that the consumer prefers coffee to coffee. This lack of consistency prevents the consumers from being able to choose in a coherent way.[2]

Note that the indifference relation $\sim_i$ satisfies reflexivity, symmetry, and transitivity. Therefore it is a class of indifference that partitions the consumption set X. That is, any element $q_i \in X$ belongs to a unique class of indifference, the intersection of any two classes of indifference is empty, and the union of all classes of indifference is the set X. Figure 2.3 illustrates these relations for an economy with two goods. The curve passing through the point q_i^1 represents the indifference class of q_i^1, denoted $I_i(q_i^1)$; all points located above the curve represent consumption plans strictly preferred to q_i^1. This set is denoted as $SP_i(q_i^1)$.

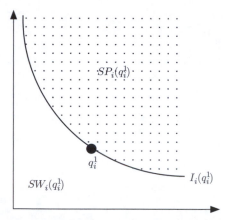

Figure 2.3 The indifference class of x_{i1}.

Finally, the bundle q_i^1 is strictly preferred to any consumption plan located below the curve. Denote those bundles as $SW_i(q_i^1)$. Formally,

$$I_i(q_i^1) = \{q_i \in X \mid q_i \sim_i q_i^1\}$$
$$SP_i(q_i^1) = \{q_i \in X \mid q_i \succ_i q_i^1\}$$
$$SW_i(q_i^1) = \{q_i \in X \mid q_i^1 \succ_i q_i\}$$

Some additional assumptions are required to formally solve the problem of the consumer. The interested reader can see the details in Jehle and Reny (2001) or Mas Colell *et al.* (1995).

2.1.2 *Utility function*

The preference ordering is a primitive component of the decision problem of the consumer introducing a criterion of comparison among consumption bundles. However, no mathematical tools exist to analytically solve the problem of the consumer working directly on the preference relation. We would like to find a way to translate the information given by the preferences into a function on which we can apply differential calculus. Such a function when it exists is termed *utility function*.

DEFINITION 2.2 (UTILITY FUNCTION). A function $U_i : X \to \mathbb{R}$ represents the preference relation $\succsim_i$ if and only if for all $(q_i^1, q_i^2) \in X$ the following holds:

$$U_i(q_i^1) \geq U_i(q_i^2) \Longleftrightarrow q_i^1 \succsim_i q_i^2.$$

Such a function U_i is called consumer i's utility function.

Note that this definition tells us that consumption bundles that are better preferred (higher in the ordering) are translated by the utility function into larger numbers. Accordingly, the consumer's problem of selecting the top bundle in his/her ordering is translated into choosing the bundle with the highest value according to the corresponding utility function. Generically, this is an optimization problem. Differential calculus has very powerful techniques to solve

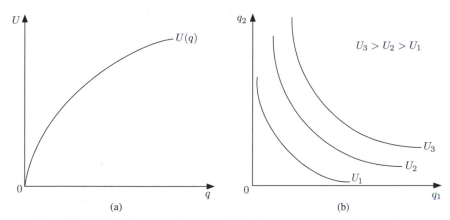

Figure 2.4 Utility function.

this type of problem. Let us assume that the utility function U_i is continuous and differentiable. Figure 2.4 represents a utility function in a one-good economy (section (a)), and in a two-good economy (section (b)). In the latter case, the utility function is depicted by means of the *map of indifference curves*. An indifference curve is a level set of the utility function. That is, the set of bundles which yield the same level of utility.

2.2 Demand function

2.2.1 *Prices and restrictions*

So far we have introduced the commodities and the utility function as the instruments to measure the level of satisfaction a consumer derives from consumption. However, there are two fundamental elements still missing to define (and solve) the consumer's problem – the *price system* and the *initial wealth* of the consumer.

DEFINITION 2.3 (PRICE SYSTEM). A price system is a vector $p \in \mathbb{R}^l_{++}$, where $p \equiv (p_1, p_2, \ldots, p_l)$, $p_k > 0$, $k = 1, 2, \ldots, l$.

This definition assumes that (i) each commodity has one and only one price and (ii) that all prices are all strictly positive. We will also assume that from the viewpoint of the consumers those prices are given, or in other words, consumers do not play any role in the mechanism of price formation. None of these assumptions are necessary in order to develop the theory of the consumer. However, they conveniently simplify the analysis while maintaining the main results.

Given a consumption bundle $q_i \in X_i$, $q_i \equiv (q_{i1}, q_{i2}, \ldots, q_{il})$ and a price system $p \in \mathbb{R}^l_{++}$, we can compute the expenditure a consumer i has to incur to consume the bundle q_i. This is,

$$pq_i^T = \sum_{k=1}^{l} p_k q_{ik}.$$

The second fundamental element to define the consumer's problem is the initial income (or equivalently, an initial bundle of goods) the consumer is endowed with. This initial "wealth" is denoted by $y_i \in \mathbb{R}_{++}$. It determines the capacity of the consumer to design the consumption bundle to obtain the highest level of satisfaction. Formally, given the price system and the initial wealth, we can define the *feasible consumption set* of consumer i.

DEFINITION 2.4   (FEASIBLE CONSUMPTION SET).   Given $(p, y_i) \in \mathbb{R}_{++}^{l+1}$, the feasible consumption set of individual i is defined as

$$B_i = \{q_i \in X_i : \sum_{k=1}^{l} p_k q_{ik} \leq y_i\} \subset X$$

This is the choice set of the consumer. It describes those bundles that are affordable to the consumer. Note that B_i is a convex and compact set. Among all the elements of B_i, we pay special attention to its frontier. This is the set $BC = \{q_i \in X_i : \sum_{k=1}^{l} p_k q_{ik} = y_i\}$. We refer to it as the *budget constraint* of consumer i. It contains those feasible bundles that exhaust the wealth of the consumer.

2.2.2   The consumer's decision problem

Formally, the decision problem a consumer i faces is

$$\max_{q_i \in X} U_i(q_i) \quad \text{s.t.} \sum_{k=1}^{l} p_k q_{ik} \leq y_i.$$

Given that B_i is compact, it can be shown that if U_i is concave, the set of solutions will be convex. Also, if U_i is strictly concave, the solution will be unique, and will belong to the budget constraint.

We denote the outcome of the decision problem of consumer i as $q_i^*(p, y_i)$, and refer to it as the *Marshallian demand function* of consumer i.

2.2.3   Marshallian demand

Figure 2.5 illustrates the solution of the problem of the consumer in a two-good economy when the utility function is concave (a) and strictly concave (b). The shaded area represents the feasible consumption set B_i, and the lines represent indifference curves. The set of solutions in case (a) is given by the thick segment. In case (b) there is a unique solution q_i^*.

Formally, consider a two-good economy and a consumer i with a utility function $U_i(q_{i1}, q_{i2})$ and income y_i. Given prices $p = (p_1, p_2)$, the individual's feasible set is given by the consumption plans $q_i = (q_{i1}, q_{i2}) \in X$ satisfying

$$y_i \geq q_{i1} p_1 + q_{i2} p_2. \tag{2.1}$$

The problem of the consumer is to select a feasible bundle q_i to maximize utility given (p, y_i), that is,

$$\max_{q_{i1}, q_{i2}} U_i(q_{i1}, q_{i2}) \quad \text{s.t. } y_i \geq q_{i1} p_1 + q_{i2} p_2.$$

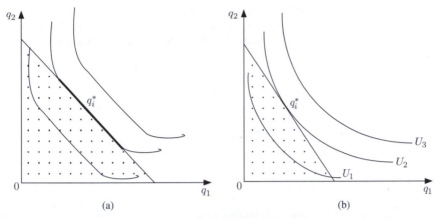

Figure 2.5 Solution to the consumer's decision problem.

Assuming the utility function is strictly concave we can use the Lagrange method of optimization and solve the following problem:[3]

$$\max_{q_{i1}, q_{i2}} L(q_{i1}, q_{i2}) = U_i(q_{i1}, q_{i2}) + \lambda(y_i - q_{i1}p_1 - q_{i2}p_2)$$

The corresponding system of first-order conditions is,

$$\frac{\partial L}{\partial q_{i1}} = \frac{\partial U_i}{\partial q_{i1}} - \lambda p_1 = 0 \tag{2.2}$$

$$\frac{\partial L}{\partial q_{i2}} = \frac{\partial U_i}{\partial q_{i2}} - \lambda p_2 = 0 \tag{2.3}$$

$$\frac{\partial L}{\partial \lambda} = y_i - q_{i1}p_1 - q_{i2}p_2 = 0 \tag{2.4}$$

From (2.2) and (2.3) we obtain,

$$\frac{\dfrac{\partial U_i}{\partial q_{i1}}}{\dfrac{\partial U_i}{\partial q_{i2}}} = \frac{p_1}{p_2} \tag{2.5}$$

This expression is of particular importance. The left-hand side of (2.5) tells us the rate at which the consumer is willing to exchange consumption of good 1 by consumption of good 2. This is called the *marginal rate of substitution*. Therefore, in equilibrium the relative prices determine the marginal adjustment of the optimal consumption bundle. Figure 2.5(b) illustrates the characterization of the optimal bundle. A variation of the relative prices means a variation of the slope of the budget constraint and thus an adjustment of the optimal consumption plan.

The remaining first-order condition (2.4) tells us that in equilibrium the consumer exhausts the income, so that the solution to the consumer's problem lies in the budget constraint. This should not be surprising because the individual does not derive utility from holding money.

Finally, the solution to the problem of the consumer is a demand function for each good $q_{i1}^*(p, y_i), q_{i2}^*(p, y_i)$ and optimal value of the *Lagrange multiplier*, $\lambda^*(p, y_i)$.

To assess the meaning of λ, let us evaluate the level of utility at the solution, $U_i^*(q_{i1}^*(p, y_i), q_{i2}^*(p, y_i))$, and differentiate it with respect to the individual's endowment of income y_i to obtain,

$$\frac{\partial U_i^*}{\partial y_i} = \frac{\partial U_i^*}{\partial q_{i1}^*}\frac{\partial q_{i1}^*}{\partial y_i} + \frac{\partial U_i^*}{\partial q_{i2}^*}\frac{\partial q_{i2}^*}{\partial y_i}. \tag{2.6}$$

Substituting (2.2) and (2.3) into (2.6) it follows that,

$$\frac{\partial U_i^*}{\partial y_i} = \lambda\left(p_1\frac{\partial q_{i1}^*}{\partial y_i} + p_2\frac{\partial q_{i2}^*}{\partial y_i}\right). \tag{2.7}$$

Next, let us differentiate (2.4) also with respect to y_i:

$$1 = p_1\frac{\partial q_{i1}^*}{\partial y_i} + p_2\frac{\partial q_{i2}^*}{\partial q_i} \tag{2.8}$$

Substituting (2.8) into (2.7) we obtain the value of λ:

$$\frac{\partial U_i^*}{\partial y_i} = \lambda$$

That is, the optimal value of the Lagrange multiplier measures the marginal utility of income: the rate of increase in maximized utility as income is increased. In other words, the Lagrange multiplier at the solution to the problem is equal to the rate of change in the maximal value of the utility function as the constraint is relaxed.

To illustrate the solution to the consumer decision problem, let us consider an economy with two goods. A consumer i has an initial wealth y_i and a Cobb–Douglas utility function:

$$U_i(q_{i1}, q_{i2}) = q_{i1}^\alpha q_{i2}^\beta, \quad \alpha, \beta > 0. \tag{2.9}$$

Given prices $p = (p_1, p_2)$, the individual's feasible set is given by $(q_{i1}, q_{i2}) \in X$ satisfying (2.1).

As the utility function is strictly concave, let us define the Lagrangian function:

$$\max_{q_{i1}, q_{i2}} L(q_{i1}, q_{i2}) = q_{i1}^\alpha q_{i2}^\beta + \lambda(y_i - q_{i1}p_1 - q_{i2}p_2)$$

The corresponding system of first-order conditions is,

$$\frac{\partial L}{\partial q_{i1}} = \alpha q_{i1}^{\alpha-1} q_{i2}^\beta - \lambda p_1 = 0 \tag{2.10}$$

$$\frac{\partial L}{\partial q_{i2}} = \beta q_{i2}^{\beta-1} q_{i1}^\alpha - \lambda p_2 = 0 \tag{2.11}$$

$$\frac{\partial L}{\partial \lambda} = y_i - q_{i1}p_1 - q_{i2}p_2 = 0 \tag{2.12}$$

From (2.10) and (2.11),

$$\frac{\alpha q_{i2}}{\beta q_{i1}} = \frac{p_1}{p_2} \tag{2.13}$$

That is,

$$q_{i2} = \frac{\beta q_{i1}}{\alpha}\frac{p_1}{p_2} \tag{2.14}$$

Substituting (2.14) in (2.12) yields

$$q_{i1}^*(p, y_i) = \frac{\alpha y_i}{p_1(\alpha + \beta)} \tag{2.15}$$

Substituting (2.15) in (2.14) yields

$$q_{i2}^*(p, y_i) = \frac{\beta y_i}{p_2(\alpha + \beta)} \tag{2.16}$$

The following example will further clarify the nature of the solution.

EXAMPLE 2.1 Consider an economy with two consumers a and b and two goods q_1 and q_2. Let,

$$U_a(q_{a1}, q_{a2}) = q_{a1}^{\frac{1}{3}} q_{a2}^{\frac{2}{3}}, \qquad U_b(q_{b1}, q_{b2}) = q_{b1}^{\frac{2}{3}} q_{b2}^{\frac{1}{3}}$$

The Marshallian demands of consumers a and b over the two goods are,

$$q_{a1}(p, y_a) = \frac{y_a}{3p_1}, \quad q_{a2}(p, y_a) = \frac{2y_a}{3p_2} \tag{2.17}$$

$$q_{b1}(p, y_b) = \frac{2y_b}{3p_1}, \quad q_{b2}(p, y_b) = \frac{y_b}{3p_2} \tag{2.18}$$

Note that the demand functions of an individual do not vary when *all* prices and the wealth are multiplied by the same factor. Accordingly, we say that the Marshallian demand functions are *homogeneous of degree zero in prices and wealth*, that is $\forall \gamma > 0, q_i(p, y_i) = q_i(\gamma p, \gamma y_i)$.

2.2.4 Comparative statics

In general, a Marshallian demand system is defined from the $(l + 1)$-dimensional space of income and prices onto the space of commodities, $q : \mathbb{R}_{++}^{l+1} \to \mathbb{R}_+^l$. This is precisely the meaning of a demand function $q_{ik}(y_i; p)$. It is a mechanism that given a vector $(y_i, p_1, \ldots, p_l) \in \mathbb{R}_+^{l+1}$ assigns the amount of good k that is optimal for consumer i. This argument is reproduced for every single commodity $k = 1, \ldots, l$ so that the outcome of consumer i's decision problem is a *demand system*,

$$q_i^* = (q_{i1}^*(y_i, p_1, \ldots, p_l), \ldots, q_{i1}^*(y_i, p_1, \ldots, p_l)), \tag{2.19}$$

indicating the optimal (utility maximizing) consumption bundle of individual i with initial wealth y_i at (market) prices $p = (p_1, \ldots, p_l)$.

At this point, we are interested in studying some properties of this demand system. In particular, we want to inquire how demand varies when the consumer's wealth varies or prices vary. This is the so-called *comparative statics* analysis of the demand. When the problem of the consumer has a multiplicity of solutions this is an exercise that is difficult to interpret. Thus, we will assume for the sake of the argument all the necessary conditions to obtain a unique solution[4] given by (2.19).

Engel curve

Let us start studying how demand $q_{ik}(y_i, p)$ varies when the initial income of the consumer varies while prices remain constant. Figure 2.6 illustrates the argument for an economy with two goods. Assume without loss of generality that the income of our consumer increases. Given that prices remain constant, it follows that the consumer is richer and thus expands the consumption of *all* goods in the same proportion as the increase of income. Graphically, the demand function *shifts outwards*.

For every possible variation of income, we can compute the corresponding optimal consumption bundle. The equation that relates the variation of income to the variation of demand is the *Engel curve*. Figure 2.7 represents different possible shapes of the Engel curve. The impact of income variations on demand provides a way of classifying goods. In most situations we expect to observe a positive relation between variation of income and consumption of a commodity k. Then, we say that commodity k is a *normal good*. Commodities 1 and 2 in sections (a) and (b) of Figure 2.7 belong to this category. Within this group we can refine the argument and distinguish two cases.

The Engel curve in section (a) is a straight line. It means that the consumer will maintain the proportion in consumption between the two goods as income varies. In other words,

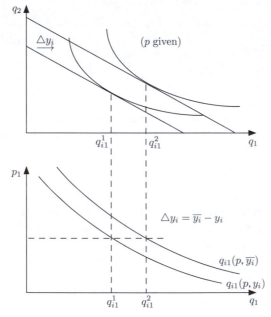

Figure 2.6 Demand and wealth variation.

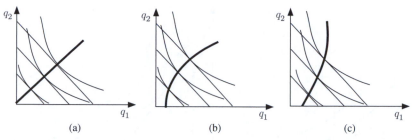

Figure 2.7 Engel curves.

$\partial\left(\frac{q_{i1}}{q_{i2}}\right)/\partial y_i = 0$. In this case we say that the demand of good k has a unit income elasticity[5] (or also that preferences are homothetic).

In section (b) we observe that as income increases consumption of the two goods increase but in different proportions. In particular, good 2 increases more than proportionally to the increase of income, and consumption of good 1 increases less than proportionally. In this case we say that good 2 is a *luxury good*, while good 1 is a *necessity good*.

Finally, section (c) in Figure 2.7 depicts a situation where an increase in income yields a contraction of the consumption of good 1. Then, we say that good 1 is an *inferior good*.

Price variations

Let us assume now that all prices but, say, p_1 remain constant, and income remains constant as well. Now we want to examine how the demand of good 1 varies when its price varies. Figure 2.8 will help to illustrate this. Assume without loss of generality, that p_1 diminishes. Since good 1 becomes relatively cheaper with respect to good 2, the budget constraint of the consumer rotates outwards on the good 2 axes so that the increase of the feasible set of the consumer is biased in favor of good 1. For every variation of the price of good 1 we can (re)compute the optimal consumption bundle of the consumer. Note that these sequences of optimal bundles move along the demand curve of good 1.

Two situations may arise. Section (a) of Figure 2.8 illustrates a scenario where the decrease of price p_1 gives rise to a demand increase. This is what we expect to happen in most markets. Accordingly, such goods are called *normal goods*.[6] Section (b) shows the opposite situation, where the decrease of the price of good 1 provokes a decrease in the demand of good 1. In such a case we refer to good 1 as a *Giffen good*.

2.2.5 *Complement and substitute goods*

The previous section studied the impact of variations of income and prices on a single good. Now we want to analyze how the variation in the consumption of one good affects the consumption of other goods in the economy. Three types of relation can be reported. Two goods may be complements, substitutes, or independent.

DEFINITION 2.5 (COMPLEMENT GOODS). We say that two goods are complements when they are consumed together.

Examples of complement goods are coffee and sugar (assuming the consumer likes to mix sugar in the coffee), pencil and paper, toner and printer, and so on. The relevant feature

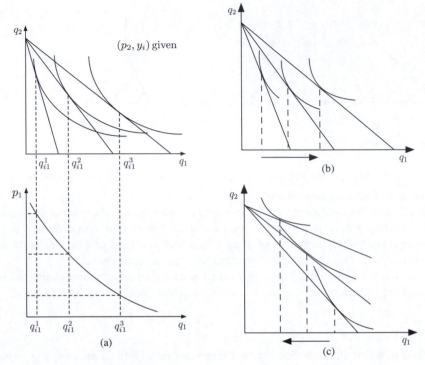

Figure 2.8 Normal and Giffen goods.

is that when the price of one good increases, its demand decreases and the demand of the complement good decreases as well.

DEFINITION 2.6 (SUBSTITUTE GOODS). Two goods are said to be substitutes when one of the goods can be consumed in place of the other.

Examples of substitute goods are butter and margarine, coffee and tea, sugar and saccharin, etc. The relevant feature is that when the price of one good increases, its demand decreases and the demand of the substitute good increases.

DEFINITION 2.7 (INDEPENDENT GOODS). Two goods are independent when their demands are not related to each other.

2.2.6 Elasticity

After studying the effects of variations of prices and income on the demand of a commodity, we need a measure to evaluate the magnitude of such variations. A good measure must be invariant to the units in which prices, income, and demand are expressed. An instrument widely used is the so-called *elasticity* of the demand function. It measures the relative variation of the demand against a relative variation of income or some prices. Accordingly, we distinguish three concepts of elasticity.

DEFINITION 2.8 (INCOME ELASTICITY). The income elasticity of demand of good k by individual i is the ratio of the percent change in demand to the percent change in income,

$$\eta_k = \frac{\% \, \Delta \, q_{ik}}{\% \, \Delta \, y_i} = \frac{\dfrac{\Delta q_{ik}}{q_{ik}}}{\dfrac{\Delta y_i}{y_i}} = \frac{\Delta q_{ik} \, y_i}{\Delta y_i \, q_{ik}}, \quad k = 1, 2, \ldots, l$$

or if the demand function is differentiable,

$$\eta_k = \frac{\partial q_{ik}}{\partial y_i} \frac{y_i}{q_{ik}}, \quad k = 1, 2, \ldots, l.$$

For normal goods we already know that there is a positive relation between a variation of income and the variation of demand. Therefore, η_k will be a positive number. The relevant question is whether it is above or below the unit. When $\eta_k > 1$ the variation of demand is more than proportional to the variation of income, and we say that the demand *overreacts* to the variation of income. When $\eta_k < 1$ the variation of demand is less than proportional to the variation of income, and we say that the demand *underreacts*. When $\eta_k = 1$ the variation of demand is of the same magnitude to the variation of income.

We can use Example 2.1 to illustrate the income elasticities of the demands of consumer a for goods 1 and 2 given by (2.17). These are,

$$\eta_1 = \frac{\partial q_{a1}}{\partial y_a} \frac{y_a}{q_{a1}} = 1, \quad \eta_2 = \frac{\partial q_{a2}}{\partial y_a} \frac{y_a}{q_{a2}} = 1.$$

DEFINITION 2.9 (OWN-PRICE ELASTICITY). The own-price elasticity of demand of good k by individual i is the ratio of the percent change in demand to the percent change in the price of good k,

$$\varepsilon_k = -\frac{\% \, \Delta \, q_{ik}}{\% \, \Delta \, p_k} = -\frac{\dfrac{\Delta q_{ik}}{q_{ik}}}{\dfrac{\Delta p_k}{p_k}} = -\frac{\Delta q_{ik} \, p_k}{\Delta p_k \, q_{ik}}$$

or if the demand function is differentiable

$$\varepsilon_k = -\frac{\partial q_{ik}}{\partial p_k} \frac{p_k}{q_{ik}}, \quad k = 1, 2, \ldots, l.$$

For normal goods we know that there is a negative relation between the variation of the price of good k and the variation of demand of good k. To avoid having to work with negative numbers, we use the convention to change the sign of the elasticity. This explains the *minus* sign in the expression of the elasticity. As before, and given this convention, the relevant question is to know whether the value of the elasticity lies above or below the unit with a parallel interpretation as in the case of the income elasticity.

Again, we can illustrate the computation of the own-price elasticity using the demands of consumer a in example 2.1.

$$\varepsilon_1 = -\frac{\partial q_{a1}}{\partial p_1} \frac{p_1}{q_{a1}} = \frac{1}{3}, \quad \varepsilon_2 = -\frac{\partial q_{a2}}{\partial p_2} \frac{p_2}{q_{a2}} = \frac{2}{3}.$$

DEFINITION 2.10   (CROSS-PRICE ELASTICITY).   The cross-price elasticity of demand of good k by individual i is the ratio of the percent change in demand to the percent change in the price of good j,

$$\varepsilon_{kj} = \frac{\% \triangle q_{ik}}{\% \triangle p_j} = \frac{\dfrac{\triangle q_{ik}}{q_{ik}}}{\dfrac{\triangle p_j}{p_j}} = \frac{\triangle q_{ik} p_j}{\triangle p_j q_{ik}}$$

or if the demand function is differentiable,

$$\varepsilon_{kj} = \frac{\partial q_{ik}}{\partial p_j} \frac{p_j}{q_{ik}}, \quad k \neq j, \, k, j = 1, 2, \ldots, l.$$

This elasticity may be positive or negative depending on the nature of goods k and j as substitutes or complements. Therefore, we are interested in learning the sign and whether in absolute value, the elasticity is above or below the unit, with the same interpretation as before.

In general when a measure of elasticity is (in absolute value) above the unit, we refer to it as an *elastic demand*, while when the elasticity falls below the unit we refer to it as an *inelastic demand*.

The empirical literature has found that the demand for health care is consistently price inelastic. Although the range of price elasticity estimates is relatively wide, it tends to center on 0.17, meaning that a 1 percent increase in the price of health care will lead to a 0.17 percent reduction in health care expenditures. Also, the demand for health is found to be income inelastic. The estimates of income elasticity of demand are in the range of 0 to 0.2. The positive sign of the elasticity measure indicates that as income increases, the demand for health care services also increases. The magnitude of the elasticity, however, suggests that the demand response is relatively small (see Ringel *et al.* 2005).

2.2.7   Inverse demand function

The demand function contains information on consumer behavior under the assumption that prices (and income) are the observed variables, and consumption levels are the relevant variables. In turn, this implies that in the economy the available information concerns the prices. We will see in Chapter 4 that when markets are oligopolistic and firms determine their behavior strategically, whether a firm decides the production level of a certain commodity or its price will be a relevant element of the analysis. However, when markets are perfectly competitive such an assumption does not matter.

Now assume that firms decide the amount of production of the commodities they produce. Then consumers when going to the market will observe quantities instead of prices. Accordingly, to describe consumers' behavior we will need to obtain a demand function where the amounts available of the different goods tell us the price at which every consumer is willing to buy them. We refer to such demand as the *inverse demand function*. Note that the variables involved in the consumer's problem are l commodities, l prices, and the level of income. Therefore, we need to fix the level of income at some level $\bar{y}_i$, to reduce the dimensionality of the decision space to l goods and prices.

Consider the utility function (2.9). To obtain the system of inverse demand functions, we can either solve the system of first order conditions (2.10), (2.11), (2.12) for (p_1, p_2), or alternatively we can solve the system of demand functions (2.15) and (2.16) for (p_1, p_2). Either way, we should obtain

$$p_1^*(q_i, \bar{y}_i) = \frac{\alpha \bar{y}_i}{(\alpha + \beta)q_{i1}}, \quad p_2^*(q_i, \bar{y}_i) = \frac{\beta \bar{y}_i}{(\alpha + \beta)q_{i2}}$$

Applying these expressions to the particular example 2.1 yields

$$p_1(q_i, \bar{y}_i) = \frac{\bar{y}_i}{3q_{i1}}, \quad p_2(q_i, \bar{y}_i) = \frac{2\bar{y}_i}{3q_{i1}}$$

2.2.8 Indirect utility function

So far we know the optimal consumption bundle of the consumer. However, this is not the answer to the original question of the consumer theory. We should remember that the problem of the consumer is to select a consumption bundle to *maximize the utility level*. Therefore, we still have to learn the level of utility associated to the demand system (2.15) and (2.16). As the optimal consumption is contingent to the price system and the level of income, the utility level the consumer can achieve will also be a function of prices and income. Such function is called *indirect utility function*, and is defined as

DEFINITION 2.11 (INDIRECT UTILITY FUNCTION). The indirect utility function $V_i \colon \mathbb{R}_+^{l+1} \to \mathbb{R}$ is given by

$$V_i(p, y_i) = \max\left\{ U_i(q_i) \,\middle/\, \sum_{k=1}^{l} p_k q_{ik} \leq y_i \right\} = U_i(q_i^*(p, y_i)).$$

Consider the utility function (2.9). Substituting the optimal consumption bundle (2.15) and (2.16), we obtain the indirect utility function as

$$V_i(p, y_i) = \left(\frac{\alpha y_i}{p_1(\alpha + \beta)} \right)^{\alpha} \left(\frac{\beta y_i}{p_2(\alpha + \beta)} \right)^{\beta} = \left(\frac{y_i}{\alpha + \beta} \right)^{\alpha + \beta} \left(\frac{\alpha}{p_1} \right)^{\alpha} \left(\frac{\beta}{p_2} \right)^{\beta}$$

The right-oriented arrows in Figure 2.9 summarize the analysis of the consumer problem.

To complete the analysis, we study the behavior of the indirect utility function with respect to its arguments, namely the price of the goods and the income. Let us start with a variation of the price of a commodity k. From the definition of $V_i(p, y_i)$ and using (2.2), it follows that

$$\frac{\partial V_i}{\partial p_k} = \lambda \sum_{k=1}^{l} p_k \frac{\partial q_i^*}{\partial p_k} \tag{2.20}$$

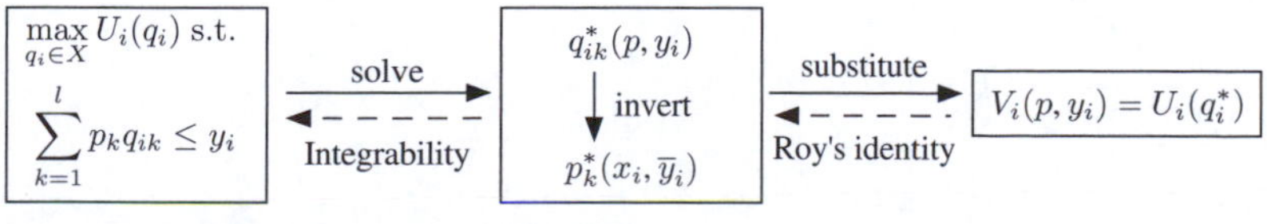

Figure 2.9 Marshallian demand theory.

Also differentiating (2.4) with respect to p_k we obtain,

$$0 = q_{ik} + \sum_{k=1}^{l} p_k \frac{\partial q_i^*}{\partial p_k} \qquad (2.21)$$

Combining (2.20) and (2.21)

$$\frac{\partial V_i}{\partial p_k} = -\lambda q_{ik}^* \qquad (2.22)$$

To interpret this expression let us consider (2.2) and multiply both sides by q_{ik}^*/p_k to obtain

$$-\frac{\partial V_i}{\partial p_k} = \lambda q_{ik}^* = \frac{q_{ik}^*}{p_k} \frac{\partial U_i^*}{\partial q_{ik}^*} \qquad (2.23)$$

Assume the price of good k decreases in one euro, and assess the increase of utility accruing to the consumer. If the consumer ignores the price variation and buys the same consumption bundle, will have q_k euros available. One possibility is to devote this extra income to the same good k. In this case the consumer can acquire an additional amount of good k given by the product of one euro times q_{ik}^*/p_k. In turn, this increase of consumption translates in an increase of utility given by the product of one euro times $(q_{ik}/p_k)(\partial U_i/\partial q_{ik})$.

Let us now study the impact of a variation of income on the indirect utility function. In a parallel way as before, we obtain

$$\frac{\partial V_i(p, y_i)}{\partial y_i} = \lambda \sum_{k=1}^{l} p_k \frac{\partial q_{ik}}{\partial y_i}. \qquad (2.24)$$

Next, we differentiate (2.4) with respect to y_i to obtain,

$$\sum_{k=1}^{l} p_k \frac{\partial q_{ik}}{\partial y_i} = 1. \qquad (2.25)$$

Finally, substituting (2.25) into (2.24) we obtain

$$\frac{\partial V_i(p, y_i)}{\partial y_i} = \lambda. \qquad (2.26)$$

This equation tells us that the Lagrange multiplier of the utility maximization problem is the marginal utility of income.

The results (2.22) and (2.26) lead to an important result known as *Roy's identity* giving a way to recover the Marshallian demand function from the indirect utility function:

Let $q_i^*(p^*, y_i^*)$ be the Marshallian demand of consumer i. Then,

$$q_{ik}^* = -\frac{\dfrac{\partial V_i(p^*, y_i^*)}{\partial p_k^*}}{\dfrac{\partial V_i(p^*, y_i^*)}{\partial y_i^*}}, \qquad k = 1, 2, \ldots, l.$$

We depict this result in Figure 2.9.

2.2.9 *Integrability*

An important problem in empirical analysis is that the demand functions derived from a utility function analytically tractable are often too complex. Therefore, it is more convenient to specify a tractable parametric form of the demand function. However, we must ensure that this parametric demand function represents the preferences of a consumer. In other words, we must be able to derive the underlying utility function.

The basic formulation assumes a well-behaved demand function that exhausts the income of the individual. The main result of the integrability problem is that such a demand function together with some additional technical assumptions allow us to obtain the utility function that would have generated the proposed demand function as the outcome of the utility maximization problem. Figure 2.9 illustrates.

2.3 Market demand

After studying the individual behavior, we are interested in the demand of the market of a certain good k. To derive it, we need to "sum" the individual demands to obtain the aggregate behavior of all consumers in the market of good k. This aggregated function is called the *aggregate demand function* of good k, or also the *market demand* of good k. From a normative viewpoint, this is the relevant function to consider to assess the welfare level of consumers (consumer surplus) and to design economic policies to affect the behavior of consumers.

DEFINITION 2.12 (MARKET DEMAND). The aggregate (market) demand for good k is the horizontal sum of individual demands.

This means that for every price p_k we compute the individual demands $q_{ak}(p_k)$ and $q_{bk}(p_k)$. The market demand at that price p_k is simply the sum of those amounts.

To illustrate, consider an economy with two individuals a and b. Their respective demand functions for a certain good k are $q_a(p_k, p_{-k}, y_a)$ and $q_b(p_k, p_{-k}, y_b)$, where p_{-k} denotes the $(l-1)$-dimensional vector of prices where the price of good k has been removed.

Figure 2.10 illustrates the technique to aggregate the demands of both consumers in the market demand. At price p_k^1 neither consumer has positive demand. Therefore the market

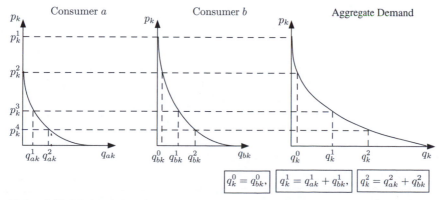

Figure 2.10 Market demand.

demand is also nil. At price p_k^2 consumer a has zero demand while consumer b demands an amount q_{bk}^0. Accordingly, market demand at price p_k^2 is $q_k^0(p_k^2) = q_{bk}^0$. At price p_k^3, demand by consumer a is q_{ak}^1, and by consumer b is q_{bk}^1. The aggregate demand is thus $q_k^1(p_k^3) = q_{ak}^1 + q_{bk}^1$. At price p_k^4, demand by consumer a is q_{ak}^2, and by consumer b is q_{bk}^2. The aggregate demand is thus $q_k^2(p_k^4) = q_{ak}^2 + q_{bk}^2$.

3   Supply

In this chapter we study the decision making of the producers in a market. We introduce the concepts of production function, cost function, and study their properties. The concepts of economies of scale and scope are also introduced. Finally, we derive the supply function of a producer, and the aggregation of individual producers supply functions into the market supply.

3.1   Introduction

Health care, be it a medical appointment, a surgery to be performed, a pharmaceutical drug, or a laboratory test, must be "produced", and resources have to be brought together. Consider surgery. Doctors, nurses, and other health professionals must be taken to a particular place, the operation theater, and instruments have to be made available. The patient has to be admitted to the hospital and then follow the protocols prior to surgery. Thus, a lot of preparation takes place before a surgery is actually performed.

   The same holds for pharmaceutical products and medical devices: once research has been successful, the products have to be produced, marketed, and distributed. The organization of resources so that patients have the opportunity to consume health care is what in economics is called the supply side of the market. In this chapter, we present the main economic concepts related to the supply side.

3.2   The set of production possibilities

The starting point of our discussion is that resources, called inputs, can be organized to achieve some outcome, called output, in various ways. The different ways inputs can be combined such that the desired output is reached define the set of production possibilities. This set is determined by the existing technological opportunities.

   To be precise, consider a certain technology F that to produce some particular good requires the use of two inputs, m_1 and m_2. The set of production possibilities of a production level q is constituted by all combinations of inputs allowing the production of q. Denote by Q the set of production possibilities. Then $Q = \{m_1, m_2 : F(m_1, m_2) \geq q\}$, where F denotes the input combinations that allow us to produce at least the quantity of output q. The shaded area in Figure 3.1 provides a graphical representation of the set of production possibilities associated with this particular output level q.

3.3   The production function

To produce an output level q of some good or service, all that is required is to select input combinations that belong to the set of production possibilities. However, points in the set

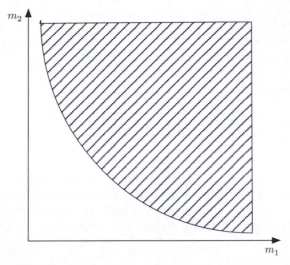

Figure 3.1 Set of production possibilities.

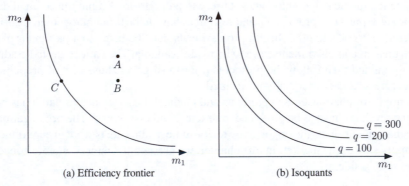

(a) Efficiency frontier   (b) Isoquants

Figure 3.2 Efficiency frontier and isoquants.

of production possibilities are not all equal. Some of these points are more interesting than others. Suppose a particular combination A in Figure 3.2(a) of m_1 and m_2, say, doctors and nurses, that allow us to visit a certain number of patients q per day. If by slightly reducing the number of nurses' hours the same number of patients can still be seen and treated, then the new combination of resources, B, is also in the set of production possibilities. More-over, it is a more interesting combination of inputs: it achieves the same objective using fewer resources. Thus, compared to the initial point A, it can attain the same output and use the remaining resources to some other end. In this sense, we say that the combination of resources B is more efficient than A, although both are feasible ways to produce q.

Still, point B can be improved upon. The above argument can be used to define a spe-cial set of points within the set of production possibilities: the combination of inputs having the property that reducing further quantities used for any input implies that output q can no longer be achieved. The points with this property are the efficiency frontier of the set of production possibilities. Graphically, the efficiency frontier is the lower envelope of the set of production possibilities (see Figure 3.2(a)). This efficiency frontier is associated with a particular volume of output q. Therefore, for each output level there will be the corresponding efficiency frontier. The collection of all these input combinations (i.e., efficiency frontiers) gives origin to the concept of production function.

The efficiency frontier defines a boundary for the set of production possibilities associated with each level of output. The graphical representation of the efficiency frontier is termed *isoquant*, as it describes all the efficient ways to achieve a certain production level. Figure 3.2(b) shows several isoquants, each corresponding to a different level of production. The further away they are from the origin (that is, the more resources are used in an efficient manner), the higher is the associated volume of production.

The slope of the isoquants provides information about the relationship between inputs. In particular, it gives information on substitution possibilities across inputs to reach a given level of output. Take as a first example a surgical procedure that requires labor input made up of nurse and physician work in a ratio of 2:1 (say, four nurses and two physicians). If this is a fixed value in the sense that adding one more physician or one more nurse does not allow us to produce more output, but withdrawing one nurse or one physician would make it impossible to do the surgical procedure, we have no substitution possibilities.

Suppose now that adding one more physician would allow us to use two fewer nurses. If such substitution possibilities exist at a fixed rate, whatever the use of inputs, then perfect substitution possibilities exist. An intermediate case of imperfect substitution can also be envisaged. The isoquants corresponding to these three cases are shown in Figure 3.3.

Note that under imperfect substitution, once a input becomes relatively scarce in use, it is far more difficult to substitute by increasing the other input.

The production function represents the most efficient way to produce: to achieve a certain output level without using more resources than those strictly needed. The production function is a technological relationship that relates inputs to outputs in the most productive way.

We typically assume several properties for the production function: (a) if no inputs are used, no production is realized; (b) if the utilization of one input increases, keeping the quantities of all other inputs constant, then total output also increases; (c) output increases due to increases in one input, holding other inputs constant, occurring at a decreasing rate.

These last two properties imply a positive but decreasing marginal return to input use. Formally, if $q = F(m_1, m_2)$ denotes the production function of q with inputs m_1 and m_2,

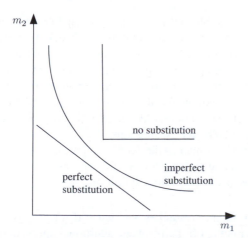

Figure 3.3 Substitution between inputs.

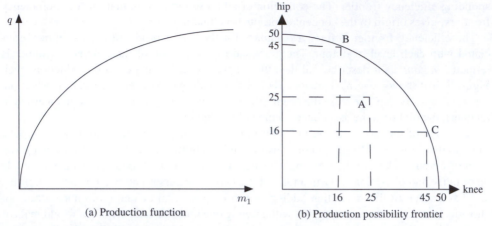

(a) Production function   (b) Production possibility frontier

Figure 3.4 Production technology.

property (a) above says $F(0,0)=0$, property (b) implies $\partial F/\partial m_j > 0$, $j=1,2$, and property (c) corresponds to $\partial^2 F/\partial m_j^2 < 0$, $j=1,2$.

Figure 3.4(a) represents a production function that requires a single input m_1 to obtain a commodity q satisfying these properties.

It is often the case that at initial stages of production, inputs become marginally more productive, in which case property (c) does not hold for low production levels. In most of our analysis, we will assume properties (a) to (c) to be valid. Whenever this is not the case, it will be mentioned explicitly.

The notion of production function can be generalized to a multiple output setting. In such a case, the use of n inputs m_j according to a production technology leads to the production of I outputs q_i. The technological relationship between inputs and outputs is the transformation function:

$$T(q_1,\ldots,q_I;m_1,\ldots,m_n)=0 \tag{3.1}$$

To illustrate, consider a hospital with 10 surgeons able to perform knee and hip interventions. If all surgeons perform knee surgery, they are able to do 50 operations per week. If instead they all devote their time to hip surgery, they perform 50 operations. Figure 3.4(b) illustrates the example. The curve represents the number of operations per week for any combination of the 10 surgeons between knee and hip interventions. Therefore, the area under the curve represents the *feasible production set*. The frontier of the feasible production set is called the *production possibilities frontier* containing (feasible) points like B and C. They represent (unlike point A) maximal activity for the hospital by the 10 surgeons.

Formally, we define the production possibility frontier as the set of maximal combinations of outputs, given the quantity of inputs available to the firm. So far we have referred to efficiency of the production process. Now we provide a formal definition.

DEFINITION 3.1 (EFFICIENCY). An allocation of resources is efficient if it is impossible to change that allocation to make a consumer better off (perform one additional intervention) without making anybody else worse off (reducing the number of operations).

There are two other related concepts particularly relevant in the realm of health economics: efficacy and effectiveness.

DEFINITION 3.2 (EFFICACY). Efficacy refers to the potential benefit of a technology. It is the probability that an individual benefits from the application of a (health) technology to solve a particular (health) problem, under ideal conditions of application.

DEFINITION 3.3 (EFFECTIVENESS). Effectiveness refers to the probability that an individual benefits from the application of a (health) technology to solve a particular (health) problem, under real conditions of application.

The distinction between efficacy and effectiveness is important because doctors and patients often do not follow the best practice in using a treatment. For instance, a patient using oral contraceptive pills to prevent pregnancy may sometimes forget to take a pill at the prescribed time; thus, while the perfect-use failure rate for this form of conception in the first year of use is just 0.3 percent, the typical-use failure rate is 8 percent. Summarizing, while efficacy may be shown in clinical trials, effectiveness is demonstrated in practice.

3.4 The cost function

The production function described earlier is a useful concept and it allows immediately for a simple type of efficiency analysis: whenever actual production does not take place at the efficiency frontier, a movement towards the efficient frontier for the same output level would save resources to be used to increase production elsewhere in the economy. Or, alternatively, the same resources if used efficiently should lead to a higher level of output.

The production function is silent about which point of the efficiency frontier is best. From a technological point of view, all points of the production function that reach the same output level are equal. To choose a point, additional criteria have to be introduced. A natural criterion to impose is to choose the combination of inputs (in the efficiency frontier) that have the least cost in achieving the desired output level. This criterion leads to the introduction of input prices in the choice process.

Let w_j be the price per unit of input m_j. Total cost is then defined by $w_1 m_1 + w_2 m_2$. The choice of inputs is then guided by the minimization of total cost subject to the constraint of being able to produce a certain level of output. The solution to this choice problem is known as the cost function. Formally, it is described by

$$C(q; m_1, m_2) = \min_{\{m_1, m_2\}} w_1 m_1 + w_2 m_2 \quad \text{subject to} \quad q = F(m_1, m_2) \tag{3.2}$$

The cost function incorporates the information from the production function and from input prices to obtain the least cost of producing an output level. Assuming that input prices are fixed (exogenous to the production entity), total cost can be represented in the (m_1, m_2) space by a line. Isocost lines represent combinations of inputs m_1 and m_2 that at prices w_1 and w_2 respectively yield the same total cost. The closer they are to the origin, the lower is the cost. So, in graphical terms, the problem can be stated as finding the point of the lowest isocost line that still reaches the level of output.

The usual properties of the cost function are,

- non-negative in $q, m : C(q; m_1, m_2) \geq 0$;
- non-decreasing in $m_j, \forall j : \partial C / \partial m_j \geq 0$;

- non-decreasing in $q : \partial C / \partial q \geq 0$;
- homogeneous of degree 1 in m_j, $\forall j : C(q; \theta m_1, \theta m_2) = \theta C(q; m_1, m_2)$. This means that when all inputs vary in the same proportion θ, the total cost also varies in this same proportion;
- concave in m_j, $\forall j$:

$$C(q; \lambda m_j^0 + (1 - \lambda) m_j^1) \geq \lambda C(q, m_j^0) + (1 - \lambda) C(q, m_j^1). \tag{3.3}$$

The result of the minimization problem (3.2) is a system of input demand functions conditional to the volume of output to be achieved q: $m_j(q)$.

3.5 Technical rate of substitution and elasticity of substitution

The characterization of the technology by isoquants allows us to define some other useful concepts associated with the substitution across inputs present in the technology. The first concept is the technical rate of substitution. This is simply the rate at which an input can be substituted by another one while keeping the production level constant. That is, if by reducing the health professionals team by one medical doctor and increasing it by two nurses achieves the same output level (quantity- and quality-wise), then the technical rate of substitution of nurses for doctors is 2:1.

Algebraically, the isoquant associated with output level q is characterized by all points at which

$$q = F(m_1, m_2) \tag{3.4}$$

holding q fixed.

Totally differentiating,

$$dq = 0 = \frac{\partial F}{\partial m_1} dm_1 + \frac{\partial F}{\partial m_2} dm_2, \tag{3.5}$$

and from this condition that requires the same output level is obtained, one gets

$$-\frac{dm_2}{dm_1} = \frac{\partial F / \partial m_1}{\partial F / \partial m_2} \tag{3.6}$$

That is, the technical rate of substitution is given by the ratio of marginal productivities of each input. To see why it is so, consider that by reducing one unit of input m_1, total output will decrease by an amount equal to marginal productivity of that input. To restore the initial output level, an increase in the other input must take place. The question is then how much that increase needs to be to compensate for an output decrease equal to the marginal productivity of the first input. If both inputs have the same marginal productivity, the answer is clear: a unit increase of the second output is enough to compensate for a unit decrease of the first input. Of course, if the marginal productivity of the second input is larger, then less than one unit of expansion is required. It should now be clear that the technical rate of substitution is determined by the ratio of marginal productivities.

The second relevant concept is the elasticity of substitution. The elasticity of substitution makes use of the characterization of the cost minimization problem, that is at the origin of the

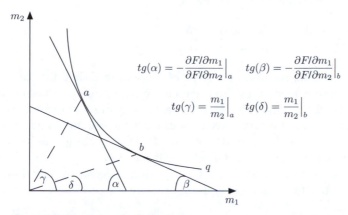

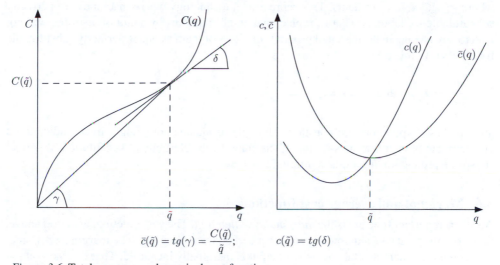

Figure 3.5 Elasticity of substitution.

Figure 3.6 Total, average, and marginal cost functions.

cost function. It has been established above that cost minimization implies that the isocost line is tangent to the isoquant corresponding to the quantity to be produced. In analytical terms, this is translated as the ratio of input prices being equal to the technical rate of substitution. The elasticity of substitution is found by measuring how much the relative use of inputs change when the relative input-price ratio changes. Consider Figure 3.5. The elasticity of substitution is effectively a measure of the curvature of an isoquant.

At point b, the slope of the line tangent to the isoquant is given by the $tg(\beta)$ (the rate of technical substitution, TRS). Moreover, the ratio of the use of inputs, m_2/m_1, is represented by the slope of the broken line $tg(\delta)$. Suppose that we move from point b to point a on the isoquant. The slope of the line tangent to the isoquant is now $tg(\alpha) > tg(\beta)$, while the ratio of inputs increases to $tg(\gamma) > tg(\delta)$. The elasticity of substitution thus compares the change in the relative use of inputs to the variation in the rate of technical substitution in percentage values.

Formally, the elasticity of substitution σ, is defined as:

$$\sigma = -\frac{d(m_1/m_2)/(m_1/m_2)}{d(TRS)/TRS} = -\frac{d(m_1/m_2)}{d(TRS)} \frac{TRS}{m_1/m_2} \tag{3.7}$$

The technical rate of substitution measures the slope of an isoquant, while the elasticity of substitution measures the curvature of the isoquant. Intuitively, the more curved or convex the isoquant is, the less the resulting change in the factor proportions will be, thus the elasticity of substitution σ is lower for very curved isoquants. In the extreme case of Leontief (no-substitution) technology, a change in RTS will not lead to any change in the factor proportions, so that isoquant are L-shaped, and $\sigma = 0$ (see Figure 3.3).

The other extreme case of perfect substitution or linear production technology is shown in Figure 3.3. Now the production function takes the form

$$q = \kappa_1 m_1 + \kappa_2 m_2,$$

where κ_1 and κ_2 are constants. This represents a technology where machines are perfectly substitutable for laborers. That is, replacing a unit of input m_1 by a unit of m_2 input will not lead to any change in the marginal products of either of them as one is perfectly substitutable for another. In this case,

$$\frac{\partial q}{\partial m_j} = \kappa_j, \quad \text{and} \quad TRS = \kappa_2/\kappa_1$$

and all these expressions are constant. Thus, the isoquants are straight lines, indicating a constant rate of technical substitution. Consequently, the elasticity of substitution of perfect substitute production functions is infinite, i.e. $\sigma = \infty$.

3.6 Marginal and average cost functions

Another important function is the *marginal cost function*. The cost function, as stated above, describes the total cost required to produce a certain level of output. The marginal cost function is the increment in total cost when output is marginally increased. That is, when output increases by one small unit, how much total cost grows defines the marginal cost of that extra unit of output. Mathematically, the marginal cost function is given by

$$c(q) = \frac{\partial C(q)}{\partial q}$$

The *average cost function* is the cost per unit produced

$$\bar{c} = \frac{C(q)}{q}.$$

The average cost function and the marginal cost function are closely related although they are different concepts. A positive marginal cost means that cost increases with output, but does not necessarily imply that average cost is increasing or decreasing. When the marginal cost is lower than average cost, the contribution to total cost of the last unit produced is smaller than unit costs, and therefore the production of that unit will contribute to reduce average cost. On the other hand, if marginal cost is above average cost, any additional production will increase average cost.

Decreasing marginal cost means that each additional output unit costs less than the previous one, while also forcing average cost to decrease whenever average cost exceeds marginal cost. These considerations can be made formal and Figure 3.6 provides an illustration of the relation between the two cost curves.

The marginal cost curve always cuts the average cost curve from below at its minimum value. To show this property note first that decreasing average cost implies a range of values of q such that $c(q) < \bar{c}(q)$:

$$\frac{\partial \bar{c}(q)}{\partial q} = \frac{\partial \frac{C(q)}{q}}{\partial q} = \frac{c(q)q - C(q)}{q^2} = \frac{c(q)}{q} - \frac{\bar{c}(q)}{q} < 0 \Leftrightarrow c(q) < \bar{c}(q)$$

Next, to show that the intersection occurs at the minimum of the average cost curve, let $\tilde{q}$ be such that $\bar{c}(\tilde{q})$ is minimum. It means,

$$\left.\frac{\partial \bar{c}(q)}{\partial q}\right|_{\tilde{q}} = \left.\frac{\partial \frac{C(q)}{q}}{\partial q}\right|_{\tilde{q}} = \left.\frac{c(q)q - C(q)}{q^2}\right|_{\tilde{q}} = \left.\frac{c(q)}{q}\right|_{\tilde{q}} - \left.\frac{\bar{c}(q)}{q}\right|_{\tilde{q}} = 0 \Leftrightarrow c(\tilde{q}) = \bar{c}(\tilde{q})$$

3.7 An example: the Cobb–Douglas production function

It is often convenient to provide a specific functional form for the production function. A very popular functional form is the Cobb–Douglas:

$$q = A m_1^{\beta_1} m_2^{\beta_2} \tag{3.8}$$

where A, β_1, β_2 are parameters characterizing the function. This functional form implies that both inputs are required for production (either $m_1 = 0$ or $m_2 = 0$ implies $q = 0$).

Taking input prices as given, the Cobb–Douglas production function allows for a simple form of the cost function. To obtain it, we solve the minimization problem:

$$\min_{\{m_1, m_2\}} C = w_1 m_1 + w_2 m_2 \quad \text{subject to } q = A m_1^{\beta_1} m_2^{\beta_2} \tag{3.9}$$

The Lagrangian function is:

$$\mathcal{L} = w_1 m_1 + w_2 m_2 + \lambda(q - A m_1^{\beta_1} m_2^{\beta_2}) \tag{3.10}$$

where λ is the Lagrange multiplier.

The first-order conditions of the problem are:

$$\frac{\partial \mathcal{L}}{\partial m_1} = w_1 - \lambda \beta_1 A m_1^{\beta_1 - 1} m_2^{\beta_2} = 0, \tag{3.11}$$

$$\frac{\partial \mathcal{L}}{\partial m_2} = w_2 - \lambda \beta_2 A m_1^{\beta_1} m_2^{\beta_2 - 1} = 0, \tag{3.12}$$

$$\frac{\partial \mathcal{L}}{\partial \lambda} = q - A m_1^{\beta_1} m_2^{\beta_2} = 0. \tag{3.13}$$

Solving the set of first-order conditions we obtain,

$$\frac{w_1}{w_2} = \frac{\beta_1 m_2}{\beta_2 m_1}, \tag{3.14}$$

$$q = A m_1^{\beta_1} m_2^{\beta_2}, \tag{3.15}$$

so that the optimal input choices are:

$$m_1 = q^{\frac{1}{\beta_1+\beta_2}} A^{\frac{-1}{\beta_1+\beta_2}} \left(\frac{\beta_2}{\beta_1}\right)^{\frac{\beta_1}{\beta_1+\beta_2}} \left(\frac{w_1}{w_2}\right)^{\frac{\beta_1}{\beta_1+\beta_2}} \tag{3.16}$$

$$m_2 = q^{\frac{1}{\beta_1+\beta_2}} A^{\frac{-1}{\beta_1+\beta_2}} \left(\frac{\beta_2}{\beta_1}\right)^{\frac{-\beta_2}{\beta_1+\beta_2}} \left(\frac{w_1}{w_2}\right)^{\frac{-\beta_2}{\beta_1+\beta_2}} \tag{3.17}$$

Substituting back into the cost function, we obtain the desired result:

$$\begin{aligned} C &= w_1 m_1 + w_2 m_2 \\ &= q^{\frac{1}{\beta_1+\beta_2}} A^{\frac{-1}{\beta_1+\beta_2}} w_1^{\frac{\beta_1}{\beta_1+\beta_2}} w_2^{\frac{\beta_2}{\beta_1+\beta_2}} \left[\left(\frac{\beta_2}{\beta_1}\right)^{\frac{\beta_1}{\beta_1+\beta_2}} + \left(\frac{\beta_1}{\beta_2}\right)^{\frac{\beta_2}{\beta_1+\beta_2}} \right] = c q^{\frac{1}{\beta_1+\beta_2}} \end{aligned} \tag{3.18}$$

3.8 Returns to scale, economies of scale, and economies of scope

We say that production exhibits increasing returns to scale when by increasing all inputs in the same proportion, output increases more than proportionately. For example, when doubling all inputs, production more than doubles. If the increase in output is in the same proportion of the increase in all inputs, then we have constant returns to scale. Finally, if the increase in output is less than proportional relative to the increase in inputs, then production exhibits decreasing returns to scale. Algebraically, suppose all inputs are multiplied by a factor $\theta > 0$, resulting the following relationship

$$F(\theta m_1, \theta m_2) = \theta^\alpha F(m_1, m_2) \tag{3.19}$$

If $\alpha > 1$, the production technology has increasing returns to scale; if $\alpha = 1$, the production technology has constant returns to scale and if $\alpha < 1$, the production technology has decreasing returns to scale.

For the Cobb–Douglas production function,

$$F(\theta m_1, \theta m_2) = A(\theta m_1)_1^\beta (\theta m_2)_2^\beta = \theta^{\beta_1+\beta_2} A m_1^{\beta_1} m_2^{\beta_2} = \theta^{\beta_1+\beta_2} F(m_1, m_2) \tag{3.20}$$

and $\alpha = \beta_1 + \beta_2$ being greater, equal or smaller than one gives the degree of returns to scale.

Economies of scale refers to the effect of increased production on the average cost of production. Whenever by increasing output, cost increases less than proportionately, the underlying technology has economies of scale. This is associated with the spreading of the fixed cost (see below) over a larger level of output. If cost increases more than proportionally, then we say that the technology presents diseconomies of scale.

Looking again at the example of the Cobb–Douglas production function, the corresponding cost function can be written, as shown above, as:

$$C = cq^{\frac{1}{\beta_1 + \beta_2}} \tag{3.21}$$

and, as before, $\beta_1 + \beta_2 > 1, < 1$ or $= 1$ implies increasing returns to scale, decreasing returns to scale or constant returns to scale.

With this cost function, we can easily compute the degree of economies of scale,

$$C(\theta q) = \theta^{\frac{1}{\beta_1 + \beta_2}} C(q) \tag{3.22}$$

and in the production function

$$F(\theta m_1, \theta m_2) = \theta^{\beta_1 + \beta_2} F(x_1, x_2) \tag{3.23}$$

Whatever the option, it is clear that for $\beta_1 + \beta_2 > 1$ we have economies of scale – output grows faster than inputs and costs grow proportionally less than output. Another interesting effect is the impact of an increase in both input prices:

$$C(q; \theta w_1, \theta w_2) = \theta C(q; w_1, w_2) \tag{3.24}$$

We see that when all inputs prices vary in the same proportion θ, the total cost also varies in the same proportion. Thus we say that the total cost function is *homogeneous of degree one* in the prices of the inputs.

The concept of economies of scale basically provides information as to whether or not increasing production is done with higher average cost. Figure 3.7 illustrates the point. In the region of production volumes exhibiting decreasing average cost, there are scale economies, whereas when average cost is increasing, production shows diseconomies of scale. The level of output associated with the minimum of the average cost is the optimal size of the firm. In

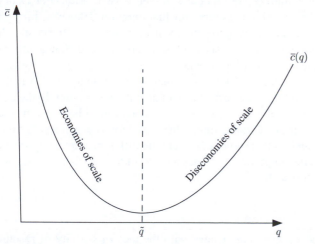

Figure 3.7 Economies of scale.

other words, a production center (say, a hospital) should always operate (i.e., the size of the hospital) as close as possible to its minimum of the average cost.

Another relevant concept is economies of scope. This concept applies only when the firm produces more than one output. Whenever joint production entails lower costs than separate production, economies of scope are said to exist. For example, considering hospitals as an economic agent, one may think of patients admitted for treatment and emergency room episodes as two (very broad) outputs. Economies of scope exist if the same entity providing both types of output has lower cost than having one facility devoted to admitting patients for programmed interventions and another different facility dedicated only to emergency cases.

Mathematically, using the cost function, economies of scope in the case of two outputs are present when

$$C(q_1, q_2) < C(q_1, 0) + C(0, q_2) \tag{3.25}$$

The definition of economies of scope can be easily extended to an arbitrary number of outputs. To illustrate, we say that a hospital exhibits scope economies if the joint production of pediatric and cancer care allows for savings in the hospital's management structure, administration systems, management of hospital capacity, nurses, and non-sanitary personnel, etc. Otherwise, it would be cheaper to set up two hospitals – one for pediatric care, the other for cancer treatments.

3.9 Variable and fixed costs

Two important concepts related to the cost function are the notions of fixed costs and of variable costs. In our construction of the cost function, the health care unit was free to choose the level of inputs it wanted. This corresponds to a long-run situation, defined by total flexibility of *all* inputs.

However, in the short-run, it is often the case that some inputs are fixed, that is, are not easily scalable and do not depend on the level of production. For example, administrative expenses tend to be constant, whatever the level of production. On the other hand, consumables are directly linked to the level of production – more production means more use of consumables. Other uses of resources are less clear in their classification. For example, hiring a doctor for a year makes it a fixed resource for that duration. However, hiring and paying a doctor per hour of consultation given to patients turns it into a variable cost. A hospital that has its own kitchen has more fixed costs and fewer variable costs than another one that outsources and pays per meal provided to patients.

Thus, the dividing line is often blurred. The time horizon for the analysis also helps to distinguish between fixed costs and variable costs. Scale of activity does matter. In the doctor example, if too many patients demand a visit, then a second doctor must be hired. In such a case, the number of doctors becomes a variable input (thus, fixed for a certain level of output but variable according to production thresholds). The crucial difference between fixed and variable costs is the relation to the output level. It does not preclude other factors influencing the level of the fixed (or variable) cost.

3.10 Opportunity cost

The concept of opportunity cost appears associated with the idea of scarcity of resources. A consumer, a producer, and any economic agent in general makes decisions under constraints. Accordingly, these decisions imply a choice among different mutually exclusive alternatives.

DEFINITION 3.4 (OPPORTUNITY COST). Opportunity cost is defined as the benefit given up by not choosing an alternative option. In other words, is the cost of an alternative that must be forgone in order to pursue a certain action.

For example, consider a city that decides to build a hospital on a vacant land lot of its property. In that very lot of land, other services could have been provided, such as a school, a parking area, a sports facility, or could also have been sold. Therefore, the opportunity cost of building a hospital is the value of the benefits foregone of the next best alternative that will not materialize.

   Some remarks are in order at this point. First, the opportunity cost is in contrast to an accounting cost in that the latter does not consider these foregone alternative choices. Second, the total opportunity costs of an action can never be known with certainty as what has been prevented from being produced cannot be seen or known. Third, opportunity cost is typically expressed as a relative price defined by the price of the alternative taken with respect to the next-best option. In this sense it is most used when evaluating cost and benefits of choices.

3.11 Supply

Having considered the characterization of cost structures, we can now define the supply function. In general, "supply" in economic terms means how much of a certain output a firm is willing to sell at a given price. Consider first the decision process of a firm that faces a price per unit of output sold that it cannot influence. That is, the firm is a price taker. How much output should the firm produce? As long as the price received from producing and selling one extra unit of output exceeds its production cost, it is worth expanding production. The decision on expanding production is linked to the comparison between marginal revenue (the price) and marginal cost. The cost of production concept relevant for this decision is the marginal cost function – the cost associated with the last unit produced. The firm follows a very simple rule: whenever the price is above marginal cost it is worth producing and supplying one more unit of the good, whenever the price is below marginal cost the firm faces a loss in the last unit produced. It will then reduce its production. An equilibrium point, that is a production plan the firm does not want to change, is reached when the price equals marginal cost. The quantity supplied by a firm is therefore the quantity that makes marginal cost equal to price.

   Again, this can be made precise. Assuming that firms maximize profits (an objective that will be discussed in a later chapter with respect to health care providers), the decision problem can be stated as:

$$\max_{q} \Pi(q) = pq - C(q) \tag{3.26}$$

The first-order condition describing the solution to this problem is:[1]

$$p - \frac{\partial C}{\partial q}(q) = 0, \tag{3.27}$$

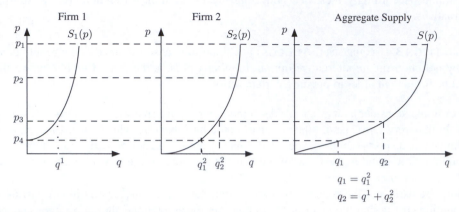

Figure 3.8 Market supply.

so that an output level $S(p) = q^*(p)$ emerges, thus configuring the supply function of the firm. A higher price allows for a higher marginal cost at the last unit produced. Since typically a higher marginal cost will be reached with a larger production level, the firm is willing to supply the market with more output for higher prices. The supply curve is a positive, upward sloped function of price.

The market supply is simply the horizontal sum of all individual supplies. Figure 3.8 illustrates the computation of the market supply for a two-firm case. Firm 1 faces a fixed cost, so that unless a minimum (p_4) prevails in the market, it does not find it profitable to produce. Accordingly, for prices below p_4 only firm 2 is active and aggregate supply coincides with the firm's 2 supply function. At, say, price p_3 both firms are active in the market. Firm 1 produces a quantity q^1 and firm 2 produces q_2^2, so that at the market place consumers find an aggregate quantity $q_2 = q^1 + q_2^2$.

The way the supply side of a market is generated implies that all firms have the same marginal cost for the equilibrium output level, even if they have different cost structures. More efficient, lower-cost firms will produce more in equilibrium. At the margin, nonetheless, the last unit of output must have the same marginal cost over all price-taker firms. Therefore, we can interpret the supply curve as the marginal cost of putting in the market a certain quantity of output.

In a similar fashion as with the demand function, we can also show some comparative statics of the supply function. As has already been argued, changes in the price of the good translates to changes in the volume of output supplied *along* the supply curve. This is illustrated in panel (a) of Figure 3.9. The other reason why (market) supply may vary is found in variation of the cost conditions. The costs of the firms may vary either because the prices of the inputs vary, or because there is technological progress. In both cases, such variations will cause a *shift* in the supply function. Panel (b) of Figure 3.9 illustrates the case of an increase in the price of inputs. As a consequence, production is more expensive and the firm contracts output, so that the supply function moves inwards to the left. Panel (c), in turn, illustrates the case of a technological development yielding a more efficient technology. Then production becomes cheaper and the firm expands production. Accordingly, the supply function moves outwards to the right.

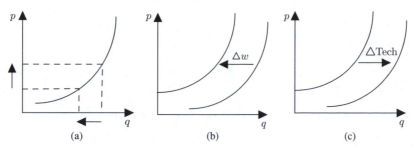

Figure 3.9 Effects on supply.

To complete the discussion, let us consider the following example: consider a firm (hospital) with a production function of health services $q(l) = l^\delta$, where l denote working hours and q health services.

The associated cost function $C(w, q) = wl(q)$ where $l(q) = q^{1/\delta}$ is

$$C(q, w) = wq^{\frac{1}{\delta}}$$

The (competitive) profit function is

$$\Pi(q) = qp - C(q)$$

The problem of the hospital is to determine the level of q to maximize profits. Formally,

$$\max_q qp - wq^{\frac{1}{\delta}} \tag{3.28}$$

First-order condition:

$$\frac{\partial \Pi}{\partial q} = p - \frac{1}{\delta} wq^{\frac{1-\delta}{\delta}} = 0.$$

Thus, the supply function of the hospital is

$$q(p, w) = \left(\frac{\delta p}{w}\right)^{\frac{\delta}{1-\delta}}$$

A second example computing the market demand will also serve the purpose of computing the elasticity of the supply function: consider a society with two (competitive) firms 1 and 2 and a good q.

$$q_1(l) = l^{1/3}$$
$$q_2(l) = l^{1/2}$$

The individual supply functions obtained from profit maximization are

$$q_1(p, w) = \left(\frac{p}{3w}\right)^{\frac{1}{2}}$$

$$q_2(p, w) = \frac{p}{2w}$$

We can compute the elasticities of these supply functions. These are given by,

$$\varepsilon_{q_1} = \frac{\partial q_1}{\partial p}\frac{p}{q_1} = \frac{1}{2}$$

$$\varepsilon_{q_2} = \frac{\partial q_2}{\partial p}\frac{p}{q_2} = 1$$

Finally, the aggregate supply is given by,

$$q(p, w) = \left(\frac{p}{3w}\right)^{\frac{1}{2}} + \frac{p}{2w} = \frac{2wp^{1/2} + 3wp}{2w(3w)^{1/2}}.$$

4   Markets

This chapter presents the interaction between supply and demand in the market. We describe different market configurations and study in detail three of them: perfect competition, monopoly, and oligopoly.

The concept of a market refers to the interaction between buyers and sellers. Such interaction may be real or virtual, may occur in a single location (and we refer to it as a *concentrated market*), or in several locations simultaneously (what we call a *dispersed market*). The outcome of this interaction is a pricing system and an allocation of goods and services among the participants in the market. A complete definition of a market must specify how prices are formed and what goods are exchanged. The latter question is rather delicate. It can be handled from a demand-oriented viewpoint or from a supply-oriented perspective.

Following the criterion of demand, a market is usually defined as the set of goods (and services) satisfying similar needs. Technically, we group those goods showing a sufficiently high cross-price elasticity among them and sufficiently low with the rest of goods and services of the economy. This definition is ambiguous because it does not contain a definition of the meaning of sufficiently high and low cross-price elasticity. To illustrate, consider the cross-price elasticity between 95-octane and 98-octane gasoline. A casual look at the statistical data will tell us that such elasticity is "high", so that both goods should be included in the same market. Consider also the cross-price elasticity between consumption of gasoline and mineral water. Presumably, it should be "low". Thus, these two goods belong to different markets.

The ambiguity in appraising the meaning of high or low cross-price elasticity severely limits the usefulness of the demand-oriented criterion in the rigorous study of the behavior of the agents in the market. Let us turn towards the supply-oriented viewpoint to see whether it proves more useful.

From the viewpoint of supply, the criterion simply consists of using the classification of economic activities. This is a way to divide the goods and services produced in a country (or more generally, in an economic area) so that each establishment can be allocated to a relevant site in the classification on the basis of its principal activity. Often these classification systems are used as proxies for market definitions. Every country has its own classification system. For instance, the USA has the NAICS (North-American Industry Classification System) with a six-digit coding system, the European Union has the NACE (Nomenclature statistique des Activités économiques dans la Communauté Européenne) with a four-digit coding system, the UK has the UKSIC (UK Standard Industrial Classification of economic activities), the CAE in Portugal, the CNAE in Spain, etc. The very fact of using a classification system conveys the precision in the description of the production of goods and services.

Table 4.1 Taxonomy of market structures

Sellers/Buyers	Many	Few	One
Many	Perfect competition	Oligopsony	Monopsony
Few	Oligopoly	Bilateral oligopoly	
One	Monopoly		Bilateral monopoly

However the very advantage of using a coding system also turns into a disadvantage, because the coding systems are designed with technological criteria that need not coincide with the demand criteria of the cross-price elasticity. For instance, producing wine and champagne have assigned different codes; however from the viewpoint of the consumer they present a high cross-price elasticity.

The supply side aspects in the definition of a market offer some advantages from the Industrial Organization point of view. A well-known example is provided by McKie (1985) (see Cabral 2000, p. 21): In 1964 the US Air Force opened a contract for the provision of a certain type of radar. The contract was assigned to Bendix an enterprise that maintained a monopoly status for some years. This situation led a second firm, Wilcox, to sue Bendix for abuse of monopoly position. The Federal Trade Commission decided in favor of Bendix. The reason was that from the demand point of view, looking at the elasticity of demand, Bendix can be considered a monopoly. Nevertheless, according to the classification of industrial activities we find a certain number of firms with similar technological capacity to Bendix. Therefore, any of them could win the next contract when it becomes public. Actually, this is what happened in 1969 when Honeywell obtained the new contract.

These considerations lead us to two conclusions. First, to study the behavior of the economic agents in a market, a precise definition of the set of goods and services is mandatory. Second, the set of goods and services included in a market should offer a compromise between demand and supply criteria.[1]

Assuming that we are able to come up with a precise definition of a market, the next assumption to be introduced is that of *rational behavior* of the economic agents participating in that market. This means that each and every agent is assumed to follow a decision-making procedure to select the best option among those available. For a consumer this means that the goods and services purchased should maximize their satisfaction. For an enterprise, the goods and services sold should maximize profits. Kreps (1990, Chapter 1) describes the behavior of the economic agents based on alternative assumptions to rational behavior such as Bayesian behavior, or limited rationality.

How the interaction between supply and demand materializes depends on the number of agents (sellers and buyers). This is the structure of the market. Table 4.1 shows the different structures that may appear in an economy.

We will only refer to the structures in the first column, i.e. perfect competition, oligopoly, and monopoly.[2]

4.1   The perfectly competitive market

A perfectly competitive market is characterized by a large number of buyers and sellers, so that none of them has the capacity to affect the market price at which transactions take place. There are very few markets in the real economies that fit in this pattern, however there are several reasons that justify its study. On the one hand, it is a market with a simple functioning mechanism that can be used as a reference to elaborate more complex models closer to real situations. On the other hand, the equilibrium of a perfectly competitive market (that is, the market price and the market allocation) shows two important properties: the allocation obtained is efficient i.e. is the best possible allocation of resources, and this equilibrium does not need any intervention from a public authority. To be precise, we first present the assumptions of the model and then will characterize the equilibrium.

4.1.1   Assumptions

The model of perfect competition is based on eight assumptions fully characterizing the framework where the agents take their decisions and their behavior.

Structural assumptions

ASSUMPTION 4.1   *The model is static and of partial equilibrium.*

This assumption means that the analysis does not contemplate a temporal dimension. Instead, all agents make their decisions at the same time without being able to transfer goods and services either from the past to the present, or from the present to the future. Also, the model only studies the market for a single commodity. Thus, no potential interactions among different goods and services are included in the decision-making process of the agents. In plain words, this set-up considers very simple agents only aware of the present and able to take decisions only on a single product.

ASSUMPTION 4.2   *Only real markets are considered in the analysis.*

Consistently with the previous assumption, since there is neither past nor future, there is no room for financial markets. Agents only decide on quantities of commodities to be sold or bought.

ASSUMPTION 4.3   *The goods offered by sellers are homogeneous.*

This means that from the consumers' viewpoint all products brought to the market by the different sellers are identical. That is, a consumer is unable to distinguish which manufacturer has produced what good.

ASSUMPTION 4.4   *All agents have perfect information.*

Perfect information means that every agent knows all the relevant information about any other agent. Therefore, every agent could place him/herself in the role of any other agent and think *as if* he or she would be that other agent. In particular, this amounts to assuming that every consumer knows their preferences and the preferences of all other consumers. Also, every producer knows its technology and the technologies of all other producers in the market.

ASSUMPTION 4.5   *The economy is of private property.*

Private property means that consumers have property rights on their income, and the owners of the enterprises have property rights on profits. This assumption has important implications for the behavior of agents. We comment on them below.

Behavioral assumptions

ASSUMPTION 4.6   *There are two types of agents in the market, sellers and buyers. All of them are price-takers.*

This assumption means that all agents consider the prices as given, and they do not have capacity to alter them. In other words, no agent is able to induce a change in a price through their decision of buying (in the case of a consumer) or selling (in the case of a producer). A simple way to justify this assumption is to consider markets with a large number of sellers and buyers. Thus, the decision of an individual agent has a negligible impact on the set of all agents.

Also, the fact that all agents are either sellers or buyers implies that there is no third-party type of agent with the capacity to impose restrictions on the behavior of buyers and sellers, like a public authority or more generally the state.

ASSUMPTION 4.7   *All agents are rational.*

As it has been commented above, this means that sellers aim at maximizing profits, and consumers aim at maximizing utility.

ASSUMPTION 4.8   *There is free entry and exit in the market.*

Free entry means that any producer can decide to enter a market to sell the corresponding product and can also decide to exit the market. Typically, firms are willing to enter a market as long as it offers opportunities to obtain positive profits. Consistently with the absence of the state as an economic agent, there are no legal restrictions associated with the decision on entry and exit. However, such decisions may involve costs. In a market with free entry we should expect sellers to join the market until the point where profits are driven down to zero.

To complete the description of the market, we should look at the implications of Assumption 4.5. Note that holding the property of one's own income and assets has important implications in terms of incentives on how to use those properties. In general (and well beyond the scope of the model of perfect competition), holding the property of the profits by the owners of a firm gives incentives to invest (part of) them to maintain or increase the profitability of the business. On the side of consumers, having the property of the income gives incentives to save to obtain capital rents allowing for higher consumption rates in the future. At the other extreme of the spectrum, the presence of a state owning all the rents and assets of an economy and determining how to distribute them eliminates those incentives.

There is a downside to individual incentives, though. This is that they give rise to inequalities. Usually, individual incentives induce the correct effects if they are linked to performance; that is, if incentives operating on individuals link their income to their performance as economic agents. However, when combining the individual interest and the social interest of a community there appears a trade-off. Think of a society where individual incentives are dominant. It would be the case of a community with a very light fiscal system. Accordingly, the public authority responsible for collecting taxes would have little capacity to implement social benefit programs (public health, schooling, pensions, etc.). In this case, the individual welfare is tightly related to the individual income, so that low-income individuals have very limited capacity to access social benefits and thus improve upon their situation, while high-income individuals with capacity for saving are able to improve their situation over time. Also, more efficient technology is expected to appear because of the investment possibilities induced by the savings of consumers. A society with a high solidarity level (highly progressive fiscal system) offers less individual incentives for saving, and lower production levels should be expected. However, inequalities across individuals should also be lower. Societies determine where do they want to stand through, for example, voting mechanisms in governmental elections.

4.1.2 *Equilibrium*

In the competitive market the resources are allocated through a system of prices. In general a price system allocates the available goods and services to the consumers with the highest willingness to pay for them.[3]

In a competitive market an equilibrium is described by the price at which the amount of the (homogeneous) good producers are willing to sell coinciding with the amount of goods that consumers are willing to buy. Formally,

DEFINITION 4.1 (COMPETITIVE EQUILIBRIUM). An equilibrium in a competitive market is characterized by the price that empties the market.

The question then is how that equilibrium price is determined. To obtain the answer, let us look at Figure 4.1 and consider an arbitrary price like *PED*. At this price, the supply curve tells us that producers would be willing to (produce and) sell an amount q_2, illustrated by point *D*. In a parallel fashion, at price *PED* the market demand curve tells us that consumers would be willing to buy (see point *C*) an amount q_4. As a result, not all consumers could be served. Formally, we say that at the price *PED* there in *excess demand* in the market. This means that there are consumers that would be ready to pay a higher price to consume such goods, so that producers realize that they could have sold the same quantities at a higher price. As a consequence the market experiences a pressure to increase the price.

Let us then consider what would be the situation at a higher price like *PES*. With the same logic as before, now we observe that sellers would be willing to bring to the market an amount q_3 of the good in excess of the amount q_1 consumers would be willing to buy. Now at such a price there is an *excess supply* in the market. Accordingly, prices tends to diminish.

These arguments allow us to envisage a price formation mechanism by which consumers and producers evaluate at every possible price whether the market would show excess supply or excess demand, and would proceed to adjust the price accordingly. After a sequence of trials eventually the price p^* would be hit. At this price, the decision of producers and consumers are compatible. The amount the former are willing to sell matches the quantity of product the latter are willing to buy. This amount is q^*. Therefore, when that price is called, the exchange takes place between sellers and buyers and we say that the market is in equilibrium. It is important to realize that the adjustment until the equilibrium price is reached is

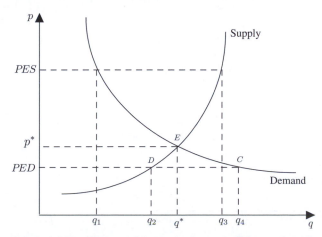

Figure 4.1 Equilibrium of the perfectly competitive market.

virtual. No exchange is observed. Agents verify in their minds whether decisions are compatible at every price, and keep on computing until the price p^* is reached. Formally, this intuitive argument allowing for identifying the equilibrium price is the result of maximizing profits taking into account that there is free entry in the market. Let us denote by q_i the production of a certain firm i, and let $C(q_i)$ be its total cost function. Let p be a price. Then the profit function of firm i is given by

$$\Pi_i(q_i) = pq_i - C(q_i).$$

The optimal (profit maximizing) output level is the solution of

$$\frac{\partial \Pi_i}{\partial q_i} = 0 = p - c(q_i) \tag{4.1}$$

where $c(q_i)$ denotes firm i's marginal cost. Accordingly, q_i^* is the output level solving

$$p = c(q_i^*).$$

Also, free entry guarantees zero profits, $\Pi_i(q_i^*) = 0$. Therefore,

$$pq_i^* = C(q_i^*), \quad \text{or} \quad p = \bar{c}(q_i^*), \tag{4.2}$$

where $\bar{c}(q_i)$ denote the average cost of firm i.

Combining (4.1) and (4.2), we characterize the competitive equilibrium as the output level q_i^* satisfying

$$p = c(q_i^*) = \bar{c}(q_i^*).$$

Figure 4.2 illustrates.

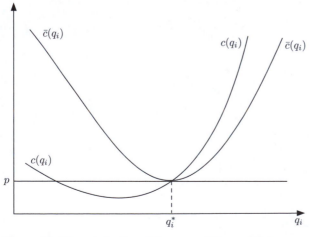

Figure 4.2 Characterization of the competitive equilibrium.

4.1.3 *Profit maximization vs. cost minimization*

In the previous chapter on the behavior of the producer, we have seen that the decision process of a firm can be studied either from the perspective of a profit maximization problem or as a cost minimization decision. An interesting property of the competitive markets is that both approaches are equivalent.

Consider a profit maximizing firm producing a certain consumption good q with a technology using two inputs, capital (K) and labor (L). Let p, r, w denote the prices of the output, capital and labor respectively. To simplify the analysis, consider a short-run decision process, so that the amount of capital is fixed at a certain level $\overline{K}$.

Formally, the problem of the firm is

$$\max_{L} \Pi_i(q) = pq - wL - r\overline{K}, \quad \text{s.t. } q = F(L, \overline{K}).$$

The left hand side of Figure 4.3 represents the solution of this problem in the space (q, L). The problem of the firm is to select the highest possible isoprofit curve compatible with the technological constraint. The firm decides optimally to hire L^* units of labor, yielding an output level of q^* units.

At the optimum, the following conditions are satisfied

$$\frac{w}{p} = \frac{\partial F}{\partial L}, \quad \text{and} \quad \frac{r}{p} = \frac{\partial F}{\partial K}$$

so that profits are maximized at

$$\frac{w}{r} = \frac{\dfrac{\partial F}{\partial L}}{\dfrac{\partial F}{\partial K}} \tag{4.3}$$

Consider next the same firm as before but deciding the amount of labor to hire to produce at the cost minimizing point. Formally the problem of this firm is

$$\min_{L} wL + r\overline{K}, \quad \text{s.t. } q = F(\overline{K}, L)$$

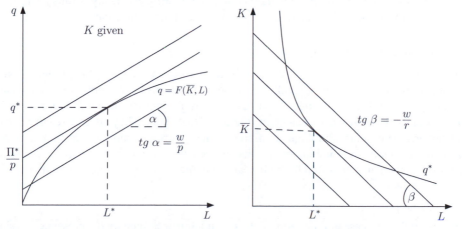

Figure 4.3 Profit maximization vs. cost minimization.

The right-hand side of Figure 4.3 represents the solution to this problem in the space (K, L). The problem of the firm is to select the lowest possible isocost curve compatible with the technological constraint. The firm decides optimally to hire L^* units of labor, yielding an output level of q^* units. With a parallel argument as before, it can be seen that the cost minimizing point is reached when the following condition holds,

$$\frac{w}{r} = \frac{\dfrac{\partial F}{\partial L}}{\dfrac{\partial F}{\partial K}} \tag{4.4}$$

Note that the optimizing conditions (4.3) and (4.4) are the same. This says that with given prices (p, r, w), maximizing profits is equivalent to minimize cost. That is, if a firm maximizes profits producing an output level q^*, it must also be minimizing cost. Otherwise, it would mean that there would be a cheaper way to produce q^* thus contradicting the claim that by producing q^* the firm maximizes profits.

4.1.4 The health care market

There are four main arguments that prevent treating the health care market as a perfectly competitive market. First, there is a difference between the health status the individual aspires to enjoy and the level of health care that (s)he is able to buy. Second, the health care sector presents an inherent difficulty in measuring its products and its costs (see Folland *et al.* 2009, ch. 4). Third, the patient does not decide the treatment to be applied (demand); the physician does it instead. This means that the physician acts as an agent of the patient. In turn, this introduces several difficulties in terms of asymmetric information, moral hazard, and adverse selection that will be examined in Chapter 11. Last but not least, individuals in the health care market can contract insurance against the illness episodes (see Chapter 10), and also there are barriers to entry imposed by, e.g., the professional associations.

As a consequence, we need to study markets where some of the assumptions defining perfect competition are not met. In the jargon of economics these are referred to as *market failures*, giving rise to imperfectly competitive markets. We will study them in the next section. Also, market imperfections convey that decisions will no longer be efficient. The role of the state intervening in the market aiming at restoring efficiency is thus justified. We refer to this market intervention as *regulation* and is examined in Chapter 5.

4.2 Imperfect competition

Looking back at Table 4.1, we will next tackle market structures with a limited number of sellers. We will see that, typically, in these markets, producers obtain strictly positive (economic) profits. The first question to ask is why no more firms enter the market. The answer points at the presence of elements impeding such entry. They are called *entry barriers* and can originate from technological differences across firms or more interestingly, from the *strategic behavior* of the incumbent producers. One way or another, we will focus on two market structures that are often found in real economies: monopoly and oligopoly.

4.2.1 Monopoly

We present first the case of monopoly. This is a situation described by the presence of a single producer aiming at maximizing profits. We are interested in assessing the decision process of such a firm both to understand its behavior, and also because it will help to comprehend the behavior of firms in an oligopolistic setting.

DEFINITION 4.2 (MONOPOLY). We say that a market has a monopoly structure, or that a market is monopolized, when there is a single firm operating in that market. We refer to such firm as the monopolist.

Note that this definition is supply-side driven. To compare this market structure with the perfectly competitive market, we maintain the structural Assumptions 4.1–4.5, and also the behavioral Assumption 4.7. The remaining assumptions are modified as follows:

ASSUMPTION 4.9 *There are two types of agents in the market, buyers and a single seller. Buyers' behavior is described by an (aggregate) market demand function. The single seller is choosing either the quantity to produce of a certain commodity or its price to maximize profits.*

This means that differently from the case of perfect competition, the situation now is asymmetric between the supply and demand sides. We will argue below that this asymmetry is harmful to consumers when compared with the case of perfect competition. Therefore, in some instances it will be necessary to limit the capacity to choose of the monopolist by appealing to a third agent (the state, or the antitrust authority, or a regulatory agency) with capacity to limit the scope of actions of the monopolist. In this way, part of the consequences of the asymmetry between the monopolist and the consumers will be corrected and the harm to consumers limited.

We have already argued that if no other competitor firm enters in a profitable market, it must be the case that these potential competitors find impediments to access the market. Leaving aside the reasons of such difficulties, we assume,

ASSUMPTION 4.10 *Entry of other competitor firms in the market is impeded.*

To characterize the equilibrium of the monopoly, let us assume that the market demand describes the behavior of consumers (see Section 2.3). Denote it as $p(q)$. Then, the problem of the monopolist is to identify the production volume q^m that given the demand function and its technology, allows to maximize profits. Formally, the problem of the monopolist is,

$$\max_q \Pi(q) = qp(q) - C(q) = R(q) - C(q),$$

where $R(q)$ denotes the revenues obtained by the monopolist from selling its production. The optimal profit maximizing output level is the solution of

$$\frac{\partial \Pi}{\partial q} = 0 = \frac{\partial R}{\partial q} - \frac{\partial C}{\partial q}, \quad \text{or} \quad \frac{\partial R}{\partial q} = c(q). \tag{4.5}$$

The first term of the last expression is the marginal revenue, that is how revenues of the monopolist vary when an additional unit of output is sold. The second term is the marginal cost and has already been defined in Section 4.1.2. To ease notation let us denote the former as $r(q)$. Then (4.5) simply says that the monopolist optimally will choose the level of

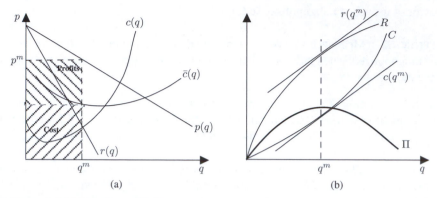

Figure 4.4 Monopoly equilibrium.

production at which marginal revenue equates marginal cost. At output levels below $r = c$ the decrease in revenue is greater than the decrease in cost ($r > c$), and at output levels above $r = c$, the increase in cost is greater than the decrease in revenue ($r < c$). Figure 4.4(a) illustrates the argument. Figure 4.4(b) shows an alternative characterization of the monopoly equilibrium. There we show the revenue function (R) and the total cost function (C). The vertical difference between both lines are the profits depicted by the thick line. The problem of the monopolist is to find the volume of output where such distance is maximum. This occurs at the point q^m where the slope of both curves coincide. Note that the slope of the total cost function at a given point is the marginal cost at that point. Similarly, the slope of the revenue function at a given point is the marginal revenue at that point. As the figure illustrates, at the point q^m both slopes also coincide consistently with (4.5).

We can also make use of Figure 4.4(a) to illustrate that the monopolist obtains strictly positive profits. Note that the revenues obtained by the monopolist from selling the volume of output q^* is given by the larger shaded rectangle. The total cost is represented by the lower shaded rectangle. Therefore, the difference between revenues and costs are the profits represented by the upper shaded rectangle.

Assumption 4.9 is the driving force behind the characterization of the equilibrium in a monopolistic market. Note that the capacity of the monopolist to announce a price (or to sell some determinate volume of output) is only limited by the fact that all consumers behave in the same way, described by the aggregate market demand. Therefore, even though the monopolist knows that is the only producer and seller of a particular commodity, it cannot obtain more income (and profits) than associated with the amount of output the consumers are willing to buy at each particular price. Equivalently, every volume of output the monopolist produces can only be sold at the price the consumers are willing to pay. The relationship between the output sold and the price is precisely the content of the aggregate demand function. To see it formally, note that we can transform the marginal revenue function into a function of the market price and the elasticity of demand in the following way. From the definition of the revenue function, it follows that the marginal revenue is

$$r(q) = p(q) + q\frac{\partial p}{\partial q}. \tag{4.6}$$

Multiplying and dividing (4.6) by p and recalling the Definition 2.9 of own price elasticity, we can rewrite (4.6) as

$$r(q) = p\left(1 - \frac{1}{\varepsilon}\right).$$

Finally, the equilibrium monopoly price is characterized by the solution of the equation $r(q) = c(q)$. Therefore,

$$p^m = \frac{c(q)}{1 - \dfrac{1}{\varepsilon}}$$

Given that $\varepsilon < 0$, it follows that the equilibrium price under monopoly is larger than the marginal cost evaluated at the equilibrium output, as it is shown in Figure 4.4(a). The more inelastic the demand function the higher the equilibrium monopoly price, and thus the higher the margin between the price and the marginal cost. This margin is usually related to the so-called monopoly power.

Let us finally compare the monopoly and perfectly competitive markets solutions. Observe Figure 4.5 where we have represented a monopoly price and a competitive equilibrium price and the corresponding volumes of output. The first observation is that under monopoly, less volume is produced and sold at a higher price with respect to the competitive solution. The monopolist by quoting a higher price is giving rise to two effects. On the one hand, it does not serve those consumers with a too low willingness to pay. Therefore the aggregate consumption decreases in an amount $q^c - q^m$. These consumers "expelled out" of the market by the monopolist were obtaining a surplus represented by the upper shaded triangle. On the other hand, those consumers that were served under perfect competition and are also served under monopoly, are now paying a higher price. And those consumers expelled out of the market are individuals willing to pay a price above marginal cost. Therefore by giving up these consumers, the monopolist is also giving up a certain amount of surplus represented by the lower shaded triangle. Formally, this area is given by,

$$\int_{q^m}^{q^c} [p(x) - c(x)]\, dx.$$

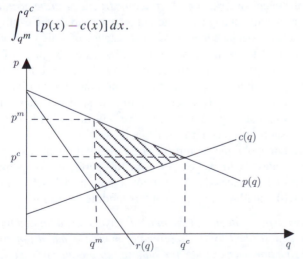

Figure 4.5 Monopoly deadweight loss.

Summarizing, the presence of a monopolist in a market gives rise to a loss of efficiency both on the demand and on the supply sides, given by the shaded triangle. We refer to the area of such triangle as the *deadweight loss* generated by the monopolist.

An underlying assumption in the analysis is that a monopolist cannot price discriminate and charge each and every consumer a different price, according to the consumer's willingness to pay for the product (or service). If such a possibility exists, then the monopolist will be able to propose a price to each consumer ensuring that all transactions with social positive value would take place (and all surplus would be appropriated by the monopolist). The objection to this allocation of resources is not on the grounds of economic efficiency but on distributive concerns.

4.2.2   Oligopoly with homogeneous product

So far we have studied two extreme market structures, perfect competition, and monopoly. A common feature of both is that firms do not interact with each other either because there are too many or only one. In other words, there are no strategic elements in the decision process of the firms. Now we introduce a market structure with a limited number of firms in the market and refer to it as oligopoly.

DEFINITION 4.3 (OLIGOPOLY).   We say that a market is an oligopoly when there is a limited number of firms in the market. In their decision process, each firm will take into account the decision of the rival firms.

The crucial element of an oligopolistic market is the interaction among the firms. This is the *strategic interaction*. Think, for instance, of a market of apples with only two sellers. Both manufacturers know that they are the only ones in the market. Therefore they know that when a consumer wants to buy an apple (s)he will buy it at either one or the other shop. Accordingly, when deciding the price at which each seller wants to sell the respective apples, it will have to guess the price of the competitor seller. If seller 1 announces a price higher enough than seller 2, consumers will know it and will patronize seller 2. The fact that one seller has to take into account the decision of the rival seller is the strategic interaction among sellers that defines the oligopolistic nature of the market.

We can distinguish two types of strategic interaction. We refer to *structural strategic interaction* as the links that firms face even without any active action on their part. In the example of the market of apples, even if seller 1 decides to ignore the existence of seller 2, it will experience an increase in its demand if for some reason seller 2 increases the price of its apples. We refer to *behavioral strategic interaction* as the actions taken by a firm fully aware of the impact they will have on its competitors. This latter interaction is the object of interest in the analysis of an oligopolistic market. Usually when studying the strategic interaction among firms we refer to the behavioral strategic interaction. We will do so here as well. Hence, strategic interaction will be short for behavioral strategic interaction.

Note that as in the case of the monopoly, the definition of an oligopoly is also supply-driven. To put the oligopoly in context with respect to both the perfectly competitive and monopolistic markets, we maintain the structural set of Assumptions 4.1–4.5 and the behavioral Assumptions 4.7 and 4.10. Finally, Assumption 4.9 is modified as follows:

ASSUMPTION 4.11   *There are two types of agents in the market, buyers and a limited number of sellers. Buyers' behavior is described by an (aggregate) market demand function. Sellers choose strategically and simultaneously either the quantity to produce of a certain commodity or its price to maximize profits.*

Note that we maintain Assumption 4.3 of homogeneous product. This means that consumers are unable to identify which seller has produced which product. Accordingly, buyers' behavior is summarized in a single aggregate demand function, and a single price for the product will prevail in the market.

Equilibrium analysis

To ease the study of the equilibrium let us consider only two sellers in the market. We refer to such situation as a duopoly. Denote sellers as 1 and 2. They produce a certain commodity in amounts q_1 and q_2 respectively. Let us also denote the aggregate production as $q = q_1 + q_2$. The aggregate demand function is $p(q)$ and satisfies the usual properties of differentiability, continuity, and decreasing monotonicity.

Sellers choose simultaneously a production level to maximize their respective profits given their own technologies, the aggregate demand function, and their respective *expectations on the decision of the rival seller*. Formally, let us denote by q_j^e firm i's expectation of the production of firm j ($i, j = 1, 2, i \neq j$). Finally, the technology of producer i is described by a total cost function $C_i(q_i)$.

The equilibrium of this duopolistic market is characterized by the solution of the following problems:

$$\max_{q_1} \Pi_1(q_1, q_2^e) = q_1 p(q_1 + q_2^e) - C_1(q_1) \tag{4.7}$$

$$\max_{q_2} \Pi_2(q_1^e, q_2) = q_2 p(q_1^e + q_2) - C_2(q_2) \tag{4.8}$$

Thus a duopoly equilibrium is a pair of volumes of output (q_1^*, q_2^*) that in turn define a market price $p(q^*)$. To see how the two competitors arrive at the determination of their respective optimal production volumes let us consider seller 1.

As in the case of the monopoly, solving (4.7) tells us that seller 1 will choose an output level q_1 that will equate marginal revenue to marginal cost, but now this equation is *conditional to the expectation it has formed on* q_2^e! Formally,

$$\frac{\partial \Pi_1}{\partial q_1} = 0 = p(q_1 + q_2^e) + q_1 \frac{\partial p(q_1 + q_2^e)}{\partial q_1} - c_1(q_1). \tag{4.9}$$

Thus, we can rewrite this condition in a compact way as

$$q_1 = f_1(q_2^e), \tag{4.10}$$

and we refer to it as the *reaction function* of firm 1. This reaction function tells us the optimal decision of firm 1 for every possible expectation it has formed on the decision of the rival firm 2.

A parallel argument can be put forward for firm 2 to conclude that its profit maximizing volume of production is given by a reaction function,

$$q_2 = f_2(q_1^e). \tag{4.11}$$

The equilibrium of the market is the pair (q_1^*, q_2^*) that satisfies simultaneously (4.10) and (4.11). This simply means that an equilibrium arises when the expectations the firms form on the behavior of the rivals are fulfilled. Figure 4.6(a) illustrates the argument.

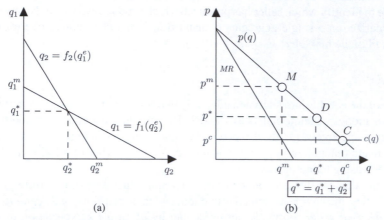

Figure 4.6 Duopoly equilibrium.

Note that we have characterized the duopoly equilibrium assuming firms determine equilibrium quantities, and the demand function determines the equilibrium market price. Given that the products are homogeneous, assuming that firms quote prices will generate a degenerate market behavior. Recall that Assumption 4.4 tells us that all agents know all the relevant information. In particular this means that if firms were setting prices, all consumers would know both prices, so that all would patronize the seller quoting the lowest price. Firms would be aware of consumers' behavior, so that they would engage in a price war. If both firms have the same technology, the price war would finish when both firms quote a price equal to the (same) marginal cost, thus reproducing a competitive equilibrium. If one firm has a better technology (i.e. a lower marginal cost) than the other, it will quote a price just under the marginal cost of the rival, and will expel it from the market.

Figure 4.6(b) compares (when marginal costs are constant) the equilibrium outputs for the three market structures presented so far. Point M represents the monopoly solution where marginal revenue equates marginal cost in accordance with (4.5). Point C represents the perfectly competitive market where price equals marginal cost in accordance with (4.1). Finally, point D is the duopoly equilibrium just studied. We see that the equilibrium price is highest under monopoly and lowest under perfect competition. This is a consequence of the capacity of the sellers to manipulate the functioning of the market, i.e. of the *monopoly power* of the firms.

Monopoly power

The question that we want to tackle next is how to assess the market power or the monopoly power of a firm. To do it, consider the solution of the profit maximization problem of an oligopolistic firm i like (4.7). Abstracting from the expectations, write it as

$$p(q) + q_i \frac{\partial p(q)}{\partial q_i} - c_i(q_i) = 0.$$

Rearranging terms, we obtain,

$$p(q) - c_i(q_i) = -q_i \frac{\partial p(q)}{\partial q_i}.$$

Next, dividing both sides by $p(q)$ and multiplying and dividing the right-hand side by q we obtain,

$$\frac{p(q) - c_i(q_i)}{p(q)} = -\frac{\partial p(q)}{\partial q_i}\frac{1}{p(q)}q\frac{q_i}{q}. \tag{4.12}$$

The left-hand side of (4.12) tells us the capacity of firm i to price above its marginal cost in relative terms. This expression is called the *Lerner index* of monopoly power, denoted as $\mathcal{L}_i$. This index takes value zero when the firm is perfectly competitive, and approaches a value of 1 in the limit case of a pure monopoly. Therefore the higher the value of the Lerner index the higher the monopoly power of the firm. One difficulty in measuring the Lerner index of a firm is obtaining accurate enough information regarding its technology. However, we already know that the price an oligopolistic firm will quote in the market is related to the elasticity of demand. Therefore, we can relate the Lerner index to the elasticity of the market demand as a way of obtaining estimates of the market power of a firm. Let us take back (4.12) and recalling Definition 2.9 of own price elasticity, we can rewrite is as

$$\mathcal{L}_i = \frac{1}{\varepsilon}\frac{q_i}{q}. \tag{4.13}$$

Finally, defining the market share of firm i as the proportion of output with respect to the total output produced, and denoting it as m_i, we can rewrite (4.13) as,

$$\mathcal{L}_i = \frac{1}{\varepsilon}m_i. \tag{4.14}$$

Thus we see that we can assess the monopoly power of a firm from the information about its market share and the elasticity of demand.

4.2.3 Oligopoly with differentiated products

So far we have assumed that the consumer's decision is to buy a certain product without being able to distinguish among the products offered by the different sellers. In other words, all goods offered in the market are identical in the eyes of the consumers. There are very few markets satisfying this assumption. Usually, consumers' preferences are "fine" enough to let them identify which firm has produced which model of the product. We will now allow consumers to be able to read the "label" attached to each product identifying the producer, and thus to *differentiate* one variety from another among all those available in the market. We refer to the models including this feature as models of product differentiation.

We next introduce a variation of the oligopoly model including differentiated products. Technically, we maintain structural Assumptions 4.1, 4.2, 4.4, and 4.5 and introduce the following one:

ASSUMPTION 4.12 *Consumers are able to identify the variety of the commodity that has been produced by each firm.*

In turn, the presence of differentiated products also introduces modifications in the set of behavioral assumptions. In particular we maintain Assumptions 4.7 and 4.10, and introduce,

ASSUMPTION 4.13 *There are two types of agents in the market, buyers and sellers. Buyers' behavior is described by an (aggregate) market demand function for each variety. Each seller chooses strategically and simultaneously a different variety and determines either the quantity to produce or its price to maximize profits.*

Note that Assumption 4.13 implies that every producer selects only one variety, so that we consider single-product firms. We can also allow to each producer to select a subset of varieties to produce. In that case firms would be multi-product.

It is important to understand that even though we consider different firms producing different varieties, we maintain the scope of the analysis in a single product market. Considering again the market for apples, now we say that consumers are allowed to distinguish among the different types of apples, e.g. Red delicious, Golden, Granny Smith, etc. Therefore, instead of buying just apples, now consumers will determine a demand function for each type of apple as a function of *the prices of all varieties of apples*.

Before proceeding with the analysis of oligopoly with differentiated products, let us summarize in Figure 4.7 all the market structures introduced so far classified according to the set of assumptions required.

The first consequence of introducing differentiated products is that in contrast with the models of homogeneous product, now there will be a set of different varieties of a certain commodity. Accordingly, there will be a set of demand functions in the market one for each variety.

There are two big families of oligopoly models with product differentiation. One of them considers all consumers identical in preferences and income, so that the analysis is developed in terms of a *representative consumer*. In this family of models, the utility of the representative consumer is increasing in the number of varieties, so that in equilibrium the consumer chooses a *bundle with all varieties*. The amount of each variety depends on the relative prices among the varieties. A particular feature of this family of models is that the (representative) consumer does not decide *what* to consume but *how much* of each variety to consume. The pioneer analysis of these models with a large number of firms is found in Chamberlin (1933) and Dixit and Stiglitz (1977) who consider a large number of competitors in the so-called *monopolistic competition* model. The study of oligopoly with a limited number of firms is due to (among others) Singh and Vives (1984).

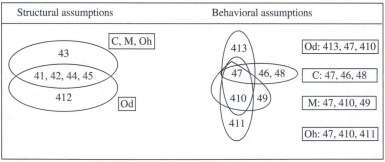

Legend:
C: Perfect competition;   Oh: Oligopoly w/ homogeneous products
M: Monopoly;   Od: Oligopoly w/ differentiated products

Figure 4.7 Taxonomy of market structures.

The second approach to product differentiation is associated with Hotelling (1929) who in contrast with Chamberlin's analysis considers that each consumer has different preferences but all have the same level of income. Then, each consumer decides to buy his or her most preferred variety, given the prices of all varieties. That is, each consumer buys a single variety, thus leading to a theory of product selection. This family of models are known as location models, or address models, and also as models of horizontal product differentiation. A variation within this approach is the so-called models of vertical product differentiation where consumers have different preferences and also different income levels. This analysis is associated with the names of Gabszewicz, Shaked, Sutton, and Thisse in a series of contributions during the 1980s.

Representative consumer models

Chamberlin (1933) proposed to model an industry where a large number of firms were producing similar goods with the same technology. Given that each firm is the only producer of its particular variety, the model has some features of the monopoly model. Given the large number of firms, the model also shares some characteristics of perfect competition. Chamberlin's approach is known as the model of *monopolistic competition*. Dixit and Stiglitz (1977) proposed the modern analytical formulation of this model. To be precise, we qualify Assumption 4.13 as,

ASSUMPTION 4.14 *The model of monopolistic competition contains a representative consumer and a large number of firms. The representative consumer has preferences (uniformly) distributed among all the varieties available in the market. These preferences are translated in a system of demand functions, one for each variety. Every demand function depends on the prices of all varieties available. Each firm produces a single variety and is the only one producing it. All firms use the same technology. Consumers choose a bundle of varieties to maximize utility. The composition of that bundle is determined by the relative prices of the varieties. Firms decide simultaneously the price of their corresponding varieties being aware that small variations of that price have a negligible impact on the decision process of the rival competitors.*

The equilibrium of this model, given the symmetry among firms (they all use the same technology) and among consumers (there is a representative consumer), is symmetric. That is, all firms announce the same price for its variety and produce the same amount. More interestingly, each firm faces a downward sloping demand, and the arbitrarily large number of firms guarantees that profits will be zero. Assuming a technology where average costs are U-shaped, the equilibrium is characterized by the tangency between the average cost and the demand curves as depicted in Figure 4.8. Note that the equilibrium output is lower than what would correspond to the minimum of the average cost. Therefore, it would be possible (keeping consumers' income constant) to diminish the number of firms and expand the production of the remaining ones in such a way as to increase the aggregate production, lower the price and increase profits. This argument leads to the standard conclusion that the model of monopolistic competition conveys too much variety, and therefore is not efficient. However, this analysis is incomplete because it does not take into account the loss of utility of consumers when they are prevented from buying those varieties that have been eliminated. Thus, *ex-ante* the overall effect is ambiguous. An empirical appraisal of the question is necessary to solve the ambiguity.

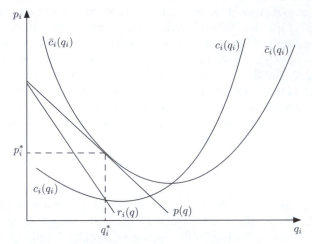

Figure 4.8 Monopolistic competition equilibrium.

The model of monopolistic competition just described lacks the strategic interaction characterizing the models of oligopoly. Therefore, let us consider that entry restrictions limit the number of active firms in the market, while maintaining all the other features in of Assumption 4.14. This true oligopoly model of product differentiation allows us to study firms' decision processes where the strategic variable may be either the volume of output (as in the case of homogeneous products) or the price (without obtaining the degenerate outcome found in the case of homogeneous products). Then, a question arises regarding comparing the equilibrium in both cases.

To make the analysis tractable, let us follow Singh and Vives (1984). These authors consider a system of linear demand functions and compute the equilibrium in prices and the equilibrium in quantities. It turns out that the equilibrium in quantities leads to higher prices and lower output volumes than the price equilibrium. Singh and Vives then say that competition in quantities is more monopolistic (in the sense that it gives the producers higher capacity to increase the price with respect to the marginal cost, i.e. higher Lerner index) than the competition in prices. Also, the difference in prices between both equilibria depend on the degree of differentiation between the two products.

One question remains in the analysis. Given that firms are allowed to choose to compete in prices or in quantities, there are various possible types of competition in the market: both firms may decide (unilaterally) to choose prices; both firms may decide to choose quantities; and one firm may decide to choose the price while the other decides to choose the quantity. Singh and Vives also show that when the two varieties are substitute goods, both firms find it optimal to select quantities as their strategic variable (in the sense that obtain a higher level of profits than with the other three alternatives). This gives consistency to the equilibrium in quantities in the models of oligopoly with product differentiation characterized by the presence of a representative consumer.

Location

We now introduce the second family of models of product differentiation characterized by the distinguishing feature that every consumer decides to purchase just one unit of one of the available varieties. Also, these models contemplate a small number of firms all using the same (constant marginal cost) technology. Therefore, they are demand-driven models of product selection.

In these models, consumers face a situation where their most preferred variety is not available (except for a set of consumers of measure zero), so that each one has to choose the second best option which depends on the relative prices of the available varieties and the loss of utility between the best and the second best varieties.

Two subfamilies are identified according to the modeling of the consumers. They are labeled as models of *horizontal product differentiation*, and *vertical product differentiation* (see Phlips and Thisse 1982).

Models of horizontal product differentiation originated in Hotelling (1929). The modern approach is due to d'Aspremont *et al.* (1979) and was developed mainly in the 1980s. An appealing survey of this literature is that of Gabszewicz and Thisse (1986a).

The distinguishing assumption is that there is a continuum of consumers and each individual consumer is assumed to have different preferences over the space of varieties of a certain commodity. Therefore, Assumption 4.13 needs to be qualified as follows:

ASSUMPTION 4.15 *In the models of horizontal product differentiation, there is a continuum of consumers. Each consumer is endowed with different preferences defined over a space of varieties in such a way that a consumer can be identified by his or her most preferred variety. All consumers are endowed with the same level of income. A small number of firms are active in the market, each producing one variety using the same constant marginal cost technology. Thus, we can also identify a firm with the variety it produces. Each consumer chooses one unit of the variety maximizing his preferences. Firms decide simultaneously the variety to produce and its price to maximize profits.*

An equivalent (and more intuitive) interpretation of this type of models is the following. Think of a city where its inhabitants are distributed uniformly along a single street. Each consumer is thus identified with his address. In this city there are also some producers that can also be identified with their address. Except for those few consumers whose location coincides with one of the producers (and this is a set of measure zero), all consumers will have to travel to the outlet where the variety he or she has decided to produce is available. Therefore, the variety a consumer decides to purchase will be determined by the prices of all available varieties *and* the transport cost to arrive at the shop. The analysis of the equilibrium relies heavily on the modeling of this transport cost. Formally, a consumer's utility located at a point x_i in the space and patronizing a firm y_j selling its variety at a price p_j is given by

$$U_i = -p_j - td(x_i, y_j)$$

where $d(x_i, y_j)$ represent a distance function between the consumer and the seller, and t is the transport cost per unit of distance. The consumer's problem is to choose the seller that, given the prices and distances maximizes utility, that is to patronize producer j satisfying

$$\max\{-p_1 - td(x_i, y_1), \ldots, -p_j - td(x_i, y_j), \ldots, -p_m - td(x_i, y_m)\}$$

where m denotes the number of firms in the market. Producers in turn, know this choice rule of consumers and announce the price that maximizes their profits.

Assume there are two firms in the market whose locations are fixed and transport costs are linear. Let the segment $[0, 1]$ represent the location space. Figure 4.9 illustrates the split

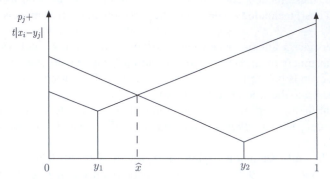

Figure 4.9 Hotelling model.

of the market between the sellers for a given pair of prices (p_1, p_2). Consumers to the left of $\hat{x}$ (the so-called indifferent consumer) obtain higher utility addressing their demands to producer y_1, and consumers to the right of $\hat{x}$ obtain higher utility addressing their demands to producer y_2.

The equilibrium analysis shows that a price equilibrium exists only when firms are located far enough apart. At this price equilibrium, the profit functions of the firms are increasing as firms locate closer one to the other. Hotelling concluded that firms have incentives to locate as close as possible around the center of the market. This is a famous result in this literature called the *principle of minimum differentiation* after Boulding (1948). However, as d'Aspremont *et al.* (1979) pointed out this principle does not hold, because when firms locate close enough, competition in prices is too harsh destroying the equilibrium. However, the principle of minimum differentiation is so appealing (as it conforms with empirical observations), that many efforts have been developed trying to find conditions under which the principle would hold. Technically, the problem is that the profit function is not quasi-concave. With a uniform distribution of consumers on the space and constant marginal cost technologies, only a quadratic transport cost function allows us to obtain quasi-concave profits functions (see Gabszewicz and Thisse 1986a). However, in that case firms soften price competition locating as far apart as possible, thus obtaining the opposite of the principle of minimum differentiation. The literature goes on using different price strategies, different distribution of consumers, different number of firms, different transport cost functions, etc. Summarizing, Hotelling's approach to the modeling of product differentiation has generated an enormous stream of analysis of horizontal product differentiation, concluding that this analysis is appealing but difficult and hardly able to generate general results.

A different approach to the modeling of product differentiation is associated with the idea that individuals consume different varieties because not all of them can afford their most preferred variety. To illustrate the idea, think of two car manufacturers, and assume consumers are only able to identify the size of a car and its quality. Consider two models of the same size. If both were priced equally, it would be expected that all consumer would buy the high quality model. Thus, if not everybody buys it, it is simply because not all consumers have enough income to afford the high quality car, and can only buy the low quality one. This idea of quality as distinguishing feature of product differentiation is behind the models of *vertical product differentiation* (see Gabszewicz and Thisse 1982).

ASSUMPTION 4.16 *In the models of vertical product differentiation, there is a continuum of consumers. Each consumer is endowed with different income. All consumers are endowed with the same preferences. A small number of firms are active in the market, each producing one of the varieties using the same constant marginal cost technology. Each consumer chooses one unit of the variety maximizing his preferences. Firms decide simultaneously the variety to produce and its price to maximize profits.*

A nice property of this model is that profits functions are quasi-concave for a large family of transport cost functions, so that there are no technical difficulties in characterizing the equilibrium of the model in terms of prices and locations of firms. Gabszewicz and Thisse (1986b) compare the strategic properties of the two models and provide the rationale for the different strategic properties of the models of horizontal and vertical product differentiation.

Finally Gabszewicz and Thisse (1980) and Shaked and Sutton (1982, 1983, 1984) show that there is an upper limit to the number of firms that can be active in the market regardless of its size. They called this feature "natural oligopolies."

5   Regulation

In this chapter, we analyze the different forms of government intervention in the market. The central issue addressed is the need for regulating the economy. The departure of real markets from perfect competition conditions introduces distortions in the resource allocation in the economy, calling for some correction mechanisms. We put special emphasis on natural monopoly, the presence of externalities, and the notion of incentive regulation.

Government intervention in the economy takes many forms: taxes and subsidies, regulations, direct action through public provision, etc. The same characterization holds with respect to government intervention in the health care market. The definition of the legal framework also affects the behavior of economic agents. It is another tool for governments to influence economic activity. Some types of regulation are universally accepted, like the minimum age to access the labor market, or safety in the workplace, but many others are controversial like the application of positive action for gender or race, antitrust laws, price discrimination practices, patents, waste disposal, environmental pollution, etc. The generic question that we tackle in this chapter is: Why regulate?

The most well-known model of economic theory is the perfect competition paradigm. In that ideal world, there is no scope for regulation. Large numbers of buyers and sellers, all of whom with complete and perfect information of each and every product or service, would achieve an efficient allocation of resources. Equity concerns would be addressed by suitable redistributions.

However, most markets and sectors do not comply with the strong conditions required by the perfect competition paradigm. The motives from economic theory for government intervention and regulation are based on market failures. The existence of market failure, however, is not a sufficient condition for government intervention. In a similar way to market failure, government failure may also occur. Bureaucracies may have their own objectives and distortions in their actions. It is necessary to show that intervention, under perfect and/or imperfect conditions, will improve the resource allocation, whatever the evaluation criterion defined for that purpose.

There are several theories justifying the existence of regulation. Without going into details on each of them, two main ones can be identified. The first one is the *public interest theory*. According to this theory, regulation exists because there are market failures. The second theory is known as the *capture theory*. Its central point is that regulation creates rents, and demand and supply of regulation establish how such rents are distributed. Although it may not explain why regulation appeared in the first place, it suggests that it may face problems. This view started with Stigler (1971), who pointed out the importance of coercive power held by governments. This coercive power can be used to generate economic rents. Regulation results from pressure groups using the coercive power of governments to their advantage.[1]

Regarding the health sector, in answer to the question of why the state regulates the health care market, a typology of answers arise. Among them we highlight the following ones: (a) market complexity allows providers to take advantage of patients; (b) health is too fundamental a good for letting the market operate freely; and (c) health care generates externalities; (d) poor people must have access to the health care market; and (e) asymmetric information between physician and patient calls for patient protection. Also, it is argued that the health care marketplace is very different from perfect competition conditions. Large sellers, few in number, and large buyers do exist, together with other forms of entry barriers like licenses, patents, and professional associations; information problems are common; externalities and important equity concerns are present; and there is public provision of health care. These arguments lie behind the regulation of the health care market. One market in health care in which we find extensive regulation is the pharmaceutical market. We can observe direct regulation of prices, minimum quality standards, authorization of entry, and definition of market rules (internal price referencing, international price referencing, possibility of pharmacists to substitute generic for branded drugs). Regulation in the pharmaceutical market will be discussed later on in more detail.

5.1 Natural monopoly

The existence of market power can also be seen as a motive for government intervention. The exercise of market power creates distortions in the allocation of resources. The standard example is the case of a monopolist as studied in Section 4.2.1. Government intervention in this market can take several forms. One is price regulation, imposing the requirement that prices cannot be above a certain value, or ruling out possibilities for price discrimination. Of course, if the regulator has perfect knowledge regarding demand conditions and cost structure, it can set the price equal to the marginal cost of production. However, this is not a common situation. Regulation, when the cost and/or demand conditions are known only imperfectly, is discussed below. Another type of intervention by governments is easing entry of other providers so that competition among them will reduce prices and efficiency distortion.

A case of particular relevance in the study of regulation is the natural monopoly.

DEFINITION 5.1 (NATURAL MONOPOLY). A natural monopoly arises when a firm's technology exhibits scale economies so large relative to the size of the market that it is not profitable for a second firm to enter the market and compete.

This technological characteristic thus generates a "natural" barrier to entry because the ratio of fixed to variable cost is high. Traditional examples of natural monopolies are public utilities such as water services and electricity where building the distribution network (fixed cost) is very expensive but the marginal (variable) cost of supplying an additional consumer is low. The notion of natural monopoly is also closely related to the concept of decreasing marginal cost. It is easy to see that with decreasing marginal cost, average cost of production is also decreasing (as the cost of the last unit produced is below the average cost of all previous units and therefore the resulting average cost after its production will be smaller than before). Under such technological conditions, it is always better to keep producing with a single firm (or institution) instead of splitting it between several institutions, from the viewpoint

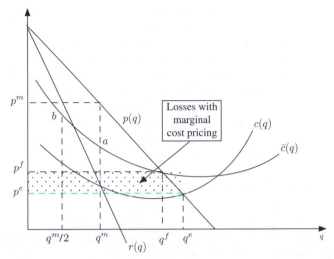

Figure 5.1 Natural monopoly.

of minimizing average cost of production. Figure 5.1 illustrates this. A monopolist producing q^m faces an average cost $\bar{c}(q^m) = a$. If this production level was to be shared between two (symmetric) firms, then producing $q^m/2$ entails an average cost of $\bar{c}(q^m/2) = b > a$. In a simple way, a natural monopoly market structure is present whenever it is cheaper to produce the desired level of output of the good or service with a single firm (or institution).

The concept of natural monopoly cannot be seen independently of demand conditions. For sufficiently high levels of demand for the service (or good), diseconomies of scale will start to matter and more than one provider of the health care service (or good) may lead to a total average cost of production lower than concentrating all production in a single unit. Low levels of demand relative to the point where economies of scale vanish will be associated with natural monopoly conditions, while large demand levels will destroy such conditions.

A frequent case of natural monopoly occurs with hospital care. In more remote, rural areas, the quantity of hospital care to be provided does not exhaust economies of scale. From an economic point of view, it is optimal to have a single hospital in those areas. This example illustrates nicely the role of demand and its relation to technological conditions in the definition of natural monopoly conditions. In large cities, the density and size of population that can potentially use the hospital usually allow for the co-existence of several hospitals in the same area.

One needs to be careful when presenting a precise definition of natural monopoly. It might seem that as long as economies of scale exist, a natural monopoly is present. Although this is true, the absence of economies of scale does not preclude the existence of natural monopoly conditions. To see why, consider a provider of health care that is producing a good or service at the point where it faces the minimum marginal cost available under the current technology.

Since marginal cost has been decreasing, it is certainly below average cost and producing more of the service (or good) with the same firm will still decrease the average cost, even if marginal cost is already increasing. The next crucial point relates to the minimum of average cost. As long as average cost decreases, it is worthwhile, for a fixed price, to keep producing and selling more units with the entity. Thus it becomes clear that economies of scale need to be exhausted before the conditions characterizing a natural monopoly situation disappear.

However, at the output level corresponding to the minimum of average cost, is it better to start producing with a second firm or to continue production with the same firm? The comparison that has to be made is between the cost of producing the additional unit in the same firm or in a new one. Whenever the average cost of production of a small amount in a new firm is higher than increasing average cost in the existing single firm, no new firm should enter the market and the natural monopoly conditions are still fulfilled. Therefore, a natural monopoly situation may exist for production levels above the one that leads to the lowest average cost. This condition is technically known as sub-additivity of the cost function.

Let us now formally introduce the concept of natural monopoly. As before let $C(q)$ denote the cost function associated with a provision of q units of the good or service. Let $c(q) = \partial C(q)/\partial q$ denote the marginal cost and let $\bar{c}(q) = C(q)/q$ denote average (unit) cost.

To formally define the concept of sub-additive cost function, consider a single-product cost function $c(q)$, where q is the output produced. Assume the cost function to be continuous and twice differentiable.

DEFINITION 5.2 (SUB-ADDITIVE COST FUNCTION).   A cost function $C(q)$ is sub-additive at $q = q^*$ if for all q_i, $i = 1, 2, \ldots, n$, such that $\sum_i q_i = q^*$,

$$C(q^*) \leq C(q_1) + \cdots + C(q_n). \tag{5.1}$$

The cost function is sub-additive if it is sub-additive at all possible output levels.

To verify if a given industry operates under the conditions defining a natural monopoly, take the socially optimal quantity (i.e. q^e in Figure 5.1). If the cost function is sub-additive at that optimal quantity, then the industry is a natural monopoly.

Since a single producer is better under natural monopoly conditions, the absence of regulation would allow a private monopolist to charge a higher price p^m to the consumers and to distort the quantity of service (or good) provided, q^m. A monopolist able to price discriminate perfectly across consumers (set a different price to each one) would not distort quantity produced but instead would collect all consumers' valuation for the good or service it provides.

Either through efficiency or equity concerns, natural monopolies are seldom left unregulated. A natural instrument to use is therefore price regulation.[2] The control of prices can be done directly (or indirectly, by profit regulation, for example). The main aim is to set a price such that the market outcome is the best possible one from the society's perspective. The first step is naturally to define the meaning of society's perspective. As in most economic analysis, here it is defined as the total valuation generated, irrespective of whether the value created is appropriated by consumers or by the firm.

Two traditional ways to price-regulate a natural monopoly are so-called *marginal cost pricing* and the *average cost pricing*.

Marginal cost pricing consists of regulating the firm so that it sets its price at the level of the marginal cost. In Figure 5.1 this gives the efficient output q^e that is sold at the price p^e.

Average cost pricing consists of regulating the firm to obtain zero profits by quoting a price equal to average cost. This is also known as a fair price and is represented in Figure 5.1 by p^f and its corresponding output q^f.

The problem with these methods is that they require accurate information on demand and cost conditions. However, if the firm does not justify its operation on efficiency grounds – that is, if a firm even quoting the monopoly price suffers losses, marginal and average cost pricing would only worsen the losses, so that regulating the price maintaining the firm in the market would be unjustified. This argument requires some qualification on welfare terms. On the one hand, it may happen that the subsidy necessary to keep the firm operative is offset by the increase in consumer surplus; on the other hand, the argument is somewhat incomplete in the sense that in does not consider the cost of the very regulation in terms of the capacity of the regulator to raise funds without incurring any distortionary costs from the tax system.

Unfortunately, these ideal conditions regarding demand and costs are seldom satisfied and different approaches have to be considered. The oldest one is the *rate of return regulation*. In this approach, regulated providers are allowed to earn a pre-determined rate of return over their physical assets. The regulation by rate of return requires information on costs and investments by the regulated entity. It is more adequate for activities that do not face any sort of competition. The rate of return regulation was consistently found to introduce incentives for too much investment, as the way to increase returns to the regulated firm. Equivalently, rate of return regulation provides low incentives for cost reductions. This argument suggests that a regulation inducing powerful incentives for cost reduction would be setting a price beforehand, together with a commitment to maintain it during a period of time even if costs changes. This is known as *price-cap regulation*.

In price-cap regulation the price is obtained after indexing according to inflation minus a so-called X-factor reflecting the deviation of the firm with respect to the average in the market. Under this type of regulation, from the point of view of the regulated firm, every euro that it saves in cost, is a euro that increases its profits. The problem with this regulation arises because the firm may anticipate that at the end of the period its effort to reduce cost will be taken into account by the regulator to define the new price for the next period, thus weakening the incentives for cost reduction. Therefore, it appears that introducing price regulation may generate perverse incentives. Section 5.2 looks into this issue.

Apart from prices, it is sometimes possible to regulate entry as well. The licensing for new providers in health care or the restrictions in the opening of pharmacies that exist in several countries are two examples.

If the government or the health authorities had perfect information, it would be easy to regulate. But most, if not all, regulatory decisions take place under conditions of asymmetric information. Regulated firms and institutions know more about demand for their services and cost structures than regulators do. Regulated providers and institutions will take advantage of their superior information, and the regulatory authority needs to recognize it in the use of its regulatory tools.

5.2   The Averch–Johnson effect

Economic regulation can also create perverse incentives. An important effect from rate of return regulation was pointed out by Averch and Johnson (1962). The point made was that rate of return regulation introduces a bias in the choice of inputs by firms. Since the rate of return is applied to physical assets owned by the regulated entity, the latter has an incentive to bias its choice of inputs. The bias will have an efficiency cost, as production costs will be higher than the minimum value possible for the output level produced.

Formally, the effect can be described in the context of a profit maximizing entity subject to a rate of return regulation. Let $R(K, L)$ be the revenues of the regulated entity, which depend on the choices of capital and equipment (K) and labor (L) to produce the output. Both inputs contribute positively to generate revenues, though at a decreasing rate. The rate of return regulation[3] constraint implies that

$$\frac{R(K, L) - wL}{K} \leq s$$

where w is the wage paid and s is the allowed rate of return. Let r be the opportunity cost of capital and equipment. Whenever $s < r$ the regulated entity prefers not to operate, whereas when $r = s$ there are zero (economic) profits. Thus, the interesting case occurs when $s > r$. Note that this regulation imposes a distortion in the relative prices of the inputs, making capital cheaper relative to labor. The maximization problem faced by the regulated entity is

$$\max_{\{K,L\}} \quad \Pi = R(K, L) - wL - rK$$

$$\text{s.t.} \quad R(K, L) - wL = sK$$

The constraint is set to equality, otherwise it would mean regulation would not impose any significant constraint upon the regulated entity. The first-order conditions of this problem are

$$\begin{cases} (1 - \lambda)\left(\dfrac{\partial R}{\partial K}\right) - r + \lambda s = 0, \\[2mm] (1 - \lambda)\left(\dfrac{\partial R}{\partial L} - w\right) = 0, \\[2mm] R(K, L) - wL = sK, \end{cases}$$

where λ stands for the Lagrange multiplier of the maximization problem.

Using the first two equations from the set of first-order conditions, we obtain

$$\frac{\partial R/\partial K}{\partial R/\partial L} = \frac{r - \lambda s}{w} \frac{1}{1 - \lambda} = \frac{r}{w} - \frac{\lambda}{1 - \lambda} \frac{s - r}{w} < \frac{r}{w} \tag{5.2}$$

From this different way of writing the expression, it becomes clear that the perceived cost of capital to firm is lower than the true one. Therefore, the level of capital and equipment chosen will be higher than the one that should be selected if the true opportunity cost is considered. Figure 5.2 illustrates this argument.

Let us examine panel (a) where we represent the isocost curves corresponding to the unregulated and regulated markets. Define $\rho \equiv \lambda(s - r)/(1 - \lambda)$ so that condition (5.2) becomes

$$\frac{r - \rho}{w} < \frac{r}{w}.$$

Let E be the efficient point characterized by the tangency between the isocost line with slope $-r/w$ and the corresponding isoquant. The distortion in the relative prices of the inputs varies the slope of the isocost curve to $-(r - \rho)/w$ so that the tangency under regulation appears now at point AJ, characterizing the Averch–Johnson point. The regulation induces a distortion in the capital to labor ratio that prevents profit maximization. This is shown in panel (b) of Figure 5.2.

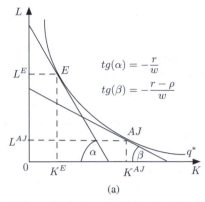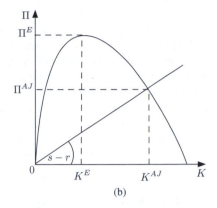

(a)   (b)

Figure 5.2 The Averch–Johnson effect.

5.3 Multi-product monopolist

A single-product natural monopoly is rare. Most situations of natural monopoly involve companies and institutions that produce more than one good or service. The idea of sub-additivity of the cost function extends to multi-product settings. The major difference, on conceptual grounds, is that sub-additivity in the cost function neither requires nor implies economies of scale. A multi-product monopolist leads to the simultaneous consideration of economies of scale and economies of scope.

The discussion on pricing regulation in a natural monopoly has considered so far a single-output monopolist. Take now the case of the multi-product monopolist. In the single output case, when costs have to be covered by the linear price charged, a departure from the perfect competition model result of price equal to marginal cost is required to ensure non-negative profits to the firm. In the presence of several outputs, the process of setting the 'right' prices is less obvious: should one only distort the price of one product and maintain the rule of price equal to marginal cost in all other products? Should all prices be distorted in the same proportional amount? Should a fixed amount be added to each and every price?

The answer to establishing the optimal pricing structure in the presence of several products offered by a natural monopoly – under the constraints that revenues must cover costs and a linear price has to be set for each product – was given by Frank Ramsey. The optimal pricing rule has the form:

$$\frac{p_i - c_i}{p_i} = \frac{k}{\varepsilon_i} \tag{5.3}$$

where k is a constant term, p_i is the price of product or service i, c_i is the marginal cost of production of product or service i and ε_i is the price elasticity of demand for product i. Thus, the optimal pricing rule states that prices should increase more for products that have a less sensitive demand. The logic is as follows. To cover costs, price must be greater than marginal cost. The distortion cost of a price increase is smaller when demand responds less to price. The efficiency distortion comes from changes in the consumption pattern. Less sensitive demands imply smaller changes in output. Note that no weight is given in this argument to the fairness (or its absence) of consumers from one product facing a higher price distortion over consumers of another product or service.

The Ramsey optimal pricing rule is based solely on efficiency grounds and it is silent on equity issues. A different way to present the Ramsey pricing rule is to state that starting from the situation where price equals marginal cost, to cover existing cost, cut all outputs in the same proportion until revenues cover total costs. By cutting all outputs in the same proportion, the prices of each product will change according to the corresponding price elasticities of demand. Low elasticity of demand leads to a higher price increase and a larger contribution to the funding of costs.

Formally, consider the problem of optimally setting prices of a (natural) monopolist producing n goods using a cost function $C(q_1, \ldots, q_n)$. Assume that each product is sold in independent markets. Demand in market j is given by $q_j(p_j)$ so that inverse demand for good j is given by $p_j(q_j)$. The revenue function of the monopolist is $R(q_1, \ldots, q_n) = \sum_j p_j q_j(p_j)$. Accordingly, the profit function of the monopolist is

$$\Pi(q_1, \ldots, q_n) = R(q_1, \ldots, q_n) - C(q_1, \ldots, q_n),$$

and the consumer surplus in market j is

$$CS_j = \int_0^{q_j} p_j(q_j) dq_j - p_j(q_j) q_j, \quad j = 1, \ldots, n.$$

From a society's perspective, total surplus is given by,

$$W(q_1, \ldots, q_n) = \sum_{j=1}^{n} CS_j + \Pi_j \tag{5.4}$$

The problem of the regulator is to maximize (5.4) subject to the restriction that monopolist does not suffer losses, i.e. $\Pi = 0$. The first order condition on the output volumes of the problem

$$\max_{\{q_1, \ldots, q_n\}} W(q_1, \ldots, q_n) \quad \text{s.t. } \Pi(q_1, \ldots, q_n) = 0,$$

is given by

$$p_j(q_j) - \frac{\partial C}{\partial q_j} + \lambda \left(p_j(q_j) + q_j \frac{\partial p_j}{\partial q_j} - \frac{\partial C}{\partial q_j} \right) = 0 \tag{5.5}$$

where λ denotes the Lagrange multiplier. Dividing (5.5) by $p_j(q_j)/(1 + \lambda)$ we obtain

$$\frac{p_j(q_j) - c(q)}{p_j(q_j)} = -\frac{\lambda}{1 + \lambda} \frac{q_j}{p_j(q_j)} \frac{\partial p_j}{\partial q_j} = \frac{-\lambda}{1 + \lambda} \frac{1}{\varepsilon_j}.$$

which is expression (5.3) with $k \equiv -\lambda/(1 + \lambda)$.

5.4   Public firms

An alternative to regulation of private firms and institutions is direct operation by the government. In health care, we often see government-run institutions. Countries like the United Kingdom, Canada, Portugal, and Spain, among others, have a health care system based on public provision of care, usually termed the national health service. Even in the United States, a large public provider of care is present. It is the Department of Veterans Affairs.

The use of direct provision of a good or service has obvious advantages: just let the government tell managers what objective they should have (say, maximize social welfare) and no further regulation is needed.

Despite this apparent simplicity, many regulated industries have resulted from government-backed direct operation. Countries with national health services are often changing their organization many times in the direction of introducing competition and private agents. Thus, direct operation by governments faces problems as well.

A first important element to take into account is the separation between ownership and management. It is true that in many private companies there is also a separation between ownership and management and therefore owners and managers have different objectives. However, the implicit controls that exist for private firms do not operate for direct government intervention in provision of goods and services.

A first reason results from the objectives of private and public firms. Assuming, somewhat simplistically, that private firms and institutions aim for profits; this is an objective easier to measure and monitor than social welfare (the "simple" objective of public firms). In other words, assessing the performance of a manager on the basis of profits raised for the company is quite different from, and much easier than, assessing performance based on social welfare.

A second way of implicit control (in the private market) of managers looking to pursue their own objectives is the discipline of the market for corporate control. A poorly-run company is easily acquired by others that believe they will be able to manage it better. The control by acquisition simply does not exist in the case of public firms. There is more room for management discretion in public institutions than in private companies.

Sometimes, to contain such discretion, managers of government-run institutions are subject to specific rules and laws. Typically, these take away important tools from the control of the public managers, harming their ability to effectively manage the organization. It is widely acknowledged that controls and incentives for efficiency are lower in the public enterprise. The resulting lower efficiency of operation is likely to drive prices up. Therefore, the comparison of the regulated private company with the public enterprise cannot be resolved solely on theoretical grounds. The answer is ultimately an empirical one.

5.5 Public goods

A different motive for regulation and government intervention is the existence of public goods. A public good is defined by two characteristics: non-rivalry in consumption and non-excludability. The first characteristic, non-rivalry, means that consumption by one economic agent does not affect the amount of the good consumed by any other agent in the economy. The second characteristic, non-excludability, means that no agent can be excluded from the consumption of the good. There are very few examples of pure public goods. National defense, public recreational areas, and knowledge are usual examples.

These two characteristics have important implications for the way a private market would provide the good. Since no individual can be excluded from consumption, it is difficult to ask consumers to pay a positive price since they can use the good for free. This is referred to as the *free-rider problem.*

They also imply that social value of one unit of the good is given by the sum of marginal valuations of all consumers. Thus, while the usual condition that maximizes social value generated in a market is price equal to marginal cost – as price is equal to the marginal utility of consuming the good to consumers – in the case of a public good this is no longer true. The price is not equal to the valuation of consumption of a unit of the good or service. Since one unit consumed by a consumer does not preclude another consumer from benefiting from the consumption of the same unit (by definition of a public good), the social surplus is maximum when the marginal cost of production equals the sum of marginal benefits to all consumers.[4] Due to this particular feature, private markets will not provide public goods. Accordingly, the *provision* of public goods is the responsibility of the state as otherwise those goods would not exist in the economy. However, the state need not *produce* public goods. It may buy them instead.

In the health sector, the conditions required for a public good are not easily satisfied. Some health-related interventions, like ensuring clean air or basic medical research, approach the characteristics of a public good. As in many other fields, basic knowledge when "consumed" by a person does not exclude others from gaining the same knowledge. Excluding someone from that knowledge is likely to be very costly. Most health care provided has both rivalry in consumption (health care resources used by one individual cannot be freely used by another) and excludability (people can be denied health care; objections to care denial are based on ethical reasons, not on technological conditions).

5.6   Externalities

A motive for government intervention is the existence of externalities. An externality is present when an economic agent directly affects utility or production possibilities of another economic agent. More precisely (and see Mas-Colell *et al.* 1995, p. 352):

DEFINITION 5.3   (EXTERNALITY).   An externality arises whenever the well-being of a consumer or the production possibilities of a firm are directly affected by the actions of another agent in the economy.

The important point of the definition is that the effect of one agent on the other must be direct and not induced though a variation of prices. Quoting Mas-Colell *et al.* (1995),

> an externality is present if, say, a fishery's productivity is affected by the emissions from a nearby refinery, but not simply because the fishery's productivity is affected by the price of oil (which, in turn, is to some degree affected by the oil refinery's output of oil).

(p. 352)

Externalities can be either positive (when they benefit others) or negative (when they harm others). On the positive externalities side, the surge of swine flu in the first decade of the twenty-first century makes self-care (washing hands properly) and vaccination a good example of a positive externality. Tobacco consumption in a closed room and pollution are examples of negative externalities. With externalities, perfect competition does not lead to optimal resource allocation because producers in the private market do not take into account the social costs and benefits of its production. Therefore, in the presence of a negative externality (pollution) it will not take into account the social cost, just its private production cost and thus will produce beyond the efficient level. A parallel argument leads to under-provision in the presence of a positive externality.

To study the distortion in the market allocation of resources induced by the presence of externalities, we will first look at the case of externalities that only affect the behavior of firms. Next we will extend the analysis to include consumers as well.

5.6.1 *Externalities among firms*

Consider an economy with the two firms, a fishery (f) and an oil refinery (r) quoted above. Both firms produce using a single input m hired in the input market at a price w. The production functions are

$$q_r = F_r(m_r), \tag{5.6}$$

$$q_f = F_f(m_f, q_r), \tag{5.7}$$

where to simplify the exposition we assume that one unit of production of oil generates one unit of pollution. To compute the optimal allocation, we must consider the joint surplus of the firms. Thus, define

$$\Pi \equiv \Pi_r + \Pi_f = p_r q_r + p_f q_f - w(m_r + m_f), \tag{5.8}$$

where q_r and q_f are defined by (5.6) and (5.7) respectively. The first-order conditions with respect to the inputs are given by

$$\frac{\partial \Pi}{\partial m_r} = p_r \frac{\partial q_r}{\partial m_r} + p_f \frac{\partial q_f}{\partial q_r} \frac{\partial q_r}{\partial m_r} - w = 0$$

$$\frac{\partial \Pi}{\partial m_f} = p_f \frac{\partial q_f}{\partial m_f} - w = 0$$

The term $\partial q_f / \partial q_r$ captures the externality of the refinery on the fishery. Given that it is a negative externality, $\partial q_f / \partial q_r < 0$. Solving for the prices we obtain,

$$p_f = \frac{w}{\dfrac{\partial q_f}{\partial m_f}}, \tag{5.9}$$

$$p_r = \frac{w}{\dfrac{\partial q_r}{\partial m_r}} - p_f \frac{\partial q_f}{\partial q_r} \tag{5.10}$$

Equation (5.9) tells us that the fishery sells its output at the competitive price or, in other words, the price of the input (w) corresponds to the value of its marginal productivity. Equation (5.10) shows that the price of oil is distorted away from the competitive price by the value of the marginal damage that the refinery imposes on the fishery. That is to say, the production externality is *internalized* through an increase in the relative prices p_r / p_f. Accordingly, the optimal allocation is characterized by a lower production of q_r than what would arise if the oil refinery does not internalize the externality and only considers its private (input) costs.

The case of a positive externality is captured by $\partial q_f / \partial q_r > 0$, while the rest of the analysis goes through. In such a case, the optimal allocation would show a higher volume of q_r

than the corresponding one should the externality not be internalized. Naturally, we need to reinterpret the meaning of q_r and q_f to accommodate the interpretation of a positive externality. To illustrate, consider that firm r produces some knowledge allowing to improve the production of firm f.

5.6.2   Externalities in the marketplace

We propose to take a step further in the analysis of externalities, and consider that, say, pollution by one firm affects not only its competitor but consumers as well. That is, we take a general equilibrium approach. The simplest general equilibrium model is the so-called *Robinson Crusoe economy*.[5] In it one agent, Robinson Crusoe, combines the decisions of production and consumption.

Consider the following Robinson Crusoe economy. Robinson is endowed with labor capacity ($\bar{m}$) used to catch coconuts (q_c) and fish (q_f). Unfortunately, cooking fish produces smoke (s) thus generating a (negative) externality. More formally, the decision of the Robinson producer is summarized in the following production function: $q_c = F_c(m_c)$, $q_f = F_f(m_f)$, $s = F_s(q_f)$, with the restriction $m_c + m_f = \bar{m}$. Also, the Robinson consumer obtains satisfaction from consumption summarized in the following utility function $U(q_c, q_f, s)$.

Robinson's problem is to determine the consumption bundle (q_c, q_f, s) yielding the maximum level of satisfaction given the production functions, and the labor endowment. Formally,

$$\max_{\{q_c, q_f, s\}} U(q_c, q_f, s) \quad \text{s.t.} \quad \begin{cases} q_c = F_c(m_c), \\ q_f = F_f(m_f), \\ s = F_s(q_f), \\ \bar{m} = m_c + m_f \end{cases}$$

where we assume $\partial U/\partial q_c > 0$, $\partial U/\partial q_f > 0$, $\partial U/\partial s < 0$.

Substituting the restrictions into the utility function, the problem simplifies to

$$\max_{m_f} U(F_f(m_f), F_c(\bar{m} - m_f), F_s(F_f(m_f))) \tag{5.11}$$

The first-order condition for the optimal choice of m_f is,

$$\frac{dU}{dm_f} = \frac{\partial U}{\partial q_f} \frac{dq_f}{dm_f} - \frac{\partial U}{\partial q_c} \frac{dq_c}{dm_f} + \frac{\partial U}{\partial q_s} \frac{dq_s}{dq_f} \frac{dq_f}{dm_f} = 0.$$

Rearranging terms we obtain,

$$\frac{dq_f}{dm_f} \left(\frac{\partial U}{\partial q_f} + \frac{\partial U}{\partial q_s} \frac{dq_s}{dq_f} \right) = \frac{\partial U}{\partial q_c} \frac{dq_c}{dm_f},$$

that can be rewritten as

$$\frac{\dfrac{dq_c}{dm_f}}{\dfrac{dq_f}{dm_f}} = \frac{\dfrac{\partial U}{\partial q_f} + \dfrac{\partial U}{\partial q_s}\dfrac{dq_s}{dq_f}}{\dfrac{\partial U}{\partial q_c}}. \tag{5.12}$$

Recalling the definitions of marginal rate of substitution (Chapter 2) and marginal rate of transformation (Chapter 3), we can rewrite (5.12) as,

$$MRT = MRS_{cf} + MRS_{cs}\frac{dq_s}{dq_f}. \tag{5.13}$$

In the absence of externalities, the optimal allocation of resources is achieved when $MRT = MRS_{cf}$. Now, equation (5.13) tells us that the externality, $dq_s/dq_f < 0$ induces a distortion preventing reaching the optimal allocation of resources. In turn, this induces a distortion in the relative prices of the consumption goods. In Chapter 2 we showed that when prices are given, the marginal rate of substitution between two goods equals its relative price. Therefore, using (5.13) we obtain,

$$\frac{p_f}{p_c} = MRS_{cf} = MRT - MRS_{cs}\frac{dq_s}{dq_f}.$$

so that the externality induces a higher relative price with respect to corresponding relative price in the absence of externalities. Again, as in the previous section, internalizing the externality induces an increase of the price of the fish, so that its consumption diminishes and so does the production of smoke.

5.7 Asymmetric information

Asymmetric information is a major constraint to regulatory activity. The regulator will have less knowledge than the regulated firms about demand intensity or cost structures or both. The regulator has to take this differential information into account when setting up the regulatory action.

Take the following example of asymmetry about costs. There are two possible levels of cost: high or low. When the regulated firm has low costs, the regulator would like to set a low price. In the same way, the regulator would like to set a high price if the firm has high costs. A regulated company prefers a high price even if it has a low cost. Relying on each type of firm announcing its type of cost structure would result in every firm stating that it has high costs. Thus, announcements of regulated firms do not reveal any information and a high price is always set. The issue is whether the regulator can improve its regulatory structure. By enlarging the set of instruments it uses, the regulator can improve the allocation of resources. If the regulator specifies both a price and a quantity of the good to be delivered, it can reduce total payments to be made or increase consumers' surplus.

The regulator faces two sets of constraints in the definition of the optimal regulatory structure. The first is that regulated firms want to produce under regulatory conditions, irrespective of being low or high cost (this is known as the *participation constraint*). The second is that the price-quantity pair set for the low-cost firm is better for this type of firm than the price–quantity pair intended for the high-cost firm (this is the *incentive compatible constraint*). This implies a distortion in the contract offered to high-cost firms.

Regulation under asymmetry of information implies that some information rents will always remain. A good regulatory design can mitigate the information rents but cannot bring them to zero.

Information asymmetries are common in the health care market. In health care finance it is often the case that a person has better information about his (or her) health status and health care needs than the insurer. In health care delivery, providers will have superior information about the adequate treatment to be adopted.

An important concept in modern theory of regulation is the notion of *incentive regulation* – set the regulatory instruments to induce the highest possible level of effort by the regulated firm. Setting incentives is often associated with imposing risk on the provider of health care. By facing risk, the health care provider will want to exert effort to avoid the costs of being identified. The argument can be easily seen with a simple example. Suppose the regulatory authority announces that it will reimburse all costs incurred by the health care provider. Then, the regulated firm will have no incentive to exert effort to achieve a lower-cost structure.

To make these arguments more precise, consider the following model. Let $p = a - q$ denote the (inverse) demand function of some good or service, with p being the price, q the quantity provided and a being a parameter. Let c be the marginal cost of production of the good (or service).

The value c is known by the regulated entity but not by the regulator. To simplify matters, assume that marginal cost can take one of two possible values: high cost, $\bar{c}$; or low cost, $\underline{c}$. The regulated entity knows whether $\bar{c}$ or $\underline{c}$ is the true marginal cost of operation. The regulator only knows that $\bar{c}$ occurs with probability π (and $\underline{c}$ occurs with probability $1 - \pi$).

Before making any payment, the regulator receives information about costs, c^*. The announcement the regulated entity makes about its costs is either $\underline{c}$ or $\bar{c}$. Naturally, since the regulator does not know the true cost, the regulated firm has an incentive to announce the level of cost that brings the highest surplus. A fairly general result from the economics literature establishes that the best a regulator can do is to specify rules that induce truthful announcements by the regulated entity. That is, the minimum efficiency cost of regulating under uncertainty is achieved when the regulatory mechanism induces the regulated entity to announce its true cost of operation, even if for that to happen some rent that would not exist under perfect information about costs has to be left to the regulated entity. This argument is the basis of the *revelation principle*.[6]

The regulator is assumed to maximize social welfare, defined as the sum of consumers' surplus and profits. Consider first a naive regulatory policy in which the regulator sets the marginal cost pricing to be followed. That is, the regulated price is equal to the (marginal) cost announced by the regulated entity. Then, the optimal strategy of the regulated entity is to always announce it has high cost. It never has an incentive to announce the lower cost, even if it is a low-cost case. The high-cost regulated entity has no economic rent, but the low-cost regulated entity benefits from an economic rent resulting from the information asymmetry.

The economic rent is given by:

$$(\bar{c} - \underline{c})(a - \bar{c})$$

as the regulated price is $p = \bar{c}$ and demand at such a price is $(a - \bar{c})$.

The question is whether or not the regulator can do better than this naive regulatory policy. What is the optimal regulatory policy, knowing that the regulated entity may have an incentive to misrepresent the true level of its costs? The first step in the analysis is to define the instruments the regulator can use. Assume that the regulator is able to set a price and a lump-sum subsidy. Both instruments can have different values, according to the value for marginal costs announced by the regulated entity. Denote by $p(c^*)$ and $s(c^*)$ the price and lump-sum subsidy, respectively. Let $\Pi(c^*, c)$ be the surplus to the regulated entity when it announces c^* while having true marginal cost c. In our framework,

$$\Pi(c^*, c) = (p(c^*) - c)(a - p(c^*)) + s(c^*)$$

The regulatory policy adopted has to satisfy two types of constraints. First, the regulated entity has to have non-negative profits. This constraint must hold for both low and high-cost regulated entities. These constraints are usually termed participation constraints or individual rationality constraints. Second, the regulatory policy must not allow regulated entities to increase their surplus by misrepresenting their operation costs. These are called incentive compatibility constraints as they must be set in a way that makes truthful revelation of costs compatible with incentives faced by the regulated entity.

Formally, the incentive-compatibility constraints require

$$\Pi(c, c) \geq \Pi(c^*, c), \forall c^*, c$$

The individual rationality constraints require

$$\Pi(c, c) \geq 0, \forall c$$

In the context of the two-types marginal cost example, the incentive compatibility constraints can be written as

$$\Pi(\bar{c}, \bar{c}) \geq \Pi(\underline{c}, \bar{c})$$
$$\Pi(\underline{c}, \underline{c}) \geq \Pi(\bar{c}, \underline{c})$$

The first condition states that a high-cost regulated entity prefers to announce a high-cost structure, while the second condition requires that a low cost firm has a higher surplus from announcing a low-cost structure. Using the surplus definitions from above

$$(p(\bar{c}) - \bar{c})(a - p(\bar{c})) + s(\bar{c}) \geq (p(\underline{c}) - \bar{c})(a - p(\underline{c})) + s(\underline{c})$$
$$(p(\underline{c}) - \underline{c})(a - p(\underline{c})) + s(\underline{c}) \geq (p(\bar{c}) - \underline{c})(a - p(\bar{c})) + s(\bar{c})$$

In a similar way, the participation constraints can be written as:

$$(p(\bar{c}) - \bar{c})(a - p(\bar{c})) + s(\bar{c}) \geq 0$$
$$(p(\underline{c}) - \underline{c})(a - p(\underline{c})) + s(\underline{c}) \geq 0$$

The problem is to find the socially optimal values for $p(\bar{c}), p(\underline{c}), s(\bar{c}), s(\underline{c})$. In the absence of information asymmetries, it would be optimal to set $p(\bar{c}) = \bar{c}$ and $p(\underline{c}) = \underline{c}$. Let's set the regulated prices to such values. From the naive regulatory policy discussed above, the low-cost regulated entity has an interest in misrepresenting its true cost. But now the regulator has an extra instrument, the lump-sum subsidy, which can be used to counteract this incentive to misrepresent costs.

Under these regulated prices, the four constraints can be written as

$$s(\bar{c}) \geq s(\underline{c}) + (\underline{c} - \bar{c})(a - \underline{c})$$

$$s(\underline{c}) \geq (\bar{c} - \underline{c})(a - \bar{c}) + s(\bar{c})$$

$$s(\bar{c}) \geq 0$$

$$s(\underline{c}) \geq 0$$

From the first two conditions, it is clear that $s(\underline{c}) > s(\bar{c})$, so that from the last two conditions the regulator may set $s(\bar{c}) = 0$ but it will have to announce $s(\underline{c}) > 0$.

Under $s(\bar{c}) = 0$, the two first conditions simplify to,

$$s(\underline{c}) \geq (\bar{c} - \underline{c})(a - \bar{c}) > 0 > -(\bar{c} - \underline{c})(a - \underline{c}).$$

The last inequality is satisfied automatically and the lowest lump-sum subsidy that needs to be given to the regulated entity with a low cost is $s(\underline{c}) = (\bar{c} - \underline{c})(a - \bar{c})$, which is exactly equal in this example to the misrepresentation value under the naive regulatory policy. There is, however, an important difference. While under the naive regulatory policy, both types of regulated entities were announced to be high cost, and the regulated price was equal to $\bar{c}$, under this optimal regulatory policy, the low-cost regulated entity announced to be low cost faces a regulated price $p = \underline{c}$ and produces a higher quantity to satisfy the larger demand due to the lower price. Thus, there is a higher social surplus.

The information advantage of the regulated entities generates an economic rent for the low-cost one. This rent cannot be reduced. The optimal regulatory policy obtains however a higher social surplus by inducing the low-cost regulated entity to announce its true cost and produce a higher output. The regulated entity with high cost, on the other hand, faces exactly the same policy as under perfect information. The interested reader is addressed to Chapter 11 for an in-depth analysis of the consequences of asymmetric information in the marketplace.

5.7.1   *Consumer ignorance*

Asymmetric information is one of the arguments for market failure. In particular, consumer ignorance has been argued to justify patient protection as asserted at the beginning of this chapter. This disadvantageous informational situation of the consumer has given rise, particularly in health care, to drawing a distinction among search, reputation, experience, credence, and merit goods.

DEFINITION 5.4   (SEARCH GOOD).   A search good is a product or service for which a prospective buyer can determine its characteristics (value) prior to making the purchase decision.

Nelson (1970) originally introduced the concept of search good to refer to situations when the consumer is able to evaluate its properties at a reasonable cost either because its physical characteristics can be directly checked, of because there is good information available about them. Consumer reports and specialized magazines (as well as the simple word of mouth) play the role of disseminating information about consumption goods. Similarly, public agencies like the Food and Drug Administration in the US and their counterparts in the EU countries require the disclosure of information on the characteristics of consumption goods (composition, calories, fat content, etc. information in the labels) and drugs (in the prospectus). Otherwise, it would be too costly for the consumer to obtain the information. In health care, and particularly in the pharmaceutical industry, most goods can be considered search goods.

A variation of search goods are reputation goods where the information on the commodities are spread word of mouth. Satterthwaite (1979, p. 483), defines reputation goods as,

DEFINITION 5.5 (REPUTATION GOODS). A reputation good is any product or service for which sellers' products are differentiated and consumers' search among sellers consists of a series of inquiries to relatives, friends, and associates for recommendations.

Traditional examples of reputation goods are personal legal services and primary medical care.

Another type of goods, in contrast to search goods, are the experience goods also introduced by Nelson (1970). These are goods for which it pays the consumer to evaluate them by consuming rather than by searching. In Nelson's words, "[t]o evaluate brands of canned tunafish, for example, the consumer would almost certainly purchase brands of tunafish for consumption. He could, then, determine from several purchases which brand he preferred. We will call this information process 'experience'." (p. 312). More formally,

DEFINITION 5.6 (EXPERIENCE GOODS). An experience good is a product or service whose characteristics are difficult to observe in advance, but can be determined after consumption.

In contrast with consumption goods of the food industry where calorie content can be ascertained from the label, determining taste requires consumption. Most food industry goods are both search and experience goods. Similarly, primary care services are both reputation and experience goods. Besides obtaining information from a physician word of mouth, an individual will only be able to accurately assess the quality of the physician after a visit.

Also, we can identify goods whose quality cannot even be determined after consumption. These are the so-called post-experience or credence goods.

DEFINITION 5.7 (CREDENCE GOODS). A credence good is a product or service whose utility is difficult or impossible to be ascertained by the individual, even after consumption. It is up to the consumer to trust that the product is worth consuming.

Example of credence goods are education, car repairs, home maintenance services, and in the context of medical care, vitamin supplements, or medical treatment. The promotion of professional morals is thus a fundamental issue in credence goods markets. In the health care market, a patient will often be able to judge whether a particular treatment is favorable or unfavorable, but will never be sure whether the physician actually affected the outcome. This is the reason why quality of health care services is not contractible. Also, public provision of health care limits the physicians' financial incentives to skimp on resources. Sloan and Hall (2002) provide an overall appraisal on these types of goods in managed care regulation.

A somewhat different type of goods are merit goods, introduced by Musgrave (1959). These goods are linked to the concept of need, in the sense that they are judged by individuals or society as necessary.

DEFINITION 5.8   (MERIT GOODS).   A merit good is any product or service that society considers its members should have even though they have not expressed any demand for it.

In this sense it is argued that the consumption of a merit good is better for an individual than what (s)he is able to perceive. Based on this idea governments carry out actions that are not justified on economic reasons. Typical examples are food stamps to support nutrition, subsidized education, and in the health care sector, free vaccination for children, and other provision of health care services to improve quality of life and reduce morbidity (such as programs on drug addiction, prostitution, or the handicapped). It is important not to confuse merit goods with equity issues in the sense that a society may consider universal access to some goods regardless of income levels, as desirable. Finally, it is also important to distinguish merit (and demerit) goods from positive (and negative) externalities. A free vaccination campaign may be a merit good generating an externality. The merit good characteristic arises from the information failure on the part of the consumer to judge how good or bad such policy is. As a by-product, a vaccination campaign against a contagious disease prevents its transmission. Examples of demerit goods are tobacco, alcoholic beverages consumption, recreational drugs, gambling, or prostitution. Social qualification as demerit goods justifies the levy of taxes and consumption bans on these goods by the government. This regulation on top also attempts to reduce the negative externality on members of the society who do not consume those goods.

5.8   Yardstick competition

In a previous section it was argued that asymmetries of information between the regulated entity and the regulator allow the former to enjoy economic rents under some circumstances. Now we assess the role of comparison between similar regulated institutions in mitigating the information asymmetries. When there are several regulated institutions, the regulator may try to use "competitive" mechanisms to achieve a better allocation of resources (similar to those obtained under perfect information of the regulator). This is known in the jargon as "yardstick competition" and was introduced by Schleifer (1985). The existence of similarly regulated institutions allows for a sort of performance-based regulation. Using information from other regulated firms, the regulator can create additional pressure upon the regulated entity.

The starting point is the existence of identical regulated entities (say, hospitals that are natural monopolies in their regions). A more common term to designate yardstick competition is relative performance evaluation. The payment to a hospital is often based on average costs over similar hospitals, for example.

In our simple setting, the yardstick competition simply consists of asking the regulated entity to use the cost level to regulate another one. Unless regulated entities collude, they have no interest in misrepresenting their true costs. As long as the costs are highly correlated across entities, this procedure will give the regulator information to eliminate to a great extent the informational rents from asymmetric information. The idea of relative performance evaluation is actually carried out to a more complex scenario.

Consider a series of natural monopolies, say, hospitals. Their cost structure is composed by a cost part common to all regulated entities, an individual cost component specific to each hospital and the cost-efficiency effort exerted by the staff of the hospital. Under asymmetric information, the regulator is not able to distinguish the high cost due to a intrinsic cost component and not making efficiency effort. Still, even if the regulator does not have much information about each firm, using relative performance may be able to induce the right amount of efficiency effort. Setting the price for each hospital (regulated entity, in general) equal to the average cost of all others would make prices converge to minimum average cost.

The reason is that the price faced by each company is independent of its cost. Given that prices are set exogenously to the firm, prices are independent of the firm's costs which provides regulated entities with strong incentives for efficiency and achieving low costs. Since all regulated entities face the same incentives, prices tend to the efficient level. The information needed to set prices close to the efficient level of cost is given by the relative performance assessment. Its accuracy is naturally highly dependent on the correlation of costs across regulated entities.

To formalize the argument, consider two similar regulated entities. The cost structure of each regulated entity is given by:

$$C_i = b + b_i - e_i \tag{5.14}$$

where b is a cost component common to both regulated entities, b_i is a cost component that differs across entities and e_i is the result from effort by the regulated entity to achieve efficiency.

The objective function of the regulated entity is

$$\Pi_i = T_i - C_i - k(e_i) \tag{5.15}$$

where T_i is the transfer made by the regulator and $k(e_i)$ is the cost of exerting efficiency effort, such that costs decrease in an amount e_i.

The surplus to the regulator from the activity of each regulated entity is denoted by S. Let λ be the cost of raising funds to pay transfers to the regulated entities. A value $\lambda > 0$ means that collecting funds entails a distortionary cost and the regulator wants to minimize transfers.

The objective function of the regulator is total social surplus:

$$W = S - C_i - \lambda T_i \tag{5.16}$$

Consider the extreme situation of $b_i = 0, b > 0$: costs are similar across regulated entities, differing only in the efficiency gains associated with the effort exerted by each regulated entity.

Under these conditions, the main result is that the first-best allocation of resources can be achieved. To see it, define the transfer to each regulated entity i to be:

$$T_i = k(e^*) + C_j \tag{5.17}$$

where $k(e^*)$ is the cost of efficiency effort evaluated at the optimal value e^*. The second component in the transfer rule is the relative cost performance according to the realized costs of other regulated entities j, $(j \neq i)$. In the case of more than two entities, this term could be the average costs of the comparable entities. The crucial feature is that excludes the cost of the regulated entity that is going to receive this particular transfer.

Under this transfer rule, the problem of the regulated entity can be written as

$$\max_{e_i} \Pi_i = k(e^*) + C_j - C_i - k(e_i) \tag{5.18}$$

The regulated entity generates a positive surplus as long as it has a lower cost than the other regulated entity. The problem can be re-written as

$$\max_{e_i} \Pi_i = k(e^*) + (b - e_i) - (b - e_j) - k(e_i) \tag{5.19}$$

The corresponding first-order condition is:

$$1 - k'(e^*) = 0 \tag{5.20}$$

The resulting level of efficiency effort is exactly equal to the choice of efficient effort by the social planner. The relative comparison provides enough information to set a transfer which induces high effort by the regulated entities. Efficiency in this case can be achieved even if the regulator does not have information about the effort done by each regulated entity and about the common cost component. The relative cost comparison extracts the relevant information, and the fixed payment creates the right incentives. In this simple example, perfect correlation across regulated entities on the cost parameter was the crucial element. Under imperfectly correlated cost structures, that is, $b_i \neq 0$, relative performance comparison extracts some information but not all. And in the limiting case of independence of cost structures, there is no information to be gained from relative performance comparison.

5.9   Competition for the market

Can competition *for* the market be a substitute for competition *in* the market? When market conditions dictate the existence of a natural monopoly situation (say, a hospital in a remote region), an available instrument to authorities is to auction the right to be the monopolist (or one of the few providers the market can sustain). By giving the right to provide the good or service to the institution proposing the lowest price (under pre-determined conditions for quality of service), the regulator could approximate competition in the market with competition for the market. If it is optimal to have only one (or just a few) firm(s), then entry should be regulated in a way that promotes a better allocation of resources. In other words, regulation should induce competition at the entry stage.

The most common types of auction are the English auction and the Vickrey auction. In an English auction the participants (potential providers of the service being auctioned) submit their proposals (bids) publicly (open bid auction) or privately (sealed bid auction). The highest bid wins the auction and its proposer obtains the concession of the service. In a Vickrey auction all firms submit their bids and the firm with the best bid wins, but receives the price of the second lowest bidder.

An auction is successful when it achieves two goals: the winner of the auction is the most efficient firm, and it gives up most of its monopoly profits. To be successful, the auction must be transparent and the mechanism to evaluate the bids must be objective. Also, the design of the subsequent contracts is also a crucial element for the successful implementation of a competition-for-the-market policy.[7]

5.10   Instruments

Regulation is implemented among economic agents with distinct and often conflicting objectives. Regulation will be effective when consumers receive their maximum benefit. We have examined several instruments of the so-called incentive regulation like rate of return regulation, price-cap regulation and yardstick competition (or benchmarking). Jamison and Berg (2008) provide a nice overview of infrastructure regulation and of these instruments in particular.

We have also mentioned simple instruments available to governments like taxes and subsidies. We devote this closing section to the study of their impact on the equilibrium characterization of the market.

A tax may take two forms. It can be a *per-unit* tax, or it can be an *ad valorem* tax. In the former case, the tax is fixed in euros per unit of output, while in the latter case the tax rate is a fixed percentage of value. In either case, the tax may be levied on the buyer or on the seller.

Consider an perfectly competitive economy described by a demand function $D(p)$ and a supply function $S(p)$. The equilibrium is characterized by the quantity q^c and the price p^c. In general, it does not matter who pays the tax (consumers or producer) in the sense that the impact of the tax will be determined by the slope (i.e. the elasticity) of supply and demand functions.

Consider first that the government levies a per-unit tax t on the producers. This means that now the producers' revenues diminish in t euros per unit sold. Accordingly, producers reduce supply, so that the new supply function $S(p - t)$ shifts upwards as shown in Figure 5.3(a). The after-tax equilibrium is represented by the pair (q^t, p^t) at the intersection of the demand function and the new supply function. To examine the effects of the tax on consumers and producers, let us identify the price $\tilde{p}$ corresponding to the point where the after-tax output q^t meets the pre-tax supply function $S(p)$. Note that the per-unit tax t is equivalent to the price difference $p^t - \tilde{p}$. Accordingly, the incidence of the tax is that consumers bear an increase in price $p^t - p^c$ and producers bear a decrease in price $p^c - \tilde{p}$.

Suppose next that the tax is imposed on consumers, so that consumers' expenditures increase in t euros per unit purchased. This is equivalent to a decrease in consumers' income so that the demand function shifts downwards to $D(p + t)$ as represented in Figure 5.3(b). The new equilibrium is again represented by pair (q^t, p^t) at the intersection of the new demand function $D(p + t)$ and the supply function $S(p)$. Define $\tilde{p}$ as the price corresponding to the after-tax output q^t on the old demand function $D(p)$. Comparing panels (a) and (b) on Figure 5.3 we can verify that the only change is the exchange of position between $\tilde{p}$ and p^t. Therefore, the incidence of the tax is the same as before: suppliers bears a price decrease of $p^c - p^t$ and consumers bear an increase in price of $\tilde{p} - p^c$.

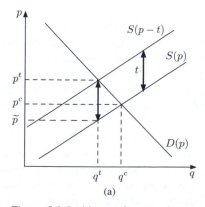
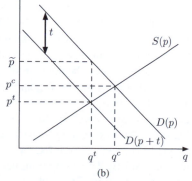

Figure 5.3 Incidence of a per-unit tax.

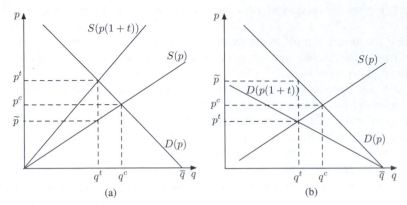

Figure 5.4 Incidence of an *ad-valorem* tax.

Let us next look at the effects of an *ad-valorem* tax levied on consumers. This means that now consumers pay a price $p(1+t)$. This means a change on the slope of the demand function, so that the new demand pivots inwards around the volume of output $\bar{q}$ corresponding to the (maximum possible) demand that would accrue at zero price. Figure 5.4(b) illustrates this. The initial pre-tax situation is represented by the intersection between supply and demand at the point (q^c, p^c). The after-tax demand is given by $D(p(1+t))$, so that the new equilibrium is represented by the pair (q^t, p^t). As before, let $\tilde{p}$ denote the price associated to the output q^t on the original demand. The impact of the tax is thus shared by consumers and producers. This impact is equivalent to the one arising when the tax is levied on producers as shown in Figure 5.4(b).

The analysis of the impact of a subsidy is essentially the same as the incidence of a tax. A subsidy is merely a negative tax. Accordingly, the effect of a subsidy on a producer is to shift the supply curve downward by the amount of the subsidy. Similarly, the incidence of a subsidy on consumers shifts the demand function outwards consistent with the increase in available income induced by the subsidy.

5.11 Regulating the health care market

One of the main regulation issues in the health care sector is the design of the reimbursement mechanism to providers in a NHS-like health care organization. There are two basic mechanisms. The first is a *retrospective reimbursement system* where the third-party payer of the health care system reimburses *ex-post* the expenses of the provider. This system was widely used until the budgets of the health care sector placed unbearable strain on the public budget of the developed countries. The fundamental problem is the lack of incentives for cost control on the side of providers.

Trying to cope with the public expenditures restrictions imposed by the Treaty of Maastricht in the EU, governments designed *prospective reimbursement systems*, where payment rates for different medical services were fixed *prior* to the period health care was provided. This is the second mechanism. This system induces incentives for cost containment similar to those of a price-cap regulation. The problem is how to calculate those prices. The most popular instrument has been the so-called diagnostic-related groups (DRGs).

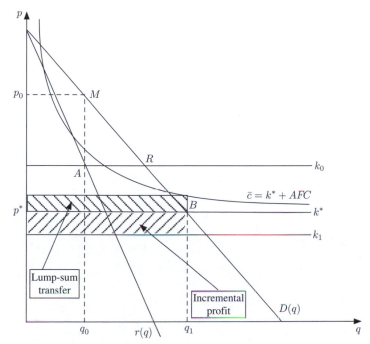

Figure 5.5 Regulation in the health care marketplace.

A DRG is an attempt to represent a case type that identifies patients with similar conditions and processes of care. Each DRG is given a flat payment rate calculated in part on the basis of costs incurred for that DRG across providers nationwide.

To illustrate, let us consider the following example.

Consider a community with n hospitals and let us focus on hospital 1. It faces a demand $D(q)$ and marginal cost equals average cost $c(q) = \bar{c}(q) = k_0$. Figure 5.5 illustrates the argument.

A monopolist provider would supply q_0 units of care at a price p_0 (point M). A hospital in a NHS subject to retrospective reimbursement would produce at point R, i.e. $\bar{c} = p$ so that profits would be nil ($\Pi = 0$).

To study the behavior of a hospital in a NHS subject to prospective reimbursement based on DRGs, let us introduce the following additional assumptions: there is a single sickness; the hospital's effort to reduce cost is a fixed cost; reimbursement rates are fixed at the average marginal cost of competitors $(2, \dots, n) = k^*$; the fixed cost is reimbursed as a lump-sum transfer so that average cost is defined as the sum of the variable average cost and the average fixed cost (AFC). That is $\bar{c}(q) = k^* + AFC$. Then, the equilibrium configuration is given by point B where $k^* = D(q)$, i.e. the pair (q_1, p^*) satisfying a zero-profit condition because $p = \bar{c}$ and the fixed cost is provided for by means of a transfer.

Assume cost reduction yields a "new" marginal cost k^* so that the hospital obtains zero (incremental) profits. If instead the cost reduction yields a "new" marginal cost $k_1 < k^*$, the hospital obtains incremental profits $q_1(k^* - k_1)$. Finally, if the cost reduction yields a "new" marginal cost $k \in (k^*, k_0)$ the hospital will face losses. This example serves the purpose of illustrating the main conclusion: as the hospital's costs do not enter into the price it receives, the reimbursement system induces a big incentive on the hospital to lower its costs.

6 Mergers and acquisitions

This chapter studies the reasons different producers may have to merge their business activities or for one producer to take over another. We distinguish among horizontal, vertical, and conglomerate mergers, and the key factors for the success or failure of a merger or an acquisition.

6.1 Introduction

There is a wide agreement among economists that mergers and acquisitions are one of the topics in industrial economics generating the most controversy and disagreement. Mueller (1989) and Salop (1987) review some of the elements of the controversy. Recently, the *Review of Industrial Organization*,[1] and *The Journal of Industrial Economics*[2] have devoted special issues to antitrust and regulatory review and to merger policy design respectively. Why mergers occur, what are their causes and consequences, and what public policies toward mergers should be are some questions of hot debate, particularly in the last twenty years (although the debate goes as far back as far the 1930s).

To fix ideas let us start by defining the concepts of *merger* and *acquisition*. Both terms as well as *takeover*, and *buyout* are usually treated as synonymous, and referred to as M&A. However, they allude to slightly different situations.

DEFINITION 6.1 (ACQUISITION). An acquisition occurs when one firm assumes all the assets and all the liabilities of another. The acquiring firm retains its identity, while the acquired firm ceases to exist.

DEFINITION 6.2 (MERGER). A merger occurs when two companies agree to go forward as a single new company. The assets and liabilities of both companies are surrendered and converted in the new company stock that is issued in their place.

In short, a merger is the result of the combination of two (or more) firms to form a new one, while an acquisition is the purchase of one company by another. Acquisitions may be friendly or hostile, while mergers are always friendly. More often than not, whether a "purchase" is considered a merger or an acquisition depends simply on its friendly or hostile character, and the way it is announced to the stockholders, the board of directors of the company, and to society. Caves (1989), DePamphilis (2008), and Collins (2009) provide a throughout analysis of M&A. Also modern textbooks of industrial organization cover this topic. See for example Martin (2002, ch. 12) and Waldman and Jensen (2007, ch. 4).

6.1.1   Motives for mergers

Two companies get involved in a M&A procedure hoping to realize some gains. That is, the resulting company should be worth more than the sum of the two firms apart. The question is thus why and how those gains can arise. Following Waldman and Jensen (2007) we will distinguish some of the most common arguments.

Market power   Mergers may increase market power and thus the national antitrust agencies are particularly careful in analyzing their potential anticompetitive effects. Horizontal mergers always increase concentration and are the mergers where more attention is paid to their effects on the competitiveness of the market. Vertical and conglomerate mergers may also reduce potential competition.

Efficiency gains   Mergers may increase efficiency by exploiting economies of scale, economies of scope, and synergies. Also, mergers may eliminate X-inefficiencies (a situation where costs are not minimized because of mismanagement of inputs. See Leibenstein, 1969, 1973).

Financial motives   A merger may also be induced by lower taxes, changes in capital requirements, or lower cost of capital.

Risk reduction   A merger may reduce risk if it increases diversification in the sources of profits. Such diversification requires that the merging firms are not too interdependent. Accordingly, we find this motive mostly in conglomerate mergers (see below).

Other motives   Empire building, bankruptcy threat, and aging owners are also other motives reported in the literature triggering mergers.

6.1.2   Types of M&A

There are three types of M&A according to the relationship between the merging parties. These are *horizontal mergers*, *vertical mergers*, and *conglomerate mergers*. A horizontal merger occurs when the two merging firms are in the same sector of economic activity. A vertical merger involves two firms in the chain of distribution from the source of raw materials to the ultimate consumer. Finally, a conglomerate merger arises when the two firms belong to unrelated sectors of the economy.

6.2   Horizontal mergers

Horizontal mergers defined as the union of two firms in the same market, may exploit efficiency gains in the form of scale and scope economies, but also may give rise to negative effects in the form of elimination of competition yielding an increase in market power to the unified firm. Also, merger activity in a sector may facilitate tacit collusion as the number of firms in the market is reduced. Williamson (1968) provides an early (static) analysis of the trade-off between positive and negative aspects of a horizontal merger. The starting point illustrated in Figure 6.1 (see Waldman and Jensen 2007, p. 120) is a competitive industry where the price (p_1) equals marginal cost (c_1), and output is q_1. All firms in the industry merge so that the resulting firm is a monopoly, with reduced marginal cost c_2. The monopoly equilibrium occurs at q_2 where marginal revenue ($r(q)$) equals marginal cost. From the consumers' viewpoint, the merger reduces their surplus in the area $p_2 p_1 B A$, where the rectangle $p_2 p_1 A C$ represents a transfer from consumers to the monopoly and the triangle ABC is

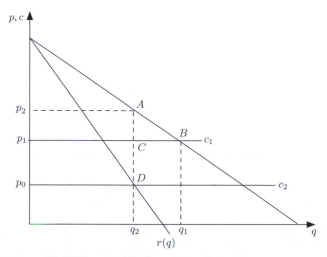

Figure 6.1 Williamson (1968) analysis of mergers.

the deadweight loss induced by the merger. However, the merger reduces the cost of producing the q_2 units. This is represented by the rectangle $p_1 p_0 DC$. To evaluate the welfare consequences of the merger we compare the deadweight loss with the efficiency gain in production, that is we compute the trade-off of market power for cost efficiency. If the former is larger (smaller) than the latter, the merger has a negative (positive) net effect.

6.2.1 *Market equilibrium effects*

To obtain more insight on the causes and consequences of mergers, we should remark that depending on the assumptions and the equilibrium concepts used, the literature offers results that range from the impossibility of the merger to the monopolization of the market (see Kamien and Zang 1990, 1991, 1993; Salant *et al.* 1983). The general idea is that in a n-firm Cournot oligopoly model with symmetric firms, linear demand, constant marginal costs, and absence of fixed costs, merger of a subset of firms is not profitable. This is so because the merger lowers the level of competition in the market, thus allowing the new firm to reduce output. In turn, this allows the firms outside the merger to be better off because they can increase production and profits (see also Stigler 1950). However, the new firm earns more profits than the sum of profits of the former firms before the merger under quite a restrictive condition. Martin (2002, pp. 399–400) shows the technical details of this argument.

Under Bertrand competition, Deneckere and Davidson (1985) show that mergers are always profitable because now the reaction of the firms outside the merger reinforces the price increase associated with the merger.

Finally, product differentiation reinforces the results obtained under price competition and also provides conditions for profitable merger under Cournot competition (see Daughety 1990; Fauli-Oller 1997; Hennessy 2000).

The modern analysis of the welfare effects of mergers is rooted in Farrell and Shapiro (1990, 1991) and Werden (1991). To illustrate their argument, consider a simplified version of their model where as before the industry is described as a n-firm Cournot oligopoly model with symmetric firms, linear demand $p(q) = 1 - q$ (where $q = \sum_i q_i$ denotes aggregate output), constant (zero) marginal costs, and absence of fixed costs. The symmetric Cournot equilibrium is given by,

$$q_i = \frac{1}{n+1}, \quad q = \frac{n}{n+1}, \quad p = \frac{1}{n+1}.$$

for $i = 1, 2, \ldots n$. Consumer surplus is

$$CS(n) = \frac{1}{2}(1 - p)q = \frac{1}{2}\left(\frac{n}{n+1}\right)^2. \tag{6.1}$$

Let $n > 2$ and assume that k firms consider the possibility of a merger. Denote by $S \equiv n - k$ the subset of firms that will remain independent.

In the pre-merger situation, the producer surplus of the subset S of firms is given by,

$$PS_S(n) = \sum_{i=1}^{S} pq_i = S\left(\frac{1}{n+1}\right)^2, \tag{6.2}$$

so that the total surplus of consumers and the S-firms is given by the sum of (6.1) and (6.2),

$$W(n) = CS(n) + PS_S(n) = \frac{n^2 + 2S}{2(n+1)^2}. \tag{6.3}$$

Now, we are interested in the number of firms in the industry such that the merger of a subset k of them is socially beneficial. Note that a merger implies a decrease in the number of competitors in the market. Accordingly, we are looking for those numbers n such that a decrease in n conveys an increase in the welfare function $W(n)$. Formally, we are evaluating the values of n such that

$$\frac{\partial W(n)}{\partial n} = \frac{n - 2S}{(1+n)^3} < 0.$$

Accordingly, the merger will be beneficial when $(1/2) < (S/n)$. Given the symmetry across firms, S/n represents the market share of the firms outside the merger. Therefore, the merger is socially beneficial when the market share of the merging firms is below 50 percent. In general Farrell and Shapiro (1990) find an upper bound of the market share of the merging firms for the merger to be socially beneficial.

The main drawback of the described analysis is that (i) the resulting firm after the merger continues to be a symmetric firm with respect to the firms that have not participated in the merger and (ii) the analysis is static. Davidson and Deneckere (1984) deal with the size effect of the merger introducing restrictions in the production capacity, so that the new firm has a higher production capacity than the firms outside the merger. Pindyck (1985) proposes a dynamic analysis of the effect of a merger on market power. He defines a global marginal cost in a period t (GMC_t) as composed of two elements, the traditional concept of marginal cost, and the present value of the future benefits lost as a consequence of today's increase in the aggregate production volume. Next, Pindyck defines the instantaneous Lerner index for a firm as,

$$L_t^* = \frac{p_t - GMC_t}{p_t} = 1 - \frac{GMC_t}{p_t},$$

and the aggregate in time Lerner index for a firm as,

$$I_m = 1 - \frac{\int_0^\infty e^{-rt} GMC_t q_t dt}{\int_0^\infty e^{-rt} p_t q_t dt}. \tag{6.4}$$

The index (6.4) describes the monopoly power of a firm towards the future measured in a particular moment in time. Naturally, its value depends on the initial competitive conditions ($t = 0$). When the industry is perfectly competitive, the index takes the value of zero, and increases as the price deviates from the global marginal cost.

6.2.2   *Evidence from the health care sector (hospitals)*

There is a large literature providing estimates of the effects of mergers in health care markets particularly since the mid 1990s in the United States. To grasp the relevance of the phenomenon it suffices to mention that in the period 1994–2000 there were 900 hospital mergers. Brouselle *et al.* (1999) and Zimmerman (2009) provide reviews of the literature on hospital mergers. Here, we will simply highlight the main arguments and conclusions of this literature.

The issues discussed are fundamentally whether mergers enhance efficiency or instead increase market power. Lower competition is typically harmful to consumers because price increases and also because in the post-merger situation accessibility usually declines and the geographical distance to the hospital may increase if the mergers yield to close down hospitals, or relocate services. Also, mergers may damage the level of quality of hospital services.

A large proportion of articles indicate the efficiency gains from mergers are possible but not guaranteed. Groff *et al.* (2007), Wicks *et al.* (1998), and Kwoka and Pollit (2010) report that improvements in efficiency do not appear in the short-run. Some reasons suggested are related to the re-organization of the firm that limit the possibilities to focus on business. From a different perspective, Brouselle *et al.* (1999) present references where problems of governance, organizational difficulties, and reallocation of physicians may jeopardize the potential economic benefits of a merger.

Another important strand of literature is devoted to assessing the impact of mergers on prices. Economic theory predicts that a firm (hospital) that increases its market power is able to charge higher prices. Therefore, the empirical approach focuses on the level of the price increase and the corresponding harm to consumers. For instance, Gaynor and Vogt (2003) argue that post-merger prices in the hospital industry in California increased as much as 53 percent, with little difference between for-profit and nonprofit hospitals. These price increases are faced by the insurance companies who, in turn, raise their rates. Vogt (2009) finds that hospital prices to private payers increased 20 percent between 1994 and 2001, and the increased reached 42 percent between 2001 and 2008. Vogt argues that these price increases are due to a wave of mergers that resulted in many cities being dominated by two or three large health care providers. These results are in line with the analysis of Krishnan and Krishnan (2003). These large increases in prices are not distributed uniformly in the hospital market. Spang *et al.* (2001) find that merging hospitals generally have lower growth in costs and prices compared with their rivals and also non-merging non-rival hospitals. Finally, Dafny (2009) reports that the impact of the price increase contains a geographical element. It occurs just after a rival's merger, and the greatest increase appears among the hospitals nearest to those that have merged. All this evidence refer to the US hospital market. Evidence from the European market is scarce and mostly not available. As an example, DutchNews.nl of December 31, 2009 refers to an unpublished report by the Dutch competition authority where it is found that "[h]ospital mergers lead to higher prices because patients are unwilling to travel longer distances to a cheaper hospital".[3]

The impact of mergers on the level of quality of hospital services is the third issue the empirical literature has studied. Ho and Hamilton (2000) compare the quality of hospital care before and after mergers and acquisitions in California between 1992 and 1995, to conclude that "[t]he adverse consequences of increased market power on the quality of care require further substantiation." Vogt (2009) also reports ambiguous predictions in the sense that different studies obtain all the possible conclusions: from the lack of impact of mergers on quality, to a positive impact, and to a negative impact. From the legal perspective, Kristin Madison (2007) reports on the discussion among scholars regarding the possibility of abandoning quality-of-care defenses because they are too difficult to prove. However, he argues that the introduction of new quality measurement techniques make such defenses potentially viable. "At the same time, imposing burdens on parties seeking to defend mergers on the basis of quality improvement may promote further advances in quality measurement and, ultimately, in the quality of care."

From a welfare perspective, Town *et al.* (2006) estimate the impact of the wave of hospital mergers in the 1990s on welfare, focusing on the impact on consumer surplus for the under-65 population. They find a modest impact: "[o]ur estimates imply that hospital mergers resulted in a cumulative consumer surplus loss of over $42.2 billion between 1990 and 2001. It is estimated that all but a modest $95.4 million of the loss in consumer surplus is transferred from consumers to providers."

Finally, Harrison (2006) classifies mergers according to the ownership status. She finds that mergers between non-teaching, nonprofit, or for-profit hospital occur more often, and concludes that after controlling for other merger pair characteristics (e.g. geographical distance), the dominant determinant of merger pairs is the ownership status.

6.2.3 Antitrust merger law

Mergers and acquisitions are very complex procedures. Evaluating their costs and benefits and potential anticompetitive consequences is a difficult task. Antitrust merger law tries to prevent mergers whose anticompetitive effects offset their potential benefits. Accordingly, markets trends and future effects must be forecasted. In other words, the antitrust agencies need accurate dynamic assessments of the particular efficiency/market power trade-off to determine whether or not to challenge a merger.

Salop (1987) describes the US Department of Justice horizontal mergers guidelines as a five-part protocol.

> First, a relevant market is determined for evaluating competitive effects. Second, concentration in the market is calculated, using the Herfindahl-Hirshman Index (HHI). [. . .] Third, the likelihood of entry into the market is evaluated. Fourth, other competitive factors that might affect the likelihood of successful collusion are evaluated, including producer information exchanges and contracting practices. Fifth, any efficiency benefits, primarily cost savings, are analyzed. These five elements then are balanced. [. . .]
>
> It is the weights the guidelines place on these factors in this balancing, and the methodology by which to measure the factors, that are disputed.

The particular applications of those guidelines to hospital mergers are studied in several contributions. The analysis of Capps *et al.* (2002) challenges the decisions by district courts to allow hospital mergers based on a definition of the relevant geographical market given by the analysis of patient flow data. Their argument is two-fold. On the one hand, generally there is no theoretical link between patient flows and the presence or absence of market power. On the other hand, both the standard merger guidelines and the hospital-specific guidelines of the US Department of Justice and the Federal Trade Commission, advocate using the *small (5 percent) but significant non-transitory (1 year) increase in price (SSNIP) criterion*. The SSNIP is theoretically appealing; however patient flow analysis remains the main tool to define geographic markets for hospital mergers because it is easy to obtain and analyze patient flow data. In contrast the data needed to apply the SSNIP standard are often unavailable because negotiated prices are secret, and prices faced by patients are not observed. The aim of the research is thus to assess whether inferences using patient flow data are close to the inferences using the SSNIP criteria. The main conclusion of the analysis is that "for a wide range of plausible situations, patient flow data provide a highly inaccurate view of the appropriate market boundaries. (. . .) Hence, we advocate eliminating the use of flow data (. . .) in any situation where their inferences are ambiguous, which is, practically speaking, all courtroom procedures." Leibenluft (2007) expresses the view of the Federal Trade Commission on the importance to preserve competition in the hospital market:

> The bottom line is that hospital mergers in some markets can lead to higher prices, preclude future price reductions, reduce quality, and diminish the incentives for hospitals to operate more efficiently and to participate in innovative financial arrangements. They can preclude future entry or growth of managed care organizations. Moreover, such mergers can reduce competitive pressure on hospitals to innovate – for example, by developing methods of clinical, physician/hospital, and other integration that could produce additional efficiencies in the delivery of the entire spectrum of health care services. Accordingly, protection of hospital competition is vital.

McCarthy and Thomas (2003) and Haas-Wilson and Gaynor (1998) argue that the relevant geographic market is important because it describes the geographic reach of those suppliers that significantly constrain the behavior of the merging firms. Therefore, a proper identification of the relevant market is often critical to hospital merger analysis.

The European Union legislation on merger decisions includes the EC Merger Regulation and the Implementing Regulation.[4] They are described in Bumgardner (2005). Zhu (2006) and Bergman *et al.* (2010) present the comparison between the EU and US antitrust legislation. The Federal Trade Commission (2004) reports on the concerns about the impact on competition of the horizontal consolidation in hospital markets in the US.

In a recent contribution Farrell and Shapiro (2010) acknowledge that using market concentration as an indicator may be misleading in some industries. They propose a different approach based on whether a proposed merger between rivals in a differentiated product industry will generate net upward pricing pressure (UPP). Such effect on prices is the outcome of two opposing forces: the loss of direct competition between the merging parties, and marginal-cost savings from the merger. The former pushes the price up, while the latter pulls the price down. If the net effect manifests in an increase in price, the merger is flagged for further scrutiny.

6.3 Vertical mergers

Vertical mergers may involve a firm buying a customer, and we will refer to this as *forward (downstream) integration*. Alternatively, a firm may acquire a supplier thus defining a

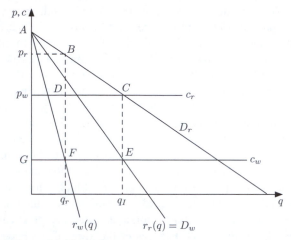

Figure 6.2 Vertical merger.

backward (upstream) integration. Also, we refer to *balanced integration* when a company controls from the supply of raw materials to the final delivery of consumer products. Thus, the integration is both upstream and downstream.

A vertical merger internalizes all transactions between the acquirer and acquired firms, so that the potential strategic effects between them are turned into a partnership. Also, the internalization can improve performance by reducing uncertainty over availability and quality of supplies, or the demand of output. A second reason for vertical mergers is to reduce transaction costs like sales and marketing expenses. In contrast with horizontal mergers, a vertical merger does not reduce the number of competitors. However, it may vary the behavior of the industry because the acquired firm may decide to deal exclusively with the acquiring firm thus altering the competitive status of the market. This raises the concern that vertical mergers may foreclosure competitors by limiting their access to either supply sources or consumers. In addition, another anticompetitive effect may appear in the form of the entry barrier of potential competitors in the market.

To illustrate the effects of a vertical integration of two firms, consider the simplest vertical structure where an upstream firm sells an input to a downstream company. Let us also assume that those firms may be either perfectly competitive or monopolists, and information is complete. Waldman and Jensen (2007, ch. 16) argue that vertical integration of the two firms only has an impact on the market price if both are monopolists. Before the integration, the crucial feature to realize is that the marginal revenue of the retailer ($r_r(q)$) is precisely the demand curve of the wholesaler (D_w). Given D_w, the associated marginal revenue curve is $r_w(q)$. The profit maximizing output of the wholesaler is determined by the equation of marginal revenue and marginal cost (c_w), so that it charges a price p_w. Next, the retailer takes p_w as its marginal cost (c_r). Again the retailer's optimal decision stems from equating marginal revenue and marginal cost, so that it charges a price p_r. Wholesaler's profits are given by the area $p_w DFG$, retailer's profits are described by the area $p_r BDp_w$, and consumer surplus is given by the triangle ABp_r. Figure 6.2 illustrates this argument.

Let us assume that the two firms merge. The new company would now consider the marginal cost of the wholesale input to be c_w so that it would charge a retail price of p_w, and would obtain profits corresponding to the area p_wCEG. Consumer surplus would be the triangle ACp_w.

From the consumers' perspective, the vertically integrated firm yields higher surplus ($ACp_w > ABp_r$). Also, from the firms' viewpoint, the integration has the effect of obtaining larger profits ($p_wCEG > p_wDFG + p_rBDp_r = p_rBFG$). In this example, the vertical merger should be encouraged from a policy perspective. The superiority of the vertical integration outcome comes from what is called the *double marginalization* problem. When firms are independent, each successive stage of monopoly causes a distortion that pushes the price up. By vertically integrating, one distortion disappears (the new integrated firm internalizes the effect) allowing for a lower price and larger quantity.

In general, vertical mergers are closely scrutinized by the antitrust authorities because the associated lower transaction costs and lower uncertainty for the firm may yield higher market power that can manifest in market foreclosure (that is the prevention to old suppliers of the former downstream firm from selling inputs to it (see Rey and Tirole 2007) and entry barriers (a vertically integrated firm controlling the upstream price of a necessary input can prevent entry of nonintegrated rivals, or can place nonintegrated rivals in the downstream market at a competitive disadvantage by artificially increasing the price of that input. This is known as a *price squeeze* effect). Vickers and Waterson (1991) and Martin (2002, ch. 12) offer a complete analysis of these elements. The whole analysis should incorporate other elements such as oligopolistic market structures and downstream product differentiation.

Salop and Scheffman (1987), Ordover *et al.* (1990), Hart and Tirole (1990), Chen (2001), Motta (2004), and Church (2009a) discuss the modern equilibrium approach to the analysis of vertical mergers. The main conclusion of the analysis is ambiguous. Given that integration may enhance efficiency but may also have anticompetitive effects, general results are difficult to obtain. Rather, results are specific to the different sets of assumptions behind the different models.

In November 2008, the EU issued its guidelines on the assessment of non-horizontal mergers containing the principles applied by the European Commission in its assessment of vertical and conglomerate mergers. Wolf (2009) and Ablasser-Neuhuber and Plank (2010) extensively survey its content. Empirical literature on the effects of vertical integration is relatively scarce and concentrated in a number of markets (see Gaynor 2006 for a list of references).

6.3.1　Vertical restraints vs. vertical mergers

Following Motta (2004, ch. 6), *vertical restraints* refer to the different types of contracts signed between vertically related firms to reduce transaction costs, guarantee stability of supplies, and better coordinate actions. Vertical restraints are enforced to serve the interest of the downstream firm, upstream firm, or both. *Vertical mergers* refer to a particular type of vertical restraint where the two vertically related firms merge.

The literature seeks to distinguish between restraints based upon agreements and those based upon dominance and analyses restraints in terms of their effects at the manufacturer level and at the retailer level competition to consider their social welfare implications. This distinction is relevant because it amounts to differentiate between restraints with positive welfare effects (removal of pricing distortions, optimizing investment levels, or eliminating avoidable transaction costs), from those with adverse effects on welfare (market foreclosure to new entrants, or dampening competition between rivals in the market through restrictions on competition).

The most common forms of vertical restraints are: *nonlinear pricing* (average cost is decreasing to the number of units bought). Examples of nonlinear pricing are franchise fees, two-part tariffs, quantity discounts, and progressive rebates; *resale price maintenance, RPM* (manufacturer affects the pricing decision of the retailer to the final consumers). Examples of RPM are recommended prices and minimum/maximum resale prices; *quantity fixing* (manufacturer affects the number of units bought by the retailer); *exclusivity clauses* (manufacturer and retailer sign exclusivity agreement distribution in for example a geographical area [exclusive territory], or in particular brand [exclusive dealing]). Depending on the capacity of monitoring that the two parts may have, some types of vertical restraints may be more effective than others. However, the implementation of any of these restraints requires as a necessary condition the presence of market power at one of both contracting parts. Precisely because of the necessary presence of market power, the issue with vertical restraints is the "trade-off" between the efficiency motives and the anticompetitive effects.

When manufacturers find it difficult to close contracts with retailers, they may attempt to merge with or take over the retailers. In this sense a vertical merger is a limited case of vertical restraint. This means than from a policy viewpoint regulation of vertical restraints and vertical merger must go hand-in-hand. Motta (2004) and Dobson and Waterson (1996) provide a complete analysis of vertical restraints and competition policy.

6.3.2   *Vertical mergers in health care*

Vertical integration activity appeared in the US health care market in the 1990s as a response to the development of managed care organizations. There is clear evidence of the downward pressure on hospital prices exerted by managed care. Therefore, hospitals only had two ways out: either to increase efficiency or to design a strategy to gain bargaining power with insurers. Two types of mergers are observed: integration between hospitals and physicians, and mergers between hospitals and insurers.[5]

Hospitals and physicians sell complementary products. Therefore, technically speaking they are not vertical to each other. However, by coordinating their pricing decisions they internalize their interaction yielding to an efficiency gain. What we cannot observe is the double marginalization problem. The potentially anticompetitive effect of the hospital–physician integration is due to a foreclosure effect preventing rival hospitals from accessing physician services (and vice versa).

Burns and Pauly (2002) and Haas-Wilson and Gaynor (1998) report that these activities were raised until the mid 1990s and have declined ever since. Cuellar and Gertler (2006) examine whether hospital–physician integration leads to efficiency gains from transaction cost economies, or whether it is a strategy to improve bargaining power. They conclude that integration has little effect on efficiency, but it is associated with an increase in prices. In contrast Ciliberto and Dranove (2006) observe that during the 1990s hospital–physician agreements were formed and also broke up. However, they conclude that these integration-and-disintegration episodes did not have any impact on hospital pricing. Huckman (2006) studies the impact of hospital acquisitions on market power to find small effects on total welfare. Gal-Or (1999a, b) studied the impact on the bargaining position of the hospital–physician integration *vis-à-vis* the insurer. She finds that the integrated hospital–physician firm improves its bargaining power when the degree of competitiveness of the hospital and physicians markets is comparable. "Overall, it is hard to say what to expect the effect of hospital–physician integration to be. Many things are possible – nothing is definite" (Gaynor 2006a, p. 177).

6.4   Conglomerate mergers

We refer to *conglomerate mergers* in a situation where the merging firms are neither horizontally nor vertically related. In other words, in a conglomerate merger the acquiring and the acquired firms are not competitors in any respect. The conglomerate merger brings together two companies with no previous connections. A recent example of this type of merger occurred in September 2009 when China's State-owned Assets Supervision and Administration Commission (SASAC) announced the merger of China National Pharmaceutical Group Corp (Sinopharm) and China National Biotec Group (CNBG), under which CNBG was to be completely incorporated into Sinopharm.

There are two types of conglomerate mergers: pure and mixed. *Pure conglomerate mergers* involve firms with nothing in common, while *mixed conglomerate mergers* involve firms that are looking for product extensions or market extensions. They may involve complementary products, or neighboring products (i.e. products that are purchased by a common pool of buyers).

A conglomerate transaction ordinarily has no direct effect on competition. There is no reduction or other change in the number of firms in either the acquiring or acquired firm's market. Rather, the threat of a takeover may induce improvements in efficiency in competitive markets. However, conglomerate merger potentially may have anticompetitive effects by increasing *entry barriers* in the market, or by converting a large firm into a dominant corporation with a decisive competitive advantage. Also, a conglomerate merger may facilitate the use of *bundling strategies*. Other arguments against conglomerate mergers are *reciprocity* and *cross-subsidization*. The former refers to the possibility that the newly created corporation "encourages" the suppliers of a division to purchase inputs from another division in the corporation. The latter refers to the use of profits obtained in one market to implement a more aggressive pricing strategy in the other market. Church (2009b) thoroughly reviews the literature on the competitive effects of conglomerate mergers.

In a similar way as in the case of vertical mergers, conglomerate mergers face a trade off between increased efficiency and increased market power. This is recognized in the antitrust legislation that distinguishes between horizontal and non-horizontal mergers, thus putting together vertical and conglomerate mergers. From a policy viewpoint, there is a general consensus both in the US and in Europe on the need to control corporate mergers. The consensus also extends to the serious doubts about the improvements in efficiency induced by conglomerate mergers, although the economic presumption is that they are typically procompetitive. However controversy appears on whether such control should concentrate on the elimination of competition in behavioral aspects such as the use of bundling strategies (see Church 2009b, Sections 3 and 8).

6.4.1   Empirical evidence from health care

Hutchens and Pettit (2009) studied 1,750 health care deals over the 1998–2008 period. They find that,

> Pharmaceuticals saw heavy action in the late 90s driven primarily by consolidation. Health care equipment saw a similar trend in between 2005 and 2007. Before 2009, there had been no blockbuster deals since 2004. There is already increased deal activity in what's categorized as the pharmaceutical and biotechnology segments. [...] While much of the activity remains within health care silos, there are some signs of convergence themes. Most deals are consolidation efforts within the same sector. But in certain

pockets we see cross-sector consolidation, motivated by slower growth or increasing operating pressure, to realize higher margins and growth prospects, acquire new lines of business or capabilities for complementary offerings, or offset declining R&D productivity. Many of these deals represent a combination of leveraging existing, and building new, capabilities.

Some examples of conglomerate mergers in that period are,

- Proctor & Gamble-Clorox. The acquisition of Clorox by Proctor & Gamble eliminated P&G as a prime potential entrant in the market for household bleach.
- Johnson & Johnson-Pfizer's consumer health care division. Without the divestiture remedies imposed by the European Commission, the transaction would have given J&J control over key inputs for nicotine patches produced by its main competitor, GlaxoSmithKline. The Commission's concern was that consumers attempting to quit smoking otherwise could have suffered higher prices and less innovative products.
- Clarient-Applied Genomics. According to Clarient CEO Ron Andrews, "Applied Genomics brings a new lung cancer panel as well as several cancer tests that are in development. (. . .) The acquisition puts Clarient in a position to grow in 2010 and later."
- Kimberly-Clark-I-Flow. This acquisition is part of KC's effort to expand its health care business to include high-growth, higher-margin medical devices, according to KC CEO Donald M. Earhart, who added that it "will enable future growth, and provide a platform to more broadly deliver pain relief and surgical site care, which is important for patients, physicians and health care providers."
- GE health care-Wipro JV. This merger turns into a new company Wipro GE health care, which distributes 85 percent of GE's various health care and medical diagnostic products in India. GE chairman and CEO Jeffrey R. Immelt declared that "[t]he integration will simplify the structure and help us focus on the Indian market. It will help us in developing new products for India and in entering more markets."

6.5 M&A failure

Outcomes of M&A in the health care sector as measured by the one-year excess return is approximately normally distributed around the zero percent excess return, according to Hutchens and Pettit (2009). They find that consolidation in the market, capability building, and diversification are the main drivers of the success or failure of a merge:

> Looking at the left tail of the distribution, we find that despite the goal of performance improvement, many empirical studies report high failure rates of M&A. Post-M&A performance is measured by synergy realization, relative performance compared to competition, and absolute performance.

Straub (2007) also analyzes the reasons for merger failure from a multidimensional viewpoint. According to his analysis, there are three key factors for a successful deal: (i) Strategic logic which is reflected by six determinants: market similarities, market complementarities, operational similarities, operational complementarities, market power, and purchasing power; (ii) Organizational integration which is reflected by three determinants: acquisition experience, relative size, cultural compatibility; and (iii) Financial/price perspective which is reflected by three determinants: acquisition premium, bidding process, and due diligence.

From a policy perspective, Mueller (1989) offers some reflections for the design of a merger policy. The starting point is the recognition that all mergers are different and thus, the aim of the merger policy should be to retain the socially beneficial mergers and reduce as much as possible the efficiency-reducing ones. An important factor behind M&A failure is managerial hubris or managerial pursuit of goals other than stockholder benefit. Merger policy should limit managerial discretion by sharing more information with stockholders, and promote an accurate evaluation of the anticompetitive and efficiency-enhancing effects of the merger. The EU and US merger guidelines already contemplate these issues. The main problems in implementing the merger policy are (i) the capacity of the regulatory agencies to assess the potential impact on efficiency of a merger, and (ii) the lobbying capacity of the large firms and concentrated industries. Mergers only increase the capacity of those large corporations to bend the rules to their own advantage.

7 For-profit and nonprofit organizations

In this chapter, we address the presence and relevance of nonprofit organizations in the economy in general and in the health care sector in particular. We define and describe the main characteristics of these type of organizations, and argue why an institution may choose this institutional choice over alternative ones. We concentrate the analysis in several proposals to model hospital behavior.

This chapter focuses on the presence and relevance of nonprofit organizations in the health care sector. Hospitals, nursing homes, psychiatric care facilities, or facilities for the mentally handicapped are examples of organizations often with the status of nonprofit. To fix ideas let us start by defining a nonprofit organization,

DEFINITION 7.1 (NONPROFIT ORGANIZATION). A nonprofit organization (NPO) is an entity where nobody holds property rights on the profits generated with its activity.

Other concepts synonymous to the nonprofit sector are "social economy," "third sector," and "third system." They all refer to a sector inbetween the market and the state pursuing the general interest and whose final objective is neither the generation nor the distribution of profits.

The literature on NPOs in the health care sector is by far richer in the US than in Europe, Canada, or Australia, to mention some examples. The main reason is the organization of the health care sector. In countries where health care is (mostly) publicly provided through a national health service, a high share of the facilities, particularly hospitals, are public and nonprofit and universal coverage dims the need for private (for-profit) provision of community services.

The literature on nonprofit organizations deals with two types of questions regarding their existence and their behavior particularly as compared with that of the for-profit organizations. OECD (2003), Sloan (1998, 2000), and Needleman (2001) review these issues thoroughly.[1]

In an economy there may coexist three types of organizational forms: for-profit, public, and nonprofit. They differ in their behavior in the market because although they all face the same population of individuals and households, their interests in identifying needs (i.e. demands) and their willingness to satisfy them may be different. Often consumers have less information on market conditions (prices, availability of substitute goods, etc.) than producers. This opens the possibility for opportunistic behavior on the side of sellers to extract higher rents from the (under-informed) consumers. Nonprofit organizations are assumed less likely to exploit these opportunistic types of behavior because there is nobody to profit from them. Thus, nonprofit institutions may help to correct market inefficiencies.

This is one of the main reasons why governments favor the existence and development of nonprofit organizations through a favorable tax regime on corporate income, on subsidies and donations, and the like. Also, it is often the very governments that allocate subsidies and donations to nonprofit organizations to carry out activities that they are not able (or willing) to do.

The choice of the institutional form is also driven by a second motive. Nonprofit organizations manage differently levels of information for buyers and sellers in the market. In this sense, we face essentially a social welfare problem. Following Weisbrod (1994, ch. 3), if consumers are well informed, they will direct their demands to those producers satisfying them at the least cost. Thus, private for-profit firms seem to be the best alternative. However, if consumers are poorly informed, the profit incentive yields inefficient and inequitable market outcomes. This does not mean that for-profit organizations necessarily perform worse in the long run. After purchasing, individuals obtain information that narrows down the initial informational gap. Accordingly, one criterion to favor either organizational form is to study how fast consumers become informed. In those markets where acquiring information is difficult, nonprofit institutions are more likely to satisfy better social demands. Also, the presence of consumers with different degrees of information opens the possibility for the coexistence of for-profit and nonprofit organizations in the same market.

In the remaining sections of the chapter, we will look more closely at these two arguments for the creation and support of nonprofit organizations, and will examine some alternatives to the modeling of nonprofit institutions. The lack of common criteria to determine the behavior of nonprofit organizations is consistent with the inconclusiveness of the empirical literature regarding the relative performance of nonprofit vs. for-profit organizations.

7.1 Why do nonprofit organizations exist?

The analysis of the role of nonprofit organizations in the health care market is inspired in Arrow (1963, pp. 950, 965) when arguing that the physician acting as an agent for the patient considers some form of ethical behavior leading to the relative unimportance of for-profit hospitals.

The development of the literature of industrial economics considering the strategic behavior of the agents, information, and agency relationships, has dealt with Arrow's suggestions in various ways. Hansmann (1980, 1996) argues that in situations where consumers cannot properly evaluate the goods and services offered (as is the case in the health care market), nonprofit institutions have an advantageous position. This is the case because nonprofit organizations are free of the incentives for exploiting their market power. In contrast with profit-seeking providers, nonprofit institutions include in their objective functions some form of *altruism*. Rose-Ackerman (1996) offers a complete discussion of altruism emphasizing its importance to properly understand the behavior of nonprofit firms.

Typically, modeling of nonprofit providers point towards better performance (lower prices, higher output, and higher quality) than the for-profit providers. Also, if profits are obtained, they are used to subsidize unprofitable care (e.g. trauma services, burnt units, neonatal intensive care), unsponsored research, and medical education. Summarizing, poorly informed consumers gain by knowing whether an organization is for-profit or nonprofit. Thus, in markets where consumers are under informed and acquiring information is difficult, coexistence of nonprofit and for-profit institutions is to be expected. *A senso contrario*, in markets with well-informed consumers, there is no reason to prefer a nonprofit organization over a for-profit one. A similar argument is applicable to the founding of nonprofit organizations by governments of the First World to manage aid to the Third World, or to countries suffering from natural disasters.

However, evaluating performance is difficult on two grounds. On the one hand, measures of output are not always available and proxies have to be used. On the other hand, it is often the case in health care provision that it is impossible to evaluate the consequences for the patient should he or she have received an alternative treatment, or patronized another provider. Quoting Sloan (2000), "If, in the case of health care, the patient improved, was it because of, or in spite of, the care received?"

Donations and subsidies are two elements often put forward for nonprofit institutions. Donations are a manifestation of an inefficiency in the typically public provision of goods and services. Consider as an illustrative example a community where the public provision of child care is regarded insufficient by those families with three or more children. Those families may found a nonprofit organization to build a hospital for child care, thus complementing the public supply of such type of care, or alternatively may donate funds to the existing hospital to enlarge its capacity. This phenomenon seems to be behind the upsurge on nongovernmental organizations like Greenpeace, Medicus Mundi, Médecins Sans Frontières, and the like.

We have already mentioned the preferential public policies directed towards nonprofit organizations, such as tax exemptions and subsidies. Arrow argues that these policies reflect the preferences of consumers for nonprofit institutions. A different justification relates to the disadvantageous position of nonprofit institutions in the market to compete against for-profit suppliers. Either way, there is a strategically oriented approach, where firms decide to acquire the status of for-profit or nonprofit comparing the advantages of the latter against the (expected) profit opportunities. This literature offers two approaches. One of them considers that the proportion of one type of institution over the other in the market is constantly evolving. The second approach considers that market dynamics induce nonprofit organizations to converge towards a profit seeking behavior leaving aside more socially oriented goals. A quick summary of these arguments can be found in Culyer (2005, pp. 162–164).

7.2   Modeling nonprofit organizations

We have already argued that a fundamental concern in economics is the efficient use of resources. Given that most hospitals are nonprofit, we should not expect hospitals' decision making to be driven by producing at minimum cost. Therefore, in modeling hospital behavior the first difficulty to solve is to define the hospital output. In essence, a hospital aims at improving the health state of its patients.[2] How well a patient improves, how much of the improvement is due to the treatment, can only be measured in approximate terms, and more often than not by means of indirect variables (proxies). Among them we highlight the number of cases treated, the number of patient days, the quantity of medical examinations, operations, working hours of physicians and nurses, and the turnover of stocks of the hospital pharmacy. Also, in measuring those variables the patients' characteristics, the type of illnesses and their severity, introduce additional complications that are particularly relevant when these measurements are used in comparative performance assessments across hospitals. The development of classification systems like the *International Classification of Diseases* or the *diagnostic-related groups* are attempts to normalize criteria in computing the output of a hospital.

McGuire *et al.* (1999, ch. 11), Phelps (2009, chs. 8, 9), and Zweifel and Breyer (1997, ch. 9) offer general economic models of a hospital somehow summarizing the attempts proposed in the literature since Newhouse's pioneering contribution in 1970. There is some consensus in that a nonprofit hospital has a different objective from profit maximization. However, there is little agreement on what the objective of a nonprofit hospital is. Without attempting to be comprehensive, several types of proposals include the following: Gaynor and Vogt (2003) and Calem *et al.* (1999) propose output maximization; Newhouse (1970) and Sloan and Steinwald (1980) consider output and quality as objectives; Ma and Burguess (1993) and Brekke *et al.* (2011) analyze price and quality; Pauly and Redisch (1973) propose a hospital as a cooperative of doctors maximizing income per member of the cooperative; Dranove (1988) and Deneffe and Masson (2002) propose output and profits; finally, Pauly (1987) and Harrison and Lybecker (2005) claim that hospitals maximize a utility function with profits and something else as arguments. It may be quantity, quality, or uncompensated care.

Lakdawalla and Philipson (2006) study the performance of nonprofit firms at the industry level. Their main finding is that positive and normative implications are very different at the industry level than at the firm level analysis. In particular, under perfect competition and homogeneous technology, the existence of a nonprofit sector has a limited impact on industry performance. More generally, nonprofit regulations matter only insofar as they influence the behavior of the for-profit sector. Therefore, they may have a limited impact if any on overall industry performance.

All these alternative proposals yield different pricing behavior for the nonprofit hospitals that are not comparable as they arise from different frameworks. To summarize we can quote Needleman (2001, p. 1120): "There are many nonprofits, and the lack of agreement on the objective function of these organizations may reflect the reality that these objectives will vary widely from one nonprofit to another."

7.2.1 Zweifel and Breyer hospital model

We will first review Zweifel and Breyer's (1997, ch. 9.3) general proposal of a model of a hospital. Next, we will review some proposals as particular cases.

Assume that there is only one illness, and consider the notation of Table 7.1. The *technology* used by the hospital describes a quality of treatment that depends on the medical services per patient, that is

$$Q = g\left(\frac{Y}{X}\right)$$

where it is assumed that g is concave and there is an upper bound α on Y/X so that $g^1 \gtreqless 0$ if $\alpha \lesseqgtr 0$.

The *cost function* of the hospital is defined by two aggregate inputs, labor (L) and capital (K). The labor input comprises both medical and non-medical types of labor, and it has a given unit price w. The capital input summarizes all the other inputs used by the hospital: capital, energy, medical supplies, etc. and it has a constant unit price r. For a given size of the hospital (Z) and level of services provided (Y), cost minimization yields optimal levels of inputs $L^*(Y, Z)$ and $K^*(Y, Z)$, so that $C(Y, Z) = wL^*(Y, Z) + rK^*(Y, Z)$.

However, the hospital (as a nonprofit institution) need not operate at the cost-minimizing solution. Instead, it may allow for some slackness in the inputs (L^s, K^s), for instance to transmit to the population the feeling of readiness against any emergency. Therefore, the actual use of inputs by the hospital is,

$$L = L^*(Y, Z) + L^s \quad \text{and} \quad K = K^*(Y, Z) + K^s$$

so that the *actual expenditure function* of the hospital is given by,

$$A(Y, Z) = C(Y, Z) + wL^s + rK^s \tag{7.1}$$

The *revenues* of the hospital are given by a revenue function that generically, it is denoted as,

$$R(X, Y, Z, A) \tag{7.2}$$

When the hospital belongs to a NHS-type of system, the payment scheme is defined by the health authority. Otherwise, the reimbursement will follow from negotiations with third-party payers and the competition among hospitals in the marketplace. Regardless of the organization of health care provision, the problem of the nonprofit hospital is to determine (Y, A).

To compute the *demand function* of the hospital, let us assume that the size of the hospital has already been decided, so that Z is exogenous. The number of cases treated in the hospital (X) is determined by the referrals from physicians and from other hospitals, and by the patients themselves. Also, if the hospital competes for patients through the quality of the services provided, the number of patients treated is also determined within some bounds, by the very hospital. Thus,

$$X = \phi(Q) = \phi\left[g\left(\frac{Y}{X}\right)\right], \quad \text{with } X \in [\underline{X}, \overline{X}]$$

Assuming $\phi' > 0$ and solving for X, we obtain the demand for patients as

$$X = \begin{cases} \underline{X} & \text{if } f(Y) < \underline{X} \\ f(Y) & \text{if } \underline{X} \le f(Y) \le \overline{X} \\ \overline{X} & \text{if } f(Y) > \underline{X} \end{cases}$$

where $f(Y)$ illustrates the dependence of X of hospital's ultimate decision Y, and $f' > 0$.

The generic *profit function* of the hospital is defined as

$$\Pi(Y, L^s, K^s) = R(f(Y), Y, A; Z) - A(Y; Z) \tag{7.3}$$

Table 7.1 Variables in Zweifel and Breyer hospital model

Q	quality of treatment	L	labor input
Y	medical services provided	L^s	slack labor
X	number of cases	K	capital input
Z	number of beds	K^s	slack capital
A	actual expenditure of hospital	w	price of labor
Π	profits of hospital	r	price of capital
R	revenue of hospital	C	minimal costs of hospital

Finally, the hospital's *objective function* is described by a utility function defined in terms of quality and profits, $U(Q, \Pi)$. The hospital aims at maximizing its utility subject to the profit constraint given by (7.3).

Naturally, the properties of the utility function depend on the payment system, i.e. the revenue function (7.2), and the agent holding the property rights on profits.

Zweifel and Breyer envisage a hospital as an organization composed of four groups of agents: physicians, nurses and other staff, the managerial team, and the owners. The utility function of the hospital aggregates the preferences of these agents where different weights may be attributed to the different types of agents.

If the hospital is for-profit, the owners are the residual claimants of the profits generated, and the usual profit-maximizing arguments apply. If the hospital is nonprofit, all agents agree that the hospital must not bear losses. The question arises when the hospital generates profits. Then the use of those profits depends on whether it is regulated by the health authority or whether the hospital has freedom to use them. In the latter case, the hospital may use profits as an incentive device to its personnel paying premiums, financing training courses, etc. to enhance efficiency.

7.2.2 Newhouse proposal

In a pioneering contribution, Newhouse (1970) proposes a hospital model where the administrator is the decision maker. In terms of the general framework of Zweifel and Breyer this amounts to considering that in defining the utility function of the hospital, all the weight falls on the managerial team. The objective of this administrator is to choose the output and the quality of the services provided yielding the maximum level of utility subject to a zero-profit constraint. Formally, (see Folland *et al.* 2009; Phelps 2009), the problem of the hospital according to Newhouse can be written as,

$$\max_{Q,Y} U(Q, Y) \quad \text{s.t. } \Pi = 0$$

where U is increasing in both arguments.

In defining profits, Newhouse considers an inverse demand function $P(X, Y)$ and a cost function $C(X, Y)$, so that everything else held constant, profits are defined as

$$\Pi(Q, Y) = P(Q, Y)Y - C(Q, Y)$$

where

$$\frac{\partial P}{\partial Q} > 0; \quad \frac{\partial P}{\partial Y} < 0; \quad \frac{\partial C}{\partial Q} > 0; \quad \frac{\partial C}{\partial Y} > 0.$$

Assuming U-shaped average cost curves, Figure 7.1 illustrates the demand and average cost of the hospital.

To solve this problem we construct an auxiliary Lagrangian function (see Section 2.2.3) defined on (Q, Y) as follows,

$$\mathcal{L}(Q, Y) = U(Q; Y) + \lambda(P(Q, Y)Y - C(Q; Y))$$

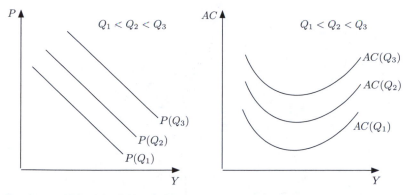

Figure 7.1 Newhouse (1970) demand and average cost of the hospital.

and solve the system of first-order conditions

$$\frac{\partial \mathcal{L}}{\partial Q} = \frac{\partial U}{\partial Q} + \lambda \left(\frac{\partial P}{\partial Q} Y - \frac{\partial C}{\partial Q} \right) = 0 \tag{7.4}$$

$$\frac{\partial \mathcal{L}}{\partial Y} = \frac{\partial U}{\partial Y} + \lambda \left(\frac{\partial P}{\partial Y} Y + P - \frac{\partial C}{\partial Y} \right) = 0 \tag{7.5}$$

$$\frac{\partial \mathcal{L}}{\partial \lambda} = \frac{\partial P}{\partial Q} Y - \frac{\partial C}{\partial Q} = 0 \tag{7.6}$$

We can rewrite (7.4) and (7.5) as,

$$\lambda = \frac{\dfrac{\partial U}{\partial Q}}{\dfrac{\partial P}{\partial Q} Y - \dfrac{\partial C}{\partial Q}} \tag{7.7}$$

$$\lambda = \frac{\dfrac{\partial U}{\partial Y}}{\dfrac{\partial P}{\partial Y} Y + P - \dfrac{\partial C}{\partial Y}} \tag{7.8}$$

To understand the meaning of conditions (7.7) and (7.8), let us define the *net cost of Q* as the difference between its marginal cost and marginal revenue. Similarly, we define the corresponding *net cost of Y*. These net costs are the denominators of (7.7) and (7.8) respectively. Accordingly, the utility-maximizing solution of the hospital is characterized by the set of points (Q, Y) where the ratio of marginal utility to net cost is equal for both decision variables.

Note that as we have assumed positive marginal utilities, the denominators of (7.7) and (7.8) must also be positive. In turn, this means that in equilibrium marginal cost is larger than marginal revenue in the provision of both quality and quantity of health care services. This implies that the (nonprofit) hospital does not operate at the monopoly solution (equality of marginal revenue and marginal cost) but it rather offers higher levels of quality and activity. We can think of this solution as a situation where the manager of the hospital devotes the potential profit to expand the scale of operation in terms of quality and quantity.

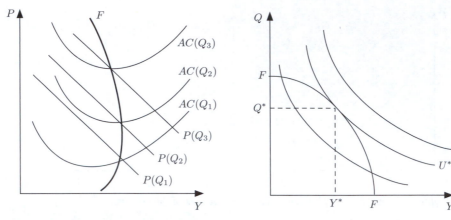

Figure 7.2 Optimal choice of the hospital.

Intuitively, the content of these conditions can be put forward with the help of Figure 7.2. Given that the problem of the hospital is to choose a combination (Q, Y) to maximize its utility, we can first identify the feasible combinations of quality and quantity of services. These are determined by the technology of the hospital and its demand. Consider a certain quality level Q_1. Then, compute the corresponding average cost curve $AC(Q_1)$ and demand curve $P(Q_1)$. The intersection of both curves corresponds to the point satisfying (7.6). We can do this exercise for all quality levels, and then draw the line identifying the set of quality–quantity points satisfying the zero-profit constraint. This is the thick line F on the left-hand side of Figure 7.2. It is a continuous line because quality, quantity, and price are assumed to be continuous variables.

Next, we plot the curve F thus obtained on the space (Q, Y) as depicted in the right-hand side of Figure 7.2. Note that this argument is parallel to the one offered in the analysis of the firm in Chapter 3. The line F represents the *production possibility frontier* of the hospital and captures the constraint of the utility maximization problem of the hospital. Finally, we represent the *indifference map* associated with the utility function of the hospital. Any point (Q, Y) where the production possibility frontier is tangent to an indifference curve, is a solution of the problem of the hospital. In general, the shape of the frontier F and of the indifference curves depend on the primitives of the model. As Newhouse assumes that cost is increasing both in Q and Y, it implies that the hospital faces decreasing returns to scale in obtaining utility in Q and Y. Therefore, the production possibility frontier must be concave to the origin. Figure 7.2 illustrates a situation with a unique equilibrium at the point (Q^*, Y^*) where the hospital obtains a maximum level of utility U^*.

7.2.3 *The approach of Pauly and Redisch*

A different way to look at the organization of a hospital was proposed by Pauly and Redisch (1973). In contrast with Newhouse, they identify the physician staff as the decision makers of the hospital, and their objective to maximize their own net income. In terms of Zweifel and Breyer, a distinction is introduced between medical (M) and non-medical labor (L), and it is the medical labor who carries all the weight in the definition of the utility function of the hospital. This approach considers the medical staff as a cooperative unit aiming at maximizing the income per doctor in the cooperative. To justify their proposal, Pauly and Redisch (1973) argue that

> [t]he staff physicians can determine, within rather broad limits, what use of the hospital will be made in treating a patient; they control many of the production decisions. They have indirect control over many other aspects of the hospital's operation, such as capital investment and the level of nursing care, in the sense that no administrator can afford to incur the displeasure of the medical staff, interfere with medical staff prerogatives, or make decisions which will deter large numbers of physicians from remaining on the hospital's staff or using that hospital for their patients.
>
> (p. 89)

Formally, medical services are provided by means of a technology using labor and capital as inputs:

$$Y = Y(K, L, M) \tag{7.9}$$

This provision is regarded as a combined activity of the medical services of physicians and the hospital services of non-medical labor and capital. Patients' demand for medical services is described by a continuous and decreasing function

$$P_T = P_T(Y), \tag{7.10}$$

where P_T denotes the combined price paid by the patient for the physician and hospital services. The hospital sets the price of its services P_h (a component of P_T), to break even that is, P_h satisfies

$$P_h Y = wL + rK \tag{7.11}$$

The physicians' cooperative may be closed (the decision to admit a new member is taken by the existing members) or open (no restriction to entry to any physician willing to do so).

Closed staff

Given a number M of physicians in the staff of the hospital, their collective revenue (R_M) is given by

$$M R_M = (P_T - P_h)Y = P_T Y - wL - rK$$

The physicians' problem is to determine the values of (K, L, M) that maximize the per capita revenue of the medical staff subject to the production function (7.9) and the demand function (7.10):

$$\max_{K,L,M} R_M = \frac{(P_T - P_h)Y = P_T Y - wL - rK}{M} \quad \text{s.t.} \begin{cases} Y = Y(K, L, M) \\ P_T = P_T(Y) \end{cases} \tag{7.12}$$

The first-order conditions are,

$$w = \frac{\partial Y}{\partial L}\left(P_T + \frac{\partial P_T}{\partial Y}Y\right)$$

$$r = \frac{\partial Y}{\partial K}\left(P_T + \frac{\partial P_T}{\partial Y}Y\right)$$

$$R_M = \frac{\partial Y}{\partial M}\left(P_T + \frac{\partial P_T}{\partial Y}Y\right) \tag{7.13}$$

These conditions simply tell us that the corresponding optimal values of each variable result from equating marginal revenue to marginal cost. Regarding the size of the cooperative, its members will allow new physicians as long as their contribution to the net revenues offsets the payment they receive. In other words, the medical staff admit new members while the revenue per physician increases.

An implicit assumption in the model is that there is a population of physicians willing to join the cooperative because their outside option is given by a competitive supply (S) at a lower level than the revenue possibilities in that hospital. Figure 7.3 illustrates the determination of the optimal value of the size of the cooperative M^c given by (7.13) and the competitive supply curve, and the corresponding earnings per member of the staff R_M^c.

Open staff

If no restrictions are imposed on entry of physicians in the hospital staff, then the equilibrium would arise at point M^o in Figure 7.3, where average income per physician in the staff equates to the marginal supply price of physicians' services.

7.2.4   Cost-shifting

The analysis presented shows that nonprofit hospitals do not operate at the profit-maximizing level. Also, income to these hospitals may originate both from the public health agency as well as from private payers. A question that has attracted considerable attention is whether

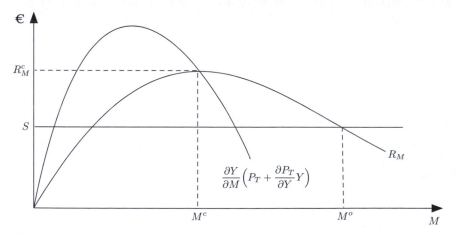

Figure 7.3 Optimal size of the staff.

a shock in the form of a cost increase or a demand decrease, or a decrease in the revenues from the public health authority would yield an increase in the price to private payers. In other words, the hospital recovers from the privately insured patients (part of) the losses from the patients under public insurance. This behavior termed as *cost-shifting*. Dranove (1988) provides a theoretical model of cost-shifting (and an empirical application) where the manager of the hospital aims at maximizing a utility function defined in terms of profitability and output. There are two types of patients: those privately insured, identified with a subindex i, and those insured by the government, identified with a subindex j.

Let $\Pi_k(p_k, \bar{c}_k)$ denote profits originated in market k, $k = i, j$, where p_k denotes the price in market k and $\bar{c}_k$ represents the (constant) average cost of providing services in market k. Define

$$\Pi(p_i, p_j, \bar{c}_i, \bar{c}_j) \equiv \Pi_i(p_i, \bar{c}_i) + \Pi_j(p_j, \bar{c}_j)$$

Let finally denote by $q_k(p_k)$ the demand of medical services in market k. Then, the utility function of the hospital is given by

$$U\left(\Pi(p_i, p_j, \bar{c}_i, \bar{c}_j), q_i(p_i), q_j(p_j)\right) \tag{7.14}$$

where $\partial U/\partial \Pi > 0$, $\partial^2 U/\partial \Pi^2 \leq 0$, $\partial U/\partial q_k > 0$. Also, profit functions satisfy the following properties: $\partial^2 \Pi_k/\partial p_k^2 < 0$, $\partial \Pi_k/\partial \bar{c}_k < 0$, $\partial^2 \Pi_k/\partial p_k \partial \bar{c}_k \geq 0$.

Demand of publicly insured individuals for medical services is exogenously given, and it is also assumed that average cost is the same for both types of patients. Then, the problem of the hospital is to choose the price p_i to be charged to the patients holding private insurance to maximize the utility function (7.14). The first- and second-order conditions are,

$$\frac{\partial U}{\partial p_i} = \frac{\partial U}{\partial \Pi}\frac{\partial \Pi}{\partial p_i} + \frac{\partial U}{\partial q_i}\frac{\partial q_i}{\partial p_i} = 0 \tag{7.15}$$

$$\frac{\partial^2 U}{\partial p_i^2} = \frac{\partial^2 U}{\partial \Pi^2}\left(\frac{\partial \Pi}{\partial p_i}\right)^2 + \frac{\partial U}{\partial \Pi}\frac{\partial^2 \Pi}{\partial p_i^2} + \frac{\partial^2 U}{\partial \Pi \partial q_i}\frac{\partial \Pi}{\partial p_i}\frac{\partial q_i}{\partial p_i}$$

$$+ \frac{\partial^2 U}{\partial q_i^2}\left(\frac{\partial q_i}{\partial p_i}\right)^2 + \frac{\partial U}{\partial q_i}\frac{\partial^2 q_i}{\partial p_i^2} < 0 \tag{7.16}$$

The presence of cost-shifting in this model is identified from the study of the impact on p_i of a cutback in p_j. Totally differentiating (7.15) we obtain,

$$\frac{dp_i}{dp_j} = -\frac{\dfrac{\partial^2 U}{\partial \Pi^2}\dfrac{\partial \Pi_i}{\partial p_i}\dfrac{\partial \Pi_j}{\partial p_j} + \dfrac{\partial q_i}{\partial p_i}\dfrac{\partial^2 U}{\partial \Pi \partial q_i}\dfrac{\partial \Pi_j}{\partial p_j}}{\dfrac{\partial^2 U}{\partial p_i^2}} \tag{7.17}$$

The hospital cost-shifts if $dp_i/dp_j < 0$. The denominator of (7.17) is negative from (7.16). Therefore, the sign of dp_i/dp_j coincides with the sign of the numerator of (7.17).

- Assume that the hospital is a profit-maximizing institution. This means $\partial U/\partial q_i = 0$. In turn, it implies $\partial^2 U/\partial \Pi \partial q_i = 0$ and, from (7.15) $\partial \Pi/\partial p_i = 0$. Substituting in (7.17) it follows that $dp_i/dp_j = 0$ and the hospital does not cost-shift. Accordingly, *a hospital will cost-shift only if it is not a profit maximizer.*

Next, if $\partial \Pi_k/\partial p_k > 0$, then a sufficient condition for the hospital to cost-shift is $\partial^2 U/\partial \Pi \partial q_i \geq 0$.

- Recall from Chapter 4 that the Lerner index tells us that the elasticity of demand is linked to the market power of a firm. In particular, the higher the elasticity of demand the lower the capacity to quote a price above marginal cost (i.e. the lower the market power), and thus the higher the impact on profits of a change of the price (i.e. the higher the value of $\partial \Pi_i/\partial p_i$).

  Note also that as $\partial \Pi_i/\partial p_i \to \infty$, $dp_i/dp_j \to 0$ because the numerator grows in $\partial \Pi/\partial p_i$ while the denominator grows in $(\partial \Pi/\partial p_i)^2$. Accordingly, *a hospital will cost-shift only if it has market power.*

These two features allow for a relatively simple way to test for cost-shifting in the market for hospital services.

7.3   Empirical evidence

Weisbrod (1994) claims a differentiated role for nonprofit and for-profit institutions induced by their different ability to obtain information on social wants, and the incentives to act on them. Accordingly, each type of institution "has a distinct niche to fill in an economic system."

The empirical literature assessing whether performance between for-profit and nonprofit differs is vast. Sloan (2000) provides a nice overview of the relevant issues. Here, we will report on some recent contributions thus complementing Sloan's Chapter in the *Handbook of Health Economics.*

There are different ways to measure differences in performance between for-profit and nonprofit organizations. Efficiency, quality, accessibility, pricing, diffusion of technology, and others. Sloan's (2000) general message is that evidence is not conclusive in any of those aspects. No systematic differences in efficiency among for-profit and nonprofit hospitals is found, no conclusive evidence of cost-shifting by nonprofit hospitals, only minor differences in uncompensated care, and no statistically significant differences in quality of care and technology adoption between for-profit and nonprofit hospitals.

Needleman (2001) also supports these findings and reports no conclusive evidence of for-profit hospitals exploiting their customers and influencing physicians to participate in it, although there is room for concern. Along this line, Melichar (2009) studies whether physicians alter their treatment behavior at the margin in response to their reimbursement. The evidence shows that physicians with capitated managed care contracts spend less time with their capitated patients than with their non-capitated patients, a decision that is not inconsistent with profit maximization.

Regarding community benefits, Needleman (2001) looks at several aspects: charity care shows high variation across states (in the US) and some of these differences are due to the location of the hospitals; also a wide variability in the provision of unprofitable services is found across for-profit hospitals, although price differences seem narrower since the 1990s. It is unclear whether it is due to market pressures squeezing prices or to more aggressive pricing by the nonprofit hospitals. The most clear difference appears in the commitment of the hospital to the place. Needleman reports that nonprofit hospitals view themselves as serving the community and not just their patients, while for-profit hospitals have played less of a leadership and view their relationship to their communities as commercial. Similarly, Sloan *et al.* (2001) find no evidence of difference in cost and quality outcomes by hospital ownership status.

Malani and David (2008) provide a test of the theory that claims that firms use the non-profit status as a signal of quality. The authors argue that if the theory is true, we should observe nonprofit firms advertising their status to consumers. A survey of over 2,800 firms in the hospital, nursing home, or child care industries is conducted to inquire whether nonprofit firms communicate their status to consumers on their websites or Yellow Pages listings. The evidence obtained does not support the hypothesis that nonprofit status is a signal of quality.

A different line of research assesses whether the nonprofit organizations return the benefits they enjoy to society. Greaney and Boozang (2005) argue that the measures of price, cost, profit margin, efficiency, quality and access do not support the claim that historically non-profit hospitals have returned benefits to society. In other words, the evidence that nonprofit hospitals contribute more benefits to society than their social cost (measured in terms of tax exemptions, volunteer labor, donations, etc.) is not convincing. "Evidence further suggests that characteristics of the local market, such as the presence of other hospitals, managed care penetration, and socio-economic status of the community, are far more powerful pre-dictors of performance than the nonprofit form" (p. 12). Schlesinger and Gray (2006b) argue that a full assessment of the impact that health care organizations have on the communities is difficult because not all activities are measurable. "The real challenge here is to clarify expectations for all forms of community benefit. Until we have better measures of the scope and impact of community-benefit activities, a tension will exist between accountability and flexibility in responding to community needs" (p. 294).

Last but not least, there is a stream of the literature dealing with the impact of the own-ership form, the provision of medical services, and the operating margins. Castaneda and Falaschetti (2008) evaluate the scope of medical services provided by a hospital according to its nonprofit or for-profit status. Their main result is that the local demographics is a much more important determinant of the mix of services than the ownership status. However, Hor-witz and Nichols (2009) find strong evidence of spillover effects between the ownership mix in the market and the supply of services by nonprofit hospitals. No significant effect appears between the market mix and the operating margins of nonprofit hospitals. David (2009) proposes a model of ownership choice to explain the convergence in size (number of beds) between for-profit and nonprofit hospitals. In contrast with many contributions, the driver of the decision on the (change of) ownership type hinges on the incentives provided by the economic environment (regulatory and tax regimes, and demographic factors). These ownership conversions together with entry and exit explain the convergence in size better than expansions or downsizing of existing hospitals.

7.4   What do nonprofit hospitals maximize?

We have mentioned at the beginning of this chapter the spread of proposals to model the behavior of a nonprofit hospital. The models presented so far do not address the issue (among others) of how competition among hospitals for-profit and nonprofit affect their decisions. Harrison and Lybecker (2005) propose a theoretical set up to examine competition (in prices) between a for-profit and a nonprofit hospital. The nonprofit hospital has an objective function defined as a linear combination of profit and a nonprofit motive that can be either quantity, or quality, or charity (provision of medical services to poor uninsured individuals). Not sur-prisingly, the results differ across the different nonprofit motives, and the authors conclude that the spread in the empirical literature may be associated with the different assumptions on the nonprofit motive.

In this field, Schlesinger and Gray (2006a, b) present a critical appraisal of the empirical literature and focus on the factors that may explain the apparent inconsistencies in the findings of empirical studies of different types of health care organizations. These factors include the fragmentation of the research literature, misidentifications of ownership, and differences in regulatory and competitive environments. They propose to revise ownership-related policies to define both the appropriate forms of community benefit and the appropriate mix of ownership in terms of local markets and communities.

To conclude, let us mention Place's (2007) proposal:

> [I]f we agree that the only criterion of our distinctiveness is some metric of direct dollar value compared to some other dollar value such as uncollected taxes, then most likely we will never be able to conclusively justify our special privileges. In effect we would be accepting the suspicion of many that we are no different than any other business in that our goal is to meet a certain rate of return. The only difference is that our rate of return is defined by the singular criterion of how well we meet or exceed the cash value of forgiven taxes. [...] We need a vocabulary not of the market but of health care as a social good that allows us to demonstrate how we fulfill our mandate to promote human dignity by being an agent of social change as we provide for the health of individuals and communities.
>
> (p. 6)

Part II
Health care

8 Essential concepts in health economics

In this chapter, we introduce the fundamental concepts of health and health care. We also define health economics and argue why it has developed into a discipline in itself. We propose two arguments: the differential characteristics of the health care sector in the economy, and its size. We present a description of the organization of the health care market, and the agents interacting in it. The chapter closes with a description of some canonical forms of structure of a health care system.

In modern societies the level of health of the population is determined by a complex set of activities developed in the framework of a social structure. This has led the World Health Organization to refer to the *health system* as a set of interrelated elements (environment, education, labor conditions, etc.) having as an objective the transformation of some sanitary resources (inputs) into a health status (final output) through the production of health services (intermediate output).

In other words, in health economics, *health* is the variable to maximize. In turn, health is the outcome of the sanitary services (intermediate output) obtained from the combination of factors of production of health. This approach is what Ortún Rubio (1990) labels as "the approach of enlarged welfare" as an alternative to the approach of strict welfare where the sanitary services are the final output. The enlarged welfare approach illustrates the difficulty of defining the concept of health, while the strict welfare approach has to be restricted to purely economic considerations. In the former approach health, health care, and health status are to be distinguished (see McGuire *et al.* 1999, pp. 1–5). *Health* is a difficult concept to frame. A usual way to define it is as the lack of illness, leading us to the definition of illness. Again different definitions of illness are used by the medical profession (pathologically based), or according to the restrictions imposed on the development of daily activities (functionally based). The broadest definition of health encompasses all aspects affecting the *health status* of the individual. Under this view, health has value in use but has no value in exchange as it cannot be traded. *Health care* instead can be purchased and offered. Accordingly, it can be treated as a regular commodity in the economy with the peculiarity that it is only consumed by individuals in order to improve their health status. As we will analyze in Chapter 9, demand for health care is linked to the wish for health by the individual. In the pages that follow, we will treat health and health care as synonyms for simplicity. Nevertheless, the reader should bear in mind that strictly speaking these two concepts have different meanings.

A working definition of health economics would refer to the study of how resources are *allocated* to and within the health care sector in the economy, as well as the functioning of the health care markets. The pathbreaking contribution giving rise to health economics as a separate discipline is that of Arrow (1963).

It is important to emphasize that the interest of health economics lies in the allocation of resources rather than in the amount of expenditure on health care services. Thus, the rules governing the allocation are crucial to generate the proper incentives to providers and individuals to use the (scarce) resources in the best possible (e.g. welfare maximizing) way.

As in general economics, we can distinguish a *normative* and a *positive* approach to health economics. The normative approach deals with the use of the resources devoted to the health sector by the government (health policy) to achieve the maximum level of welfare, equity, and efficiency. In this respect health economics aims at providing the health authority with (theoretically based) sound rules to implement those decisions. The positive approach deals with the rational choice of the agents in the health care sector.

We will mainly concentrate on the positive aspect of health economics. Following Zweifel *et al.* (2009, pp. 4–7) and Phelps (2009, pp. 10–13) a convenient way of thinking of health and health care consists of assuming that every individual when born is endowed with a certain stock of health. That is a health status in the same way that consumer theory assumes consumers are initially endowed with a bundle of goods. The individual obtains satisfaction (utility) from the flow of services produced by the stock of health and from the flow of services (consumption) of a bundle of goods. In describing individuals' preferences for stocks of health or consumption levels, it should be clear that the satisfaction the individual can obtain from "consuming" is linked to his or her health state. In particular, when the ratio of health to consumption becomes small (for instance due to a poor health status) additional consumption does not increase utility.

Also, it seems reasonable to consider that only healthy enough people can be employed and thus earn some income. Income is spent on medical care and consumer goods. Taking prices as exogenous, we can define a budget constraint dependent on the heath status of the individual.

One preliminary question though is why health economics has developed into a discipline in itself. The answer contains two elements. On the one hand, we find the differential characteristics of the health care sector within the economy. On the other hand, we have the importance, in terms of size, of the health care sector in the economy. Trends in the health spending to GDP ratio are the result of the combined effect of trends in both GDP and health expenditure. In most OECD countries health spending grew more quickly than GDP in the period 1995–2007 (see OECD 2010). This has resulted in a higher share of GDP allocated to health. According to OECD (2009), the share of health expenditure to GDP is likely to increase further, following the recession that started in many countries in 2008 and became widespread in 2009. As a reference, in 2007 the share of health spending to GDP for the set of OECD countries ranged from less than 6 percent up to 16 percent of GDP.

This trend in spending, in the context of the OECD countries, is consistent with the aging of populations and technological development. In 2007, life expectancy[1] at age 65 in OECD countries stood, on average, at over 20 years for women and close to 17 years for men (OECD 2009, 2010). Similarly, in 2007 life expectancy for women at age 80 stood at 9.2 years on average in OECD countries, and at 7.6 years for men. In both cases these figures represent a significant increase over the last 30 years.

Pharmaceutical expenditure is an important component of the increase in health budgets. Across OECD countries in 2007 it is estimated to surpass 650 billion US$, accounting for around 15 percent of total health spending. Also, over the last ten years, average spending per capita on pharmaceuticals has risen by almost 50 percent in real terms. Relative to the

GDP, pharmaceutical spending accounted for 1.5 percent of GDP on average across OECD countries.

The recent history of modern societies has allowed an obvious progress in the access and equity of health systems. This access, in turn, has generated a variation in the population pyramid with a higher participation of the elder population (that together with infancy are the most demanding groups of medical services). As is well-known, there is a positive relationship between health status and income. There are two explanations for this phenomenon. One is that because of technological innovations and investment in public infrastructures, higher health levels are easier to attain and maintain over time. The second explanation appeals to changing preferences of individuals over time. Accordingly, for a given level of income, individuals become more concerned about their health status as they age. Either way, this relation bears two consequences. Following Jack (1999, Chapter 3), on the one hand, as populations become healthier, they also age. This is known as the demographic transition. On the other hand, the pattern of diseases changes. This is known as the epidemiological transition.

Finally, we should not forget the technological progress that has made available to physicians more efficient treatment possibilities and diagnosis techniques (e.g. nuclear medicine procedures). All these factors have generated a substantial increase in the expenses in the health care sector threatening the future of the so-called welfare state. Therefore, we face a dilemma between efficiency and equity in the health system that has generated a debate on the reform of the health systems in western countries.

Figure 8.1 adapted from Culyer and Newhouse (2000) summarizes all the elements appearing in health economics. We can read the scheme as composed of three parts; the economic analysis, the economic evaluation, and the policy analysis. The starting point of the *economic analysis* is box *A*, "What is health?". From here we move to study the elements of the demand for health care (box *C*) and other elements influencing health (box *B*). Next come the elements of the supply of health care (box *D*). The combination of demand and

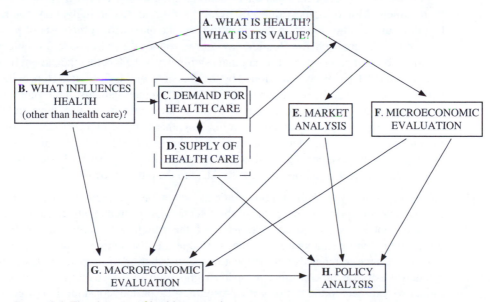

Figure 8.1 The elements of health economics.

supply leads us to the analysis of the health care market equilibrium (box E). The *economic evaluation* contemplates both the microeconomic level (box F) and the macroeconomic level (box G). Finally, *policy analysis* is found in box H. Also, Fuchs (1993) provides a nice description of the scope of health economics.

8.1   Differential characteristics of health economics

What makes health economics different from economics? What features of the health care sector make it sufficiently different from other sectors in the economy? Before precisely answering these questions, it is important to mention that although health care has some distinctive features, it is not unique in any of them. Rather, it is the combination of these features that makes the sector unique. These features are:[2]

The presence of uncertainty.   There is uncertainty in both demand (health status of the population) and in supply (e.g. availability and efficacy of treatments). Health status is uncertain in the sense that it is unpredictable. As a consequence, demand (and supply) of health care services do not follow any foreseeable trend. This uncertainty makes decision making difficult in that agents want to avoid taking a wrong decision leading to adverse outcomes. Nevertheless, some actions may lower the probability of an ill-episode, such as healthy habits or preventive health care measures.

The relevance of insurance.   The uncertainty regarding the moment when an individual gets ill gives rise to the possibility of insurance against the occurrence of a sickness. Insurance breaks the relationship between the price and the cost of provision of health care services giving rise to situations of moral hazard (associated with the shifting outwards of the budget constraint of the consumer) and of adverse selection (associated with the selection of profiles of risk by the insurers). Intervention by the state tries to generate the right incentives to minimize the perverse effects of the uncertainty.

   Patients in the health care market buy information on the illness they suffer and its treatment. Moreover, individuals often are risk averse. Accordingly, they contract health insurance, thus lowering the incentives to take into account the costs of provision of health care services. This fact lays at the root of the moral hazard problems. Another consequence of this informational asymmetry is the fact that the patient in his or her demand decisions is conditioned by the decisions of the physician. Hence, there is the possibility that the physician induces demand on their patients in the sense that a patient demands more services than they would have done should they have had the same information as the physician. Therefore, together with the moral hazard problem mentioned above, we also face an adverse selection problem in the form of rejection of patients with some peculiar pathologies or, alternatively, the shift of patients with expensive treatments from the private providers to the public provider.

The presence of (asymmetric) information.   Patients do not have perfect information about, for example, the quality of hospitals or the effectiveness of treatments. In turn, physicians do not know all the characteristics of the patients. This together with the uncertainty mentioned above raises the issue that the distribution of property rights may show some differences with respect to the distribution of property rights in the standard theory of the consumer. Property rights refer to the position of each individual with respect to the use of scarce resources. Regarding consumption of goods, traditional consumer theory assumes that each individual uses their resources in their own best interest. In health care, there appear many situations where the sovereignty of the patient in properly evaluating the costs and benefits of the decision-making process is at least questionable.

The role of nonprofit institutions.   The prevalence of nonprofit institutions in the provision of health care services is particularly important in the health care sector.

The extent of regulation in the market.   There are restrictions to competition in the health care sector, such as the compulsory license for physicians, or the restriction on advertising, that are accepted to guarantee a minimum level of quality towards patients. We can also refer here (although we will not analyze it) to the presence of patents, reference prices, or the development of generics in the pharmaceutical sector.

The existence of need.   Although need is a difficult concept to pin down in a definition, it is generally understood as the amount of medical care that medical experts believe a person should obtain to remain or become as healthy as possible, based on current medical knowledge. Generically it is widely accepted as a principle that people should have access to the health care services they need regardless of their level of income.

The public provision and financing of health care services.   Social security in European countries represents a massive presence of the government in the provision and financing of health care services and also in the organization of the health care market.

The presence of externalities.   Externalities appear when the actions of some agents in the market have an impact (positive or negative) on the behavior of other agents. For instance, vaccination programs may avoid the spread of epidemics (positive externality), pollution may generate illnesses to individuals exposed to that pollution (negative externality). Then, the social benefits (from vaccination) often differ from the private benefits (reduced risk). Externalities refer to the interdependence of the utility functions of the individuals. One of the main interdependencies appear when tackling the issue of equity.

All these elements imply that the market will not be able to assign resources efficiently in the health care sector. Thus, there is room for regulation.

The characteristics just listed make health care appear to be a private good[3] provided by the state (other examples of this type of good are education and social security).

It is important to point out that there are other markets showing similar problems as the ones described (a typical example is the food market) where regulation when it exists is minimal. What argument then justifies this differentiated attention to the health care market? Usually, the answer appeals to a "moral" argument. This is the universal access to the health care system.

State intervention appears in different ways. The lowest level of intervention is in the US model (also Ireland) where health care is privately provided except for poor people whose income does not reach a minimum level (Medicare), and the elder population (Medicaid). At the other extreme we find a public model of provision of health care in countries like Spain. In between we find mixed systems with reference prices as in Germany, Japan, Canada, France, and Belgium. In these systems, the state finances the patient a (constant) part of the cost of any medical service. Whenever the patient patronizes a provider with a higher tariff, he or she must bear the difference.

The alternative system is the provision of health care centralized by the state. This scenario is not free of difficulties. Following Ortún Rubio (1990),

> The non-market health care systems present four failures: lack of relation between revenues and costs, lack of objectives of the organization, externalities induced by the action of the State, and distributive inequalities.[4]

It is important to point out that the role of the state in the economy must not be reduced to its relative size, or to the discussion between liberalism and socialism. In this sense Calsamiglia (1994) says,

> Regarding the State intervention the problem is neither how much nor what, but how. This is the fundamental problem. It is necessary to be aware of the limitations of the State and the objectives pursued to determine the type of intervention allowing to improve performance. [...] The important factor is not the size of the public sector, but its management.[5]

8.2   The organization of the health care market

A proper description of the health care market must start with the description of the agents interacting in it. Figure 8.2, borrowed from Narciso (2004), illustrates. These include the health authority, the national health service, providers, third-party payers, patients, and the pharmaceutical sector.

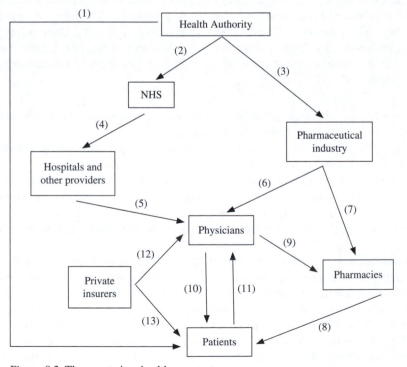

Figure 8.2 The agents in a health care system.

Quoting Narciso, the *Health Authority* has a strong regulation role that works in several directions. One task of this Health Authority is to stipulate the type and/or value that patients have to pay for medicines and for the several services in the *NHS* providers (arrow 1). It also defines the organization of this public health system (arrow 2), for example, it decides which types of appointments and treatments are provided in the hospitals or by other providers and the geographical distribution of the patients through the health providers (arrow 4). Finally, the Health Authority regulates the pharmaceutical sector (arrow 3) concerning the prices of medicines, both the pricing to the pharmacies and also the prices that patients must pay.

Both *hospitals and other public providers* (such as health centers) hire physicians, nurses, and other staff (arrow 5), who deal directly with patients.

The *Pharmaceutical industry* produces and sells the medicines to the *pharmacies* which in turn, sell them to the patients (arrows 7 and 8). The agency relationship between physicians and patients creates in the pharmaceutical industry the incentives to promote their products to the physicians with the purpose of influencing their choice of medicines (arrow 6). Nevertheless, when the countries have substitution laws it is possible for the pharmacies to sell a medicine that is different from the one prescribed by the physician. That is, under substitution rules, when the doctor prescribes a branded drug, the pharmacy is allowed to sell a generic version of that medicine to the patient (arrow 8) and, in this case, the relationship between the pharmacists and the patients becomes closer and more important than when the pharmacist only acts as a seller. When substitution is allowed, the pharmacist is an actor in the decision process.

However, the medicines that patients consume are typically prescribed by the *physicians* who act as agents of the patients in the sense that they decide the consumption of medicines on their behalf (arrow 9). This is very peculiar to the health care market since the patients who consume the good (the medicine) are not the ones who choose the good to consume. Finally, arrows 10 and 11 represent the central relationship in this process: the interaction between patients and physicians, which gives us the final outcome of the whole system and the reason for its existence. The *patient* consults a doctor when he or she finds some symptoms of illness or when he or she is advised in a previous appointment to do so. Based on the symptoms reported by the patient and on possible additional examinations, the physician prescribes the treatment deemed appropriate.

It is still possible that patients buy *private insurance* which will be alternative or cumulative to the public one. In this case, the private insurers will contract the payment schemes both with physicians and patients (arrows 12 and 13).

A detailed overview of the relationships among those agents, also including the pharmaceutical industry and the politicians, is provided by Thurner and Kotzian (2001).

We will focus on three types of agents. *Patients* represent the part of the population that, facing a certain sickness, demand health care services. *Providers* supply health care services. Among those, we can distinguish "first-level providers" including general practitioners and primary care services, and "second-level providers" where we find the specialized health care, that is hospital and specialists. Finally, the third type of agents are the *third-party payers* that finance the provision of health care services. These may be private insurance companies or a public agency (social security). These third-party payers buy health care services from the providers on behalf on their insured, thus granting them coverage, and defining the protocols to reward providers.

Generically, a society faces two alternative ways of allocating its resources: a (decentralized) free market mechanism or a centralized system by means of the state. A free market mechanism where patients directly pay the health care services is shown in Figure 8.3 where

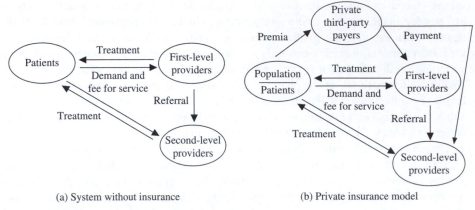

(a) System without insurance   (b) Private insurance model

Figure 8.3 Private provision with and without insurance.

section (a) shows a system without insurance and section (b) introduces private insurance companies offering health insurance contracts to the population against a premium, and patients addressing the providers when ill.

A quick glance of the health systems in western European economies presents an important participation by the state. This may just show the peculiarities by the health care services that make the proper (efficient) functioning of the health care market virtually impossible.

8.3   Structure of a health care system

State intervention[6] in the health care market consists on the one hand of regulating supply (physicians, hospitals, insurance companies) in terms of treatments, pharmaceutical products, insurance premiums, and prices for medical services; on the other hand it also regulates demand through, for example, subsidies to health care costs, fiscal advantages, or universal access to the health care system. We can distinguish three health care systems models: the reimbursement model, the contract model, and the integrated model.

8.3.1   The reimbursement model

There are two variants of this model; public (compulsory health insurance with compulsory contribution) and private. The public or private character of the model is determined by the existence of a public payer or a set of private insurance companies. In any case, the fundamental characteristic of this system is the separation between payers and providers. Patients pay the services that afterwards are reimbursed (totally or partially) by the payer. Figure 8.4 illustrates this model.

The private version of this model represents (*grosso modo*) the system in the UK. The public version is a close approach to the system in the Netherlands.

In this model the patient may patronize his or her preferred provider. In the private version, the very freedom to choose by the population guarantees tough competition among insurance companies and among providers. However, switching costs associated with changing insurance company and the adverse selection of risks are elements that soften competition. Also, among providers the induced demand effect mitigates competition.

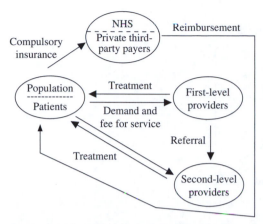

Figure 8.4 The reimbursement model.

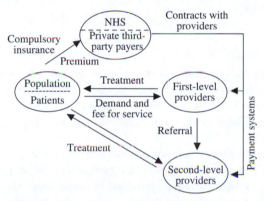

Figure 8.5 The contract model.

The public version considers compulsory health insurance either through a public system or a network of private companies and mutualities. Now there is no competition among payers, thus eliminating the adverse selection of risks. Universal access does not interfere with the freedom to choose provider.

8.3.2   *The contract model*

In contrast with the previous model, the contract model presents a link between payers and providers as shown in Figure 8.5.

When payers are private insurance companies, their clients pay premiums and are free to choose any provider in the set of providers selected by the insurance company. Insurance companies compete among themselves for consumers and also to contract with providers. Providers in turn compete among themselves to obtain the best contracts.

The public version of this model corresponds to a social security system where provision of health care is universal and free (equity) and patients have a wide array of providers to choose among. This corresponds broadly speaking to the system in Germany and Ireland. The system is financed out of compulsory contributions and taxes. Providers are reimbursed by the state or by regulated insurance companies and reimbursement rates are negotiated

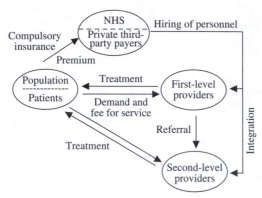

Figure 8.6 The integrated model.

at the national (regional) level. Accordingly, the only competitive element of the system (efficiency) is quality of health care services.

8.3.3 *The integrated model*

The integrated model takes its name from the integration between payers and providers both at first and second levels. That is, insurance companies and mutualities (public or private) own the hospitals and contract physicians. Thus, the insurer bears the risk not only of cost control of the system but also of the use of health care services provided as well. Figure 8.6 illustrates this.

The private version of the model contemplates a population of consumers contracting health insurance with a private company. This insurance is defined by a premium and the coverage of health care services (free or against a co-payment fee) provided by those hospitals and physicians contracted by the insurer. Competition among insurance companies and mutualities allows for compensating some tendency to restriction of use associated with providers reimbursement through salaries and closed budgets. However, limiting access because of reimbursement capacity of users seriously restricts the effects on equity and solidarity.

The public version of the model reproduces the system of social security in for example Spain or Portugal. In this framework, the state acts as main insurer and provider. This guarantees on the one hand universal access (equity) but limits the possibility of choosing coverage (except for some particular groups of civil servants in the case of Spain) implying low efficiency due to lack of competition among providers and lack of incentives for physicians reimbursed through salaries.

To summarize the different characteristics of the several systems presented, public systems fulfill the equity and solidarity principles as they ensure universal access to the health care system. However, those systems do not typically satisfy the principle of efficiency as cost control is difficult to implement. It is precisely this difficulty of budget containment in the public systems of health care that has given rise to the discussion on the design of mechanisms of cost control both on the demand and supply sides.

On the demand side, incentives to cost containment appear in the introduction of co-payments. The main forms in which co-payments are implemented are co-insurance, sharing the payment of the services, and deductibles. The co-insurance usually takes the form of a payment by the patients of a fixed proportion of their expenses in health care services.

Sharing the payment means that patients pay a fixed amount regardless of the amount spent. Finally, a deductible means that patients pay the full cost of the health care services and the payer reimburses (a fixed or proportional part) of this bill.

Cost containment on the supply side is usually more effective. Here we find prospective budgets on hospitals and first-level providers, together with the introduction of incentives to efficiency and productivity through decentralization and encouragement of competition among providers. These measures often found in private systems are being also implemented in public systems.

8.3.4   NHS vs. Bismarckian health systems

An alternative, but complementary, view of health care systems distinguishes between the so-called NHS and Bismarckian systems.

The NHS system is characterized by the government controlling the funding, provision, allocation, and regulation of health care. The role of the market is reduced to a separation between payers and providers. Price competition is typically absent, and providers compete for patients in non-price dimensions like quality, waiting times, and complementary services (such as hotel facilities, visiting times, etc.). The United Kingdom, Spain, Portugal, and the Nordic countries are served by this type of health care system.

In most of the remaining western European countries (such as France, Germany, Switzerland, the Netherlands, and others) health systems are insurance based. They show greater plurality in provision, and the government plays the role of a regulator guaranteeing universal coverage and access to health care insurance, determining reimbursement schemes, monitoring minimum quality standards, and the like. The major difference in the health care systems in these countries concerns the organization of the market for health insurance.

9 Demand for health and health care

This chapter begins with the concerns and difficulties of the valuation of life from an individual and aggregate perspective. The notion of statistical value of life is particularly based on the notion of willingness to pay. Similarly, the chapter introduces the most popular measure of valuation of quality of life. These ideas help to pin down the concept of demand for health care services based on Grossman's contributions. The chapter presents an in-depth analysis of Grossman's approach; its characteristics, results, extensions, criticisms, and applications. Finally, uncertainty is introduced in the analysis for health care.

9.1 Value of life and of quality of life

The value of life (and the value of health) is one of the difficult issues addressed by health economics. Valuing health from an economic perspective requires valuing life and valuing quality of life. This is not an easy matter and no broad consensus exists.

Several ways of measuring the economic value of life, the quality of life, and changes in health have been proposed. Some have gained wider support than others, some are now less used than they were in the past.

The valuation of life from an economic perspective is necessary on two grounds. On the one hand, to assess benefits from policy interventions, the variable of interest is often the well being of people, which is basically related to life years and quality of life. Empirically, this is a major concern. On the other hand, most of the theoretical analysis is based on concepts of value from consumption of goods and services and satisfaction resulting from it. In the health care sector, the main "good" is health. Objectives of economic agents do require that valuation of life and of health is not an empty concept, to ensure internal consistency of the analysis apparatus.

The valuation of life is also a difficult issue due to the ethical aspects involved and the "strangeness" to many people of the idea of putting an economic value on life. It is common to hear that life is priceless, that health has an infinite value. Economic analysis and evidence do contradict such assertions. Imagine yourself conducting an experiment where people in the street have to declare their agreement or disagreement to the statement "life is priceless". More often than not you would find agreements to that statement. As economists, though, we should ask ourselves about the meaning of that expression. Literally, it says that an individual agreeing to it would be willing to pay any arbitrary large amount of money to avoid the risk of death (regardless of his or her unavoidable budget constraint). Obviously, such a statement does not have any content: on the one hand it is inconsistent. Consider an individual paying all their present and future income to avoid death (and this is still far from any arbitrarily large amount of money). On what means would (s)he continue living afterwards? On the other hand, it is quite likely that when expressing the agreement to the statement, the individual would be thinking in extreme risk situations where staying alive would depend on having access to a particular treatment. In most situations though, risk is not so extreme. Think of regular illnesses where one's health status is diminished only temporarily. In such cases, the individual would declare their willingness to pay a *finite* amount of money to diminish such risk.

To make the economic valuation of life and of health precise, definitions of these concepts need to be established. While life extent and life years are easy to define, the concept of quality of life is not.

Health, on the other hand, has been defined in several ways. The most commonly accepted definition of health is the one proposed by the World Health Organization: health is a state of complete physical, mental, and social well-being and not merely the absence of disease or infirmity.

Health is, under this view, a very broad concept, including not only the working of the human body but also the ability of the individual to operate within society.

9.1.1   The value of life: individual vs. society's perspective

One of the more important aspects of the economic analysis of the value of life is the change from an individual perspective of the valuation of one's own life to the society's view on the valuation of its population's health.

Surely from one's own perspective, life carries a very high value and "priceless" may not be a bad approximation to such a feeling. However, from a global perspective the opportunity cost of replacing one life in a large population is actually quite small.

Society's perspective is the relevant approximation from both health policy design and the analysis of the health care sector. For example, when the health authority carries out an intervention to save the lives of victims of road traffic accidents, it does not put a name on which lives to save. A policy decision aimed at ensuring access to health care in case of need of treatment does not carry a name tag either. Similarly, economic analysis is about a general representative individual or group of individuals. Anonymity is the rule. It helps to overcome the ethical dilemmas in valuing each and every particular life. Economic analysis adopts, most of the time, the concept of value of a *statistical* life. This concept does not go without criticisms. Nonetheless, it provides a useful instrument and allows economic analysis to be made.

Once we accept the notion of value of a statistical life as the main approach to valuation of life, its measurement becomes the relevant issue. Several empirical approaches have been proposed and are used. A first (simple) technique is to value a statistical life by the present value of future earnings, as a proxy to human capital. While it is popular in court cases deciding on compensation for life losses, it is widely regarded as inappropriate at the population level. Another approach is based on the implicit valuation made by people when they take (require) different wages for jobs having distinct health (mortality) risks. In this case, choices about wages and jobs fatalities do provide us with information about life valuation.

A more popular method to obtain the value of a statistical life is based on the *willingness to pay* for risk reductions of the individuals. This information is usually obtained by way of surveys where individuals are asked about their willingness to pay, framing different risk conditions. The willingness-to-pay approach is rooted in the microeconomics of the individual's preferences. It can be described in a simple way. Consider a risky prospect, where a population faces a common survival probability π_0 (that is, all individuals in the population face the same death risk under the same probability). Let y denote the consumption bundle of each individual in society, expressed in monetary units (or equivalently, individual's income), and let H_0 be the initial health status of the individual.

Satisfaction of consuming bundle y with health condition H_0 is given by the utility function $U(y, H_0)$ for a representative individual from the population. Expected utility is:

$$\pi_0 U(y, H_0) + (1 - \pi_0)U(y, 0)$$

where $H = 0$ denotes the situation of death and $U(y, 0)$ stands for utility in that case (which we can normalize to a zero value).

Propose now a new risky prospect to the individual, characterized by a survival probability $\pi_1 > \pi_0$. The valuation of this change in risk results from asking the individual how much he or she is willing to pay to move from one prospect to the other. Let M be the maximum value the individual is willing to pay for that change. This value is defined by,

$$\pi_0 U(y, H_0) + (1 - \pi_0)U(y, 0) = \pi_1 U(y - M, H_0) + (1 - \pi_1)U(y - M, 0)$$

Taking first-order approximations to the right-hand side around $U(y, H_0)$ and $U(y, 0)$ respectively and rearranging, results in

$$M = (\pi_1 - \pi_0)\frac{U(y, H_0) - U(y, 0)}{\pi_1 U'(y, H_0) + (1 - \pi_1)U'(y, 0)}$$

The numerator is the increase in utility associated with the change in health status. The denominator is simply the expected marginal utility of income consumption.

Define the value of a statistical life (*VSL*) in monetary values as,

$$VSL \equiv \frac{U(y, H_0) - U(y, 0)}{\pi_1 U'(y, H_0) + (1 - \pi_1)U'(y, 0)}.$$

Then, we have $VSL = M/(\pi_1 - \pi_0)$. Note that the value of a statistical life computed in this way results from an assessment of risk changes and not from the valuation of a particular life. Thus, the value of a statistical life is particularly useful in the assessment of health intervention programs and policy measures.

There are several surveys on the results obtained for *VSL* under different conditions and settings. The broad regularity are values in the range 5 to 10 million US$. While the particular values may be disputed, it is clearly below 15 million US$ and far from infinite or even 100 million.[1]

In a different, but interesting direction, Becker *et al.* (2005) use more directly the "utility value" of consumption to measure the gains from longevity. Instead of using an "approximation" as in the above definition for the value of a statistical life, the authors calibrate directly a specific functional form for the (indirect) utility function.

Define the indirect utility function, V, of an individual with lifetime income $\hat{y}$ and survival function $S(t)$ as,

$$V(\hat{y}, S) = \max_{\{c(t)\}} \int_0^\infty \exp(-rt) S(t) u(c(t)) \, dt$$

$$\text{s.t.} \quad \int_0^\infty \exp(-rt) S(t) y(t) \, dt = \int_0^\infty \exp(-rt) S(t) c(t),$$

where $S(t)$ indicates the probability that the individual is alive in period t, $y(t)$ is income at t, $c(t)$ is consumption at t, and r is the interest rate. Lifetime income $\hat{y}$ denotes the profile of income $y(t)$ in each period t. The budget constraint holds in lifetime terms. Consumption must equal income over the life period, accounting for the likelihood of survival. Taking the lifetime to be infinity is not restrictive as for $t > T$ one may have $S(t) = 0$.

Life expectancy is defined as $LE = \int_0^\infty S(t) t \, dt$. Changes in longevity imply that a new survival function $S'(t)$ replaces $S(t)$. Income growth in the economy increases $\hat{y}$ to $\hat{y}' > \hat{y}$. The value of the new survival function, M, is defined as

$$V(\hat{y}', S') = V(\hat{y}' + M, S)$$

where M is interpreted as being the monetary amount that makes the individual indifferent to the new and old survival functions, at the new income level. Another way to read it is as the amount that should be given to the individual to compensate him for not having $S'(t)$ instead of $S(t)$.

To obtain an explicit value for M, Becker *et al.* (2005) make the following simplifying assumptions. First, they consider a representative agent, who receives the average per capita, income ($\bar{y}$) in all the years; and second, the representative individual is characterized by the survival probability of the population at each age, in any given year.

These two assumptions allow us to write

$$V(\bar{y}, S) = U(\bar{y}) \times A(S), \quad \text{where } A(S) = \int_0^\infty \exp(-rt) S(t) \, dt$$

and the above expression becomes

$$U(\bar{y}' + M) A(S) = U(\bar{y}') A(S')$$

The value M does not include aspects like the value of leisure time, consumption of goods and services without explicit markets, family consumption and production, happiness, etc. The value comes solely from consumption. Assuming a particular utility function and calibrating it using parameters from existing studies, Becker *et al.* (2005) report estimates for the value of longevity gains.

9.1.2 The value of the quality of life

The previous section offered a technique to evaluate the compensation to offer to an individual to accept a variation in his or her mortality risk. Now we want to study the valuation for an individual facing a variation of his *morbidity* risk, i.e. a change in his health status or in other words, a change in his quality of life.

This issue is also related to the discussion about the non-equivalence between cost–benefit and cost-effectiveness analyses. The latter is the most common tool in the evaluation of health care, where the concept of QALY (to be defined below) is used as the output measure. In contrast, cost-benefit analysis has its foundation in economic welfare theory.

Consider an individual with a health status H. Assume that we have been able to obtain the information on the set of their possible health states, and identified their ideal one H^*. We normalize this "perfect health" state, $H^* = 1$, to be used as the reference to measure all other possible health states. Then, the expected quality of life is a probability measure of the weighted average of quality of life scores associated with each possible state of health the individual may face. This idea allows us to evaluate the benefits of different health programs by weighting the years a patient will survive with the expected health state. The index thus obtained was developed by Zeckhauser and Shepard (1976) and Weinstein and Stason (1977). They refer to it as the index of "quality-adjusted life years" (QALY).

DEFINITION 9.1 (QALY). Consider an individual with a lifetime horizon of T years along which he will enjoy a health status H_t. The quality-adjusted life years index is a measure of the utility of health outcomes defined as a weighting scheme where each period of expected life is adjusted by the health state in which it is spent.

Note that this definition implicitly assumes that life duration and health status are separable. Often, QALY models are referred to as multiplicative utility models. Formally, let the health profile of an individual be $(H_1, t_1; H_2, t_2; \ldots, H_n, t_n)$ where health status H_τ is maintained for t_τ periods, and $t_1 + t_2 + \cdots + t_n = T$. Let r denote the discount (interest) rate. Then, the QALY index will be defined as

$$U(H_1, t_1; H_2, t_2; \ldots, H_n, t_n) = \sum_{\tau=1}^{n} \frac{H_\tau t_\tau}{(1+r)^\tau}.$$

Typically, weights are defined assigning value one to the perfect health state, and zero to death. This does not prevent us from assigning negative weights to health states that the patient value as worse than death. There is no consensus on the predictive validity of various classes of QALY models. On this issue see Abellán *et al.* (2004).

To clarify the way to use the QALY index to evaluate different health programs, consider the following examples:

- *Example 1* [Individual level]

  Consider a 70-year-old individual whose life expectation is 20 more years. The first ten years of his health will be perfect, so that the weight attached to those periods will be 1; the second 10 years his quality of life will be half of his perfect health status, i.e. the weight will be 0.5. The computation of QALYs will be $QALY = (10 \times 1) + (10 \times 0.5) = 15$ discounted years (i.e. 15 years equivalent with perfect health)

- *Example 2* [Evaluation of alternative health care programs]

  This example is borrowed from Getzen (1997, pp. 51–52). Consider a patient with a health status rated at 60 percent of perfect health. If such a patient is treated with medications alone, he can expect to live for three years. Alternatively, if surgery is successful he can expect to live five more years, and have a better quality of life. Surgery rate of success is 40 percent. Also, there is a chance of 3 percent of surgical mortality causing immediate

Table 9.1 Computing QALYs

	year 1	year 2	year 3	year 4	year 5	total
Time discount	1.00	0.95	0.91	0.86	0.82	
Medication						
Quality of life	0.60	0.50	0.40	0.00	0.00	
Discounted value	0.60	0.48	0.36	0.00	0.00	*1.44*
Successful surgery						
Quality of life	0.90	0.80	0.70	0.60	0.50	
Discounted value	0.90	0.76	0.63	0.52	0.41	*3.23*

death. Surgery costs are 30,000 EUR. Finally, the discount rate is set at 5 percent. Table 9.1 illustrates all the relevant information.

The costs of medical care can be compared to the benefits by calculating the cost per QALY gained between the two alternative programs. On the benefit side, each additional life year is discounted for risk, time, and quality of life. Accordingly, the QALY index associated with medication is 1.44 discounted years, while it is 3.23 discounted years in the case of successful surgery. Therefore, the (gross) expected gain in QALY between both treatments, taking into account that surgery success rate is 40 percent is given by $(3.23 - 1.44)(0.40) = 0.72$ adjusted years. To this figure we have to subtract the risk of death during surgery. Given the 3 percent probability of death, it is given by $(3.23)(0.03) = 0.09$ discounted years. Accordingly, the net expected gain in QALY between both treatments is given by $0.72 - 0.09 = 0.63$ adjusted years.

On the cost side we have the cost of surgery of 30,000 EUR, that represents a cost per QALY gained of $47,620(= 30,000/0.63)$ EUR.

We thus conclude that the net gain of 0.63 adjusted years is achieved at a cost of 47,620 EUR per QALY gained.

- *Example 3* [Resource allocation]

The QALY index can also be used in the resource allocation problem. Consider a society composed of two individuals A and B. Figure 9.1 represents the situation depicting A's and B's QALYs.

The starting point is that both individuals enjoy the same level of quality of life $A_1 = B_1$ at point M. Society has some additional resources able to improve both individuals' health. The level of health of the society is defined as $A^* + B^*$. This sum is maximized at point R. Moving along the frontier from point R, an additional QALY for individual A (or B) reduces individual B's (A's) QALYs by more than 1, thus reducing the sum. This is so as such reallocation goes under the line with slope -1.

Now the relevant question is whether such an allocation is cost-efficient and/or egalitarian for the society. Note that since $B_{max} > A_{max}$ the same resources will provide more additional QALYs to individual B than to individual A. Therefore, point R is the most cost-efficient allocation for society, although it provides more QALYs for individual B than for individual A.

An alternative egalitarian allocation is given by point Q where both individuals obtain the same level of QALYs as it lies on the 45-degree line.

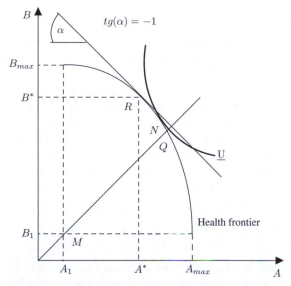

Figure 9.1 Allocation of resources using QALYs.

Still another criterion society may decide to use is to choose the allocation maximizing a social welfare function U. This is point N defined by the tangency between a social indifference curve and the health frontier. At this allocation, again individual B obtains more QALYs than individual A. At this point though the asymmetry of the allocation of QALYS is less intense than in point R.

The basic QALY model presented assumes that lifetime utility depends solely on health status. As we have mentioned before, this poses a problem for the consistency of QALY-based decision making when we broaden the scope to consider that patients not only take decisions on their health status but also that these decisions are interrelated with their consumption decisions. It is beyond the scope of this chapter to go into the details of how the notion of QALY should be reformulated to accommodate this new environment. The interested reader can address Bleichrodt and Quiggin (1999) for an investigation on the set of necessary and sufficient conditions for the consistency of QALY-based decision making with life-cycle preferences over consumption and health status.

9.1.3   Criticisms of the QALY model

The concept of QALY and its use as an evaluation tool has been object of several criticisms (see McGuire *et al.* 1999).

- As we have mentioned above, the information on the preferences of the individuals is obtained directly by means of interviews or indirectly from the observation of the decisions of the individual in the market. Either way, this information need not reflect individuals' true behavior as typically, those decisions are made under imperfect and/or incomplete information on the consequences of those decisions. Also, preferences may change as individuals get more and better information. In addition, Torrance (1986) points out that the valuations obtained are not robust to the phrasing of the questions that the individuals are asked.

- The valuations are always unidirectional, that is, from a certain health state to a worse one. If we assume that health exhibits diminishing marginal utility, then also valuing situations where an improvement in the health state arises may have important consequences in the policy design.
- The appreciation of the loss of utility depends on the personal circumstances of every subject (patient, expert, non-expert) and also on the expected duration of the health condition being evaluated. In this sense, Sackett and Torrance (1982) provide evidence where dialysis patients weighted the loss of utility less than people not affected by the illness. Both collectives though showed an increasing utility loss as the period of duration increased.
- Finally, QALYs capture only the benefits directly related to the patient. Other benefits related to the valuation of the relatives of patients, the value of information provided by physicians, etc. are not taken into account.

9.2 Demand for health

The early studies of demand for health care were based on the revealed preference approach, which demonstrated that demand could be analyzed from the observation of how individuals' decisions were affected by variations in prices and income.

A new approach proposed by Grossman (1972a, b) regards the demand for health as an application of the theory of consumer demand. A fundamental distinction under this approach is that the individual demands health and not health care. The demand for health care is thus a derived demand. The crucial assumption in Grossman's analysis is the removal of the separation between consumption and production necessary to allow price and income to enter as the major independent explanatory variables in the household consumption function. The individual demands health for two basic reasons: as consumption as it is a component of the utility function, and as an investment that determines the distribution of time between labor and leisure and thus the disposable income. In this sense, demand for health is also a derived demand. Following Feldstein (2002), demand for health is increasing in age, is increasing in income, and is decreasing in education (as more educated people are supposed to be more efficient in producing health).

This approach departs from the fact that the health status of an individual is, in part, his own responsibility. In other words, the individual may not determine his health state (as nature sets the initial conditions) but can definitively influence it. Thus, we are concerned with the actions that the individual should pursue to obtain a given improvement of his health. More precisely, we are interested in the optimal distribution of resources between health and other goods. This approach is also labeled as the individual being the producer of his health or as the *human capital model* because it is inspired by human capital theory. The main departure from human capital theory though is that Grossman argues that health capital differs from other forms of human capital in that an individual's stock of knowledge (human capital) affects his market and non-market productivity. Health capital instead determines the total amount of time the individual can devote to producing money earnings and commodities (see Grossman 2000, pp. 349–350 for a more detailed argument.)

In Grossman's model, health care is purchased solely to yield a flow of illness-free days each year for the rest of the consumer's life. The purchase is, therefore, not made to alleviate sickness but rather to invest in health. This characteristic justifies the reference to Grossman model as a health production model. Important characteristics of the model are that it is deterministic and that there is no uncertainty. Thus, no room is left for the health care insurance market.

In summary, the treatment of health in the Grossman model as endogenous meant breaking away from the previous health models. Those were insurance-driven. That is, the occurrence of bad health episodes is an stochastic element and medical services are demanded to recover from illness. By contrast, in the Grossman model individuals weigh up the costs and benefits of investing in their health status to determine their demand of health, i.e. how much of a stochastic loss to offset.

9.2.1 Grossman model – a static version

We follow Zweifel *et al.* (2009, pp. 79–83), and Wagstaff (1986a). Think of an economy composed of a health sector and a consumption sector. In this economy, and for every individual, we distinguish between health stock (H) and health care (medical) services (M), the latter being an input for the former through a production technology $H = H(M)$. More precisely, we can think of M as a composite of time and market health services (health care, gymnasium membership, time exercising, etc.) yielding a health output H by means of a health production function $H(M)$. Quadrant IV in Figure 9.2 illustrates this.

In a similar way, the consumption sector contains consumption services (C) and non-health inputs (X). These inputs are a composite of other time and market goods consumption that are transformed into consumption services through a production technology $C = C(X)$ (think of a car as an input to produce transportation services). This is depicted in quadrant II of Figure 9.2.

The individual obtains satisfaction (utility) from his stock of health and the flow of consumption services. That is, the utility function representing the individual's preferences is given by,

$$U = U(H, C),$$

increasing in both arguments and quasi-concave.

In describing preferences between H and C, it should be clear that the satisfaction the individual can obtain from consumption is linked to his health state. In particular, when the ratio of health to consumption becomes small (for instance due to a poor health status) additional consumption does not increase utility. Accordingly, the indifference curves become vertical. Also, the frontier of the set of feasible combinations (H, C) can be assumed (strictly) concave. We provide an argument for this statement below. Quadrant I in Figure 9.2 illustrates, where $\bar{u} > u$.

Finally, the individual is endowed with an initial health stock that induces an income level $Y(H)$. It seems reasonable to consider that only healthy enough people can be employed and thus earn income. Income (Y) is spent between medical care (M) and consumption goods, whose prices, denoted by p and q respectively, are exogenous. Hence, we can construct a budget constraint dependent on the heath status of the individual as

$$Y(H) = qX + pM.$$

This budget constraint will be *concave* rather than linear. It will depart from the argument that an individual in a very poor healthy condition ($H \sim 0$) will earn no income. The other extreme appears where the individual spends all his/her income in buying medical care. Starting at $H = 0$, as the individual improves his/her health condition, the increase in income is

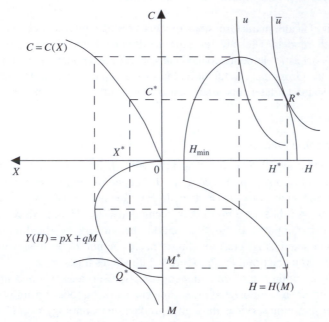

Figure 9.2 The simplified Grossman model.

more than proportional to the increase in medical care. Thus, the individual can expand his/her consumption. This expansion of consumption will occur at a decreasing rate as the capacity to work (and the associated earning of income) reaches a maximum. Further expenses in medical care can only be done sacrificing consumption of goods. This is shown in quadrant III of Figure 9.2. Also in this quadrant we can depict input indifference curves, where preferences over inputs are derived from the relationships in the other quadrants.

The tangency point $R^* = (C^*, H^*)$ in quadrant I shows the maximum utility attainable by the individual. To reach it, (s)he has to acquire the input combination Q^* (in quadrant III), that is purchase M^* units of medical care and X^* units of the consumption good. Finally, Q^* gives (as a consistency condition) the optimal budget allocation.

The formal analysis of the decision of the individual requires a bit more of structure. We need to explicitly introduce the distribution of time within the period among the alternative activities. Let Ω denote the total available time of the individual. Part of this time is devoted to the production of the health stock (TH). Similarly, another share of time is devoted to the production of the consumption good (T). The remaining time is divided between working time (TW) and sick time (TL). Therefore,

$$\Omega = TH + T + TW + TL \tag{9.1}$$

For future reference, define $h \equiv TH + T + TW$ as the total healthy time.

The production technologies of the health stock and consumption good are given by,

$$H = H(M, TH; E), \tag{9.2}$$

$$C = C(X, T; E), \tag{9.3}$$

where E denotes the education level of the individual. It is exogenous and conveys the assumption that more educated people are more efficient in production activities.

The objective function of the individual is the following utility function,

$$U = U(H, C, \phi). \tag{9.4}$$

We assume that the individual can only perform his/her activities as long as (s)he is healthy. Accordingly, let ϕ stand for the healthy time per unit of health stock, so that $h = \phi H$ represents total healthy time, and the utility function can be rewritten as,

$$U = U(h, C).$$

From the definition of the healthy time h, we obtain that sick time is defined as,

$$TL = \Omega - h \tag{9.5}$$

Finally, we need to introduce the budget constraint of the individual. Let working time (*TW*) be remunerated at unit price w. The individual obtains income from his working time. This income is spent in the purchasing of the health care services and non-health inputs, that is

$$wTW = pM + qX. \tag{9.6}$$

The problem of the individual is to maximize (9.4) subject to (9.1) (9.2), (9.3), (9.5), and (9.6). Formally,

$$\max_{TH,T,TW,TL,X,M} U(H, C, \phi), \quad \text{s.t.} \begin{cases} H = H(M, TH; E) \\ C = C(X, T; E) \\ wTW = pM + qX \\ \Omega = TH + T + TW + TL \\ h = \Omega - TL \\ \phi = h/H \end{cases}$$

We can combine constraints (9.1), (9.5), and (9.6) to obtain.

$$w\Omega = w(TH + T + \Omega - h) + pM + qX,$$

so that the maximization program can be rewritten as,

$$\max_{TH,T,X,M} U(H, C, \phi), \quad \text{s.t.} \begin{cases} H = H(M, TH; E) \\ C = C(X, T; E) \\ w\Omega = w(TH + T + \Omega - h) + pM + qX \end{cases}$$

The first two constraints define the production possibilities frontier depicted in quadrant I in Figure 9.2. The last constraint summarizes the budget constraint depicted in quadrant III in Figure 9.2.

9.2.2   *Grossman model – a dynamic approach*

Consider an individual with a life horizon of n periods from now. Time (age) is denoted by $t = 0, 1, \ldots, n$. The inter-temporal utility function of the individual, as presented in Grossman (2000), is given by[2]

$$U = U(\phi_t, H_t, C_t), \quad t = 0, 1, \ldots, n \tag{9.7}$$

where n is the individual's time horizon, H_t denotes the stock of health in period t, ϕ_t is the service flow per unit stock (that is, healthy time derived per unit of health stock), and C_t is consumption in period t.

The total initial stock of health, H_0, is given. The length of life as of the planning date n is endogenous. That is, death occurs when $H_t \leq H_{\min}$. Accordingly, the length of life is determined by the quantities that maximize utility subject to production and budget constraints.

The crucial component of the model is the evolution of health stock over time. The individual may decide to invest in health by purchasing medical care (M_t). Such investment is costly in terms of money and time. Examples of such investments are healthy diets, performing physical exercise (in gyms, or in the open air), refraining from smoking, or regular visits to the doctor. This gross investment I_t would give rise to a positive rate of change of the stock of health, causing the individual to become healthier and healthier all the time. The counter-force is given by the depreciation during the period of the stock of health at a rate $\delta_t \in (0, 1)$. This depreciation is exogenous but increases with time to reflect aging. Accordingly, the evolution of the health stock is a constraint in the decision process of the individual. It is given by,

$$H_{t+1} - H_t = I_t - \delta_t H_t. \tag{9.8}$$

Similarly, individuals also invest in the consumption good C_t. These investment decisions constitute the set of household *production functions*. They are defined as

$$I_t = I_t(M_t, TH_t; E), \tag{9.9}$$

$$C_t = C_t(X_t, T_t; E), \tag{9.10}$$

where M_t is a vector of inputs purchased in the goods market that contribute to gross investment in health (i.e. health-related goods and services) as described above, X_t is another vector of inputs that contribute to the production of C_t, TH_t is the time spent investing in health, and T_t denotes the time input in the production of C_t. Finally, E, assumed constant and exogenous over the life span, is the stock of human capital *exclusive of* health capital. To simplify, think of E as education. It affects efficiency of the individual production in a similar way as technology affects the efficiency of an industrial production process. Leibowitz (2004) reviews the importance of education and time (in non-medical uses) in Grossman's model. Summarizing, this problem can be thought of as a reduced form of a larger problem after the consumer has determined his optimal stock of human (knowledge) capital. Grossman also assumes that production functions I_t and C_t are homogeneous of degree one in the endogenous market goods and own time inputs.

Medical care, M_t, usually has associated a positive price p_t and non-health input, X_t, a positive price q_t. The expenses in these goods must be offset by labor and property income.

Let w_t denote the price of labor in period t, TW_t represent hours of work in the period, r is the market rate of interest (i.e. the opportunity cost of capital), and A_0 the discounted value of capital income generated by the initial assets of the individual. Then, the *lifetime budget constraint* equates the present value of the expenses in the composite consumption good and health-related goods and services to the present value of earnings income along the n periods plus initial assets endowment:

$$\sum_{t=0}^{n} \frac{p_t M_t + q_t X_t}{(1+r)^t} = \sum_{t=0}^{n} \frac{w_t TW_t}{(1+r)^t} + A_0. \tag{9.11}$$

Also, the time available in any period is fixed. The total amount of time available in period t, denoted by Ω_t must be completely distributed among the time used as inputs (TH_t, T_t), working time (TW_t), sick time (TL_t). That is,

$$\Omega_t = TW_t + TL_t + T_t + TH_t. \tag{9.12}$$

Sick time is assumed to be inversely related to the stock of health, i.e. $\partial TL_t / \partial H_t < 0$. Let $h_t = \phi_t H_t$ define total healthy time of the individual. Then, we can write,

$$TL_t = \Omega_t - h_t.$$

Solving (9.12) for TW_t and substituting it into (9.11), allows us to summarize the two constraints into a single one as,

$$\sum_{t=0}^{n} \frac{p_t M_t + q_t X_t + w_t (TL_t + TH_t + T_t)}{(1+r)^t} = \sum_{t=0}^{n} \frac{w_t \Omega_t}{(1+r)^t} + A_0. \tag{9.13}$$

This restriction equates the individual's full wealth [lhs of (9.13)] to his initial assets plus the discounted value of the earnings the individual would obtain should he spend all of his time at work [rhs of (9.13)]. Part of this time is spent on market goods, part on non-market production, and part is lost due to illness.

Before formalizing the problem of the individual, the elements determining the behavior of a rational consumer are as follows. Assume a consumer, in period t, wants to increase his health capital stock in one unit. The gain (in money terms) is given by the marginal product of health capital in period t times the wage rate (i.e. the increase in income in the next period). The cost is given (in money terms) by the product of the cost per unit health investment (i.e. the marginal cost) in $t-1$ times the rate of growth of the health capital (i.e. the ratio between capital and investment). Therefore, the period t optimization condition simply equates both magnitudes. Over the n-period horizon, we have to take into account the depreciation of health capital, δ, and the time preference given by the rate of interest r. Accordingly, in the steady state the rate of growth of health capital must be equal to the depreciation rate corrected by discounting, i.e. $\delta + r$. In other words, the payoff per euro invested in health capital corrected by its depreciation rate should be equal to the marginal efficiency of any other investment. In equilibrium those investments obtain the payoff of r per euro invested.

Let us write (9.7) as $U(h_t, C_t)$, $t = 0, 1, \ldots, n$. The problem of the individual is to choose investment and consumption over time that maximizes the utility function $U(h_t, C_t)$, subject to the constraints given by (9.8), (9.9), and (9.13). That is,

$$\max_{I_{t-1}, C_t} \quad U(h_t, C_t), \quad (t = 0, 1, \ldots, n)$$

$$\text{s.t.} \quad \begin{cases} H_{t+1} - H_t = I_t(M_t, TH_t; E) - \delta_t H_t, \\[2mm] \sum_{t=0}^{n} \dfrac{P_t M_t + Q_t X_t + W_t(TL_t + TH_t + T_t)}{(1+r)^t} = \kappa \\[2mm] C_t = C_t(X_t, T_t; E) \end{cases} \qquad (9.14)$$

where $\kappa \equiv \sum_{t=0}^{n} w_t \Omega_t / (1+r)^t + A_0$ is a constant in the optimization program. The first (technological) restriction illustrates on the relationship between H_{t-1} and I_t, or equivalently between H_t and I_{t-1}. This information will be necessary to compute the impact on the utility function in period t of a variation in the investment in period $t - 1$.

Since the inherited stock of health (H_0) and the rates of depreciation (δ_t) are given, the optimal quantities of gross investment determine the optimal quantities of health capital. Thus, differentiating with respect to I_{t-1}, we obtain,

$$\frac{\partial U}{\partial h_t} \frac{\partial h_t}{\partial H_t} \frac{\partial H_t}{\partial I_{t-1}} + \cdots + \frac{\partial U}{\partial h_n} \frac{\partial h_n}{\partial H_n} \frac{\partial H_n}{\partial I_{t-1}} - \lambda \left[\frac{\pi_{t-1}}{(1+r)^{t-1}} + \frac{w_t}{(1+r)^t} \frac{\partial TL_t}{\partial H_t} \frac{\partial H_t}{\partial I_{t-1}} + \cdots \right.$$

$$\left. + \frac{w_n}{(1+r)^n} \frac{\partial TL_n}{\partial H_n} \frac{\partial H_n}{\partial I_{t-1}} \right] = 0, \qquad (9.15)$$

where $\partial U / \partial h_t$ denotes the marginal utility of healthy time; the Lagrangian multiplier, λ, is the marginal utility of wealth; $\partial h_t / \partial H_t = -\partial TL_t / \partial H_t$ represents the marginal product of the stock of health measured by healthy time;[3] and π_{t-1} is the marginal cost of gross investment in health in period $t - 1$.

To compute the value of the marginal cost of investment, recall that we have assumed that the production function of health investment given by (9.9) satisfies constant returns to scale. Accordingly, we can rewrite it as,

$$I_t = M_t g \left(\frac{TH_t}{M_t} \right). \qquad (9.16)$$

Then, the marginal products of time and medical care in the production of gross investment are,

$$\frac{\partial I_t}{\partial TH_t} = \frac{\partial g}{\partial \frac{TH_t}{M_t}} = g', \qquad (9.17)$$

$$\frac{\partial I_t}{\partial M_t} = g - g' \frac{TH_t}{M_t}. \qquad (9.18)$$

The marginal cost of gross investment can be computed from the equilibrium condition that equates the price of a factor and the value of its marginal product. That is $w_t = \pi_{t-1} g'$.

The first order condition (9.15) is defined by three components. First, the elements arising from differentiating the utility function with respect to its health variables; next, we find an element giving us the effects on the cost of the investment in $t-1$; finally, a third group of elements show the effects of the investment in $t-1$ on the budget constraint in the following periods. This is an induced effect arising from the effect of the health capital stock on the available time to the consumer.

Note that, an increase in the gross investment in period $t-1$ increases the stock of health in all future periods. These increases are

$$\frac{\partial H_t}{\partial I_{t-1}} = 1,$$

$$\frac{\partial H_{t+1}}{\partial I_{t-1}} = 1 - \delta_t,$$

$$\frac{\partial H_{t+2}}{\partial I_{t-1}} = (1 - \delta_t)(1 - \delta_{t+1}),$$

$$\vdots$$

$$\frac{\partial H_n}{\partial I_{t-1}} = (1 - \delta_t)(1 - \delta_{t+1}) \ldots (1 - \delta_{n-1}).$$

Substituting these expressions into the first-order condition (9.15), recalling that $\partial h_t / \partial H_t = -\partial TL_t / \partial H_t$, and rearranging we obtain,

$$\frac{\pi_{t-1}}{(1+r)^{t-1}} = \frac{1}{\lambda} \left[\frac{\partial U}{\partial h_t} \frac{\partial h_t}{\partial H_t} + \cdots + \frac{\partial U}{\partial h_n} \frac{\partial h_n}{\partial H_n} (1 - \delta_t)(1 - \delta_{t+1}) \cdots (1 - \delta_{n-1}) \right]$$

$$+ \frac{w_t}{(1+r)^t} \frac{\partial H_t}{\partial h_t} + (1 - \delta_t) \frac{w_{t+1}}{(1+r)^{t+1}} \frac{\partial H_{t+1}}{\partial h_{t+1}}$$

$$+ \cdots + \frac{w_n}{(1+r)^n} \frac{\partial H_n}{\partial h_n} (1 - \delta_t)(1 - \delta_{t+1}) \cdots (1 - \delta_{n-1}). \tag{9.19}$$

First-order condition (9.15) says that the present value of marginal utility of a gross investment in health in period $t-1$ must be equal to the present value of its marginal cost. Thus, the optimal amount of gross investment in period $t-1$ is determined. The equivalent expression (9.19) gives the discounted marginal cost of an investment in period $t-1$.

To better understand the forces affecting consumers' investment decisions, we follow Keiding (*c.* 2000) and compute the discounted marginal cost of an investment in period t. This is given by,

$$\frac{\pi_t}{(1+r)^t} = \frac{1}{\lambda} \left[\frac{\partial U}{\partial h_{t+1}} \frac{\partial h_{t+1}}{\partial H_{t+1}} + \cdots + \frac{\partial U}{\partial h_n} \frac{\partial h_n}{\partial H_n} (1 - \delta_{t+1}) \cdots (1 - \delta_{n-1}) \right]$$

$$+ \frac{w_t}{(1+r)^{t+1}} \frac{\partial H_t}{\partial h_t} + \cdots + \frac{w_n}{(1+r)^n} \frac{\partial H_n}{\partial h_n} (1 - \delta_{t+1}) \cdots (1 - \delta_{n-1}). \tag{9.20}$$

Now subtract (9.20) from (9.19) to obtain,

$$
\frac{\pi_t}{(1+r)^t} - \frac{\pi_{t-1}}{(1+r)^{t-1}}
$$

$$
= -\frac{w_t}{(1+r)^t}\frac{\partial h_t}{\partial H_t} - \frac{1}{\lambda}\frac{\partial U}{\partial h_t}\frac{\partial h_t}{\partial H_t}
$$

$$
+ \delta_t\left[\frac{w_{t+1}}{(1+r)^{t+1}}\frac{\partial h_{t+1}}{\partial H_{t+1}} + \cdots + \frac{w_n}{(1+r)^n}\frac{\partial h_n}{\partial H_n}(1-\delta_{t+1})\cdots(1-\delta_{n-1})\right.
$$

$$
\left. + \frac{1}{\lambda}\frac{\partial U}{\partial h_{t+1}}\frac{\partial h_{t+1}}{\partial H_{t+1}} + \cdots + \frac{1}{\lambda}\frac{\partial U}{\partial h_n}\frac{\partial h_n}{\partial H_n}(1-\delta_{t+1})\cdots(1-\delta_{n-1})\right]
$$

Note that the terms in square brackets is precisely (9.20). Accordingly, we can simplify this expression to

$$
\frac{\pi_t}{(1+r)^t} - \frac{\pi_{t-1}}{(1+r)^{t-1}} = -\frac{w_t}{(1+r)^t}\frac{\partial h_t}{\partial H_t} - \frac{1}{\lambda}\frac{\partial U}{\partial h_t}\frac{\partial h_t}{\partial H_t} + \delta_t\frac{\pi_t}{(1+r)^t},
$$

and rearranging terms we obtain,

$$
\frac{\pi_{t-1}}{(1+r)^{t-1}} = \frac{\partial h_t}{\partial H_t}\left[\frac{w_t}{(1+r)^t} + \frac{1}{\lambda}\frac{\partial U}{\partial h_t}\right] + (1-\delta_t)\frac{\pi_t}{(1+r)^t}.
$$

Next, multiplying both sides by $(1+r)^t$ we get,

$$
\pi_{t-1}(1+r) - \pi_t(1-\delta_t) = \frac{\partial h_t}{\partial H_t}\left[w_t + \frac{(1+r)^t}{\lambda}\frac{\partial U}{\partial h_t}\right].
$$

Define $\bar{\pi}_{t-1} = (\pi_t - \pi_{t-1})/\pi_{t-1}$. This is the percentage rate of change in marginal cost between period $t-1$ and t. Assume also, $\delta_t\pi_t \approx \delta_t\pi_{t-1}$. Then,

$$
\pi_{t-1}(1+r) - \pi_t(1-\delta_t) = \pi_{t-1} + r\pi_{t-1} - \pi_t - \delta_t\pi_t
$$

$$
= -\pi_{t-1}\bar{\pi}_{t-1} + r\pi_{t-1} + \delta_t\pi_{t-1}
$$

$$
= \pi_{t-1}(r - \bar{\pi}_{t-1} + \delta_t).
$$

Therefore, we end up with the following expression,

$$
\frac{\partial h_t}{\partial H_t}\left[w_t + \frac{(1+r)^t}{\lambda}\frac{\partial U}{\partial h_t}\right] = \pi_{t-1}(r - \bar{\pi}_{t-1} + \delta_t), \tag{9.21}
$$

This is an equation determining the optimal stock of health in period t. It tells us that the undiscounted value of the marginal product of the optimal stock of health at any period must equal the supply price of capital $\pi_{t-1}(r - \bar{\pi}_{t-1} + \delta_t)$.

Alternatively, and for future reference, assuming that the horizon n is exogenous, we can rewrite the first-order condition (9.21) as

$$\frac{\partial h_t}{\partial H_t}\left[w_t + \frac{(1+r)^t}{\lambda}\frac{\partial U}{\partial h_t}\right] = \pi_{t-1}(r - \bar{\pi}_{t-1} + \delta_t), \quad t < n, \tag{9.22}$$

$$\frac{\partial h_n}{\partial H_n}\left[w_n + \frac{(1+r)^n}{\lambda}\frac{\partial U}{\partial h_n}\right] = \pi_{n-1}(r + 1). \tag{9.23}$$

Equation (9.23) stems from the fact that investment in $n - 1$ yields returns for one period only, so that the individual behaves as if the rate of depreciation of the stock of health is equal to 1 in period n.

The rationale behind expression (9.21) is readily obtained after rewriting it as,

$$\frac{(1+r)^t}{\lambda}\frac{\partial U}{\partial h_t}\frac{\partial h_t}{\partial H_t}\frac{1}{\pi_{t-1}} + \frac{w_t}{\pi_{t-1}}\frac{\partial h_t}{\partial H_t} = r - \bar{\pi}_{t-1} + \delta_t. \tag{9.24}$$

The first term on the left-hand side of the equation expresses the consumption benefit, also called the "psychic" rate of return, while the second term expresses the marginal monetary return on an investment in health (i.e. the investment benefit). The right-hand side contains the user cost of capital defined by the sum of the real own-rate of return $(r - \bar{\pi}_{t-1})$ and the depreciation rate. Accordingly, this equation sets at the margin the equality between the user cost of health capital and the discounted marginal benefits of health. In other words, the sum of the monetary rate of return and the "psychic" rate of return to an investment in health must equal the user cost of that capital as expressed by the price of gross investment.

Grossman assumes that the consumer is alive until period n (i.e. $H_n > H_{min}$) and dies in period $n + 1$ (i.e. $H_{n+1} \leq H_{min}$), so that the individual lives for $n + 1$ periods, $t = 0, 1, \ldots, n$. The first-order conditions (9.14) and (9.15) do not provide an explicit condition determining n. To close the model, we need to show that those conditions guarantee that n is the optimal length of life. The argument to solve this problem is an iterative process that runs as follows: we start by maximizing lifetime utility for a fixed horizon n and verify whether $H_{n+1} \leq H_{min}$. If so, we are done. Otherwise, we add one period to the horizon, remaximize the utility function, and verify whether $H_{n+2} \leq H_{min}$, and so on until we identify the optimal horizon.

9.2.3   Comparative statics of the Grossman model

Once the model is solved and the optimal levels of the stock of health, gross investment in health, and health inputs have been determined, we want to study how these variables react to variations in exogenous variables. For the sake of simplicity, Grossman examines two polar cases obtained by abstracting out separately the consumption benefits and the investment benefits to be obtained from the capital stock of health. To analyze consumption effects, the second term on the left-hand side of equation (9.24) is set to zero. To analyze investment benefits, the first term on the left-hand side of equation (9.24) is set to zero.

Pure investment model

Let us ignore consumption benefits. That is, assume that the marginal utility of healthy time $(\partial U/\partial h_t)$ is zero. Then, health would be solely an investment commodity and we can obtain

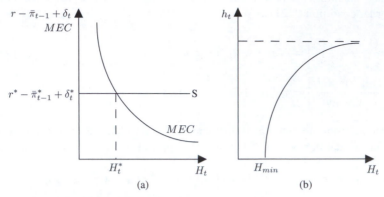

Figure 9.3 Equilibrium in the pure investment model.

the optimal values of H_t from equations (9.22), and (9.23) as,

$$\frac{w_t}{\pi_{t-1}} \frac{\partial h_t}{\partial H_t} = r - \bar{\pi}_{t-1} + \delta_t, \quad \text{for } t < n, \tag{9.25}$$

$$\frac{w_n}{\pi_{n-1}} \frac{\partial h_n}{\partial H_n} = r + 1, \quad \text{for } t = n. \tag{9.26}$$

The right-hand side of equation (9.25) denotes the marginal monetary rate of return on an investment in health. Thus, for $t < n$, the optimal amount of health capital H_t arises from the equality between the marginal monetary rate of return on an investment in health and the opportunity cost of capital. Figure 9.3(a) illustrates the determination of the optimal stock of health capital. The supply curve S shows the relationship between the stock of health and the cost of capital. Since $r - \bar{\pi}_{t-1}$ and δ_t are independent of the stock, the supply curve is infinitely elastic. The demand curve, MEC (marginal efficiency of capital) is downward sloping because (given that neither the wage rate W_t nor the marginal cost of gross investment $\bar{\pi}_{t-1}$ depend on the stock of health) as already assumed, the marginal product of health capital diminishes as the stock increases, i.e. $\partial^2 h_t / \partial H_t^2 < 0$. The equilibrium stock of health H_t^* is given by the intersection of supply and demand.

Figure 9.3(b) shows a possible relationship between the stock of health and the amount of healthy time (production function of healthy time). The slope of that curve at a given point gives the marginal product of health capital. Naturally, to the left of $H_{\min}$ healthy time is zero. To the right of this threshold, healthy time increases at a decreasing rate as the stock of health increases. There is an upper bound to the healthy time given by the total time available (e.g. 365 days in a year).

VARIATIONS OF δ_t

Assume δ_t is age-dependent and in particular, assume that it increases with age. This means that as individuals age, their stock of health falls. This turns into a shift upwards of the supply function, so that the optimal stock of health capital in every period is lower than in the previous one. The greater the elasticity of the demand curve (MEC) the greater the decrease in the optimal stock with age. Figure 9.4 illustrates this.

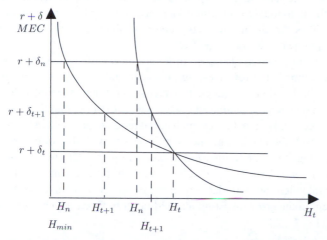

Figure 9.4 Increasing δ with age, demand elasticity, and optimal *H*.

As marginal cost of gross investment $\bar{\pi}_{t-1}$ is assumed constant, equation (9.25) reduces to,

$$\frac{w_t}{\pi_{t-1}} \frac{\partial h_t}{\partial H_t} = r + \delta_t. \tag{9.27}$$

As δ_t increases, equation (9.27) is violated because the marginal cost of producing healthy days becomes larger than the benefits. Recall that we have assumed $\partial h_t / \partial H_t > 0$ and $\partial^2 h_t / \partial H_t^2 < 0$. To restore the equilibrium, the individual will demand a lower stock of health so that its marginal productivity will increase and eventually will offset the increase in the marginal cost. Note that in this model there is no uncertainty, so that we can assume the adjustment process to be instantaneous.

Also, the increase in δ_t has an impact on the gross investment. The rise in the depreciation rate reduces the amount of capital supplied to consumers by a given amount of gross investment. As the cost of investment increases the supply of health capital reduces. If the change in supply exceeds that change in demand, individuals have an incentive to close the gap by increasing gross investment. Otherwise, gross investment will fall.[4] If demand for health is *inelastic*, gross investment and the depreciation rate are positively correlated, while gross investment and the stock of health are negatively correlated. This conclusion predicts that less healthy (old) people will make larger gross investments in health than healthy (young) people. Thus, estimating the elasticity of the demand turns out to be crucial in the derivation of policy conclusions from the model.

The changes in δ_t give rise to movements *along* the demand curve. Now we will examine two elements that will *shift* the demand curve. These are changes in the value of the marginal product of health capital induced by changes in w_t, and changes in human capital other than health capital (e.g. education), i.e. changes in *E*.

VARIATIONS OF W_t

The value of the marginal product of heath is given by $w_t(\partial h_t / \partial H_t)$. Accordingly, an increase in the wage rate raises the monetary equivalent of the marginal product of a given stock. That is, the higher the wage rate, the higher the value of an increase in healthy time. Also, a high wage induces the individual to substitute market goods for his own time in the production of commodities. This substitution will continue until the monetary value of the marginal product of consumption equates the wage rate.

Note that the gross investment function also uses time as input, so that if more time is spent in the labor market, less time is left for investing in health, and the cost of investment must increase. Assume, that the fraction of total cost of gross investment accounted for by time is denoted by K. Then, a one percent increase in wage would increase marginal cost of gross investment, π, by K percent. Given that other inputs than time are involved in the gross investment schedule (i.e. $K < 1$), the percentage increase in wages will always be greater, at the margin, than the percentage increase in investment costs. In particular, the percentage growth in $(W_t/\pi_{t-1})(\partial h_t/\partial H_t)$ will be $1 - K > 0$. The exact rise in the quantity of health capital demand as the wage rate increases will depend on the elasticity of demand for health and on the share of time spent in the gross investment schedule. It will be given by the wage elasticity of capital: $e_{HW} = (1 - K)\varepsilon$.

VARIATIONS OF E

Education behaves in a similar way as technology. It shifts the production function. That is, education increases productivity. Accordingly, it reduces the quantity of inputs required to produce a given amount of gross investment. In turn, this more efficient production (reduction of costs) translates in a shift upwards of the demand curve for health and thus raises the optimal stock of health. The percentage increase in the amount of health capital for a given increase in E depends on the elasticity of demand and on the elasticity of investment with respect to education.

Kennedy (2004) provides three explanations (and empirical evidence) for the positive relationship between education and health for Australia and Canada. These are, technical efficiency, allocative efficiency, and time preference explanations. Grossman (2004) reviews seven recent studies on the effects of schooling on health.

Pure consumption model

The pure consumption model assumes that the cost of health capital is large relative to the monetary rate of return on an investment in health (i.e. the second term on the left hand side of equation (9.24) is set to zero), and also assuming that $\bar{\pi}_{t-1} = 0$ for all t. Then, equation (9.24) becomes,

$$\frac{1}{\lambda}\frac{\partial U}{\partial h_t}\frac{\partial h_t}{\partial H_t} = \frac{\pi(r + \delta_t)}{(1 + r)^t}.$$

Now, the monetary equivalent of the marginal utility of health capital equals the discounted user cost of H_t. As in the pure investment model, we are interested in assessing aging, wage, and education effects.

As McGuire *et al.* (1999, p. 141) point out, the process of aging causes individuals to substitute away from future health until death is chosen, in line with the pure investment model. However, now the existence of time preference for the future might outweigh the rise in the depreciation rate that accompanies age and lead to a temporary increase in health capital. The elasticity of substitution between present and future health, rather than the elasticity of the marginal efficiency of capital schedule, becomes the parameter determining life-cycle behavior.

Wage effects are ambiguous as wages affect both the marginal cost of gross investments and the marginal cost of consumption goods. Similarly, a variation of E generates wealth and substitution effects operating in different directions, so that the overall effect is again ambiguous.

Kverndokk (2000) proposes an extension of the pure consumption model containing psychological aspects such as status seeking, identity seeking, and health adaption.

9.2.4   Criticisms

Before going into the criticisms of the model, we should emphasize that Grossman's model is a pathbreaking attempt to apply rigorous economic analysis to the study of health economics. As such, several aspects of the model deserve comment.

As a general approach, the model assumes a fully rational consumer when making utility-maximizing choices regarding the investment in health care and health stock, including its depreciation and the knowledge of future technical changes. This highly demanding rationality and information capacity of the general setting is rooted in the certainty nature of the model. This allows Grossman to avoid going into the market for insurance, and the questions of risk-bearing in the analysis of the demand for health and health care.

The next criticisms are related to particular assumptions of the model.

(A)   The certainty assumption leads to assuming that the depreciation rate is known, so that every individual is able to choose his or her own death time. Although Grossman himself acknowledges this assumption is restrictive, there is debate on how to overcome it. Phelps (1973) and Cropper (1977) introduce a probability distribution to the depreciation rate in each period, thus creating dispersion in time of death expectations. Dowie (1975) argues that uncertainty should be incorporated on the gross investment variables as aging is a continuous process largely determined. Instead, the effect of an input on a specified health stock is largely uncertain.

(B)   Muurinen (1982) argues that Grossman treats consumption and investment benefits as substitutes. She proposes to treat those health benefits as complements because it is both types of benefits are at the basis of the demand for health.

(C)   Also, Muurinen (1982) argues that the health stock is not the only durable capital good producing flows of services. The stock of education and wealth also produces flows of services. To a certain extent, she argues, the three capital stocks are interchangeable.

9.2.5   On demand elasticity – concept and difficulties

The elasticity of demand for a product is an index of the sensibility of that demand to variations in its determinants individually considered. Typically, among those determinants we find the own price of the product, the prices of related products, and the income of the individual demanding the product.

The demand for health is no exception in this regard. However, two comments are in order here. First, in line with Grossman's view, individuals demand health but cannot directly purchase it. Individuals when ill buy those health care services (treatment) intended to produce health. In other words, demand for health is derived from demand for health care services. Accordingly, it is the demand for health care (and not demand for health) that can be studied. This demand can be measured either by the quantity of services (inpatient days, outpatient visits, prescriptions, etc.), or by the total cost of the services.

Second, following Keiding (*c*. 2000, p. 40) demand for health care services may be determined by the need for treatment rather than by prices. That is when an individual suffers from a particular disease, they need a particular (and often well-defined) treatment. Changes in the price of this treatment only mean that whoever has to afford it (insurance company, individual himself, or both) will retain less surplus, but the treatment will be delivered. Thus, we should expect demand for health care services to be strongly inelastic. We will leave these considerations aside in our discussion.

From now on, we will refer to demand for health care rather than demand for health. Having solved the first difficulty (specifying the type of demand), we still have more difficulties to tackle before proceeding to estimate the elasticity of that demand. Following Ringel *et al.* (2005, ch. 2),

Health care insurance   An important consideration is the fact that the price of a health care service may differ from the "perceived" price the patient will effectively pay as the patient may hold a health insurance contract limiting his out-of-pocket expenses. That is, the "discussion of the elasticity of demand for health with respect to price cannot be separated from the discussion of the methods for financing health expenditure." (Keiding *c*. 2000, p. 41). There are two effects that should be pointed out in the demand for health insurance in relation with the demand for health care. If the price of the insurance (premium, deductible, co-payment) falls, more consumers will contract health insurance. Also, those already holding the insurance will use more services than before. Accordingly, the total impact of the variation in the price of the insurance on the demand for health care will be the sum of the elasticities corresponding to these two components. The empirical studies tend to concentrate on the change in the demand for health care of the previously insured, thus underestimating the impact in a variation of the out-of-pocket costs of health care services.

Waiting time   Waiting time can have a significant impact in the demand for health care services. Waiting time may refer either to the delay in obtaining an appointment, or to the time spent waiting in the physician's office. In general, it is this latter interpretation that is considered in the measurement of the own-price elasticity of demand. While waiting in the physician's office, the patient cannot perform any other activity, so waiting may have a high opportunity cost for the individual. We should expect to see individuals with lower opportunity costs using more intensively medical services than those with high opportunity costs of time (usually measured by the individual's market wage). Accordingly, when studying health care demand both the monetary cost and the time cost must be taken into account.

Adverse selection and moral hazard   Adverse selection in the provision of health care appears when individuals with poor health are able to enroll in health plans with high benefits, and people with good health avoid these plans because of their high cost. Then, elasticity estimates will be distorted because they will capture not only the response to a price change but the difference in needs of people with different health status. Disentangling these two elements in the estimations require highly sophisticated econometric techniques (see Olivella and Vera-Hernandez 2006).

Moral hazard appears when the individual is willing to incur higher risk because they are covered by an insurance contract. This attitude toward risk may appear before the need for health care (*ex-ante* moral hazard) or after with an inaccurate compliance of the treatment (*ex-post* moral hazard). The presence of moral hazard induces more consumption of health services than would appear without health care insurance. As before, the elasticity estimates will incorporate the effects of a price variation and the effects of moral hazard.

Supply-induced demand   An important and controversial argument in the demand for health care comes from the behavior of the suppliers (physicians, hospitals, primary care services). Physicians act as agents for patients. Thus, they have the capacity to induce demand (prescribing more intense treatments, ordering unnecessary tests, extending stays in hospital, or outpatient visits, etc.), particularly when patients are little sensitive to prices because they are protected by an insurance contract. This is particularly relevant when increased cost-sharing leads to lower demand for their services. A more detailed analysis of this phenomenon is found in the last section of Chapter 11.

Types of health care   Usually the impact of price variations in different treatments will have different impacts on the demand for those treatments. Accordingly, whenever possible, it will be useful to estimate separately the elasticities of demand for different treatments.

9.2.6   On demand elasticity – empirical results

The empirical literature can be divided between those studies looking at general health care services or at specific types of medical studies. Those studies are also organized around three types of methodologies: experimental studies, natural experiments, and observational studies.

Experimental studies use random assignment into treatment and control groups to infer the effects of a particular treatment. This methodology does not present any selection bias given the randomization of people into different treatments. However it suffers from several drawbacks. Experiments are difficult to design and implement, may be very costly, take a long time until the results can be fully evaluated, and results need not be generalizable.

Natural experiments are particular type of experiments where individuals are not randomly assigned to treatments. They consider an economic environment and try to identify the effects of a treatment controlling for all factors that may have changed during the time period of analysis. For instance, we may want to study the effects of introducing a co-payment in the insured of a particular (control) insurance company to estimate the effects of price on demand for health care.

Finally, observational studies are based on survey or administrative data. These studies use mainly econometric models and have several advantages over experimental studies. They are less costly to implement and provide results more quickly. Also, results are more generalizable.

ELASTICITY OF DEMAND FOR HEALTH CARE IN GENERAL

The many studies estimating health care demand elasticities seems to point to the same qualitative conclusions, regardless of the spread of methodologies used and data sources. These conclusions are: (i) demand for health care is price inelastic, although the range of price elasticity estimates is fairly wide; and (ii) demand for health is also income inelastic. The estimates of income elasticity of demand are in the range of 0 to 0.2. However, studies based on long time series data tend to report higher income elasticities.

ELASTICITY OF DEMAND FOR SPECIFIC CLASSES OF HEALTH CARE SERVICES

Preventive care and pharmacy benefits are among those medical services with larger price elasticities. This is not surprising given the number of available substitutes. In the case of preventive care, consumers are able to substitute it with other goods and services that promote health such as nutritional supplements and healthy foods. Also, there is the argument classifying preventative care as a luxury good and thus highly (in relative terms) sensitive to price increases. Other arguments supporting a higher elasticity are (i) the fact that the benefits of preventive care accrue in the long term so that they are heavily discounted, and (ii) the fact that preventive care services and prescription drugs are typically either not covered by insurance or subject to high co-payment rates.

ELASTICITY OF DEMAND IN DEVELOPING COUNTRIES

The studies concentrating in different types of services in developing countries show even a wider spread than those in developed countries. Some demands may well be highly elastic.

ELASTICITY OF DEMAND FOR HEALTH INSURANCE

Most studies focus on the demand for health care services provided by a particular health plan. Any change in the out-of-pocket costs of services or premium costs will have an effect on the number of plan enrollees and, thus, on the demand for health care services paid for by that plan. According to Royalty and Solomon (1999), there is no definitely established range of price elasticities [of health plan choice] in the literature. Econometric studies of health care plan choice vary dramatically not only in their price elasticity estimates but also in the data sources, econometric methods, and experimental design.

9.2.7 An application of the Grossman model: health promotion

Health promotion is a growing field in economic activity in the health care sector and represents an increasing share of health sector spending in developed countries. The rationale behind these increases is that public authorities expect that the marginal product of health promotion will overcome the marginal allocation in acute and curative medical care. In other words, efficiency of national health care systems may be enhanced by transferring resources from curative medicine to prevention and early detection.

Following Connelly (2002, 2004) there are several definitions of health promotion from a non-economic as well as an economic viewpoint. The non-economic definition following the ideas of the WHO are summarized by Connelly (2002, pp. 3–5) as those programs designed to modify health status via non-clinical means, particularly by modifying individual's lifestyle and behavior. The European Commission (2003, pp. 39–42) in a similar way states that effective health promotion leads to changes in the impact of the determinants of health. Health promotion activities are addressed from four intervention perspectives: health protection, disease-oriented, risk-oriented, and settings-based.

From an economic perspective Connelly (2002, pp. 6–7) proposes a definition based on the consumption of goods and services to improve the health status. Health promotion is "that set of activities that is designed to affect the consumption of goods and services, primarily for the purposes of enhancing health, or preventing illness."

Health promotion programs can be motivated from a *non-welfarist* perspective. This means that the public agency has its own objectives e.g. maximizing health, prestige, pay, power, etc. In contrast a *welfarist* planner would aim at maximizing social welfare defined as the aggregation of individual welfare states. Assume individual j's utility function is given by,

$$U_j = \alpha_j H_j + (1 - \alpha_j)C_j,$$

where α_j represents the weight individual j attaches to his health stock H_j, and C_j his non-health consumption. The non-welfarist health planner's utility function would be given by,

$$U_{hp}^{nw} = \alpha_{hp} \sum_j H_j + (1 - \alpha_{hp}) \sum_j C_j.$$

That is, the health planner derives utility from the pattern and levels of consumption, and the weights reflect his own weights for H and C.

In contrast, a welfarist health planner would maximize,

$$U_{hp}^{w} = \sum_j U_j = \sum_j \alpha_j H_j + \sum_j (1 - \alpha_j)C_j,$$

where now the health planner derives utility not from consumption patterns, but from the utility that each consumer derives from their consumption. In other words, health planners' interests are aligned with those of the consumers in the design of the optimal bundle. The immediate consequence is that a welfarist health planner will only implement health promotion programs to correct market inefficiencies (due to externalities, market power, information asymmetries, etc.) as long as the benefits of the program in helping individuals to attain their efficient allocations overcome the costs of implementing the programs.

Health promotion programs

Connelly (2004) illustrates the role of health promotion programs (both welfare maximizing and health stock maximizing) in a context of problems of information using the static version of the Grossman model depicted in Figure 9.2. There the optimal bundle (H^*, C^*) was obtained under the assumption that the individual had perfect information about the technologies to produce health $(H(M))$ and other goods $(C(X))$. Assume now the individual has imperfect information about the health production technology, and he thinks that it is given by $H_D(M)$. Other than this, the individual has perfect information of the production of the composite non-health consumption good. Figure 9.5 illustrates the situation. Output preferences are not affected by the misinformation on the production technology. However, it distorts the preferences over inputs. The indifference curve in the (X, M)-space reflects this distortion. The new optimal input combination is given by P^* that corresponds to bundle D where the indifference curve is tangent to the corresponding production possibilities frontier. Finally, the individual realizes their mistake when the input combination P^* allows them to obtain the bundle F instead. Although it yields higher utility than D, the individual still suffers a utility loss as the optimal bundle C^* associated with perfect information is superior to F. Note that because the health stock is non-tradable, the consumer cannot move along the production possibilities frontier by making *ex-post* trades.

This sub-optimal outcome provides a necessary (but not sufficient) condition for public intervention. Policies to be used may be information campaigns, public production, quantity controls, or subsidies and taxes.

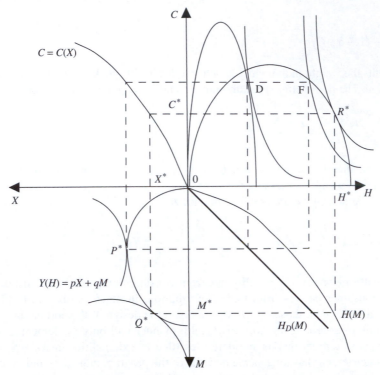

Figure 9.5 Welfare loss by misinformation in health production.

Health promotion policies involving information dissemination are programs designed to provide "accurate information about the relationships between health and diet, exercise, consumption of medical and preventive health care services ... Insomuch as these programmes are designed to correct imperfect knowledge about the relationship between behaviour and health, they may constitute second-best efficient responses by government" (Connelly 2004, p. 239). In terms of Figure 9.5, it turns out that $U(R^*) > U(F)$ and H^* is also larger than the health stock associated with F. This later characteristic of our example need not always be the case. Figure 2 in Connelly (2004) is an example where H^* is lower than the resulting health stock at the corresponding bundle F. Accordingly, the outcome of this policy is to be expected utility-increasing but not necessarily health-increasing. If the policy gives full information to the consumer, then it will not only be necessary but also sufficient for each consumer obtaining his maximizing utility consumption bundle.

An alternative policy to help the consumer attain the bundle R^* is the combination of taxes and subsidies on inputs. Figure 9.6 illustrates the situation. Assume again that the individual has imperfect information on the health production technology as given by $H_D(M)$. Given this technology and the budget constraint, the individual chooses a combination P^* of inputs given by the tangency of the distorted input indifference curve with the initial budget constraint. With this input combination the consumer expects to obtain, through the production technology $C(X)$, a bundle D. However, as D is not feasible, the resulting output bundle is F, containing the same amount on non-health consumption and a lower amount of the health stock (consistent with the overestimation of the productivity of health inputs). Again,

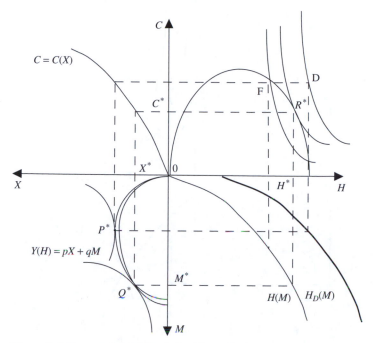

Figure 9.6 Taxes and subsidies in health production.

bundle *F* is suboptimal. The government by manipulating the relative price of the health and non-health inputs may bring the consumer back to the choice of Q^* yielding the utility maximizing output bundle R^*. In our particular example, the government by introducing a subsidy on non-health inputs and/or a tax on health inputs distorts the budget constraint in such a way to obtain a tangency at Q^*.

Finally, a third policy alternative consists of introducing quotas on non-health inputs as Figure 9.7 illustrates. The situation is the same as before where the individual has a distorted perception of the health production technology. It makes the consumer choose an input combination P^* in the expectation of achieving the consumption bundle *D*, while really obtaining *F*. Now the intervention of the government consists in introducing a quantity control X^* (think of place-specific bans on smoking or bans on consumption of drugs, etc.) that induces a new production possibilities frontier and the optimal bundle R^*.

9.2.8   *The "contingent claims" approach to demand for health*

Grossman's view of the demand for health abstracts from uncertainty and uses "conventional" demand theory in the sense that maintains the consumer's sovereignty, i.e. individual demand is determined by willingness to pay and the budget constraint. Let us now change the paradigm to study the demand for health under uncertainty.

Consider an individual facing two states of nature, "sick" (*s*) or "healthy" (*h*). Along the life of the individual the sequence of the realizations of the states of nature is random. All the individual can do is to affect the transition probabilities between the two states along the periods. That is, the individual cannot choose to catch a cold (*s* state) or not (*h* state), but through his actions can influence the likelihood of the sequence of healthy and sick periods.

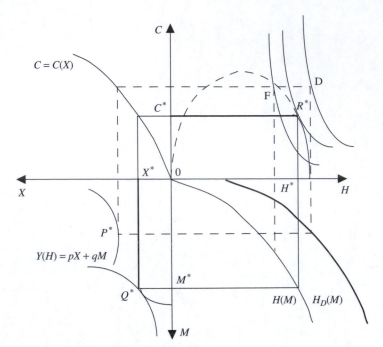

Figure 9.7 Quotas in health promotion.

To simplify matters, assume our individual lives for two periods. Accordingly, the possible sequence of states are hh, hs, sh, ss. Let π_t denote the state probability of being sick in period t. Also, ϕ_{hs} denotes the transition probability of being sick in period 2 after having been healthy in period 1. Similarly, let ϕ_{ss} be the transition probability of being sick in period 2 after having already been sick in period 1.[5] For instance, the probability of being healthy in period 2 is given by,

$$(1 - \pi_2) = (1 - \pi_1)(1 - \phi_{hs}) + \pi_1(1 - \phi_{ss}). \tag{9.28}$$

This is the sum of the probability of staying healthy in period 2 after having been healthy in period 1 plus the probability of turning healthy in period 2 having been sick in period 1. We assume that the individual values being healthy, so that if they are healthy in period 1, the only way to increase $(1 - \pi_2)$ is to lower ϕ_{hs} by means of, say, prevention measures (i.e. healthy habits) that require some time, t^h, to implement. If the individual is sick in period 1, he has to invest in medical services, M, to reduce ϕ_{ss} thus increasing $(1 - \pi_2)$. Therefore, the factors influencing the probability of being healthy in period 2 are contingent on the state of the individual in period 1. Formally (see Zweifel *et al.* 2009, Section 3.4.2),

$$(1 - \pi_2) = \begin{cases} (1 - \pi_2)[\phi_{hs}(t^h, \ldots)] \\ (1 - \pi_2)[\phi_{sh}(M, \ldots)], \end{cases}$$

where, as just described, the probability of falling sick in period 2 can be affected by the time t^h devoted to health maintenance if initially healthy, and by the contracting of medical services (obtained after investing time t^M and paying unit price q) if initially sick,

$$\pi_2 = \pi(t^h), \quad \text{with } \frac{\partial \pi}{\partial t^h} < 0, \text{ if healthy} \tag{9.29}$$

$$\pi_2 = \pi(M), \quad \text{with } \frac{\partial \pi}{\partial M} < 0, \text{ if sick} \tag{9.30}$$

We assume the individual derives utility from consumption. As consumption is dependent on the health state, the utility function will also be state dependent. The individual prefers to stay healthy, so that we assume that in each period

$$u(C_{ht}, h) > u(C_{st}, s),$$

where C_{kt} denotes consumption services in period t given the state k. Figure 9.8, borrowed from Zweifel *et al.* (2009, p. 95), illustrates the arguments presented so far.

To obtain consumption services C_{kt} the individual needs to purchase consumption goods X at price p, and devote time to consumption, t^C. Formally,

$$C_{kt} = C_{kt}(X, t^C), \quad \text{with } \frac{\partial C_{kt}}{\partial X} > 0, \quad \text{and } \frac{\partial C_{kt}}{\partial t^C} > 0.$$

When the individual is healthy, (s)he obtains income from working. A share of the overall time available in the period is devoted to work, t^W, at a salary w, so that income wt^W is used to purchase input consumption good,

$$wt^W = pX_h. \tag{9.31}$$

However, when the individual is sick, (s)he cannot work. Instead, a social security scheme guarantees a replacement income Y. This income is used in purchasing medical services and input consumption good,

$$Y = pX_s + qM. \tag{9.32}$$

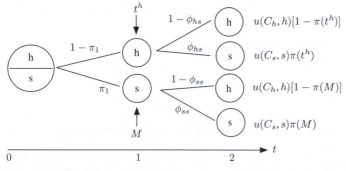

Figure 9.8 Sequence of health states.

Finally, the available time is distributed among the different activities of the individual, contingent on being healthy or sick,

$$\Omega = \begin{cases} t_h^C + t^h + t^W, & \text{if healthy} \\ t_s^C + t^M, & \text{if sick.} \end{cases} \tag{9.33}$$

In contrast with the Grossman model, in this approach production possibilities are different in both states. Hence, we are interested in deriving a joint objective function for the individual over the planning horizon of the two periods. Also, the output of the decision process of the individual is an increased probability of being healthy in the second period, instead of a stock of health. This model lies in the tradition of the "contingent claims" literature, started by Arrow (1951) and Debreu (1959, ch. 7).

The objective function of the individual is thus two-fold contingent on the realization of the initial state. As Figure 9.8 shows, the expected utility of the individual over his two-period planning horizon is given by,

$$EU = (1 - \pi_1)u(C_{h1}, h) + \pi_1 u(C_{s1}, s) + (1 - \pi_2)u(C_{h2}, h) + \pi_2 u(C_{s2}, s), \tag{9.34}$$

where π_2 takes different values (see (9.29) and (9.30)) contingent on the initial state of the individual. In particular, let us consider only the extreme cases $\pi_1 = \{0, 1\}$. Then, if the initial state of the individual is healthy, that is $\pi_1 = 0$, it follows that $\pi_2 = (1 - \pi_1)\phi_{hs} = \phi_{hs} \equiv \pi(t^h)$. If in turn, the initial state of the individual is sick, that is, the state probability $\pi_1 = 1$, then $\pi_2 = \pi_1 \phi_{ss} = \phi_{ss} \equiv \pi(M)$.

The problem of the individual is to decide how to optimally allocate resources between the probability of being healthy and consumption when they are initially in the healthy state or in the sick state.

Initial healthy state

The trade-off between health and consumption arises because the overall amount of time is given. Accordingly, an increase in the time devoted to health maintenance implies less time for the remaining activities (consumption and probability of healthy state) that determine the amount of consumption services. In technical terms, this means that we can identify a production possibilities frontier in the space $(C_h, 1 - \pi)$ whose shape is determined by the sign of the marginal rate of transformation, $dC_h/d(1 - \pi)$ (where let us recall $C_h = C_h(X_h, t^C)$).

Let us start by differentiating (9.29) to obtain,

$$d(1 - \pi) = -d\pi = -\frac{\partial \pi}{\partial t^h} dt^h. \tag{9.35}$$

Similarly, total differentiation of the consumption services function, C_h, yields,

$$dC_h = \frac{\partial C_h}{\partial X} dX_h + \frac{\partial C_h}{\partial t^C} dt^C. \tag{9.36}$$

The budget constraint (9.31) tells us that consumption can only be augmented by expanding labor income, which in turn, implies expanding working time,

$$dX = \frac{w}{p} dt^W.$$
(9.37)

Finally, from the time constraint (9.33) we derive,

$$dt^C = -dt^h - dt^W.$$
(9.38)

Substituting (9.37) and (9.38) into (9.36), we obtain,

$$dC_h = \frac{\partial C_h}{\partial X}\left(\frac{w}{p} dt^W\right) - \frac{\partial C_h}{\partial t^C}(dt^h + dt^W) = -\frac{\partial C_h}{\partial t^C} dt^h + \left(\frac{\partial C_h}{\partial X}\frac{w}{p} - \frac{\partial C_h}{\partial t^C}\right) dt^W.$$
(9.39)

Given that in the optimum, the marginal rate of transformation equals the relative prices,

$$\frac{\frac{\partial C_h}{\partial t^C}}{\frac{\partial C_h}{\partial X}} = \frac{w}{p},$$

it follows that (9.39) reduces to,

$$dC_h = -\frac{\partial C_h}{\partial t^C} dt^h.$$
(9.40)

Finally, dividing (9.40) by (9.35) we obtain,

$$\frac{dC_h}{d(1-\pi)} = \frac{\frac{\partial C_h}{\partial t^C}}{\frac{\partial \pi}{\partial t^h}} < 0.$$
(9.41)

To verify the concavity of this frontier, we must examine the negativity of the second derivative. This is

$$\frac{d^2 C_h}{d(1-\pi)^2} = \frac{d}{dt^h}\left(\frac{dC_h}{d(1-\pi)}\right)\frac{dt^h}{d(1-\pi)} = \frac{d}{dt^h}\left(\frac{\frac{\partial C_h}{\partial t^C}}{\frac{\partial \pi}{\partial t^h}}\right)\left(\frac{-1}{\frac{\partial \pi}{\partial t^h}}\right),$$
(9.42)

where (9.35) and (9.41) have been used. Assuming C_h is linear in t^C, (9.42) simplifies to yield,

$$\frac{d^2 C_h}{d(1-\pi)^2} = \frac{-\frac{\partial C_h}{\partial t^C}\frac{\partial^2 \pi}{(\partial t^h)^2}}{\left(\frac{\partial \pi}{\partial t^h}\right)^2}\left(\frac{-1}{\frac{\partial \pi}{\partial t^h}}\right) = \frac{\frac{\partial C_h}{\partial t^C}\frac{\partial^2 \pi}{(\partial t^h)^2}}{\left(\frac{\partial \pi}{\partial t^h}\right)^3} < 0.$$

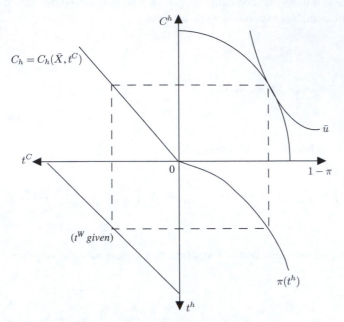

Figure 9.9 Optimal consumption and health choice under $\pi = 0$.

Figure 9.9 summarizes the discussion. A parallel argument can be developed for the case where the initial state of the individual is sick. In that case again the transformation frontier is concave.

10 Insurance

The inherent uncertainty on the moment and circumstances when a health problem may arise leads to the demand for insurance as a protection mechanism. This chapter starts by introducing the basic concepts needed to study the demand for health insurance. Next, the notions of risk and uncertainty are introduced, leading to an analysis of the elements of an insurance contract. The optimal demand of insurance is studied under several institutional scenarios.

The uncertainty about the moment and intensity of health care required leads in a natural way to the demand for protection mechanisms. In particular, when protection against the financial cost associated with health care provision is demanded by individuals, we have demand for insurance.

Insurance protection is simply a transfer of the financial responsibility associated with health care, when needed, to a third party – the insurer. In exchange, the individual makes a fixed payment (premium) to this third party. This payment is independent of the demand for health care and is typically made at the beginning of the health insurance coverage.

The insurer is willing to take individual risks as the aggregation of many individuals with uncorrelated sickness episodes result in some requiring health care, and being net recipients of funds, while others do not require health care and are net contributors. The crucial element is that not all people will be sick at the same time. The third party is thus an instrument of redistribution of income from the healthy to the sick.

A quick reality check informs us that many people differ in their risk characteristics. Thus, different insurance decisions may easily result. It will make a difference whether or not knowledge of the risk characteristics is such that both the individual and the third party know it.

Another potential problem in this market for health care insurance is that people may take actions that potentially affect both the probability and the magnitude of health problems.

The issues arising from strategic use of information in the context of asymmetric information are treated in Chapter 11. The current chapter introduces the basic concepts underlying the demand for insurance in general and some particular aspects of the demand for health care insurance.

10.1 Basic concepts

This section introduces the basic concepts needed to study the optimal demand for health care insurance. These are: *expected income*, *utility of expected income*, *expected utility*, and *state-dependent utility*.[1]

Consider an individual that obtains a certain income y from, say, his labor activity. This income allows the individual to consume goods and services in accordance with his preferences thus obtaining a certain level of satisfaction that is represented by means of a utility function $U(y)$ where abusing notation we assimilate income to consumption (see Chapter 2).

The individual faces the uncertainty of falling sick with a certain probability π. In such circumstance assume for simplicity that (s)he is unable to work, so that his/her income is reduced to y_s. Naturally, with probability $(1 - \pi)$, the individual is healthy, develops normal activity and obtains income y_h.

DEFINITION 10.1 (EXPECTED INCOME). Given the probability distribution over the two states the individual may face, we define his expected income as the *ex-ante* weighted average income, that is

$$E(y) = \pi y_s + (1 - \pi)y_h.$$

To illustrate, consider an individual having a wealth of €1,000 is uncertain of whether or not he will face some loss of, say, €100. Suppose the loss occurs with probability 0.3. The individual knows that at the end of the month, he will have either €1,000 (in the case of no loss) or €900 (in case of a loss of €100). He also knows that more often than not he suffers no loss. The concept of expected income accommodates into a single measure the information about the loss and its attached probability, by weighting each possible end value by its probability of occurrence. Thus, the expected value in this example is given by:

$$E(y) = 0.3(1,000 - 100) + 0.7(1,000) = 970.$$

Note that the expected income is an *ex-ante* concept. When the individual wakes up in the morning he is either healthy or sick, so that his *ex-post* income is either y_h or y_s.

The example can be generalized to any number of possible outcomes, where for each possible situation i, usually called "state of nature", we know the associated income, y_i, and probability of occurrence, π_i. Then, the expected value is defined as

$$E(y) = \sum_{i \in Y} \pi_i y_i,$$

where Y denotes the set of possible outcomes.

It may be that the variable of interest is best characterized by a continuous variable. In that case, for each possible value of the relevant variable, there is knowledge about its density function, denoted by $f(y)$, and the expected value is defined by

$$E(y) = \int_Y y f(y) dy,$$

where Y denotes the domain of the variable.

Regardless of the situation of the individual (sick or healthy), he or she obtains some income that yields satisfaction to the individual. Therefore we can introduce the concept of *utility of the expected income*:

DEFINITION 10.2 (UTILITY OF THE EXPECTED INCOME). Let $U(\cdot)$ denote the utility function of the individual. The utility associated with the expected income $E(y)$ is

$$U(E(y)) = U(\pi y_s + (1 - \pi)y_h).$$

To continue with the illustration above, assume $U(y) = \sqrt{(y)}$. Then, the utility of the expected income is,

$$U(E(y)) = U(970) = 31.145$$

The next important issue is to describe how individuals value uncertain situations. The concept of utility function extends itself naturally to the notion of *expected utility*. The value of an uncertain situation to an individual is the expected value of utility in each of the possible outcomes. Given that with probability π the individual obtains income y_s, with this probability he obtains satisfaction $U(y_s)$. Also, with probability $(1 - \pi)$ the associated utility is $U(y_h)$. Therefore, in a similar way as we computed the expected income we can define the *expected utility* of the individual.

DEFINITION 10.3 (EXPECTED UTILITY). Let π be the probability that an individual experiences a sickness episode. Then, his expected utility is the *ex-ante* weighted average utility, that is

$$EU = \pi U(y_s) + (1 - \pi)U(y_h).$$

Using the illustration above, the expected utility of our individual is given by

$$U(E(y)) = 0.3U(900) + 0.7U(1,000) = 0.3(30) + 0.7(31.623) = 31.136.$$

As before, we can generalize the concept of expected utility to any number of possible outcomes. Then, expected utility is defined as

$$EU = \sum_{i \in Y} \pi_i U(y_i).$$

When the variable of interest is continuous, and its density function is $f(y)$, the expected utility is expressed as

$$EU = \int_Y U(y)f(y)\,dy.$$

Note the crucial difference of expected utility relative to expected income: the role of the utility function.

So far, we have assumed that the utility of the individual depends exclusively on his/her level of income/consumption. That is, the only consequence of falling sick is a drop in income that induces a drop in consumption and thus a lower utility. However, other elements than income may affect the utility of the individual. We can think for example that being in a hospital also adds some cost in terms of discomfort that can be evaluated in monetary terms. Then, the utility function itself differs when the individual is healthy and sick. Formally, we say that the utility function of the individual depends on the level of income *and* on the state of nature (sick or healthy) he bears. Let us denote these utility functions as $U_s(y_s)$ and $U_h(y_h)$ when the individual is sick and healthy respectively. These define the *state-dependent utility* in the sick state and in the healthy state respectively. Then we can define the *expected state-dependent utility* as

DEFINITION 10.4   (EXPECTED STATE-DEPENDENT UTILITY).   Let $U_s(y_s)$ and $U_h(y_h)$ denote the individual's utilities when sick and healthy respectively. Then, expected state-dependent utility is the *ex-ante* weighted average state-dependent utility, where the weights are given by the probability of each state, that is,

$$EU = \pi U_s(y_s) + (1 - \pi)U_h(y_h).$$

As in the previous definitions, the expected stated-dependent utility can be generalized to an arbitrary number of states as

$$EU = \sum_{i \in Y} \pi_i U_i(y_i).$$

These concepts will be helpful in studying the behavior of an individual under the presence of uncertainty. We are interested in assessing the decision-making process of an individual when facing the uncertainty of falling sick. To do it, we also need to introduce two additional concepts, *uncertainty* and *risk*. They provide a different angle to the situation of the individual facing a certain probability of falling sick.

10.2   Risk and uncertainty

The notions of risk and uncertainty are present in many daily events. However, they are often confused. We refer to *uncertainty* as the lack of certainty. In other words, when there are several possible outcomes to a given situation. More formally,

DEFINITION 10.5   (UNCERTAINTY).   We say that an individual makes decisions under uncertainty when the probability distribution over the possible events is exogenous and thus beyond the control of the individual.

The way to measure uncertainty as the definition already hints at is through a probability distribution defined over the set of possible results.

   To illustrate consider the following example. When an individual falls sick he can be treated by a "good" physician or by a "bad" physician. The "good" physician is characterized by a 99 percent probability of a good diagnosis, and a probability of 1 percent of a wrong diagnosis. Instead, a "bad" physician produces correct diagnoses in 90 percent of cases and produces wrong diagnoses in 10 percent of cases. From the viewpoint of the patient, the physician's ability is not a decision variable. Naturally, wrong diagnostics are observable (the patient does not recover his health status) but a mistaken diagnostic does not prove lack of ability.

DEFINITION 10.6   (RISK).   We say that an individual makes decisions under risk when he can determine (and thus, affect) the probability distribution over the different states he may face.

Usually, a situation of risk also conveys the occurrence of a loss. Consider the following example. A car driver may decide to drive prudently or aggressively. When prudent an accident occurs with probability 1/100,000. When aggressive, his/her probability of accident raises until 1/10,000. Naturally, the loss associated with the accident involves damages to the own car, to other cars, injuries to him/herself and/or to other occupants, etc. From the viewpoint of the driver his/her style of driving is his/her decision. Therefore, the driver decides the probability distribution of having an accident. Naturally, the accident is an observable event. However, the occurrence of an accident does not imply that the driver is aggressive.

The concepts of risk and uncertainty although different may be related in the sense that an individual may face an uncertain situation without risk but there is no risk without uncertainty. Consider an individual fan of football. The winner of the World Cup is *ex-ante* uncertain, and unless the individual has bet on a winner, he faces no risk. However, if the individual bets for a particular team as winner of the World Cup, then *ex-ante* he would be facing an uncertain and risky situation where some amount of money is invested/risked for a possibly large return, but with a positive probability of losing it all. The decision of betting is under the control of the individual, however the winner of the competition is not.

Most of the analyses of the health care sector that we will study will involve risk. Following healthy habits, preventive care measures, and the like, are decisions taken by the individual to reduce the risk of sickness. However, the appearance of a sickness episode is beyond the control of the individual. From the perspective of the provision of health care services, physicians manage medical risk. This justifies the presence of a professional code of ethics governing the physician–patient relationship. Also, from the viewpoint of public health, efforts in primary prevention (vaccination campaigns, etc.) are required and there is an obligation to follow some procedures by all the populations at risk.

10.2.1 *Attitudes towards risk*

The previous examples of risky situations have contemplated an aggressive driver against a prudent driver, or a football fan gambling for his candidate to win a contest. Therefore, we face individuals with different attitudes toward risk. Technically, we distinguish three types of agents: *risk-averse* individuals, *risk-neutral* individuals, and *risk-loving* individuals.

To illustrate these attitudes consider an individual with a certain income y, who has the possibility to participate in a contest. If (s)he rejects participating, (s)he keeps his/her income at y. However, if (s)he participates in the contest with a probability that π loses and his/her income reduces to y_s, while with probability $(1 - \pi)$ wins and his/her income increases to y_h. His/her expected income is $E(y)$. To simplify the example, let's assume $y = E(y)$.

Our individual has a utility function continuous increasing in income, $U(y)$. Accordingly, the utility of income when not playing is $U(E(y))$. However, if (s)he participates in the contest, his/her expected utility is (as defined before) $EU = \pi U(y_s) + (1 - \pi)U(y_h)$. Therefore, the decision of the individual regarding the contest depends on the comparison between $U(E(y))$ and EU.

DEFINITION 10.7 (RISK AVERSION). We say that an individual is risk averse if the utility of expected income is higher than the expected utility of income. Formally, if

$$U(E(y)) > EU.$$

DEFINITION 10.8 (RISK LOVING). We say that an individual is a risk lover if the utility of expected income is lower than the expected utility of income. Formally, if

$$U(E(y)) < EU.$$

DEFINITION 10.9 (RISK NEUTRALITY). We say that an individual is risk neutral if the utility of expected income is equal to the expected utility of income. Formally, if

$$U(E(y)) = EU.$$

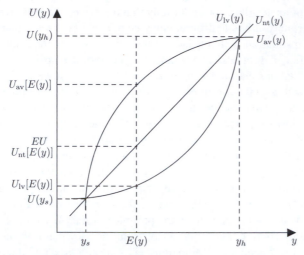

Figure 10.1 Three attitudes towards risk.

For a given individual, the comparison of those two magnitudes depends on the form of his utility function. Figure 10.1 represent the three attitudes. Consider the utility function $U_{av}(y)$. This is a strictly concave utility function: the utility of the expected income $U_{av}(E(y))$ is higher than the expected utility (of income y), EU. Therefore, a strictly concave utility function depicts a risk-averse individual. The utility function $U_{lv}(y)$ is the opposite case. It is strictly convex and the utility of the expected income $U_{lv}(E(y))$ is lower than the the expected utility (of income y), EU. Therefore, a strictly convex utility function describes a risk-loving individual. Finally, a risk-neutral individual is represented by a linear utility function.

The distinction across these types is intuitively illustrated by the following example. Take a simple game of throwing a balanced coin. Whenever heads results, the individual receives €100, whenever the result is tails, the individual pays €50. Since we are considering a balanced coin, the expected outcome from playing this game is $\frac{1}{2}(100) + \frac{1}{2}(-50) = €25$.

We can now ask people how much they are willing to pay to participate in this game. Those that announce €25 and actually pay €25 to participate are termed *risk neutral*. Those that announce more than €25 expect to sustain a loss in expected terms from participating. Then they must value the risk by itself so that the value they give to the game exceeds the resulting financial outcome. These individuals are termed *risk lovers*. Finally, we have the individuals who are willing to pay less than €25 to participate in the game. These are *risk averse* individuals.

The most common assumption is that people are risk averse and we will adopt it in the remainder of the text, unless otherwise stated.

The reason why we consider risk aversion to be a reasonable assumption is illustrated with the following example. Consider the lottery in which a coin is flipped until tails results. The lottery pays 2^n where n is the number of heads that have occurred before tails ends the lottery. Let us compute the expected value of this lottery. According to the definition of expected value, each possible outcome is weighted by its probability of occurrence:

$$E(y) = \sum_{t=1}^{\infty} 2^{t-1} \left(\frac{1}{2}\right)^t = \frac{1}{2} \sum_{t=1}^{\infty} 1 = \infty.$$

In the first throw of the coin, the individual may get 0 if tails while if heads shows, it continues. Each event occurs with probability 1/2. If the lottery continues, then with probability 1/2 tails results and the individual receives 2 (from the first throw continuation), and with probability 1/2 continues. Thus, from the start, it has probability 1/4 of receiving 2. The same reasoning can be applied to check the individual receives 4 with probability 1/8, and so on.

Computing the expected value, we obtain an infinite value. Since individuals are not continuously taking this lottery they are unwilling to pay a sizable amount to play such a lottery and thus their behavior cannot correspond to that of risk-neutral individuals.

10.2.2 Measures of risk aversion

The utility function obtained from the preferences of an individual are uniquely defined up to affine transformations (see Chapter 2). Accordingly, expected utility functions are also unique up to affine transformations.

Also, we have just associated risk aversion to a concave (expected) utility function, so that the more concave the utility function is, the more risk averse is the corresponding individual. Often, we will need to compare degrees of risk aversion of different individuals, so that we need to develop a measure of the concavity of their utility functions. This measure to be meaningful must be invariant to any affine transformation of the utility function. Arrow (1965) and Pratt (1964) proposed two measures of risk aversion. They are the *coefficient of absolute risk aversion*, also known as the *Arrow–Pratt measure of absolute risk aversion* and the *coefficient of relative risk aversion*, also known as the *Arrow–Pratt measure of relative risk aversion*.

When the utility function is concave over the whole domain of its argument, then we use the measure of absolute risk aversion. However, it may happen that for some subdomains of its argument, the utility function is concave and for other subdomains it is convex. Then, we use the measure of relative risk aversion.

DEFINITION 10.10 (ABSOLUTE RISK AVERSION). Let $U(x)$ be a utility function. The Arrow–Pratt measure of absolute risk aversion is defined by:

$$A(x) = \frac{-U''(x)}{U'(x)}$$

where U' and U'' denote the first and second derivatives respectively.

If $A(x)$ is decreasing in x, then $U(x)$ displays decreasing absolute risk aversion (DARA). If $A(x)$ is increasing in x, then $U(x)$ displays increasing absolute risk aversion (IARA). If $A(x)$ is constant in x, then $U(x)$ displays constant absolute risk aversion (CARA).

An example of a DARA utility function is $U(x) = \log(x)$, with $A(x) = 1/x$; an example of a IARA utility function is $U(X) = x - \alpha x^2$, where $\alpha > 0$. In this case, $A(x) = 2\alpha/(1 - 2\alpha x)$. Finally, an example of a CARA utility function is $U(x) = 1 - e^{-\alpha}x$ since $A(x) = \alpha$.

DEFINITION 10.11 (RELATIVE RISK AVERSION). Let $U(x)$ be a utility function. The Arrow–Pratt measure of relative risk aversion is defined by:

$$R(x) = xA(x) = \frac{-xU''(x)}{U'(x)}$$

Similarly as for absolute risk aversion, we can define constant relative risk aversion (CRRA), decreasing relative risk aversion (DRRA), and increasing relative risk aversion (IRRA).

10.3   Insurance

Generically, the health state of an individual is uncertain. Therefore, an individual faces an uncertain scenario where with some probability (s)he may fall sick and bears the risk of having to cope with an expenditure representing a significant proportion of his/her income when his/her capacity to earn income is diminished. If on top the individual is risk averse, the usual solution to such problem is insurance. Let us then start by defining an insurance contract.

DEFINITION 10.12   (INSURANCE CONTRACT).   Insurance in general refers to a contract between an individual and a third-party payer (the insurer) by which the insured agrees to pay the insurer a certain price in exchange for a payout to be made to the insured when he suffers some well-defined losses. This contract alters the variance of the income distribution of the individual.

EXAMPLE 10.1   Consider an individual owning assets valued in €21,000 (say, a car). With probability of one percent the individual faces a loss of €6,000 (due to an accident), so that with probability 0.01 his/her wealth will be €15,000 and with probability $(1 - \pi) = 0.99$ his/her wealth will be €21,000.

An insurance company offers our individual the following contract: against a payment of €60, the insurer will reimburse the individual €6,000 if an accident occurs. This contract alters the distribution of income of the individual. Now, with probability $\pi = 0.01$ the insured obtains income $21,000 - 60 + 6,000 - 6,000 = €20,940$. Also with probability $(1 - \pi) = 0.99$ the individual obtains income $21,000 - 60 = €20,940$. Therefore, in this example the individual maintains his/her income constant regardless of the occurrence of an accident.

This example has a direct translation in terms of health care insurance. Our individual with probability $\pi = 0.01$ becomes sick and suffers a loss valued at €6,000. While healthy (with probability $(1 - \pi) = 0.99$), his/her income is €21,000. The health insurance contract states that against a fixed payment of €60, the individual obtains an indemnity of €6,000 from the insurer.

An obvious question is why the insurers are willing to take up (part of) the risk that their clients are willing to pay to avoid? The answer relies on the law of large numbers. An insurance company by signing a large number of contracts is able to pool risks. The law of large numbers basically says that the larger the number of a certain type, the more precise is the average as a prediction of such an event to occur. An individual with a particular profile (age, sex, . . .) with hypertension does not know whether (s)he will suffer a stroke next year. However, the average of the population of that profile is a good approximation (the larger the population, the better) of such an event. The discrepancy between the average and the individual occurrence of the event allows the insurance company to obtain profits. The same argument applies to a public insurer but allowing for redefining a budget balance condition. For expositional simplicity we will use private insurers as our reference point.

10.3.1   The elements of an insurance contract

To be more precise, let us define the elements that characterize an insurance contract.

Premium   is the amount paid by the insured to the insurer.

Coverage   is the amount paid by the insurer to the insured when the loss materializes.

Co-insurance   is a cost-sharing mechanism by which the insured assumes a proportion of the loss when it occurs. The proportion borne by the insured is called co-payment.

Deductibles   are also a cost-sharing mechanism by which the insurer commits to bear a fixed amount of the loss irrespective of the co-insurance. The insurance does not apply until the individual pays the deductible.

Co-insurance and deductibles are often used together. A typical health insurance contract requires the patient to pay a certain amount of money out of pocket and a percentage of the remaining costs of treatment. The economic logic behind these cost-sharing mechanisms is to provide the right incentives to individuals to avoid excessive visits to the physician and at the same time to make the patient aware of the cost of the treatment provided. The effects of deductibles and co-payments on the demand for insurance are studied in Section 4.1 of Chapter 11.

Figure 10.2 will help us to understand how much individuals are willing and able to pay for insurance. Let us assume that an individual has a strictly concave utility function $U(y)$. With probability π the individual is sick and obtains income y_s yielding utility $U(y_s)$. With probability $(1 - \pi)$ the individual is healthy and obtains income y_h from which obtains utility $U(y_h)$. Accordingly, his/her expected income is $E(y)$ and the utility of this expected income is $U(E(y))$. Let $y_h - y_s$ represent the cost of treatment to recover the healthy status. We follow Morris *et al.* (2007) and define three concepts related to the insurance premium.

DEFINITION 10.13 (TOTAL PREMIUM). The total premium is the maximum amount of money the individual is prepared to pay for health insurance.

Any individual will contract insurance if it allows him/her to obtain more utility than otherwise. The maximum level of utility achievable is $U(y_h)$. The individual's expected utility without insurance is given by $\pi U(y_s) + (1 - \pi)U(y_h) = EU$. Accordingly, where the payment leaves the individual indifferent to contracting or not, insurance is precisely the one

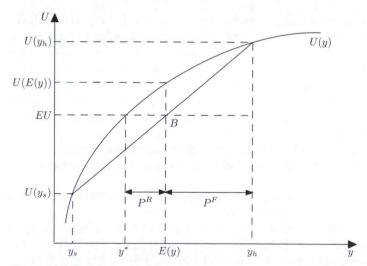

Figure 10.2 Insurance premium.

corresponding to the difference between $U(y_h)$ and EU. The level of income yielding a utility level of EU is y^*. Therefore, the individual would be willing to pay at most $y_h - y^*$ to get insured and thus maintain his/her income y_h. Any premium above this threshold would imply a net loss of utility associated with the contracting of insurance, and the individual would give insurance up. Any premium below that threshold allows the individual to obtain a net gain in utility terms by contracting insurance.

This total premium can be regarded as the composition of two types of premiums: the fair premium and the risk premium.

DEFINITION 10.14 (FAIR PREMIUM). The fair premium is the amount of income corresponding to the expected loss should the individual remain uninsured.

In terms of Figure 10.2, the expected loss of income when sick and uninsured is $\pi(y_h - y_s)$. To represent this income in the figure, note that

$$\pi(y_h - y_s) = \pi y_h - \pi y_s = y_h - ((1 - \pi)y_h + \pi y_s) = y_h - E(y).$$

Note also that the fair premium corresponds to the premium that a perfectly competitive insurer would set because it yields zero expected profits. The expected profits of the insurer $(E\Pi)$ are

$$E\Pi(P) = \pi(P - (y_h - y_s)) + (1 - \pi)P,$$

where P denotes the premium. Evaluating the expected profits at the fair premium, we obtain,

$$E\Pi(P^F) = \pi[\pi(y_h - y_s) - (y_h - y_s)] + (1 - \pi)[\pi(y_h - y_s)] = 0.$$

DEFINITION 10.15 (RISK PREMIUM). The risk premium is the amount of income that leaves the consumer indifferent to contracting insurance and guaranteeing a certain level of income with certainty.

Risk aversion implies that individuals are willing to pay more than just the expected loss from sickness. In terms of Figure 10.2, note that the level of expected utility EU corresponds to the composition of the uncertain utility levels associated with the occurrence of a sickness episode. Also the value of EU would be achieved by the individual should (s)he have had a level of income y^* with certainty. In other words, the individual is indifferent between an uncertain scenario yielding expected income $E(y)$ and a scenario where (s)he obtains income y^* with certainty. Formally, $EU = U(y^*)$. The difference among the corresponding income levels is the risk premium, $P^R = E(y) - y^*$.

We can recall the example 10.1 to illustrate the different concepts of premium. An individual owns assets value in €21,000 and with probability of one percent faces a loss of €6,000.

If the individual remains uninsured, his/her expected loss is of €6,000 with a probability one percent, that is €60. Accordingly, $P^F = 60$.

To compute the risk premium let $U(y) = \sqrt{(y)}$. Then, y^* is the solution of the equation $EU = U(y)$, where $EU = (0.01)\sqrt{15,000} + (0.99)\sqrt{21,000} = 144.7$. Therefore $y^* = 144.7^2 = 20,935$, and the risk premium $P^R = E(y) - y^* = 20,940 - 20,935 = €5$.

The total premium is the sum of fair premium and risk premium, i.e. $R^T = 60 + 5 = 65€$.

10.3.2 *Optimal demand for health care insurance*

We study the optimal demand for health care insurance of an individual. Let us assume that our individual with probability π is sick and obtains income y_s and with probability $(1 - \pi)$ is healthy and enjoys income y_h. We follow Zweifel *et al.* (2009, ch. 5) and assume that when sick the cost of treatment is M. The individual preferences are represented by a strictly concave utility function $U(y)$, so that our individual is risk averse and thus is willing to contract health care insurance. The simplest set-up describes a contract by two elements, the premium P and the indemnity $I \in [0, M]$. We assume away co-insurance and deductibles. Also, we assume that the insurer does not incur in any costs and maximizes expected profits. The individual in turn, maximizes expected utility.

After contracting insurance, the disposable income of the individual is $\hat{y}_s = y_s - P + I - M$ and $\hat{y}_h = y_h - P$, in the sick and healthy states respectively. Therefore, the problem of the individual is,

$$\max_{P,I} EU = \pi U(\hat{y}_s) + (1 - \pi)U(\hat{y}_h).$$

To further simplify the problem assume that the market for insurance is perfectly competitive so that insurer's expected profits are zero. Expected profits for the insurer are given by $\pi(P - I) + (1 - \pi)P = P - \pi I$. Therefore, a competitive insurer will set the premium proportional to the indemnity, that is $P = \pi I$, where the proportionality is given by the probability of a sickness episode. This is the *fair premium* as defined above. The logic behind the fair premium is that if the insurer sets a lower premium it will incur losses because its revenues will not cover the expected indemnities that it will face. If instead the insurer sets a premium higher than the fair premium it will obtain positive profits, thus attracting the entry of new competitors in the market.

Let us now study the optimal insurance coverage I^*. Introducing the expression of the premium in the individual's income values we obtain, $\hat{y}_s = y_s + (1 - \pi)I - M$ and $\hat{y}_h = y_h - \pi I$. The optimal demand for health insurance coverage reduces to choosing the level of indemnity solving the following problem

$$\max_{I} EU = \pi U(\hat{y}_s) + (1 - \pi)U(\hat{y}_h). \tag{10.1}$$

The first-order condition for an interior solution is

$$\frac{\partial EU}{\partial I} = \pi \frac{\partial U}{\partial y}\Big|_{\hat{y}_s} \frac{\partial y_s}{\partial I} + (1 - \pi)\frac{\partial U}{\partial y}\Big|_{\hat{y}_h} \frac{\partial y_h}{\partial I}$$

$$= (1 - \pi)\pi \frac{\partial U}{\partial y}\Big|_{\hat{y}_s} - \pi(1 - \pi)\frac{\partial U}{\partial y}\Big|_{\hat{y}_h} = 0 \tag{10.2}$$

We offer two alternative ways to visualize the optimal insurance coverage level. The first one is represented in Figure 10.3(a). Note that income in the healthy state is decreasing in the indemnity, while income in the sick state is increasing in the indemnity. Looking at the first term of (10.2) referred to as the sick state, it is easy to verify that every euro of indemnity conveys extra income when the individual falls sick. However, the marginal expected utility of every extra euro of coverage diminishes. Therefore, the expression $(1 - \pi)\pi(\partial U/\partial y)|_{\hat{y}_s}$ describes a downward sloping curve in the space represented in Figure 10.3(a).

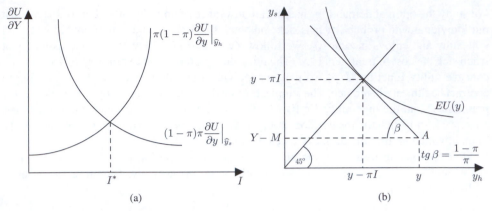

Figure 10.3 Optimal insurance coverage.

The second term of (10.2) refers to the healthy state. Every euro of coverage conveys less income for the individual while staying healthy. Given that marginal expected utility is decreasing (due to risk aversion) the decrease in income translates into higher marginal expected utility. Therefore, the expression $\pi(1-\pi)(\partial U/\partial y)|_{\hat{y}_h}$ is an increasing curve in the space represented in Figure 10.3(a).

The combination of both effects determines the optimal level of coverage at the point where the two curves intersect, thus satisfying the first order condition. The second-order condition is trivially satisfied. Note that the optimum level of coverage is characterized by the equality of the marginal expected utilities in the healthy and sick states.

The second alternative depicts the optimal coverage in the space of incomes in the healthy and sick spaces and it is illustrated in Figure 10.3(b). Recall that in the healthy state without insurance the individual enjoys an income $y_h = y$, and with insurance his/her income is $\hat{y}_h = y - \pi I$. Similarly, when sick the individual has income $y_s = y_M$ without insurance and $\hat{y}_s = y + (1-\pi)I - M$ when insured. Therefore, in the initial situation (prior to contracting insurance) the individual is at point A. Also, solving one equation for I and substituting it into the other one allows us to obtain the budget constraint. It is given by

$$y_s = \frac{y}{\pi} - M - \frac{1-\pi}{\pi} y_h.$$

Next, we represent a representative indifference curve. Its slope is given by

$$\left.\frac{dy_s}{dy_h}\right|_{dEU=0} = -\frac{\partial EU/\partial y_h}{\partial EU/\partial y_s} = -\frac{1-\pi}{\pi}\frac{(\partial U/\partial y)|_{y_h}}{(\partial U/\partial y)|_{y_s}}$$

Note that the slope of the indifference curve and of the budget line coincide at the point where $(\partial U/\partial y)|_{y_h} = (\partial U/\partial y)|_{y_s}$. Therefore, the optimal insurance coverage is characterized by the equality of incomes across the healthy and sick states. That is, the optimal indemnity satisfies $y - M + (1-\pi)I = y - \pi I$ or $I^* = M$. Accordingly, under perfect competition, the individual optimally contracts full coverage, and guarantees an income of $y^* = y - \pi M$ with certainty.

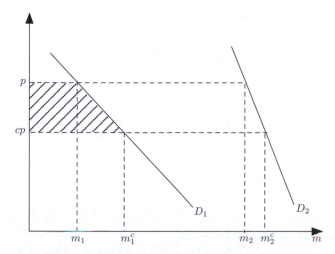

Figure 10.4 Co-payments and demand for health care (1).

10.3.3 *Insurance and demand elasticity*

We have argued that contracting insurance affects the variance of the income distribution of the individual. Therefore, we should expect that the presence of insurance also alters the demand for health care services. A consequence of contracting insurance is that the insured faces a lower price for the service. Price is zero in case of full coverage, but more generally the presence of co-payments and deductibles mean that the insured pays a price lower than the market price. Consider an insurance contract contemplating a co-payment $c \in (0, 1]$. Then, the insured pays a proportion c of the price of the service and the insurer pays the complementary proportion $(1 - c)$. Let p denote the price of the treatment for a certain illness. Figure 10.4 illustrates the effect of insurance according to the elasticity of demand. Consider two illnesses, one minor (illness 1) the other major (illness 2). For any given price, it should be expected that demand for treatment of the severe illness be more inelastic than the demand for treatment of the minor sickness. To simplify the argument, let us assume that both treatments have the same price p. The patient pays a price cp if insured and the price p otherwise. In terms of Figure 10.4 the insured patient increases demand from m_1 to m_1^c when (s)he suffers a minor sickness, for example, when (s)he suffers a migraine and is uninsured. (S)he simply stays at home and possibly buys some suitable drug. However, the insured patient may decide to go to the emergency unit of the nearest hospital. When the individual is affected by a severe sickness episode (say, a stroke), (s)he has to be treated in a hospital. If uninsured, the patient may be willing to share the room, while if insured (s)he may prefer to have a single room (this would correspond with demands m_2 and m_2^c). In both situations, mild or serious sickness, the presence of insurance increases demand because the patient pays a lower price. How much the demand increases depends on its elasticity (as we studied in Chapter 2), which in turn depends on the severity of the sickness episode.

The presence of insurance has an important additional effect on the demand for health care services. Consider an individual with a probability π of falling sick that holds an insurance contract contemplating a co-payment c. Also, assume the cost of treatment has a unit price p_1. If the demand for treatment of the individual is perfectly inelastic as shown in Figure 10.5(a), their demand for treatment will not be distorted by the presence of insurance.

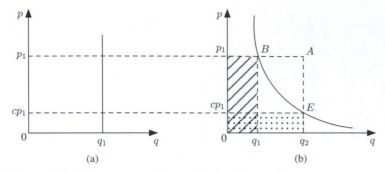

Figure 10.5 Co-payments and demand for health care (2).

However, when the demand is sensitive to the price as in Figure 10.5(b), the presence of insurance conveys a differentiated behavior of the patient.

If the patient is not insured, he or she pays the full cost of the treatment. At the price p_1, the individual demands q_1 units of treatment and the bill to be paid is represented by the shaded area $0p_1Bq_1$.

If the patient has contracted a health care insurance, (s)he pays the price cp_1. At this price the patient demands q_2 units of treatment and pays a bill of cp_1q_2€ represented by the area $0cp_1Eq_2$ (and the insurer bears the remaining cost $(1-c)p_1q_2$€). Comparing the two areas, we realize that the decision to contract insurance allows the patient to consume more treatment with a lower bill. This example illustrates three issues that are important:

- The differentiated behavior of the insured and uninsured patient identifies the moral hazard effect that will be studied in detail in Chapter 11.
- If the insurance company charges a premium cp_1q_1 it will default because the revenues will not cover the expected costs of treatment. Formally, $cp_1q_1 < cp_1q_2$.
- If the insurer charges a premium cp_1q_2 it leaves the consumer indifferent between contracting insurance or remain uninsured.

These observations support the fact the (i) insurance companies offer contracts with larger coverage for those services with more inelastic demand; (ii) insurance companies will offer contracts for those services with more inelastic demands and only in second place contracts for services with more elastic demands.

10.3.4   *Optimal partial coverage*

We have studied the optimal demand for insurance when the insurer is competitive and bears no cost. Then, the optimal contract is characterized by a fair premium and full coverage. When administrative and other costs of providing insurance are introduced in the analysis, in general they are summarized in a so-called *loading factor F*. In this case, the premium charged by the competitive insurer would be the sum of the fair premium and the loading factor. That is, the premium is no longer actuarially fair but higher, that is the premium rate P will be greater than the probability of falling sick π. The consequence of this higher premium is that the individual optimally with contract partial coverage. To see the argument let us reconsider the maximizing problem (10.1), where now $\hat{y}_s = y_s - \pi I + I - M$ and $\hat{y}_h = y_h - \pi I$.

The first-order condition for an interior solution is (see Barros 2009, ch. 11)

$$\frac{\partial EU}{\partial I} = (1-P)\pi \left.\frac{\partial U}{\partial y}\right|_{\hat{y}_s} - P(1-\pi)\left.\frac{\partial U}{\partial y}\right|_{\hat{y}_h} = 0,$$

or $\dfrac{(\partial U/\partial y)|_{y_s}}{(\partial U/\partial y)|_{y_h}} = \dfrac{P(1-\pi)}{(1-P)\pi}$

Given that $P > \pi$, it follows that $1 - \pi > 1 - P$, so that $P(1-\pi) > (1-P)\pi$ and accordingly,

$$(\partial U/\partial y)|_{y_s} > (\partial U/\partial y)|_{y_h}. \tag{10.3}$$

From the concavity of $U(\cdot)$, it follows that the inequality (10.3) can only be satisfied if $y_s < y_h$ or $I < M$. Summarizing, when the premium rate P is higher than the fair one, the individual optimally contracts partial coverage. This is a general result for private and public insurers.

10.3.5 Compulsory insurance

Compulsory insurance was initiated in Germany in the late years of the nineteenth century under the government of von Bismarck and has been widely adopted in Europe, part of Asia, and some other countries like Canada, Australia, New Zealand, and Chile.

Essentially, under a compulsory health insurance system any individual has free access (up to some cost sharing) to medical care from any provider participating in the system. In turn, the cost of medical care is financed through taxation.

There is a large body of literature debating efficiency, equity, and quality issues in the provision of health care services through compulsory insurance. Barr (1989) claims the efficiency role of social insurance based on the fact that private insurance markets fail to offer efficient cover against risks like unemployment or inflation. Then,

> social insurance in an industrialised country exists not just to facilitate any redistributive aims one may (or may not) have, but to do things which private insurance markets for technical reasons, would either not do at all, or would do inefficiently. Social insurance is necessary for efficiency reasons, and would continue to be necessary even if all distributional problems, by some process or another, had been solved.
>
> (p. 59)

One of the technical problems to achieve efficiency in private (insurance) markets is the presence of externalities. In wealthy societies one such externality shows in the form of *altruism* supporting consensus for universal access to health care services, particularly for low-income groups. Zweifel *et al.* (2009) note that the altruistic behavior give rise to free riding by individuals close to the poverty threshold, and argue that compulsory insurance solves this problem. The argument goes as follows: if society decides that low-income individuals are eligible to obtain free access to health care when falling sick, this gives incentives to individuals close enough to the income threshold not to contract insurance. If such an individual has a minor disease with a low-cost treatment, the saving of the premium offsets the cost of treatment. If the individual requires a high-cost treatment, then his/her income will fall under the threshold and will be eligible for the subsidy. Accordingly, such an individual *ex-ante* can obtain a higher level of expected utility without buying insurance and free riding on society.

To tackle this problem Zweifel *et al.* (2009, ch. 5.3) propose to include three additional assumptions to the model of demand of insurance studied above. These are: (i) all individuals are guaranteed a minimum income y_{min}; (ii) individuals are heterogeneous in their gross income, but are homogeneous in their probability of falling sick (π), and the cost of treatment (M); and (iii) treatment is provided to any sick individual. Individuals pay for the treatment and those insured obtain the indemnity (I) from the insurer. If the income of an individual after paying for the treatment is lower than y_{min}, the government covers the difference. Therefore, the income of a sick individual is now defined as

$$y_s = \max\{y - P - M + I; y_{min}\}.$$

Assuming a fair premium $P = \pi I$, the expected utility of an individual is

$$EU = (1 - \pi)U(Y - \pi I) + \pi U(\max\{y - M + I(1 - \pi); y_{min}\}).$$

To study the optimal demand for insurance coverage, we have to distinguish two types of individuals. Those whose gross income $y - M$ lies above (or at) the threshold y_{min}, and those whose gross income lies below. The former behave according to the model studied above and contract optimal coverage $I^* = M$.

Let us now look at the incentives to contract insurance of the individuals below the poverty line. For these individuals, their expected utility is,

$$EU = (1 - \pi)U(y - \pi I) + \pi U(y_{min}).$$

That is, in a sickness episode their utility is independent of I. Therefore, the incentives to contract insurance for these individuals rely on whether their expected utility increases or decreases with insurance. Let us define the following coverage threshold $\hat{I}$ characterizing the individual whose income is precisely y_{min}:

$$\hat{I} \equiv \frac{y_{min} - y + M}{1 - \pi} \tag{10.4}$$

It is straightforward to verify that the expected utility is decreasing for $I < \hat{I}$ and increasing otherwise. Technically, there are two local optima $I = 0$ and $I = M$, so that what local optimum dominates depends on the level of income of the individual. This critical level of income is characterized by the indifferent individual, that is the one whose expected utility coincides with and without insurance. Formally, we compute

$$EU[I = M] - EU[I = 0] = U(y - \pi M) - ((1 - \pi)U(y) + \pi U(y_{min})).$$

This difference is increasing in y, so that there must be a critical level $\hat{y}$ such that

$$I^* = \begin{cases} 0 & \text{if } y < \hat{y} \\ M & \text{if } y \geq \hat{y} \end{cases}$$

That is, (very) low income individuals do not contract insurance (but their health care expenses are financed by the government), while individuals whose income lies in the interval $y \in (\hat{y}, y_{\min})$ contract full insurance because the transfer they receive from the government offsets the cost of insurance.

Next, we look at the incentives of the individuals with income $y \in (y_{\min}, y_{\min} + M)$. In principle, they can afford to contract insurance. However we must distinguish two subsets, according to income being above or below $y_{\min} + \pi M$.

Consider individuals with income $y = y_{\min} + \pi M$. Following a similar argument as before, we can compute

$$EU[I = M] - EU[I = 0] = U(y_{\min}) - ((1 - \pi)U(y_{\min} + \pi M) + \pi U(y_{\min})) < 0.$$

Therefore, this segment of population gives up contracting insurance and free rides on the rest of society due to the government's commitment to guarantee a minimum level of income $y_{\min}$. The same argument holds for individuals with income larger and smaller than $y_{\min} + \pi M$. They would qualify for the government's subsidy if they would contract full insurance, but prefer the implicit insurance associated with the government's commitment to guarantee the income level $y_{\min}$. Figure 10.6 summarizes the discussion.

Note that a free rider contributes $y - y_{\min}$ to the cost of his or her treatment, so that the government covers the remaining part of the cost, that is $T = M - (y - y_{\min})$. The expected value of this transfer to maintain free riders' income above $y_{\min}$ is

$$E(T) = \pi(M - (y - y_{\min})). \tag{10.5}$$

Accordingly, a free rider's expected income is

$$E(y^{FR}) = (1 - \pi)y + \pi y_{\min} = y - \pi M + E(T), \tag{10.6}$$

and his expected utility is

$$EU^{FR} = (1 - \pi)U(y) + \pi U(y_{\min})$$

So far we have seen that guaranteeing a minimum level of income generates free-riding behavior so that some individuals able to afford insurance give it up. The question is to design a mechanism to correct this undesirable behavior. Zweifel *et al.* (2009) propose to introduce compulsory insurance. Trivially, compulsory insurance eliminates the possibility of free riding. Its virtue is that the scheme proposed allows to achieve a Pareto superior allocation, or in other words improves the efficiency of the system.

Let us now introduce compulsory insurance at premium πM. To accept the obligation of contracting insurance free riders must be given a certain small compensation τ. Accordingly, a free rider's income will be $y - \pi M + \tau$. The amount of the transfer τ must be set at the

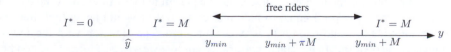

Figure 10.6 Free riding on insurance.

level at which the free rider's utility from his income equates his expected utility without insurance. In other words, τ is defined as the solution of

$$U(y - \pi M + \tau) = EU^{FR}. \tag{10.7}$$

Also risk-averse individuals are willing to pay a positive risk premium ρ in exchange for a guaranteed level of income. Given the definition of risk premium above, it is defined as

$$U(E(y^{FR}) - \rho) = EU^{FR}. \tag{10.8}$$

Combining (10.7) and (10.8) we obtain,

$$U(y - \pi M + \tau) = U(E(y^{FR}) - \rho). \tag{10.9}$$

Given the properties of the utility function, equation (10.9) can only be satisfied if

$$y - \pi M + \tau = E(y^{FR}) - \rho, \quad \text{or}$$

$$y - \pi M + \tau = y - \pi M + E(T),$$

where we have used (10.6). Solving for τ, we obtain $\tau = E(T) - \rho$. Given that $\rho > 0$, it follows that $\tau < E(T)$.

Summarizing, without compulsory insurance the expected value of the transfer, $E(T)$, to maintain free riders' income above y_{min} is given by (10.5). With compulsory insurance at premium πM, free riders must receive a transfer ρ to accept the mandate with the property that their utility is kept constant. Transfer ρ is smaller than the expected transfer $E(T)$. Given that these transfers are financed by taxpayers, it follows that the introduction of a compulsory insurance achieves a Pareto improvement.

Therefore, the free rider problem provides a rationale for compulsory health insurance. However as Zweifel *et al.* (2009, p. 171) note

> [i]t needs to be emphasized, however, that this is no inherent market failure but rather a problem caused by government interference in the first place. Without the implicit insurance provided by the government in the form of a minimum income, more individuals could be expected to buy full insurance. But those who are unable to afford health insurance would not be able to finance their treatment costs.

10.3.6   Risk selection

In any society there is a wide variety of individuals with different health conditions. We have seen that individuals' risk aversion gives rise to the demand for health care insurance. Regardless of the fact that the insurer may be profit or nonprofit, a high-risk individual will hardly be profitable for the insurer because the expected expenses will offset the premium paid. In other words, if the insurer could charge the premium that would cover the expected expenses (i.e. apply the price equal to marginal cost rule), it would be so high that most likely the individual would choose to remain uninsured. The situation with the low-risk individuals is the opposite. In general, an insurance company expects to lose money on high-risk clients and make profits on low-risk individuals. Therefore, in a competitive market we should expect the insurers to try to select low-risk individuals only or at least to have a sufficiently small proportion of high-risk individuals insured to guarantee positive profits. This activity is known in the jargon of the insurance literature as *cream-skimming*, and insurers try to perform it by offering benefit packages attractive for low-risk and unattractive for high-risk individuals. Besides cream-skimming, risk selection is also linked to adverse selection on the part of consumers. We tackle this issue in Chapter 11.

Shen and Ellis (2002) quantify the additional profit that can be gained from using risk selection mechanisms. Using data from 1992 and 1993, they find that the overall profit increase ranges from $68 to $260 million depending on the risk selection system used and the information the payer has about their own propensity to use medical services.

A side issue we are not going into is *underwriting*. This refers to risk selection and risk classification. Evaluating all available information on an applicant allows the insurer to classify him under a risk type. Then, according to this classification a contract (premium, deductibles, co-payments) is designed. The American Academy of Actuaries (2009) contains a non-technical review of the fundamentals of risk selection and risk classification.

From a societal perspective, discriminating individuals by the risk type is seen as undesirable. Regulating the insurance market banning premium discrimination would induce high risks to contract insurance. However, low risks would not be willing to contract insurance to avoid cross-subsidization of the high-risk individuals. Assume then that insurance is compulsory. Government intervention to avoid risk selection can impose an *open enrollment* policy so that insurers cannot reject high-risk applicants, and/or can regulate the content of benefit package to make it attractive for both high- and low-risk individuals. Also, the regulator can link the reimbursement scheme to the risk profile undertaken by the insurer, introducing rewards for enrolling high risks and penalizing cream-skimming activities (see Eggleston 2000). Zweifel *et al.* (2009, ch. 7) present a formal study of the impact of these measures on reducing risk selection.

The interested reader is directed to Ellis (2008), Glazer and McGuire (2006), or Van de Ven and Ellis (2000) for reviews of the literature on risk adjustment. Empirical studies on risk adjustment systems in US, Germany, the Netherlands, and Switzerland and on using supplementary insurance as a risk selection tool in Belgium, Germany, Israel, the Netherlands, and Switzerland are found in Schneider *et al.* (2008) and Paolucci *et al.* (2007) respectively.

11 Contracts and asymmetric information

The market for health care involves the interaction of three types of agents: patients, providers, and third-party payers with different levels of information. These information asymmetries give rise to the agency problem that is the central topic of this chapter. The study of how to provide incentives to the different agents to achieve the objective of an efficient provision of health care services, and the conflict of objectives due to the information asymmetry, complete the contents of the chapter. The study of the supplier-induced demand in the health care sector illustrates the main arguments.

In previous chapters we have argued that supply, demand, and financing of health care services involve three types of agents: *patients* who do not decide upon the service they receive, nor pay for it; *providers* who demand a service that they do not consume and are paid by a third party who does not consume the service demanded either; and *insurers* who pay for a service that they do not consume. These links across consumers (patients), producers (providers), and payers (insurers) appear because the level of information available to the agents differ. For instance, the insurance company has less information on the health status of the individual contracting health insurance than the individual themselves. In fact, the separation between receiving a service and paying for it has given rise to the term *third-party payer* that is unique to health care. In a similar vein, the patient has less information about his or her health condition than the physician after proper examination and diagnosis. We refer to this phenomenon as *imperfect information*. In turn, these information asymmetries imply that agents cannot decide by themselves. Instead, they have to delegate the decision to another (better-informed) party. Accordingly, there appears an *agency relationship*. Finally, to implement those cross-links, *contracts* are signed to guarantee as much as possible that the deciding party does its best to pursue the interests of the other party. The study of how to design these contracts, and what incentives have to be provided to the parties involved is the domain of the *economics of information*. Macho-Stadler and Pérez-Castrillo (2001) present a complete analysis of the elements of the economics of information. The interested reader may also see Folland *et al.* (2009, Chapters 9 and 10).

11.1 The problem of information

The differences in the information levels of the agents in a market give rise to different definitions of information. We distinguish among perfect, complete, and symmetric information.

DEFINITION 11.1 (PERFECT INFORMATION). In an economy, information is perfect if all of its agents are aware of all the history of decisions taken in the past by all agents in the market.

Perfect information in economics is similar to the assumption of a frictionless world in physics, or a zero-dimension point in geometry. It is a useful benchmark for market decision-makers.

DEFINITION 11.2 (IMPERFECT INFORMATION). Information in an economy is imperfect when it is not perfect.

This means that we only need a single agent lacking some information to be in a set-up where information is imperfect.

DEFINITION 11.3 (COMPLETE INFORMATION). An economy has complete information when there are no random elements in the relationships among its agents.

DEFINITION 11.4 (INCOMPLETE INFORMATION). An economy where there is at least one agent uncertain of any element relevant in the decision making is said to have incomplete information.

Often, consumers are uncertain about the evolution of the prices of some goods, or investors are uncertain about the price of the shares of some companies. These are examples of markets with incomplete information.

DEFINITION 11.5 (SYMMETRIC INFORMATION). Information in an economy is said to be symmetric when all agents share exactly the same information.

Note that perfect information is necessarily symmetric. Imperfect information is also symmetric when all agents share the same uncertainty.

DEFINITION 11.6 (ASYMMETRIC INFORMATION). Information is asymmetric when different agents have different levels of information.

To illustrate these definitions, let us consider the following examples.

EXAMPLE 11.1 (COMPLETE INFORMATION). Consider the interaction between two hospitals trying to attract patients. In this competitive process, let us assume that both hospitals consider the possibility of purchasing a new MRI device. If none or both buy it, patients perceive the two hospitals as identical and demand is spread evenly between them. If only one hospital acquires the MRI device, that one improves its quality image and attracts a larger share of patients. In any event, information is complete because the decision of whether or not to buy the new device is not subject to any random element. However information may be perfect or not according to whether or not each hospital observes the decision of its rival. If one hospital takes its decision before the other, then it is natural to assume that the decision is observed and thus information would be perfect. If decisions to buy the new MRI device are simultaneous, then it is hardly possible that the decision of one hospital is observed by the rival hospital. Thus, information would be imperfect. Figure 11.1 illustrates the two scenarios in a decision tree diagram. Hospitals are denoted as H1 and H2, and b and nb represent the decision to buy and not to buy the device. Finally, numbers represent the split of patients between hospitals, the top number corresponding to H1.

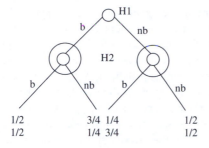

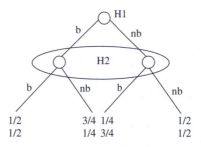

Complete and perfect information   Complete and imperfect information

Figure 11.1 Complete information.

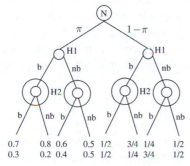

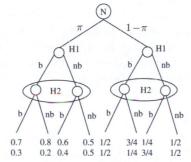

Incomplete and perfect information   Incomplete and imperfect information

Figure 11.2 Incomplete information.

EXAMPLE 11.2 (INCOMPLETE INFORMATION). Let us consider again the two hospitals deciding whether to acquire or not the new MRI device. Let us assume now that for hospital H1 the decision depends on the appointment of a new manager still to be selected. Let us assume that with probability π the new manager will have an aggressive personality, and with probability $1 - \pi$, he will have a soft personality. In this case there is a random element in the game of interaction between the two hospitals. Therefore, information is incomplete. Figure 11.2 illustrates the decision trees when information is incomplete and perfect or imperfect.

11.1.1 Information and agency

When information is *asymmetric*, it follows that one party is better informed than the other (and assume that it is too costly for the under-informed party to acquire the missing information). In this set-up, the under-informed party may be willing to hire the services of the informed party to take a decision on its behalf. In other words, the under-informed individual *delegates* to the informed one the decision making. This is called an *agency relationship*. This delegation of decision making is formalized in a *contract*, where the contracting party (the under-informed individual) is called *principal*, and the contracted party (the informed individual) is called *agent*. The contract specifies the obligations of the two parties and the transfers to be made under different contingencies. The contract can only be enforceable if its terms are verifiable, that is if the values of the variables specified in the contract are observable and can be proved before a court of law.

We say that the agency relationship is perfect, or that the *agent is perfect*, when the objectives of both parties are aligned, or, more generally, when the agent gives up his/her own interests to behave "as if" (s)he were the principal. In general, though, the interests of principal and agent will not be aligned, so that the contract will have to include incentives to minimize the deviation of the agent from the objectives of the principal. A common example of the agency relationship is that of a patient and a physician. In the event of a disease an individual (patient) contracts the diagnostic and treatment services of a physician to recover healthy status. The patient is the principal party. His or her lack of information about how to recover a health status leads him or her to delegate in the physician (the agent) the decision making. The physician is better placed *ex ante* through his/her knowledge, training and experience to evaluate the health status of the patient and the effectiveness of a treatment. Note that the objectives of the patient and the physician are not aligned. The patient wants to be healthy again regardless of any other consideration (remember that he or she is insured). However, the physician has to put in costly effort to obtain the proper diagnosis and select the adequate treatment. In other words, the patient requires the maximum effort from the physician, and the physician wants to minimize effort. Thus, the principal, in offering the contract to the agent, will have to provide enough incentives so that the interests of the principal prevail upon the interests of the agent.

11.1.2 A formal model

Consider the relation between a patient and a physician. Let $s \in [\underline{s}, \bar{s}]$ denote the health status of the patient. The patient delegates to the physician the diagnosis and treatment to recover from sickness. Therefore, the health status of the patient is an uncertain event (because it is subject to random elements) depending on the physician's effort (e). The uncertainty of s is characterized by a probability density function $f(s; e)$, where a higher effort of the physician turns into a better health state. Also, let us assume that the patient is fully insured.

The physician bears a cost $c(e)$ of exerting effort. The cost function c is strictly increasing. Also, assume the physician is paid an amount w after providing his health care services.

Then, the patient's utility (net of the insurance premium) is $v(s)$ assumed to be known to the physician. The utility of the physician is $u(w) - c(e)$. Note that these utility functions reflect the conflict of interest between the two parties. The patient is only interested in the outcome of the relation with the physician, this is his/her health status, s. In particular, the patient is not directly interested in the level of effort of the physician. In contrast, the physician is not directly interested in the outcome, but in effort that is costly to him/her. Finally, given that greater effort makes better results more likely, in an indirect way the patient (the principal in the contract) would like the maximum effort from the physician. The contract regulating the relation between principal and agent is the mechanism providing the adequate incentives to make this conflict of interest compatible.

Finally, assume that the physician is altruistic so that in determining their optimal level of effort (s)he considers a weighted sum of his/her and the patient's utilities, defined as

$$U(e) = \beta U(w) - c(e) + (1 - \beta) \int_{\underline{s}}^{\bar{s}} v(s) f(s, e) \, ds$$

where β is the weight the physician assigns to his/her utility. If $\beta = 0$, then the physician would be a perfect agent of the patient (and no conflict of interest would arise). In this case, the level of effort would be socially optimal. If $\beta = 1$ the physician would be a pure profit maximizer without any altruism. The case $\beta \in (0, 1)$ thus represents the physician as an imperfect agent.

The first-order condition of this optimization problem is,

$$\frac{\partial U}{\partial e} = -\frac{dc}{de} + (1 - \beta) \int_{\underline{s}}^{\overline{s}} v(s) \frac{\partial f}{\partial e} \, ds = 0$$

Note that for $\beta = 1$, $\partial U / \partial e < 0$, the physician exerts the minimum level of effort. This is so because the physician will be in a situation where reimbursement is independent of effort, and he or she only cares about profits. The other extreme case, $\beta = 0$, yields a level of effort where its marginal cost equates the marginal benefit of the patient, $\frac{dc}{de} = \int_{\underline{s}}^{\overline{s}} v(s) \frac{\partial f}{\partial e} \, ds$. This is the socially optimal level of effort. Finally, for intermediate values of β, the level of effort is distorted thus reflecting the imperfect agency relation between physician and patient.

11.2 Imperfect information and competition

The early analysis of the consequences of information asymmetries on market competition is due to Satterthwaite (1979) and Pauly and Satterthwaite (1981). The starting point is to recognize that the lack of information of the individuals about the providers of health care services relies on the opinion of friends and relatives. That is to say that the provision of health care services is a *reputation good* (see Chapter 5), so that consumers (patients) can differentiate each provider from the others, and the market becomes monopolistically competitive.

In this set-up Satterthwaite (1979) shows that an increase in the number of providers may lead to an increase of prices. This is so because as the number of providers increase, the average number of friends and relatives visiting a particular provider diminishes. Therefore, the average level of information about each particular provider also diminishes which induces a more inelastic demand (because the responsiveness of the individual to the price depends upon the level of information of the provider). The more inelastic demand yields more market power to each physician and as a consequence, prices increase. This pricing behavior is known as the *theory of increasing monopoly*. A conclusion that stems from this theory is that the presence of (a fraction of) informed consumers in the market induces enough discipline in the market to recover the usual economic effects.

Pauly and Satterthwaite (1981) give empirical support to the theory of increasing monopoly by regressing the average price of primary care services on a set of variables including density of physicians per geographic area, transport facilities, "social stability", number of physicians per capita, salary in the industry, demand variables and other variables to control for fixed effects.

11.3 Incentives in the health care sector

A general objective of the health authorities in all countries is to provide the maximum level of quality at the minimum cost. To reach this objective it is necessary to identify those elements of inefficiency and to provide incentives to patients and providers to correct them. Some examples will illustrate the issue.

11.3.1 Patients

Consider an individual that has contracted a full coverage health insurance. As we have argued in Chapter 10, an insured individual loses perception of the cost of the service obtained as it is paid by the insurer. As a consequence, the individual has a tendency to artificially increase their demand for (health care) services, and also increase in relative terms his/her perception of (lack of) quality.

To correct for these effects, the health authority in the case of the public insurance and the insurance companies in the case of private insurance, try to make the consumer aware of the expenses generated by their demand of health care services in different ways. Two of the most frequently used are (i) sending the individual a notification of the bill that the insurer (public or private) has paid to the provider for the health care services provided to the individual (the so-called informative bill), and (ii) the introduction of a *co-payment* in the health care insurance contract. A co-payment is a mechanism by which the insured party shares the cost of the services provided with the insurer. *Cost sharing* does not refer to or include amounts paid in premiums for the coverage.

Cost sharing mechanisms can be implemented in different ways:

- defining the contribution of the insured "up-front", such as sliding scale premiums or enrollment fees;
- defining the contribution of the insured "at-time-of-service" such as co-payments or deductibles, in order to obtain specific health care services;
- defining the contribution of the insured as a percentage of the total charges incurred for medical services. This is called "co-insurance". It is mostly found in private insurance plans.

The general difficulty in designing any cost-sharing mechanism is to preserve equity, and prevent individuals from giving up contracting insurance.

Another line of attack against inefficient use of health care resources is to look closely at the *effectiveness* of the treatments (see Chapter 3). Effectiveness refers to the probability that an individual benefits from the application of a (health) technology to solve a particular (health) problem, under *real* conditions of application. This is to be distinguished from *efficacy*. It refers to the probability that an individual benefits from the application of a (health) technology to solve a particular (health) problem, under *ideal* conditions of application.

The distinction between efficacy and effectiveness is important because doctors and patients often do not follow best practice in using a treatment. Hallfors *et al.* (2006) provide an example where positive efficacy trial findings were not replicated in the effectiveness trial in evaluating substance abuse and violence prevention programs in schools in the US.

11.3.2   *Physicians*

The role of physicians in the health care market is to provide health care services in the form of diagnosis and treatment to the patient. The asymmetry of information between patient and physician ensures that the latter determines the patient's needs. In other words, the physician is an *expert* selling a *credence good* (see Chapter 5). The patient is always unaware of whether the treatment implemented was the best one, or even if he recovered because of or despite the treatment.

Wolinsky (1993) and Dulleck *et al.* (2009) study how information asymmetries affect market behavior in a theoretical and experimental setting respectively. In markets of credence goods consumers need to delegate the evaluation of the quality of the good to the provider of the service. Accordingly, it is necessary to design an incentive mechanism to discipline experts, so they act as close as possible as perfect agents of the consumers.

Several proposals are studied in the literature. Among them we highlight customers' search for multiple opinions, reputation considerations, and the separation between diagnosis and treatment (e.g. prescription and sale of pharmaceutical drugs). This separation guarantees (in absence of collusion) that the diagnosis expert will select the best treatment, and the treatment expert will follow closely the indications of his colleague. Iizuka (2007) empirically assesses the physician–patient agency relationship in the context of the prescription drug market in Japan where physicians often both prescribe and dispense drugs. A concern is that, due to the incentive created by the markup, physicians' prescription decisions may be distorted.

A second problem that has attracted a lot of attention is the so-called *supplier-induced demand*. In general, this phenomenon is defined as the capacity of a supplier to exploit its informational advantage over the consumer to induce a higher level of demand of the good or service provided than what the consumer would have demanded should both supplier and consumer have had the same information. In the health care market, supplier-induced demand translates to the capacity of physicians to induce patients to demand health care that they do not necessarily need. We will study the design of incentives in the presence of supplier-induced demand in Section 11.6.

Finally, a third feature that is worth mentioning relates to the *reimbursement system* of physicians. The literature concentrates mainly on two generic types of mechanisms to pay physicians for their services. The first one is a *fee-for-service* reimbursement system. This means that payment is made as services are provided. Typically, it consists of a fixed fee and a variable component related to the cost borne by the physician. The main characteristic of this system is that the physician does not participate in the costs that are generated. Thus, in diagnosing and treating patients the physician does not have any incentive to contain costs. In other words, the physician does not bear any risk. It is the payer (be it the patient, the insurer, or both) who is the interested party in monitoring that the services provided correspond to the medical necessity of the patient. The second popular reimbursement system is *capitation*. Under this system, the physician is paid a fixed amount of money in advance. In turn, the physician must provide any needed health care services to all patients patronizing him or her. In other words, now the reimbursement of the physician is independent of his/her effort, and bears all the risk. If nobody demands his/her services, all the payment is profit. However, if there is an unlucky episode and extensive services are demanded, the physician may face losses. In contrast with the previous reimbursement system, now the physician tends to avoid the difficult patients requiring more effort and time.

11.3.3   Hospitals

The main problem any hospital manager faces is complying with the yearly budget. The underlying objective of the health authority is to limit the level of expenditures without sacrificing the quality of the services provided.

Historically, hospitals were reimbursed all their expenses by the public and/or private insurers. In other words, reimbursement occurred *after* the health care services were rendered and the costs were incurred. Therefore, the hospital did not bear any financial risk. This set-up is termed a *retrospective payment system*. Under this system, hospitals do not have any incentive to control costs. Fee-for-service payment falls in this category.

In the 1980s in the US a federal law mandated the development of a *prospective payment system* for Medicare reimbursement in an attempt to control government expenditures for Medicare beneficiaries. Also, the restrictions imposed on public finances by the Treaty of

Maastricht imposed the shift to prospective payment systems in the European Union. Under a prospective payment system reimbursement occurs *before* health care services are provided. In other words, each hospital is endowed with a prospective budget defined according to a set of criteria including the characteristics of the hospital, geographical data, characteristics of the population of influence and number of hospitals in the area.

A basic distinction between retrospective and prospective payment systems hinges on the role of the cost of providing the health care services. As we have described, in a (fully) retrospective payment system the payer reimburses all the costs incurred by providers. In contrast, under a prospective payment system, payers reimburse providers independent of cost. Abbey (2009) and Jegers *et al.* (2002) provide a detailed description of health care payment systems. Zweifel *et al.* (2009, ch. 10) discuss an in-depth analytical study of the payment systems to providers.

In a prospective payment system, since the provider has a given amount of money to finance its activity, incentives induce efficiency. The drawback of the system is that hospitals may attempt to achieve efficiency by lowering the quality of the services provided (the well-known "quicker but sicker" phenomenon). Also, prospective systems generate opportunities to shift costs by referring patients to other (less adequate) providers. These issues are important because they are difficult to monitor by the insurer and/or the health authority. A side issue interfering in the design of the hospitals' budgets is the random nature of illness and catastrophic episodes that may occur, requiring additional financing.

The most often used form of prospective payment is the per-case payment based on *Diagnosis-Related Groups (DRGs)*. This is a classification of patients as homogeneous as possible with respect to the resources used and the cost incurred in diagnosing and treatment. Hospitals paid by diagnosis groups try to cream-skim selecting the healthiest (least sick) patients in the group and avoid those generating costs above the revenues obtained.

Finally *capitation* consists of reimbursing the provider a fixed amount for each patient treated. It may be related to the DRG system if the reimbursement fee is differentiated according to diagnosis and treatment. In general, hospitals reimbursed on capitation basis have incentives to provide cost-effective care but not all care services with positive net benefits.

11.4   Asymmetric information and conflict of objectives

All the arguments developed so far hinge on the asymmetry of information between the provider and the patient. The sense in which information is asymmetric, that is the identification of the better-informed party, is a crucial element of the analysis of the informational asymmetry. We distinguish three types of problems. A *moral hazard* situation occurs when the informational asymmetry arises after the signature of the contract. An *adverse selection* situation occurs when the informational asymmetry arises before the contract is signed. Finally, *signaling* refers to a situation wherein the informed party can reveal private information before signing the contract.

11.4.1   Moral hazard

In a *moral hazard* situation the principal and the agent have the same information at the moment of initiating the relationship. However, once the contract is signed an informational asymmetry arises because the principal cannot observe the action of the agent. For instance, the patient (principal) cannot observe the effort exerted by the physician (agent) in the provision of health care services. A moral hazard problem also appears between an insurer (principal) and an insured individual (agent) because the insurer cannot observe how the insured individual affects the probability of illness through lifestyle. This difficulty in controlling effort inputs together with the inherent uncertainty in the health status of an individual, conditions the way the agent is remunerated for the provision of services. In particular, reimbursement cannot be linked directly to effort.

Moral hazard can be addressed from the producer and from the consumer perspectives. The former captures situations that arise for instance when physicians are remunerated on a fee-for-service regime. Then there is a financial incentive for physicians to provide health care services in excess of the quantities that fully informed patients would demand. This phenomenon is best known as *supplier-induced demand* and is studied in Section 11.6. Consumer moral hazard appears when an insured individual demands more medical services than they would should they have to pay those services themselves. Ehrlich and Becker (1972) introduce the distinction between self-insurance and self-protection that in the modern literature is known as *ex-post* and *ex-ante* moral hazard respectively. The latter arises before a sickness state materializes. It refers to the ability of an individual to reduce the probability of falling sick through the use of preventive care measures (see below). *Ex-post* moral hazard appears once a sick episode has materialized, and refers to actions that the individual takes to reduce the loss associated to an illness episode. We will examine this situation first.

Consider an individual facing two possible states of nature, *healthy* or *sick*.[1] When sick, the individual bears a disutility B^* and may contract the provision of health care services x at a constant unit price. An amount x of treatment yields utility $B(x)$, where B is concave, has a maximum at x^+, is such that $B^* - B(x^+) = M > 0$, and $B(0) = 0$. That is, treatment can never wash away the disutility of falling sick, and such disutility can only be diminished through the purchase of health care services.

Before the uncertainty over the states of nature is resolved, the individual can also invest in preventive health care programs (q), so that the probability of falling sick is $p(q)$. This action has a cost (measured in utility units) $f(q)$ but is *not verifiable*.

Finally, the individual obtains utility from consumption of a composite commodity, y, net of the consumption of health care services. Summarizing, the utility of an individual in each state of nature can be expressed as

$$U(y - x) - \mu(B^* - B(x)) - f(q),$$

where $\mu = 0$ in the healthy state of nature, and $\mu = 1$ in the sick state of nature.

This set-up allows for discussing two moral hazard problems characterized by the individual taking an action before (*ex-ante* moral hazard) or after (*ex-post* moral hazard) uncertainty is resolved (see a detailed analysis in Zweifel *et al.* 2009, ch. 6; Macho-Stadler and Pérez-Castrillo 2001, ch. 3). We want to characterize the design of the contract (that is the premium and the co-payment) and the demand for health care services. Zweifel and Manning (2000) survey this issue and the empirical evidence available: "Theoretically, *ex ante* moral hazard (a reduction of preventive effort in response to insurance coverage) is not unambiguously predicted, and there is very limited empirical evidence about it. The case for static *ex post* moral hazard (an increase in the demand for medical care of a given technology) is stronger."

Ex-post *moral hazard*

A problem of *ex-post* moral hazard arises when the individual chooses the level of medical services (x) once having fallen sick. The insurer cannot observe the health state of the

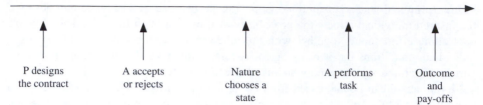

Figure 11.3 Ex-post moral hazard.

individual, and therefore is not able to assess the proper treatment. To simplify the argument, let us ignore the choice of prevention, and assume $p(q) = p$. Figure 11.3 (see Macho-Stadler and Pérez-Castrillo, 2001, ch. 3.6) illustrates the sequence of moves of the game.

Assume first that there is no insurance. The choice of the level of health care services in the sick state of nature is the solution of the following problem:

$$\max_{x} U(y - x) - B^* + B(x).$$

The first-order condition characterizing the solution x^* is

$$U'(y - x^*) = B'(x^*),\tag{11.1}$$

so that the marginal utility of consumption goods equates to the marginal utility of health care services (i.e. the marginal impact on lowering the disutility of being sick).

If nature selects the healthy state, the individual does not obtain any benefit from demanding health care services, so that the problem has a corner solution $x = 0$.

Assume next that nature determines whether the individual is healthy or sick *before* the choice of health care services. Then, the problem is to find the optimal level of services maximizing the expected utility of the individual. This is,

$$\max_{x} EU = p[U(y - x) - B^* + B(x)] + (1 - p)U(y)$$

The first-order condition characterizes the same solution as (11.1). Therefore, from the perspective of the uninsured individual, the choice of the optimal demand of health care services when sick is independent of the moment when the uncertainty is resolved.

Assume now that the individual is insured. Assume also that the insurance market is competitive and the insurance company has zero marginal cost. Then, in equilibrium the premium will be actuarially fair, that is equal to the expected value of the expenses borne by the insurer. Let the insurance contract be described by the premium P and a co-payment c borne by the insurer. Then, $P = pcx$.

The choice of health care services conditional to be in the sick state of nature is the solution of the following problem:

$$\max_{x} V = U(y - P - (1 - c)x) - B^* + B(x).$$

The first-order condition characterizing the optimal value of expenditures in health care services, z, given that the individual has signed an insurance contract (taking into account

$P = pcz)$ is,

$$(1 - c)U'(y - z + (1 - p)cz) = B'(z). \tag{11.2}$$

If nature selects the healthy state, the same argument as in the absence of insurance prevails, so that the problem has a corner solution $z = 0$.

A natural question to ask is whether the presence of insurance increases the demand of health care services, that is whether $z > x^*$. From the first-order condition it is relatively simple to obtain $\partial x / \partial c > 0$. This tells us that as insurance lowers the marginal cost of health care services in the sick state of nature, while marginal benefit remains unaltered, it is to be expected that the individual increases his consumption of health care services.

Let us study the optimal contract design without moral hazard. This will allow us to characterize the first-best optimum, and thus assess the distortion caused by the presence of moral hazard.

Assume that the insurer can observe the health state of the individual. Individuals can determine their final level of health by the choice of medical services as measure in terms of utility recovery $B(x)$. Together with x, individuals also choose a health insurance contract summarized in the co-payment rate c (given that the premium is set at its actuarially fair value).

The optimal (first-best) contract is determined by the simultaneous choice of level of health care services (x) and the co-payment rate (c) solving the problem

$$\max_{x,c} V = p[U(D(c, x)) - B^* + B(x)] + (1 - p)U(S(c, x))$$

where

$$D(c, x) = y - pcx - (1 - c)x, \tag{11.3}$$

$$S(c, x) = y - pcx, \tag{11.4}$$

represent the disposable income of the individual when sick and healthy respectively. Also, observe that we have already the equilibrium condition defining the premium in a competitive insurance market.

The first-order conditions are,

$$\frac{\partial V}{\partial c} = p(1 - p)x[U'(D) - U'(S)] = 0, \tag{11.5}$$

$$\frac{\partial V}{\partial x} = p(1 - p)c[U'(D) - U'(S)] + p[B'(x) - U'(D)] = 0 \tag{11.6}$$

The solution of (11.5) yields

$$U'(D) = U'(S). \tag{11.7}$$

In turn, this implies that $D(c, x) = S(c, x)$, and from (11.3) and (11.4), it follows that $c = 1$; that is insurance provides full coverage.

Substituting (11.7) into (11.6), and taking into account that $c = 1$, we obtain the optimal level of health care services $\tilde{x}$ as the solution of

$$B'(\tilde{x}) = U'(y - p\tilde{x}). \tag{11.8}$$

Comparing (11.1) and (11.8), it is straightforward to verify that $x^* \neq \tilde{x}$. Also, given that $U'(\cdot) > 0$, it follows that $B'(x^*) > 0$ and $B'(\tilde{x}) > 0$. Finally, the concavity of $B(\cdot)$ implies that $x^* < \tilde{x}$.[2]

Let us introduce now the moral hazard component by assuming that the insurer cannot observe the health state of the individual. Instead, the insurer uses the medical expenditure as an indicator of a sickness episode. Now the individual faces a two-stage optimization problem because his decisions are sequential rather than simultaneous. In the first place a contract is signed and secondly the demand of treatment is determined. This game is solved using backward induction, capturing the feature that when the parties sign the insurance contract, the insurer foresees the demand for health care services in case of sickness. Note also that the contract only specifies a premium and a co-payment, but not a volume of services. This is usually the case in health insurance contracts in reality. Also, we develop the argument with only two possible states of nature, while the uncertainty behind the health status of individuals is much more complex. However, this simplification allows us to capture the essential elements driving the decision making. A full analysis of the optimal insurance coverage with moral hazard is presented in Zweifel *et al.* (2009, ch. 6).

The second stage of the game consists of solving for any given co-payment rate c the demand for health care services when sick. This amounts to solving the following problem,

$$\max_x V = U(D(x)) - B^* + B(x)$$

where $D(x)$ is defined by (11.3). The first-order condition is given by

$$(1 - c)U'(D) = B'(x). \tag{11.9}$$

Let us denote the optimal demand of health care services for any given contract as

$$x = x(c), \ x' > 0.$$

In the first stage, the insurance company chooses the copayment rate c anticipating the decision of the insured individual when sick. The problem of the insurer is

$$\max_c V = p[U(y - P - (1 - c)x) - B^* + B(x)] + (1 - p)U(y - P)$$

$$\text{s.t.} \quad \begin{cases} P = cpx \\ x = x(c) \end{cases}$$

where the first restriction captures the competitive insurance market, and the second restriction characterizes the behavior of the patient. Substituting both restrictions in the objective function, we can rewrite the problem of the insurer as,

$$\max_c V = p[U(y - cpx(c) - (1 - c)x(c)) - B^* + B(x(c))] + (1 - p)U(y - cpx(c))$$

The first-order condition of this problem can be written (using (11.9)) as

$$(1 - p)x[U'(D) - U'(S)] = cx'[p(U'(D) - U'(S)) + U'(S)] \tag{11.10}$$

where D and S are defined by (11.3) and (11.4).

Note that by definition of D and S, $D \leq S$, so that the concavity of $U(\cdot)$ implies $U'(D) \geq U'(s)$. In turn, $p(U'(D) - U'(S)) + U'(S) > 0$. Given, $x'(c) > 0$, it follows that the right-hand side of (11.10) is positive. This implies that $U'(D) > U'(s)$ for the left-hand side of (11.10) to be positive as well. Finally, the concavity of $U(\cdot)$ implies $D < S$ which in turn implies $c < 1$.

Now we can compare the equilibrium level of health care services given by the solution of (11.9) with its optimal value given by the solution of (11.2). Looking at extreme cases, under full coverage ($c = 1$) the equilibrium level of health care services exceeds the the socially optimal solution. However, under absence of insurance ($c = 0$), the equilibrium level of health care services is smaller than the optimum. Therefore, by continuity of the first-order conditions, there exists a critical value of the co-payment rate for which the equilibrium level of health care services is optimal. The rationale behind this result is relatively simple. The problem of moral hazard arises because when the insurance contract is signed, the insurer does not know what the demand for health care services by the individual insured will be. Consider an individual that has signed a contract providing full coverage. In that case all the costs of the health care services are borne by the insurer, so that the individual has incentives to demand services in excess of what would be efficient from a medical point of view. In this argument there are two effects. On the one hand, there is a price effect that captures a positive link between the level of coverage and the demand of medical services ($\partial x / \partial c > 0$, as we have argued above). On the other hand, there is an efficiency effect that tends to lower the demand of services. The argument under full coverage tells us that the price effect dominates the efficiency effect. Consider now the other extreme case of absence of insurance. Now all the medical costs are borne by the individual. Accordingly, the individual confronts the medical bill of the treatment with the net loss of utility when sick. Accordingly, the individual demands the minimum amount of medical services possible, so that the efficiency effect dominates the price effect. By continuity, as the level of co-payment increases, the efficiency effect loses ground against the price effect, and above a certain critical level the latter effect dominates the former.

The presence of moral hazard distorts the design of the insurance contract away from full coverage (socially optimal). The insurer uses the co-payment in the insurance contract as a cost-sharing mechanism to involve the patient in the financing of the excess demand of health care expenses generated by him.

Ex-ante *moral hazard*

Individuals often can influence the probability of falling ill investing in preventive care. The *ex-ante* moral hazard problem arises because the insurer cannot observe the involvement of the individual in, say, "good lifestyle habits," and thus cannot be taken into account in the design of the insurance contract. As Figure 11.4 illustrates (see Macho-Stadler and Pérez-Castrillo, 2001, ch. 3), the action is taken before the uncertainty is resolved but after signing the insurance contract.

To simplify the analysis, we assume that the probability of falling sick is decreasing in the volume of preventive care services (q), that is $p = p(q)$, $p' < 0$. Also, to isolate the problem of *ex-ante* moral hazard from the problem of *ex-post* moral hazard, we assume that once a sickness episode occurs, the demand for health care services is fixed $x = x^*$ in such a way as to exactly offset the disutility of sickness, $B^* = B(x^*)$. Finally we also assume that preventive care has a cost that we can express in utility terms as $f(q)$, $f' > 0$, $f'' > 0$.

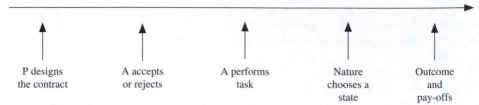

Figure 11.4 Ex-ante moral hazard.

We will follow the same structure of analysis as before. Thus, let us start assuming first that there is no insurance. The problem to solve is given by,

$$\max_{q} V = p(q)U(y-x) + (1-p(q))U(y) - f(q).$$

The first-order condition characterizing the optimal volume of preventive care is

$$p'(q)[U(y-x) - U(y)] = f'(q),$$

so that the marginal impact on lowering the probability of sickness equates the marginal cost of investment in preventive care.

Next, assume that the individual is insured, and as before assume the insurance market is competitive and the insurance company has zero constant marginal cost. Accordingly, the insurance premium will be actuarially fair $P = cp(q)x$. The optimal contract without moral hazard will characterize the first-best optimum. In other words, let us assume that the insurer can observe the preventive care actions undertaken by the individual. Then, the optimal first-best contract is characterized by the simultaneous choice of the effort in preventive care (q) and the co-payment rate (c) solving the problem

$$\max_{q,c} V = p(q)U(D(q,c)) + (1-p(q))U(S(q,c)) - f(q).$$

where

$$D(q,c) = y - x(1-c) - cp(q)x, \tag{11.11}$$

$$S(q,c) = y - cp(q)x, \tag{11.12}$$

have the same interpretation as in the previous section.

The first-order conditions are,

$$\frac{\partial V}{\partial q} = p'(q)[U(D) - U(S)]$$

$$- cp'(q)x[p(q)U'(D) + (1-p(q))U'(S)] - f'(q) = 0 \tag{11.13}$$

$$\frac{\partial V}{\partial c} = p(q)x(1-p(q))[U'(D) - U'(S)] = 0 \tag{11.14}$$

The solution of (11.14) yields

$$U'(D) = U'(S).$$

In turn, it implies that $D(q, c) = S(q, c)$, and from (11.11) and (11.12) it follows that $c = 1$, so that insurance provides full coverage.

Finally, substituting (11.14) into (11.13) and taking into account that $c = 1$, we obtain the optimal level of preventive care as the solution of,

$$-p'(q)x = f'(q).$$

Let us introduce the moral hazard element in the model by assuming that the insurer cannot observe the actions taken by the individual to lower their probability of falling sick. A first consequence of the inability of the insurer to observe q is that the premium (P) cannot depend on the level of prevention. Again, the *ex-ante* moral hazard problem can be viewed as a two-stage optimization problem where the insurer chooses first the co-payment rate, and then after signing the contract the individual chooses his level of preventive care.

The second stage of the game consists in solving for any co-payment rate c the following problem:

$$\max_{q} V = p(q)U(y - P - (1 - c)x) + (1 - p(q))U(y - P) - f(q)$$

The first-order condition is,

$$\frac{\partial V}{\partial q} = p'(q)[U(y - P - (1 - c)x) - U(y - P)] - f'(q) = 0 \tag{11.15}$$

It characterizes the optimal level of prevention as a decreasing function of the co-payment rate, $q(c)$, $q' < 0$. More generous insurance coverage (higher c) reduces the incentive of the individual to invest in prevention, because the utility loss from sickness is smaller.

In the first stage of the optimization problem, the insurance company chooses its optimal co-payment rate c anticipating the reaction of the individual's effort in prevention $q(c)$. Formally, the problem of the insurer is,

$$\max_{c} V = p(q(c))U(D(c)) + (1 - p(q(c)))U(S(c)) - f(q(c)),$$

where now D and S are redefined as

$$D(c) = y - x(1 - c) - cp(q(c))x,$$
$$S(c) = y - cp(q(c))x,$$

The first-order condition (using (11.15)) is,

$$\frac{\partial V}{\partial c} = p(1 - p)x[U'(D) - U'(S)] - xcp'q'[pU'(D) + (1 - p)U'(S)] = 0 \tag{11.16}$$

Let us look at the incentives of the insured to invest in prevention as a function of the insurance coverage.

Under full coverage $(c = 1)$ we know that the individual would not incur in any preventive action. The question is whether partial coverage can be a solution of (11.16).

Under partial coverage $(c < 1)$, it follows that $D < S$ so that given the concavity of the utility function would result in $U(D) < U(S)$ and $U'(D) > U'(s)$. Then, the first and last terms of (11.16) are negative, the second term is positive, and the third term has an ambiguous sign. Again, partial coverage may be an optimal solution to the problem of the insurer.

The incentives of the individual to devote resources to preventive care thus depend on whether maximum expected utility is achieved with a contract providing full coverage together with a very high fair premium, or with a contract with partial coverage and a lower fair premium.

We have commented above that under *ex-ante* moral hazard the insurance premium cannot depend upon the level of prevention. This raises an important question about the incentives of the individual to spend at all on prevention. Helwege (1996) illustrates in a thought exercise the incentives of the insurer and insured to engage in preventive care. Conway and Cutinova (2006) look at the incentives to include prenatal care on maternal health and the associated savings. From a different perspective, Barros and Martinez-Giralt (2003) focus on the externality resulting from referral decisions from primary to acute care providers. They find that when hospitals are reimbursed according to costs, prevention efforts are unlikely to occur. However, under a capitation payment for the primary care center and prospective budget for the hospital, prevention efforts increase when shifting from an independent to an integrated management of primary and acute care services. Hennessy (2008) looks at preventive and cure efforts to assess their complementarity or substitutability.

Moral hazard, deductibles, and co-payments

We present here a graphical analysis of the effect of moral hazard in the demand of health care services. Assume an individual with probability π of falling sick that has contracted a full coverage health insurance. Assume finally that provision of health care services has a unit price of p_1€.

If the individual's demand for health care is completely inelastic as in Figure 11.5(a), his/her demand will be unaffected by the insurance even though when insured (s)he does not bear any cost.

Let us assume next that our individual has a demand for health care sensitive to the price as illustrated in Figure 11.5(b). If the individual is uninsured, he or she faces the (unit) price p_1. When sick he or she would demand q_1 units of health care services and would pay a bill represented by the shaded area $0 p_1 B q_1$. If the individual has contracted a health care insurance with full coverage, when sick demand for health care expands until q_2, and the insurer pays a bill of $p_1 q_2$€.

From the point of view of the insurer, assume the premium is actuarially fair. If the insurer computes the premium according to the demand of the individual without insurance, he/she will obtain revenues $\pi p_1 q_1$, and will go bankrupt because those revenues will not cover the costs of the treatment $\pi p_1 q_2$. However, if the premium is set in accordance to the demand q_2, then the individual would be indifferent to contracting or remain uninsured. Therefore, the insurance company needs to introduce incentives in the insurance contract to discipline the individual's demand for health care services. Two of the most often used mechanisms are *deductibles* and *co-payments*.

A *deductible* in an insurance contract is an amount of money that the insured individual bears before the insurance company starts to cover expenses. For instance, let us assume that an individual contracts an insurance with a deductible of d€. Assume that the individual has a health incidence and receives treatment generating a bill of k€. Then, the individual pays (up to) d€ and the insurer pays the remaining $k - d$€, as long as it is a positive amount.

Let us examine the effects of including a deductible in an insurance contract.

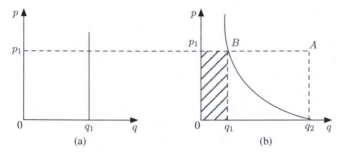

Figure 11.5 Moral hazard and demand for health care.

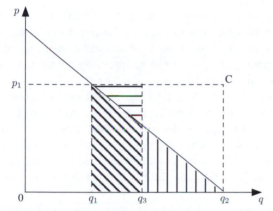

Figure 11.6 The effect of a deductible.

Consider an individual with probability π of falling sick. His/her demand for health care services is decreasing in the price. Assume that the unit price of treatment is p_1. If the insurance provides full coverage, his/her demand of health care will be of q_2 units as illustrated in Figure 11.6, and the cost of the treatment will be of $p_1 q_2$ €.

Assume next that the insurance company introduces a deductible of $d = p_1 q_1$ €. Now the individual compares the level of service that (s)he obtains with insurance (q_2 units against the premium and the deductible) and without insurance (q_1 units at a cost of $p_1 q_1$ €). The net gain is thus the triangle under the demand curve between q_1 and q_2.

Assume now that the insurer increases the deductible until $d' = p_1 q_3$€. Will the individual remain insured? Under the new contract, the individual bears q_3 units of care. That is, when sick, the insurance makes him/her demand $q_3 - q_1$ additional units of care (with respect to being uninsured) that pays at the price p_1. This is represented in Figure 11.6 by the rectangle with base $(q_3 - q_1)$ and height p_1. However, given the demand function of the individual, the cost of this increased demand is greater than his/her willingness to pay for q_3 units of treatment. The difference is represented by the triangle above the demand function between q_1 and q_3, and is a loss of welfare. But this is not the only effect. Note that once the deductible is paid, the insurer pays the remaining bill that may accrue. Accordingly, the individual expands his demand until q_2, which conveys an increase in welfare given by the triangle under the demand curve between q_2 and q_3. Again, our individual will decide whether or not to contract health insurance in accordance with the net benefits of the new deductible. If the triangle above the demand is smaller than the triangle below the demand, the individual will contract the insurance with the larger deductible.

Note that a deductible does not have an impact on the demand of health care services with respect to a full coverage insurance. In both cases the demand is of q_2 units and therefore the total cost of the health care system remains the same. The deductible is simply a transfer of resources between the insurance company and its insured individuals.

Let us examine now the effects of a *co-payment* in an insurance contract (see Cutler and Zeckhauser 2000). A co-payment is a cost-sharing mechanism defining the proportion of the cost of the health care services provided to be borne by the patient and by the insurer. Let us consider a patient who has received treatment and the corresponding bill amounts to $k€$. Denote by $c \in [0, 1]$ the proportion of the cost borne by the patient. Then, the patient pays $ck€$ and the insurer pays the remaining $(1 - c)k€$. Of course, $c = 0$ means full coverage, and $c = 1$ means that the patient is uninsured.

Consider an individual with probability π of falling sick. Demand for treatment is decreasing in the price, and assume the unit price of treatment is p_1 as illustrated in Figure 11.7 (see Folland *et al.* 2004, ch. 7). If the patient is uninsured, he/she will demand q_1 units of treatment. If alternatively, the individual has a full coverage insurance contract, his/her demand is $\bar{q}$ (the demand corresponding to a zero price).

Assume now that the individual has contracted a health insurance defined by a premium and a co-payment $c < 1$. This means that the patient faces a price cp_1 per unit of treatment, so that his/her demand function pivots to the right at the point $\bar{q}$. With this new demand function, at the price p_1 the individual reduces his/her consumption (with respect to a full coverage insurance contract) from $\bar{q}$ to q_2. The corresponding bill is p_1q_2, of which the individual pays an amount cp_1q_2, and the overall expenditure of the health system reduces by an amount of $p_1(\bar{q} - q_2)$.

We conclude that the introduction of co-payments in the insurance contract helps to contain the cost of the health care system, with respect to a situation where insurance contracts provide full coverage to the insured individual. This is the case, because the co-payment makes the consumer sensitive to the cost of the services provided through the sharing of that cost with the insurer.

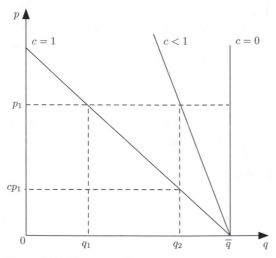

Figure 11.7 The effect of a co-payment.

11.4.2   Adverse selection

In contrast with moral hazard, we say that a problem of *adverse selection* appears when the agent has private information before initiating the relation with the principal. In other words, we face a situation with asymmetric information prior to the signature of the contract. Technically we say that nature plays first choosing the *type* of agent as Figure 11.8 (see Macho-Stadler and Pérez-Castrillo 2001, ch. 4) illustrates.

A simple example will help us to grasp the main features of the problem. Think of a society where there is only one private insurance company offering a single contract. This insurance company does not know the medical record of its potential clients. Therefore, it could only charge a price based on the average health status of the population. In this situation, this insurer would incur losses because those individuals healthier than average (people expecting low medical bills) would not contract the insurance policy, while all individuals with health state below average (people expecting high medical bills) would contract. Accordingly, the revenues of the insurer would not be enough to cover the expenses generated by its clients. High-risk individuals drive out of the insurance market low-risk individuals.

The problem of the principal (the insurer) in this set-up is to find a way to reduce its informational disadvantage. To do it, the insurance company will devote effort to *screening* applicants, selecting those expected to generate low medical bills and rejecting potential high-risk clients. More generally, the screening of applicants translate to the insurer offering a menu of contracts with the objective that the different types of individuals choose the one with a premium and co-payment rate allowing the insurance company to (at least) cover their respective expected medical bills. In short, the insurer designs the menu so that applicants self-select themselves according to their risk types.

Naturally, this selection of risks implies distortions generating inefficiencies that prevent reaching the first-best resource allocation in the market, and sometimes even the very existence of equilibrium. Note that the resources devoted to screening is the main difference between a private and a public insurer (that does not discriminate among applicants). Actually, the presence of adverse selection is one of the main arguments for the provision of compulsory public health insurance. Given that the state would have to cover the health care services of those left uninsured, it is preferable to force everybody into the same insurance pool so that healthier individuals cross-subsidize those with poorer health status.

A situation of adverse selection also appears in the design of the reimbursement mechanism for providers. Providers have better information of their case-mix than the insurance company (or the public health authority). In the negotiations over the budget of a provider, it conceals this information to obtain a higher reimbursement. Similarly, the relation between patient and physician may contain elements of adverse selection. Before being examined, the patient (principal) does not know the quality of the physician.

The literature of adverse selection was initiated by Akerlof's (1970) *lemons* model of the second-hand car market. In this market the buyer of a car does not know beforehand whether

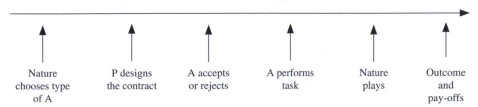

Nature	P designs	A accepts	A performs	Nature	Outcome
chooses type	the contract	or rejects	task	plays	and
of A					pay-offs

Figure 11.8 Adverse selection.

it is a good car or a defective car (a 'lemon'). Accordingly, the best that the buyer can do is to assume that the car (s)he is interested in is of average quality, and (s)he will be willing to pay the price of a car of known average quality. Therefore, an owner of a good used car will not be able to sell it at the price corresponding to the quality of the car. As a consequence, no good-quality used cars will be available in the market. This reasoning is also done by the buyer so that applying the argument iteratively, only used cars of the lowest quality can be expected in the market. But those cars yield no profits and the market disappears.

Rothschild and Stiglitz (1976) present the pathbreaking analysis of adverse selection in the insurance market. Van de ven *et al.* (2000) and Belli (2001) present surveys of the developments in the literature building on Rothschild and Stiglitz's (1976) contribution. In the remainder of this section we will present the basic ideas in the model of Rothschild and Stiglitz (RS hereafter).

RS model with symmetric information

Consider a population composed of two types of individuals characterized by their probability of falling sick, π_L (low probability) and π_H (high probability), with $\pi_L < \pi_H$. Let θ be the share of low-type individuals (L) and $(1 - \theta)$ the share of high-type individuals (H). Assume all individuals have the same gross income Y. An insurance contract is defined by the premium P and the indemnity I. When sick, the cost of treatment allowing for full recovery is denoted by M, so that $I \in [0, M]$. The individual obtains utility from his net income (y). When healthy (h), the disposable income of an individual of type $i = H, L$ is denoted by y_h^i and by y_s^i when sick. They are given by,

$$y_h^i = Y - P_i, \tag{11.17}$$

$$y_s^i = Y - P_i - M + I_i. \tag{11.18}$$

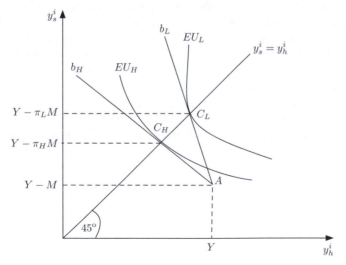

Figure 11.9 Insurance contracts with symmetric information.

Finally, the expected utility (assumed concave) of an individual of type i is given by

$$EU_i = \pi_i U(y_s^i) + (1 - \pi_i)U(y_h^i), \quad i = H, L.$$

Assume that the insurance market is competitive, so that the corresponding actuarially fair premium will be $P_i = \pi_i I_i$. Assume also that the insurer can observe the risk type of each individual (i.e. no adverse selection). Then, the problem of the insurer is,

$$\max_{I_i} EU_i = \pi_i U(y_s^i) + (1 - \pi_i)U(y_h^i) \quad \text{s.t. } P_i = \pi_i I_i$$

The first-order condition is

$$\pi_i(1 - \pi_i)[U'(y_s^i) - U'(y_h^i)] = 0.$$

The solution of this equation is an indemnity I_i^* for which marginal utilities in both states are equalized. In turn, this implies that disposable incomes in the two states must be equal, $y_h^i = y_s^i$, so that $M = I_i^*$. In other words, individuals will buy full insurance, and they will have an income $y_h^i = y_s^i = Y - \pi_i M$. Note, however, that the premiums are different for the different types of individuals:

$$P_H = \pi_H M > \pi_L M = P_L,$$

so that high-type individuals pay a higher premium than low-type individuals due to their higher probability of falling sick. Figure 11.9 (see Zweifel *et al.* 2009, p. 172) illustrates this result in the space of net incomes for type i individuals. Point A represents individuals' net income without insurance, so that endowments in the healthy and sick states are identical. The lines b_H and b_L are the budget lines for the high- and low-risk types respectively. The budget line for a type i individual is obtained by solving (11.17) (introducing $P_i = \pi_i I_i$) for I_i and substituting into (11.18). That is,

$$y_s^i = \frac{Y}{\pi_i} - M - \frac{1 - \pi_i}{\pi_i} y_h^i, \quad i = H, L \tag{11.19}$$

Given that $\pi_H > \pi_L$, it follows that the budget line b_L is steeper than the budget line b_H. The individual of type i maximizes his utility with the contract C_i characterized by the tangency of an indifference curve and the budget line. At the tangency, the slopes of both lines are the same. The slope of the indifference curve is given by,

$$\frac{dy_s^i}{dy_h^i}\bigg|_{dEU_i=0} = -\frac{\frac{\partial EU_i}{\partial y_h^i}}{\frac{\partial EU_i}{\partial y_s^i}} = -\frac{1 - \pi_i}{\pi_i}\frac{U'(y_h^i)}{U'(y_s^i)} \tag{11.20}$$

Comparing the slope of (11.19) with (11.20), they coincide when $U'(y_h^i) = U'(y_s^i)$. That is, the two optimal contracts C_H and C_L must lie on the certainty line $y_h^i = y_s^i$.

RS model with asymmetric information

Let us introduce now adverse selection by assuming that the insurer does not know the individuals' risk types. Also, we assume that a contract is a point (P, I) in the space (y_h, y_s) where I denotes a fixed reimbursement and P the premium. Finally, an individual buys exactly one insurance contract. Rothschild and Stiglitz (1976) define the equilibrium as,

> a set of contracts such that, when customers choose contracts to maximize expected utility, (i) no contract in the equilibrium set makes negative expected profits; and (ii) there is no contract outside the equilibrium set that, if offered, will make a nonnegative profit. This notion of equilibrium is of the Cournot-Nash type; each firm assumes that the contracts its competitors offer are independent of its own actions.
>
> (p. 633)

In this set-up two types of equilibria may be envisaged – a *pooling equilibrium* where the two groups of individuals buy the same insurance contract, and a *separating equilibrium* where each risk group of individuals choose different contracts (see Macho-Stadler and Pérez-Castrillo 2001, ch. 4.3).

Note first that the equilibrium (C_H, C_L) obtained under symmetric information is no longer an equilibrium under asymmetric information. This is so because although low-risk individuals do not have incentives to choose the C_H contract (it yields less expected utility because of the higher premium), the high-risk individuals would try to choose the C_L contract. With that contract they would continue to obtain full coverage at a lower premium, thus increasing their expected utility. Accordingly, all individuals would choose the same contract C_L and the insurer would incur (expected) losses.

Let us examine next the existence of a *pooling equilibrium*. The average probability of sickness in the population of individuals is $\bar{\pi} = \theta \pi_L + (1 - \theta) \pi_H$. The insurer offers a single contract $Z = (P_Z, I_Z)$, with premium $P_Z = \bar{\pi} I_Z$. This contract given that the insurance market is competitive, yields zero expected profits. If it would yield positive profits, a rival insurer would be able to offer an alternative contract offering a slightly lower premium, still yielding a positive profit when all individuals choose it. Therefore, all individuals would buy this alternative contract so that Z could not be an equilibrium. The budget line associated with the contract Z is given by

$$y_s^i = \frac{Y}{\bar{\pi}} - M - \frac{1 - \bar{\pi}}{\bar{\pi}} y_h^i, \quad i = H, L \tag{11.21}$$

and is represented by $\bar{b}$ in Figure 11.10 (see Zweifel *et al.* 2009, p. 174). Contract Z must lie on the $\bar{b}$ budget line. Note that Z is not on the $y_s^i = y_h^i$ line. Therefore, the premium P_Z is not actuarially fair for the low-risk types. Indeed, these individuals would prefer to buy a contract with partial coverage and a lower premium.

Consider an alternative contract like Q. It yields higher expected utility than Z to low-risk types, and lower expected utility to the high-risk individuals. Therefore, all low-risk individuals will shift to Q. Moreover, contract Q is profitable because it is chosen by low-risk individuals only and it lies below the budget line of low-risk individuals b_L. We can conclude that if a contract like Z is in the market, it is profitable to offer a (profitable) contract Q. In turn, it implies that Z cannot be an equilibrium because given that only high-risk individuals choose it, becomes unprofitable. Summarizing,

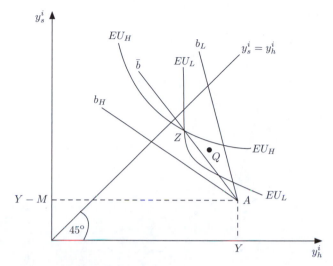

Figure 11.10 Pooling equilibrium.

PROPOSITION 11.1 *There is no pooling equilibrium in the Rothschild and Stiglitz model of asymmetric information.*

The only possible equilibrium with different risk types is a separating equilibrium. Let us look at the conditions under which a *separating equilibrium* may exist. In a separating equilibrium the insurer offers two contracts and each individual self-selects the one corresponding to his/her type. That is low-risk individuals choose the contract the insurer has designed for low-risk individuals, and high-risk individuals choose the contract the insurer has designed for high-risk individuals. We present the argument characterizing the conditions for existence of a separating equilibrium in three steps.

Step 1. In any separating equilibrium both contracts must yield zero expected profits. Therefore, we know that the contract for high-risk individuals must lie on the budget line b_H, and the contract for low-risk individuals must lie on the budget line b_L.

Let us consider the high-risk individuals. We have already seen that the best-preferred (expected utility maximizer) contract is C_H providing full insurance. Therefore, C_H must be part of any separating equilibrium. Regarding low-risk individuals, we have also seen that the best-preferred (expected utility maximizer) contract is C_L providing full insurance. However, C_L offers more consumption in each state than C_H. Accordingly, high-risk individuals prefer the contract C_L to the contract C_H. This means that if both contracts are offered by the insurer, all individuals will choose C_L and the insurer will incur in losses. Summarizing,

LEMMA 11.1 *The menu of contracts (C_H, C_L) is not a separating equilibrium.*

Step 2. The previous argument tells us that if a separating equilibrium exists, the contract for the low-risk type must not be more attractive for the high-risk individuals than C_H. In terms of Figure 11.11 this means that the contract for the low-risk individuals cannot lie above the indifference curve EU_H corresponding to the utility level obtained by the high risk individuals when choosing contract C_H. Also, the contract

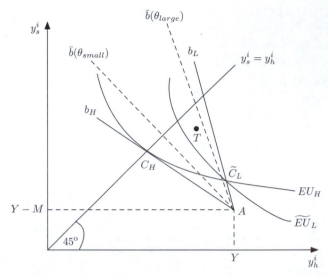

Figure 11.11 Separating equilibrium.

to be offered to low-risk individuals must lie on the budget line b_L (i.e. must yield zero expected profits). In Figure 11.11 this means that the set of contract candidates for the low-risk individuals is the segment $A\widetilde{C}_L$ of b_L. This set of contracts all lie below the certainty line $y_s^i = y_h^i$, thus implying that they offer partial coverage (with a fair premium). Among all contracts in this segment, the most preferred is $\widetilde{C}_L$ because it is the one yielding the highest level of expected utility to low-risk individuals, $\widetilde{EU}_L$. Note that high-risk individuals are indifferent to C_H and $\widetilde{C}_L$. We solve this indifference by assuming that the high-risk types stay at C_H.[3] Also note that the contract $\widetilde{C}_L$ does not correspond to a tangency point between the budget line b_L and the indifference curve $\widetilde{EU}_L$. Accordingly, it is not an optimal contract. Summarizing,

LEMMA 11.2 *The only separating equilibrium candidate is* $(C_H, \widetilde{C}_L)$.

Step 3. It remains to prove under what conditions the menu of contracts $(C_H, \widetilde{C}_L)$ is actually a separating equilibrium. Consider a contract like T in Figure 11.11. It lies above both the indifference curves $\widetilde{EU}_L$ and EU_H. Accordingly, if such a contract would be offered, all individuals would choose it over C_H and $\widetilde{C}_L$. If on top, contract T would be profitable and it would upset the candidate equilibrium $(C_H, \widetilde{C}_L)$. Hence the question left is when T is profitable, and the answer depends on the relative share of low-risk over high-risk individuals, that is on the value of θ.

Consider a population with sufficiently high-risk people, that is with θ small. As contract T pools all individuals together, the corresponding average budget line is represented by $\bar{b}(\theta_{small})$ in Figure 11.11 that lies below the indifference curve $\widetilde{EU}_L$. Then, the insurer offering contract T would incur losses (because T lies above the pooling budget line). Accordingly, the menu of contracts $(C_H, \widetilde{C}_L)$ is the only separating equilibrium.

Consider now a population with sufficiently many low-risk people, that is with θ large. As contract T pools all individuals together, the corresponding average budget line is represented by $\bar{b}(\theta_{large})$ in Figure 11.11 that crosses the indifference curve $\widehat{EU}_L$. Then, the insurer offering contract T would obtain positive profits (because T lies below the pooling budget line), thus challenging the menu of contracts $(C_H, \widetilde{C}_L)$. Since in step 2 we have already seen that this menu is the only separating equilibrium candidate, it follows that the competitive insurance market does not have an equilibrium.

We can summarize the discussion as

PROPOSITION 11.2 *In the Rothschild and Stiglitz model of asymmetric information, a separating equilibrium exists when the proportion of low-risk individuals in the population is sufficiently large. Otherwise, a competitive insurance market does not have equilibrium.*

Note that in a separating equilibrium high-risk individuals choose the same contract C_H as in the first-best. However, low-risk individuals obtain less than optimal (full) coverage. Accordingly, we should expect a welfare loss due to the negative externality that high-risk individuals impose on the low-risk ones. There is a stream of literature trying to overcome the non-existence result in the Rothschild and Stiglitz model of a competitive insurance market. Zweifel *et al.* (2009, ch. 5) and Belli (2001) survey the main contributions.

11.4.3 Signaling

The analysis of moral hazard and adverse selection shows that the principal distorts the contract to cope with the asymmetry of information. This is because the informed party will try to use their private information in their own interest. However, there exist situations where the informed party cannot take advantage of their informational advantage. In this case the informed party would be willing to disclose his/her private information. For instance in studying the adverse selection problem we have seen that one type is left unaffected by the asymmetry of information, while the other type is strictly worse off. Therefore, an agent will be willing to disclose his/her private information if by doing so the greater utility obtained offsets the cost of disclosing the information. Then, we say that the agent *sends a signal* to reveal his/her type. The action of sending the signal is called *signaling*.

To illustrate these ideas, let us think of the following question (see Macho-Stadler and Pérez-Castrillo 2001, ch. 5): why do firms advertise job vacancies announcing that they seek a recent graduate, without specifying the exact type of studies? Spence (1973) was the first to address this question. His answer was that education acts as a signal of the capacity to learn of an individual holding a university degree. It is important to note that the capacity to learn of an individual does not depend on having a degree. This is part of the personal characteristics (given by nature) of the individual. In other words, the fact that an individual has obtained a university degree is of no value *per se* to the firm. However, the firm uses the fact that the agent discloses that information to sort out candidates.

We borrow from Macho-Stadler and Pérez-Castrillo (2001, p. 188) to define a *signal* as "some activity, or some decision, that proves that the agent concerned has a certain ability or characteristic, or possesses certain information". This situation is somewhat similar to adverse selection, but now the party holding private information has the possibility to disclose it by signaling. There are two scenarios where signaling may appear according to whether the private information is held by the principal or by the agent.

When the agent is the informed party, after learning his/her type and before signing the contract, (s)he has the capacity to send a signal that is observed by the principal, aiming at

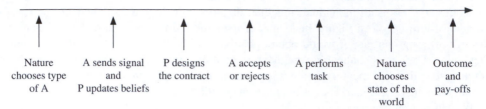

Figure 11.12 Signaling by an agent.

influencing the principal's beliefs about the agent's characteristics. Figure 11.12 (see Macho-Stadler and Pérez-Castrillo 2001, ch. 5.3) illustrates this.

This situation can be identified with, for instance, the decision of physicians to hang all their degrees and diplomas on the walls of the booth where they see patients. In this way, physicians signal their high quality and thus try to influence the patients on their capability to diagnose and design treatments. Without going into the details, the difficulty of the analysis lies in the update of the beliefs that a principal forms on the agent's type once the signal has been sent. Often these models have several equilibria, among them pooling and separating equilibria.

In a *separating equilibrium* good agents signal their characteristic, and bad agents have no interest in paying the cost of getting a degree to be identified as being good. In a separating equilibrium agents of good type incur in the signaling cost to transform an asymmetric information problem into an adverse selection problem with symmetric information.

Pooling equilibria may also exist. In a *pooling equilibrium* no agent is interested in sending a costly signal before signing a contract with the principal. In a pooling equilibrium agents give up the possibility of sending a signal, and the result is the same as that of a pure adverse selection.

Alternatively, it may be the case that the informed party is the principal. Recall Akerlof's model of the used car market. There, the seller (principal) has more information about the quality of the used cars than the buyer (agent). In this type of situation, the seller's decision to price, advertise, offer guarantees, etc. can be seen as a signaling activity to disclose information to the buyer regarding the quality of the cars. The relation between an insurance company and an insured individual can also be framed in this context. Low-risk individuals are willing to provide evidence of their type showing voluntarily (costly) medical reports when deciding whether to accept or reject a health insurance contract. Figure 11.13 (see Macho-Stadler and Pérez-Castrillo, 2001, ch. 5.5) illustrates. Now the principal uses the design of the contract to transmit information to the agent. As before, we can find separating equilibria where the contract signals the principal's type (i.e. the principal transforms an initial situation with asymmetric information into a new one with symmetric information), and pooling equilibria where contracts do not reveal any information.

11.5 Time-consistent contracts

So far we have described the behavior of a competitive insurer and an individual whom, when sick, health care allows to recover his/her healthy status. However, there is a family of illnesses whose treatment extends along time (think of AIDS, or cancer). The insurance contracts studied are not well suited for these situations because they imply large increases

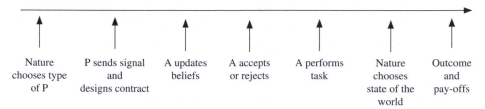

Figure 11.13 Signaling by a principal.

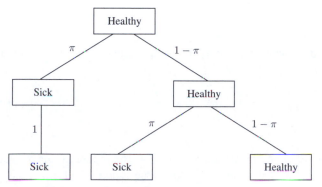

Figure 11.14 Two-period time-consistent contracts.

of the premium or simply the rejection of any coverage. Cochrane (1995) addresses this issue and describes *time-consistent contracts* providing long-term insurance.

To illustrate Cochrane's (1995) argument let us consider a model described by the following three characteristics: (i) there is a population of identical individuals living for two periods. In each period, any individual has an income y and faces a probability π of being affected by a long-term illness. That is, if the individual becomes sick in period 1, then he will be sick in period 2 with probability 1. If in period 1 the individual stays healthy, then he may be sick in period 2 with the same probability as in period 1; (ii) when an individual is ill, he generates health care expenditures for a value of M per period; and (iii) the insurance market is competitive so that premiums are actuarially fair and individuals will contract full insurance.[4] Figure 11.14 illustrates the sequence of events just described. Finally, at the end of period 1, both parties (insured and insurer) can terminate the contract.

At the beginning of the game, the risk type of an individual is not known. Therefore, insurers will offer insurance with a fair premium equal to the average health care expenditure in each period, that is in period 1, $P_1 = \pi M$ and in period 2, $P_2 = \bar{\pi} M$, so that individuals do not bear any premium risk. However, this argument has a problem. Consider an individual who is healthy in period 1. Then, in period 2 he has incentives to cancel the contract, and replace it by a new one-period contract with a premium equal to his expected cost πM, thus saving $(\bar{\pi} - \pi)M$ in period 2. As a consequence, only high-risk individuals (those ill in period 1) would maintain the two-period contract and the insurer would incur in losses. Accordingly, the insurer would never offer a long-term contract.

Let us study in detail this problem and Cochrane's proposal to design a long-term contract.

An insurance contract defines a premium and an indemnity for the first period (P_1, I_1), and a premium and indemnity for the second period contingent on having been healthy or sick in the first period, (P_{2h}, I_{2h}) or (P_{2s}, I_{2s}). We assume that the individual can save some income in the first period S, to be spent in the second period. Finally to simplify we assume that there is no discounting and that the interest rate is zero.

The expected utility of an individual over the two periods is given by

$$EU = (1 - \pi)V(y - P_1 - S) + \pi V(y - P_1 - S + I_1 - M)$$
$$+ (1 - \pi)^2 V(y - P_{2h} + S) + (1 - \pi)\pi V(y - P_{2h} + I_{2h} + S - M)$$
$$+ \pi V(y - P_{2s} + I_{2s} + S - M) \tag{11.22}$$

The zero-profit condition for the insurer induced by the competitive insurance market reads,

$$P_1 + \pi P_{2s} + (1 - \pi)P_{2h} = \pi I_1 + \pi I_{2s} + \pi(1 - \pi)I_{2h} \tag{11.23}$$

The design of the optimal intertemporal insurance contract consists in identifying the set of variables $(S, P_1, I_1, P_{2h}, I_{2h}, P_{2s}, I_{2s})$ that maximize the value function (11.22) subject to the constraint (11.23).

Let us denote the disposable income of the individual in the different scenarios as,

$$H = y - P_1 - S$$
$$S = y - P_1 - S + I_1 - M$$
$$HH = y - P_{2h} + S$$
$$HS = y - P_{2h} + S + I_{2h} - M$$
$$SS = y - P_{2s} + S + I_{2s} - M \tag{11.24}$$

Let $\mathcal{L}$ denote the Lagrangian function associated with the optimizing problem just described, and let λ represent the Lagrange multiplier associated to the constraint (11.23). Then, the first-order conditions are,

$$\frac{\partial \mathcal{L}}{\partial S} = -(1 - \pi)V'(H) - \pi V'(S) + \pi V'(SS) + \pi(1 - \pi)V'(HS)$$
$$+ (1 - \pi)^2 V'(HH) = 0, \tag{11.25}$$

$$\frac{\partial \mathcal{L}}{\partial P_1} = -(1 - \pi)V'(H) - \pi V'(S) + \lambda = 0, \tag{11.26}$$

$$\frac{\partial \mathcal{L}}{\partial I_1} = \pi V'(S) - \pi \lambda = 0, \tag{11.27}$$

$$\frac{\partial \mathcal{L}}{\partial P_{2h}} = -\pi(1-\pi)V'(HS) - (1-\pi)^2 V'(HH) + (1-\pi)\lambda = 0, \qquad (11.28)$$

$$\frac{\partial \mathcal{L}}{\partial I_{2h}} = \pi(1-\pi)V'(HS) - \pi(1-\pi)\lambda = 0, \qquad (11.29)$$

$$\frac{\partial \mathcal{L}}{\partial P_{2s}} = -\pi V'(SS) + \pi\lambda = 0, \qquad (11.30)$$

$$\frac{\partial \mathcal{L}}{\partial I_{2s}} = \pi V'(SS) - \pi\lambda = 0, \qquad (11.31)$$

$$\frac{\partial \mathcal{L}}{\partial \lambda} = P_1 + \pi P_{2s} + (1-\pi)P_{2h} - \pi I_1 - \pi I_{2s} - \pi(1-\pi)I_{2h} = 0. \qquad (11.32)$$

Note that (11.30) and (11.31) coincide and tell us that the restriction is binding. It introduces a degree of freedom that will not allow to uniquely determine the design of the optimal intertemporal contract. This is so because P_{2s} and I_{2s} only appear in the definition of disposable income SS, so that they are always linked together.

Combining (11.27), (11.29), and (11.31) it follows that $V'(S) = V'(HS) = V'(SS)$. From (11.28) and (11.29), it follows that $V'(HS) = V'(HH)$. Similarly, from (11.26) and (11.27), it follows that $V'(S) = V'(H)$. Accordingly, we find that in equilibrium marginal utilities are equalized across the different possible episodes an individual may be facing. In turn, this implies that (11.25) is trivially satisfied.

Also, the equality $V'(HS) = V'(HH)$ implies $HS = HH$ which in turn yields $I_{2h} = M$. In a similar fashion, the equality $V'(S) = V'(H)$ implies $S = H$, or $I_1 = M$. Summarizing,

$$I_1 = I_{2h} = M. \qquad (11.33)$$

Substituting the values of these indemnities into (11.32) we obtain,

$$P_1 + \pi P_{2s} + (1-\pi)P_{2h} = \pi(2-\pi)M + \pi I_{2s}, \qquad (11.34)$$

and we have five variables to determine $(P_1, P_{2s}, P_{2h}, I_{2s}, S)$. Observe that any value of S will be compatible with any solution.

Note that this argument does not take into account the possibility that at the end of period 1 the individual (and the insurer) can terminate the contract, and sign a new one-period contract with another insurer. The individual (and the insurer) will do so if by switching contracts there is a net gain. Cochrane (1995) defines a time-consistent contract as an agreement where no party has incentives to terminate the contract at the end of period 1. To design such a contract we have to take into account the *severance payment* if the contract is terminated, and the premium of the new contract. To determine the severance payment let us compute the variation of the expected expenditures in the second period. At the beginning of period 1 at the moment of signing the contract and before the realization of the state of nature, the expected medical expenses of an individual in period 2 are,

$$\pi M + \pi(1-\pi)M = \pi(2-\pi)M.$$

At the end of period 1 after nature determined the state of the individual, the expected expenditures in period 2 will be either M or πM, according to whether the individual was sick or healthy in period 1 respectively. Therefore, if in $t = 1$ the individual was sick, the variation in medical expenses in period 2 is,

$$M - \pi(2 - \pi)M = M(1 - \pi(2 - \pi)).$$
(11.35)

Alternatively, if in period 1 the individual was healthy the variation in medical expenses in period 2 is,

$$\pi M - \pi(2 - \pi)M = -\pi(1 - \pi)M.$$
(11.36)

Define now the following rule: if an individual or the insurer terminates the contract, the severance payment is given by the variation in medical expenditures just computed. An interpretation of this rule is the following. The insurer at the moment of signing the contract commits to pay the medical expenses of the individual over two periods. In particular, if the individual turns out to fall sick in period 1 and the contract is terminated, the insurer would "save" paying medical expenses by an amount given by (11.35). The rule says that the insurer should transfer such amount to the individual as a severance payment. Alternatively, if the individual was healthy in period 1, a parallel argument establishes that he should pay the insurer the amount given by (11.36) as a severance payment.

Given this rule, let us compute the total payments an individual faces when changing contracts in any state of nature. In period 2 the insurer observes whether the individual is sick or healthy. Therefore, if the individual was sick in period 1, the new one-period contract will contain a premium of M; if the individual was healthy in period 1, the fair premium of the new one-period contract will be πM. Adding up severance payments and premiums, we observe that the total payment for an individual switching contracts is of $\pi(2 - \pi)M$ regardless of whether he or she was sick or healthy in period 1.

The rule defining the severance payment leaves the parties signing the contract indifferent to terminating the contract at the end of period 1 or continuing it until the end of period 2. This indifference is at the root of the design of a time-consistent contract. Formally, the contract must contain a premium in period 2 such that the parties do not have incentives to terminate the contract, i.e.

$$P_{2s} = P_{2h} = \pi(2 - \pi)M$$
(11.37)

The determination of the equilibrium premia in period 2 given by (11.37) together with the equilibrium indemnities (11.33) will allow us to characterize the equilibrium values of the remaining variables (P_1, I_{2s}, S).

From (11.29) and (11.31) we already know that $SS = HS$. Substituting (11.37) and (11.33), we obtain,

$$I_{2s} = M.$$
(11.38)

In turn, substituting (11.37), (11.33), and (11.38) into (11.32), it follows that

$$P_1 = \pi M.$$
(11.39)

Finally, from (11.27) and (11.31) we already know that

$$S = SS.$$

Substituting all the equilibrium values of the variables implied we obtain,

$$S = \frac{\pi(1-\pi)}{2} M. \tag{11.40}$$

Summarizing, the characteristics of Cochrane's time-consistent contract are,

$$I_1 = I_{2s} = I_{2h} = M,$$

$$P_1 = \pi M,$$

$$P_{2h} = P_{2s} = \pi(2-\pi)M,$$

$$S = \frac{\pi(1-\pi)}{2} M.$$

This contract as already mentioned provides full coverage, premia are actuarially fair, and savings S guarantees the redistribution of resources across periods. Cochrane already points out that the design of these contracts hinges on the assumption that low-risk individuals (i.e., those healthy in the first period) are willing to transfer the severance payment to the insurer or equivalently, that transfer can be enforced in court. A possible way out suggested by Cochrane himself is that low-risk individuals transfer the severance payment at the beginning of the period. Zweifel *et al.* (2009) question the viability of this type of contract because in most cases of long-term illnesses, many elements of the treatment cannot be specified in the contract. As an illustration Zweifel *et al.* consider the possibility of an insured demanding intensive psychotherapy while the insurer deems occasional counseling sufficient, so that it is difficult for a court to resolve a conflict of this type.

11.6 Supplier-induced demand

In the physician–patient relationship, the physician plays a dual role. He or she provides diagnosis and treatment. As has been commented earlier in this chapter, this gives the physician an informational advantage over the patient. Now we look at the activity of a physician in his or her private practice, and study whether this informational advantage is used to distort performance away from efficiency and obtain extra profits. This phenomenon is known as *supplier-induced demand* (SID), and has been a controversial topic among economists. Although it does not apply exclusively to physicians (lawyers are another typical example of professional practice raising the same question), it is in the health care sector where the debate is hottest.

To start, we should remember that patient demand for care is determined by the physician. This would be innocuous if the physician is be a perfect agent for the patient. However, when the physician's decisions are altered so that a *systematic* increase in the physician activity results, we say that the physician is inducing (extra) demand, or that supply-induced demand occurs.

The origin of the controversy dates back to the contributions by Shain and Roemer (1959) and Roemer (1961) that can be summarized in the *Roemer effect*: "a bed built is a bed filled". This observation is motivated by the apparent correlation identified by Shain and Roemer between the availability of beds per 1,000 inhabitants and the rate of use measured by the number of days per 1,000 inhabitants in several States in the US.

The basic idea of the SID is simple (see Folland *et al.* 2009, ch. 10; McGuire 2000; Zweifel *et al.* 2009, ch. 8) and is illustrated in Figure 11.15.

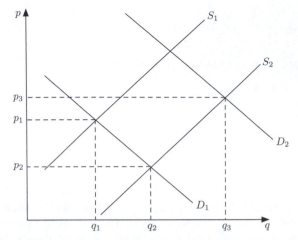

Figure 11.15 Supplier-induced demand.

DEFINITION 11.7 (SUPPLIER-INDUCED DEMAND).   Supplier-induced demand (SID) refers to a situation where the provider in acting as an agent for the patient, induces a level of consumption of health care services larger than what the patient would have demanded should he or she have been fully informed and able to choose freely.

SID is an economic concept to be distinguished from the concept of *overtreatment*. Actually, they are independent concepts. Overtreatment refers to a technical assessment of the difference between the treatment technically necessary and the treatment actually provided. For instance, a patient may demand more treatment than what would be technically necessary (a phenomenon often detected in primary care). In this case we would observe overtreatment without inducement. On the other hand, we may find patients preferring less treatment than what would technically be necessary and being induced to consume more.

11.6.1   SID in the health care market

Consider a competitive market for health care provision, and assume that the initial situation of the market is described by a demand curve D_1 and a supply curve S_1 (see Figure 11.15), characterizing an equilibrium (p_1, q_1). Assume now that for some reason the supply of physicians in the market increases, thus shifting the supply curve to the right to S_2. As we studied in Chapter 4, there will be a new equilibrium at (p_2, q_2). In this new equilibrium, the overall expenditure of the health care sector may increase or decrease depending on the elasticity of the demand. The empirical evidence points towards an inelastic demand of health care services, so that we should expect a decrease in aggregate health care spending. Also, the increase in supply, at the given demand D_1 means that the activity *per physician* diminishes and so do the profits of every physician.

If physicians are not perfect agents, but in treating their patients also pursue their own interests (profits), they can manipulate demand taking advantage of their informational advantage recommending unnecessary services (analysis, controls, visits, etc.) so that demand is artificially increased and the demand curve shifts to the right to D_2. The consequence of this inducement of demand is a new market equilibrium characterized by (p_3, q_3).

Thus, in the short run we observe a variation of the equilibrium of the market from (p_1, q_1) to (p_3, q_3).

The question that remains is how can we associate this new equilibrium to an inducement of demand by the physicians. Reinhardt (1985) proposes a partial test of demand inducement consisting of estimating the correlation between the price of medical services and the supply of health care services. If the correlation is positive as in the example in Figure 11.15, it is interpreted as evidence of inducement. Otherwise, the test is inconclusive.

Note that in a system of full health care insurance the patient does not have any incentive to resist demand inducement beyond the extra cost of time associated with the additional and unnecessary consumption of health care services. Accordingly, countries where the provision of health care is organized around a national health service (NHS), provide a natural framework in which to observe demand inducement.

11.6.2   SID and the individual physician

A different approach to study the problem of SID is to examine the physicians' individual behavior. Zweifel *et al.* (2009, ch. 8) provide a model inspired in Evans (1974) where the utility of the physician depends on income and the capacity to induce demand.

Let us consider a simplified version of the Zweifel *et al.* model where a population of n fully insured patients (therefore insensitive to the price of medical services) receive treatment from a population of a identical physicians. Let us denote by $\delta \equiv a/n$ the physician–population ratio. Assume that the (unit) price of medical services, p, is given. Assume also that each patient demands M units of care, and that each physician can "induce" $s \geq 0$ units of additional demand. In this set-up, total demand of health care services is $nM + sa$. In other words, demand per physician is

$$h(\delta, s) = \frac{M}{\delta} + s \tag{11.41}$$

and demand per patient is

$$q(\delta, s) = M + s\delta \tag{11.42}$$

Accordingly, a physician's income is given by an increasing and concave function,

$$y = ph(\delta, s), \qquad y' > 0, \, y'' < 0. \tag{11.43}$$

Finally, the physician obtains utility from his/her income and capacity to induce demand. We model it as a concave function increasing in income and decreasing in demand inducement (reflecting the ethical conflict)

$$U = U(y, s), \tag{11.44}$$

where $\partial U/\partial y > 0$, $\partial^2 U/\partial y^2 < 0$, $\partial U/\partial s < 0$, $\partial^2 U/\partial s^2 \leq 0$.

The problem of the physician is to select the level of inducement that maximizes utility. Substituting (11.43) into (11.44), we can write the problem of the physician as

$$\max_s U = U(ph(\delta, s), s), \tag{11.45}$$

so that the first-order condition is

$$\frac{\partial U}{\partial s} = p\frac{\partial U}{\partial h}\frac{\partial h}{\partial s} + \frac{\partial U}{\partial s} = 0. \tag{11.46}$$

From (11.41), it follows that $\partial h/\partial s = 1$. The first observation stemming from (11.46) is that demand inducement requires $p > 0$. In other words, demand inducement is a consequence of a fee-for-service payment system. The second observation is that we can obtain the optimal value of inducement solving the implicit function $F(s; \delta, M, p) = 0$. The solution $s^*(\delta, M, p)$ tells us that the physician induces demand until the level at which the marginal benefit of additional consumption equals the marginal utility loss (from ethical conflict) from demand inducement.

Recall that SID refers to physicians' reaction to variations in δ, the ratio of physician to patients, and p, the reimbursement fee. Therefore, we have to study the comparative statics of the model with respect to these two parameters.

Let us examine first the comparative statics with respect to δ.

Demand per patient is given by (11.42). Then,

$$\frac{\partial q}{\partial \delta} = s + \delta\frac{\partial s}{\partial \delta}.$$

This expression tells us that an increase in the physician–patient ratio (given by, say, an exogenous increase in the number of physicians) yields a non-negative direct effect in the form of inducement, and an indirect effect given by the impact of the physician–patient ratio on demand inducement. Note that a sufficient condition for a positive total effect is the positivity of the second component. The sign of $\delta(\partial s/\partial \delta)$ using the implicit function theorem, is given by

$$\frac{\partial s}{\partial \delta} = -\frac{\dfrac{\partial F(s; \delta, M, p)}{\partial \delta}}{\dfrac{\partial F(s; \delta, M, p)}{\partial s}} > 0.$$

The positive sign comes from the fact that second-order conditions ensure that the denominator is negative, and the numerator is positive (see the details in Zweifel *et al.* p. 302).

Figure 11.16 provides a graphical interpretation of the model proposed. We depict in the space (y, s) the income line of the physician as given by (11.43) in an initial situation represented by $ph(\delta, s)$, and the indifference curve tangent to this income line at the point A. This represents the optimal choice of inducement s_a yielding an income level y_a.

Next, assume an exogenous increase in the number of physicians while the population of patients remains constant. This increases the ratio δ and the demand per patient changes to $\hat{h}(\delta, s)$. Accordingly, the income function (11.43) becomes $\hat{y} = \hat{h}(\delta, s)$ that is also represented in the figure together with the corresponding tangent indifference curve at point B. The decrease of demand is compensated by the physician with an increase in inducement to s_b allowing mitigation of loss of income from $\hat{y}_b$ (if the physician would have maintained level of inducement) to y_b. The analysis proposed deserves some remarks. First, we have assumed fully insured patients. If patients are partially covered, they will be sensitive to the expenses generated and thus, it is to be expected some resistance to demand inducement. Second, we have also assumed a fee-for-service reimbursement system. Other payment systems like capitation do not generate incentives to induce demand.

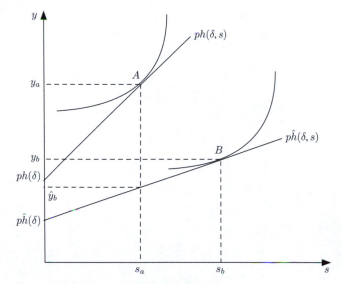

Figure 11.16 SID and physician behavior.

Comparative statics with respect to p are ambiguous.

Part III
IO in health care

12 Competition in health care markets

This chapter looks at the different dimensions in which competition takes place in the health care market. It starts by looking at price competition in terms of the payment systems stemming from the negotiations between payers and providers and their efficiency consequences. Next, the focus moves to quality competition. First we analyze the impact of financial incentives on the (re)classification of patients; next we study the effect of the market structure on the competition among providers to attract patients. The chapter ends with an appraisal of technology adoption as a major driver of the growth of health care costs.

12.1 Payment systems

As described earlier, the health care sector has a specific characteristic – there is an important role played by insurance mechanisms – leading third-party payers to negotiate directly with providers of health care regarding the prices (and sometimes volume) of care given to patients. In this context, definition of payment rules and payment values has assumed a central role in the working of the health care sector.

Historically, both passive insurance companies and national health services paid providers on the basis of their invoices of historical costs, respectively. The steep increase in health care expenditures motivated the search for payment mechanisms that would help to contain expenditures growth.

The trend in the way providers are paid is very clear: moving from simple cost reimbursement to prospective payment by sickness episode (mainly to hospitals), and even capitation payments covering all health expenditures of a beneficiary population have been adopted. The economic justification for this trend lies in the incentives for efficiency that have been pointed out regarding prospective payments relative to cost reimbursement approaches.

The rationale underlying this economic justification is that under a cost reimbursement payment system, the provider does not have incentives to be cost efficient. Any cost saving it achieves is transferred to the third-party payer, and it by definition reimburses costs.

In the other system, prospective payment defines *ex-ante* a value to be paid independently of the actual costs of health care provision. Under this payment mechanism, all cost savings achieved by the health care provider are kept by it. The health care provider therefore has strong incentives to look for ways to increase its efficiency. More efficient provision of health care allows for lower prices.

The basic argument in favor of prospective payment vs. cost reimbursement is well known from the theory of regulation.[1] The prospective payment mechanism has high-powered incentives, while cost reimbursement has low-powered incentives. This main feature is prevalent to several extensions of the analysis, considering that treatment costs have some element of uncertainty.

Although the main ideas behind the use of different payment mechanisms are already in regulation theory, particular features of the health care sector demand specific treatment and adjustments in the analysis must be done.

A relevant issue is the proper definition of the main objectives of health care providers. It has become common to assume that health care providers are concerned about both financial results and patients' benefits from treatment. This departure from pure profit motivations has implications for the design of optimal payment mechanisms. In particular, it may lead to optimal mixed payment mechanisms (the mixed payment mechanism has a prospective component and a partial cost reimbursement). We will now introduce a simple model to illustrate the above discussion.

12.1.1   A simple model of payment systems

Consider a hospital providing health care services q.[2] The production of health care services has a cost $c(q, e)$, where e is the efficiency effort performed by the hospital management.

We assume that more health care production raises costs at an increasing rate ($\partial c/\partial q > 0$, $\partial^2 c/\partial q^2 > 0$), while more efficiency effort lowers total cost and marginal cost of health care services ($\partial c/\partial e < 0$, $\partial^2 c/\partial q \partial e < 0$) but does so at a decreasing rate ($\partial^2 c/\partial e^2 < 0$, $\partial^3 c/\partial q \partial e^2 > 0$). Efficiency efforts have a cost $\phi(e)$ for the hospital management (with $\partial \phi(e)/\partial e > 0$ and $\partial^2 \phi/\partial e^2 > 0$).

The payment system is defined by $R = \alpha + \beta c(q, e)$. Total payment R to the hospital is made up by a prospective component α and a share β of costs. A fully prospective payment mechanism occurs for $\alpha > 0$, $\beta = 0$, and a full cost reimbursement payment system is characterized by $\alpha = 0$ and $\beta = 1$. A mixed payment system has $\alpha > 0$ and $\beta < 1$.

Patients' benefits from treatment are $b(q)$, with b being a concave function with a maximum value at q^*. This representation of patients' benefits can mean that too much treatment may be harmful to the patient.[3]

Consider the effort choice problem faced by the hospital management, taken as given the "quantity" of services (this assumption will be relaxed below). Then, the decision problem relates only to the effort choice:

$$\max_{\{e\}} R - c(q, e) - \phi(e) \tag{12.1}$$

where $R = \alpha + \beta c(q, e)$. The first-order condition characterizing the optimal choice of effort is:[4]

$$(\beta - 1)\frac{\partial c}{\partial e} - \frac{\partial \phi}{\partial e} = 0 \tag{12.2}$$

It becomes clear from this condition that $\beta = 1$ implies $e = 0$ (or the minimum observable value).

Thus, a pure cost reimbursement model leads to no efficiency effort. Under $\beta = 0$ (a prospective payment system), the first-order condition can be written as:

$$-c_e = \phi_e \tag{12.3}$$

and a strictly positive level of efficiency effort will be exerted.

Note the crucial difference between the two cases: under pure cost reimbursement, the health care provider does not have any gain from existing efficiency effort, and therefore it minimizes it. Under prospective payment, the hospital management keeps all efficiency gains and has an incentive to make positive effort.

We can use the same framework to address the choice of "quantity" of care by the provider. Take the efficiency effort as fixed (the discussion of a simultaneous choice of efficiency effort and quality is provided below). We assume an objective function for the provider that includes both the financial results and patients' benefits, as described above. Thus, the semi-altruistic provider has utility:

$$U = U(b(q), \Pi = R - c(q, e)) \tag{12.4}$$

The utility function U has positive marginal utilities ($\partial U / \partial b > 0$, $\partial U / \partial \Pi > 0$), at decreasing rates ($\partial^2 U / \partial b^2 < 0$, $\partial^2 U / \partial \Pi^2 < 0$), and marginal valuation of patients' benefits is greater for a better financial result for the health care provider ($\partial^2 U / \partial b \partial \Pi > 0$).

As before, we take a linear payment rule $R = \alpha + \beta c(q, e)$. The optimal choice of quantity is provided by the solution to the following first-order condition:[5]

$$\frac{\partial U}{\partial b} \frac{\partial b}{\partial q} + \frac{\partial U}{\partial \Pi} (\beta - 1) \frac{\partial c}{\partial q} = 0 \tag{12.5}$$

From this first-order condition, it follows directly that for $\beta = 1$ (full cost reimbursement), the quantity that maximizes patients' benefits is selected:

$$\frac{\partial b}{\partial q} = 0 \tag{12.6}$$

from which $q = q^*$.

At the margin, patients' benefits are zero. Under full cost reimbursement, care is provided but no additional benefit for patients exists. This result has an immediate implication: too much health care is provided from a social point of view under cost reimbursement. Marginal benefits are zero but marginal costs are strictly positive.

Let next $\beta = 0$ (a full prospective payment), then the condition defining the equilibrium quantity is:

$$\frac{\partial b}{\partial q} = \frac{\partial U / \partial \Pi}{\partial U / \partial b} \times \frac{\partial c}{\partial q} \tag{12.7}$$

This equation defines an equilibrium quantity lower than q^*, as in equilibrium marginal benefit is positive.

Thus, compared to the full cost reimbursement system, the prospective payment system leads to a lower quantity of care being provided. Since the cost reimbursement payment system implied too much health care, the prospective payment system offers the possibility of a more appropriate level of care from the social point of view. To assess whether or not this is the case, one needs to set the benchmark quantity from a social point of view.

Following Ellis and McGuire (1986), we assume a social welfare function defined by benefits to patients (valued in monetary terms) minus costs of provision:

$$SWF = b(q) - c(q, e) \tag{12.8}$$

From this social welfare function, which assumes no costs associated with the payment system and no social value given to managers' utility, it follows an optimal quantity of care given by the solution to the first-order condition for maximization of social welfare:

$$\frac{\partial b}{\partial q} = \frac{\partial c}{\partial q} \tag{12.9}$$

This condition highlights that at the social optimum, marginal benefits to patients should equal marginal costs of provision. Thus, it confirms that cost reimbursement leads to too much quantity. Prospective payment systems on the other hand may lead to the socially optimal quantity whenever

$$\frac{\partial U/\partial \Pi}{\partial U/\partial b} = 1 \tag{12.10}$$

The socially optimal quantity results if the ratio of marginal utilities in the left-hand side is equal to one. It is above (below) the optimal quantity if the same ratio is greater (smaller) than one.

Another implication, using the first-order condition (12.7) and comparing it with the condition for a social optimum, is that a mixed system with

$$(1 - \beta)\frac{\partial U/\partial \Pi}{\partial U/\partial b} = 1 \tag{12.11}$$

or

$$\beta = 1 - \frac{\partial U/\partial b}{\partial U/\partial \Pi} \tag{12.12}$$

leads to the optimal choice from the social point of view.

Under certain conditions, the socially optimal level of quantity of care can be attained with a mixed payment system.

The next logical step in the analysis is to add the efficiency decision by the hospital to the quantity decision.

Taking both decisions by hospital management, quantity and efficiency effort, as simultaneous decisions under a mixed payment system $R = \alpha + \beta c(q, e)$, the problem to be solved is

$$\max_{\{e,q\}} U(b(q), \alpha + \beta c(q, e)) - \phi(e) \tag{12.13}$$

and the first-order conditions are

$$\frac{\partial \Pi}{\partial q} = b'(q)\frac{\partial U}{\partial b} - (1 - \beta)\frac{\partial c}{\partial q}\frac{\partial U}{\partial \Pi} = 0 \tag{12.14}$$

$$\frac{\partial \Pi}{\partial e} = -(1 - \beta)\frac{\partial c}{\partial e}\frac{\partial U}{\partial \Pi} - \phi'(e) = 0 \tag{12.15}$$

The impact of the cost-sharing parameter β can be seen by total differentiation of these first-order conditions, and solving appropriately. The cross-effect $\partial^2 c/\partial q \partial e$ plays an important role. If higher efficiency effort decreases the marginal cost of providing quantity, then a more prospective rule may increase efficiency enough to lead to an increase in quantity, which is a different result relative to the previous solution.

12.1.2 Efficiency incentives vs. cream skimming

The discussion so far has concerned issues associated with homogeneous patients and superior knowledge by the health care provider relative to the payer.

The existence of heterogeneous patients, known only by the health care provider and not by the third-party payer, leads to a different set of economic problems. In particular, under prospective payment, a provider has a strong incentive to select its patients and choose to treat those involving lower costs. The lowest-cost patients provide a higher financial margin to the health care provider. Thus, health care providers have a clear incentive to pursue an active selection process.

Heterogeneous patients introduce a different trade-off to third-party payers – a more prospective payment system helps in achieving efficiency but creates incentives for selection of patients.

Under the standard model used above, this becomes simple to show. However, this trade-off actually results from having more objectives than instruments. While the prospective payment in the payment system aims at keeping revenues of providers at the minimum level that it requires to operate, the level of cost reimbursement is set to achieve the opposite goals of no risk selection and of operational efficiency.

To solve this issue Barros (2003) proposes an additional instrument, which can be interpreted as an *ex-post* adjustment fund, that allows under its specific rules to achieve efficiency without inducing risk selection of patients by the health care provider.

We consider here a simplified version of Barros (2003) to illustrate the main points. Individuals have utility

$$V_j = U(Y - T(Y) - F_i) - p_j \bar{B} \tag{12.16}$$

where Y is personal income, assumed equal across the population, $T(Y)$ is an income-based tax and F_i is a payment made directly by individual j to insurance institution i (be it a private insurance company, a public fund or the national health service). The cost of being sick is denoted by $\bar{B}$ and sickness occurs with probability p_j, which differs across members of the population.

To simplify matters, we assume this probability to be uniformly distributed in the population. The size of the population is normalized to 1. When sick a patient needs to receive health care with monetary cost X. This monetary cost depends on effort e to organize health care provision: $X = X(e)$; $X'(e) < 0, X''(e) > 0$.

Efficiency effort e is non-contractible. The cost $X(e)$ is observable and contractible. Exerting effort for cost containment implies a cost $\phi(e)$ per beneficiary of the health insurance system, with positive and increasing marginal cost, $\phi'(e) > 0, \phi''(e) > 0$. Examples of this effort are check-ups and early screening, monitoring and utilization review.

The health insurance institution maximizes expected profits, defined by

$$\Pi_i = \int_{p \in \Omega_i} (S_i(p, X(e_i)) + F_i - c(e_i) - pX(e_i)) \, dp \tag{12.17}$$

where the integral sums over all the population members that are beneficiaries of health institution i (denoted by Ω_i).[6]

The term S_i denotes the per capita transfer payment received by the health insurance institution (with no discrimination according to the underlying risk). Competition between health insurance institutions is present in their choice of F_i. The regulatory system imposes open enrollment, meaning that a consumer that accepts to pay F_i cannot be rejected.

The first decision is taken by the government and defines the payment rule S_i. Then health insurance institutions choose F_i. Consumers choose their health insurer. Finally, the health insurance institution selects its efficiency effort, nature decides who is sick in the population, health care is demanded, provided and paid.

We first characterize the optimal choice efficiency effort by the health insurance institution. Maximization of expected profit with respect to the effort, e, yields the following first-order condition:

$$\int_{p\in\Omega_i} \left(\frac{\partial S}{\partial X} X'(e_i) - \phi'(e_i) - pX'(e_i) \right) dp = 0 \tag{12.18}$$

Take now S to be a proportion of expected health care costs:

$$S_i = \beta p X(e_i), \quad \beta \leq 1 \tag{12.19}$$

(and the remaining costs must be covered by the charge F_i.)

Under this proportional payment rule, $\partial S/\partial X = \beta p$, and the first-order condition for effort choice is

$$\int_{p\in\Omega_i} ((\beta - 1)pX'(e_i) - c'(e_i)) \, dp = 0 \tag{12.20}$$

When for $\beta = 1$, it follows $e_i = 0$ (the lowest admissible value). This is a relatively general result from moral hazard contexts. The implication is the need to have $\beta < 1$ to induce a positive level of efficiency effort. Next, we have to characterize the optimal choice of F_i. Under competition between health insurance institutions (either by consumers switching between firms or "voice" pressure about fees charged), $F_i = F$ for all health insurance institutions and such that profits are washed away:

$$F = c(e) + X(e)(1 - \beta)\bar{p} \tag{12.21}$$

where $\bar{p}$ is the average probability of illness of the set of consumers who choose to contract with a given health insurance institution.[7]

The next step is the definition of the optimal transfer system set by the government. The government maximizes a utilitarian social welfare function. The maximization of this social welfare function faces three constraints: (i) behavior of health insurance institutions with respect to the choice of cost-reducing effort; (ii) the zero-profit condition for health insurance institutions (competitive equilibrium to set F_i); and (iii) the budget constraint on the funding of the system. This third constraint requires that contributions $T(Y)$ raised must be enough to pay expected transfers.

The problem of the government is

$$\max_{\{\alpha, e_i, F\}} U(Y - T(Y) - F) \tag{12.22}$$

$$\text{s.t.} \quad -X'(e_i)\bar{p}(1-\beta) = c'(e_i)$$

$$F = c(e_i) + X(e_i)\bar{p}(1-\beta)$$

$$T(Y) = \beta\bar{p}X(e_i)$$

From the above discussion, $\beta < 1$ and $F > 0$.

The proportional transfer cannot induce both the efficient provision of efficiency effort and absence of cream-skimming (selection of best cases – low probability of sickness) when the open enrollment rule is not fully enforceable.

Whenever health insurance institutions have an informational advantage over the government and are able to use it to select beneficiaries with better risk characteristics (lower probability of being sick), the definition of a payment that does not create incentives to perform such selection of beneficiaries becomes an issue. It results here from the non-price discrimination across beneficiaries in the direct contribution to the health insurance institution.

Barros (2003) proposes a simple extension to the usual payment mechanism that is able to deal with both concerns: incentives for efficiency and no incentives for risk selection.

The extended payment system can be interpreted as an *ex-post* clearing fund, though a special one as the rules for its definition differ from the ones that have been proposed. The *ex-post* clearing fund sets a stream of future financial flows. The health insurance institutions will internalize the impact of risk selection on the *ex-post* fund contributions. The incentive effect of the *ex-post* fund will differ for net contributors and for net recipients to the fund. More importantly, the *ex-post* fund will accommodate the concerns of no-risk selection without undermining the incentives for efficiency effort. It breaks the trade-off between efficiency incentives and no-selection incentives.

The transfer payment is enlarged to

$$S_i = \alpha + \beta_1\bar{p}_i X(e_i) + \beta_2\hat{p}X(e_i) \tag{12.23}$$

where $\bar{p}_i$ is the average probability of sickness in the beneficiaries of firm i and $\hat{p}$ is the average probability of sickness in the population.

The choice problem of the government regarding the parameters of the payment function is defined by

$$\max_{\{\alpha, \beta_1, \beta_2, F, e\}} U(Y - T(Y) - F) \tag{12.24}$$

$$\text{s.t.} \quad S_i = \alpha + \beta_1\bar{p}_i X(e_i) + \beta_2\hat{p}X(e_i)$$

$$NT(Y) = \sum_i \int_{p_i \in \Omega_i} S_i\, dp$$

$$-c'(e_i) + X'(e_i)(\beta_1\bar{p}_i - \bar{p}_i + \beta_2\hat{p}) = 0$$

$$\Pi_i = 0, \quad \forall i$$

$$\Pi_i/n_i = \Pi_j/n_j, \quad \forall i, j$$

The first constraint is simply the definition of the extended payment rule. The second constraint requires financial balancing in the payments made by the government – the sum of all contributions equals the sum of all capitation payments performed, N being the population size. The third constraint is the induced effort on health insurance institutions. Comparing with the previous problem, it now includes the term $\beta_2 \hat{p} X'(e_i)$, which enlarges the way the government by a suitable choice of the payment rule parameters (the β's) can influence the efficiency effort decision. The fourth constraint is the competitive constraint faced by health insurance institutions as before.

Finally, the fifth constraint requires that profits per beneficiary of the health insurance institution ($\pi i / ni$) are the same whatever set of beneficiaries it chooses to have. By refusing beneficiaries with high probability of sickness or by attracting beneficiaries with low probability of sickness, the health insurance institution is not able to increase its profits. Thus, we are requiring a payment rule that does not create incentives for selection of beneficiaries.

The solution to the problem of optimally choosing the values of β_1 and β_2 has $\beta_1 = 1$ and $\beta_2 = -1$, implying a payment rule given by

$$S_i = \alpha + X(e_i)(\bar{p}_i - \hat{p}) \tag{12.25}$$

It is worth looking in some detail at why this payment rule results. To avoid selection incentives, it is clear that $\beta_1 = 1$, as it makes profits independent of the particular set of beneficiaries (and their risk characteristics) associated with a health insurance institution. Under the traditional payment system, this value of β_1 would also make the profit of the health insurance institution insensitive to gains from efficiency effort and undermine such efforts. However, under the extended payment system, profits per beneficiary still depend on efficiency gains through the term $\hat{p} X(e_i)$.

Then, for $\alpha_2 = -1$, the socially optimal choice of effort gets implemented. This parameter value makes the health insurance institution "owner" of the full saving from cost efficiency, thus providing incentives to exert effort.

Under equilibrium values, the transfer rule can be interpreted in the following way. First, at the start of the year, each health insurance institution receives a lump-sum, pure capitation, payment. Then, at the end of the year, an *ex-post* adjustment fund is used. The *ex-post* adjustment fund is based on a net contribution rule set by $X(e_i)(\bar{p}_i - \hat{p})$.

Selection of patients resulting in a better than average mix of sickness probabilities makes the health insurance institution a net contributor to the fund. This feature reduces the incentives for selection. One may be concerned about incentives in the opposite direction: does it pay to have the sicker patients, so that the health insurance institution becomes a net recipient of transfers from the *ex-post* fund? The answer is negative for a simple reason. Having sicker patients also means that health expenditures will be larger as well, which cancels out the benefits from extra transfers from the fund.

The next issue is about efficiency effort. Whenever the health insurance institution is a net contributor, it becomes clear that the more efficient it is, the less it has to pay to the *ex-post* fund. Once again, of trickier situation may occur when the health insurance institution is a net recipient. But the same reasoning as above applies here. Being less efficient means receiving more from the fund but it also means having more expenditures overall, which is not compensated by the value received from the fund.

A second important point is that the *ex-post* fund is financially balanced (except for the costs of operating the system). Third, the information required to compute the transfers is not particularly demanding, at least not more demanding than other proposals and applications of *ex-post* funds. The necessary elements are the value of health care per capita costs of each health insurance institution, the average cost per sick beneficiary in the health insurance institution and the proportion of "sick" people in the population.

Whenever computations can be made on a disease basis or categorization by type of health risk, age, gender or any other risk adjuster, the same approach to the risk transfer can be applied. Still, a very fine classification of health risks will face the problem of how to assign health care costs to particular diseases or health problems.

Ex-post funds have both advantages and disadvantages relative to simple payment systems. The main advantage is introducing one more instrument to address the efficiency and selection concerns. The main disadvantage of an *ex-post* adjustment fund lies in the need for a balancing agent. Contribution and claims to the fund are the reasons why it balances at equilibrium values. Losses and surpluses may be present in any given year, and need to be managed by some official institution.

12.2 Upcoding

Most works assume that demand is sensitive to the level of quality and the same assumption is kept here. To address the issues of upcoding, we use a simpler version of the model of Kuhn and Siciliani (2008). Let $n = n(T)$ be the number of patients treated, where T is quality of care. Let $nq(\omega)$ be the number of patients treated measured in DRG units. The quantity of care $q(\omega)$ is to be interpreted as intensity of DRG weights. The value ω is the DRG weight that measures intensity of treatment. Let m be the manipulative effort that affects DRG weight for each given patient, $\omega = \omega(m)$. A higher ω leads to a higher q and p is price per point. Thus, choosing a higher m leads to more ω, which means a DRG with a larger price. This interpretation allows treating in a continuous way the choice of DRG, and it should be viewed as a useful approximation. Total costs increase in quality, quantity of care, and manipulative efforts at increasing rates, and are defined as $TC = n(T)c(q, T, m)$, where $c(\cdot)$ is unit cost per patient.

Hospitals are profit maximizers and risk neutral. Their profit function is:

$$\Pi = pn(T)q(\omega(m)) + \alpha - (1 - \beta)n(T)c(q, T, m) \tag{12.26}$$

where α is a lump-sum transfer (prospective payment) and β is the amount of cost sharing.

Upcoding in this context has a direct effect on costs, from manipulation effort m, and an indirect effect, as the effort m implies more resources used in the higher DRG, and more patients treated. The hospital chooses quality and the level of manipulation effort to maximize profits. The associated first-order conditions are

$$\frac{\partial \Pi}{\partial m} = pn \frac{\partial q}{\partial \omega} \frac{\partial \omega}{\partial m} - (1 - \beta)n \frac{\partial c}{\partial q} \frac{\partial q}{\partial \omega} \frac{\partial \omega}{\partial m} - (1 - \beta) \frac{\partial c}{\partial m} n = 0 \tag{12.27}$$

$$\frac{\partial \Pi}{\partial T} = pq \frac{\partial n}{\partial T} - (1 - \beta)c \frac{\partial n}{\partial T} - (1 - \beta) \frac{\partial c}{\partial T} n = 0 \tag{12.28}$$

The interest lies in the impact of the payment system on quality and upcoding (manipulation effort).

We assume the cost function is separable in its elements as an approximation,

$$c(q, T, m) = c_1(q) + c_2(T) + c_3(m) \tag{12.29}$$

then $\partial^2 \Pi / \partial T \partial m = 0$.

Total differentiation of the first-order conditions yields a system of equations to be solved. Let's take the impact of increasing the price per DRG weight (p). The same approach can be used to explore the impact of changing the payment regime parameter β. The system of equations is:

$$\frac{\partial^2 \Pi}{\partial m^2} dm + \frac{\partial^2 \Pi}{\partial m \partial T} dT + \frac{\partial \Pi^2}{\partial m \partial p} dp = 0 \qquad (12.30)$$

$$\frac{\partial^2 \Pi}{\partial T \partial m} dm + \frac{\partial^2 \Pi}{\partial T^2} dT + \frac{\partial \Pi^2}{\partial T \partial p} dp = 0 \qquad (12.31)$$

The direct second-order derivates are negative, and the cross derivative is zero due to the simplifying assumption of cost separability. It is also the case that

$$\frac{\partial^2 \Pi}{\partial m \partial p} = n \frac{\partial q}{\partial \omega} \frac{\partial \omega}{\partial m} > 0 \qquad (12.32)$$

$$\frac{\partial^2 \Pi}{\partial T \partial p} = q \frac{\partial n}{\partial T} > 0 \qquad (12.33)$$

The solution to the system of equations gives:

$$\frac{dm}{dp} > 0 \quad \frac{dT}{dp} > 0 \qquad (12.34)$$

Increasing the price per DRG weight leads to higher manipulation effort and to higher quality in equilibrium. This is an expected result, as the return from both decisions increases with a higher p.

We start the analysis assuming quality to be fixed. The only decision variable to the hospital management is the manipulation effort. In this context, more cost reimbursement (a higher β) reduces the costs to upcoding without influencing its benefits. This leads to more upcoding in equilibrium under cost reimbursement than under prospective payment. Also, increasing p, holding quality constant, leads to higher manipulation – upcoding – as the benefits from doing it are greater. The same effects hold for the choice of quality, holding "manipulation effort" constant: an increase in cost sharing and/or an increase in the price per DRG point increases quality (either marginal benefit is larger or marginal cost of investment in quality is lower). The reasoning carries through in a straightforward way to the situation of two decision variables, quality and manipulation effort, as shown by the above comparative statics exercise.

When the cost function is not separable, the more natural assumption is that more manipulation effort increases the marginal cost of providing quality. In this case, comparative statics are less clear, as an increase in one decision variable also increments the marginal costs. This will tend to reduce its use.

The main implication of upcoding is that changes in DRG prices also lead to composition changes in DRGs. Several studies, making use of US data, have found evidence of this effect. DRG classification does respond to changes in relative prices of DRGs. Taking as illustrative the empirical work regarding upcoding, consider Dafny's (2005) analysis. Making use of relative price changes of closely related DRGs, and using a difference-in-difference approach, Dafny (2005) concludes that a larger increase in the price of the top DRG (the one with higher complexity and carrying a larger price) leads to a larger increase in the proportion of patients in that DRG.

This evidence reveals the existence of upcoding in response to financial incentives to reclassification of patients. An open issue is whether or not the same incentives and reactions may occur in national health services. Traditional payment systems in national health services relied on global budgets. Recently, the last years have witnessed a move towards prospective payments based on patient classification systems, which have introduced incentives for upcoding even in national health service settings.

12.3 Competition on quality

12.3.1 The choice of quality: monopoly

One major concern in health care is quality. Quality also gets more attention because under health insurance patients become price insensitive when they demand health care. Quality differentials are then the main instrument for providers to attract demand. However, this role for quality, demand guidance, still relies on two maintained assumptions – first, that quality is observable by patients, and second, that patients do have a choice over providers. For certain medical interventions the first assumption will not hold. In a similar way, for some health systems, the second assumption will not hold.

There is a huge literature on outcomes measurement in the fields of health management and in medicine itself. That literature gives only scant attention to economic incentives, in general, and market interactions, in particular. Instead, we are interested in how market forces influence quality (be it through competition across providers or contracting between a payer and a health care provider).

Our first distinction regarding quality is between horizontal and vertical differentiation. Under vertical differentiation, all consumers have the same preferences. They rank products in the exact same way according to preference.[8]

A starting point in the discussion about the choice of quality is the comparison of the socially optimal level of quality and the choice by a monopolist. Gaynor (2006) provides a general discussion and we adapt here the following example, originally from Pepall *et al.* (2005) and also used by Gaynor. Patients' demand is described by the following inverse demand function:

$$p = T(\theta - q) \tag{12.35}$$

where θ is the intensity of preference for the health care treatment, and T is quality. The reservation price is $T\theta$, increasing in quality.

Health care providers have quality and quantity costs, which we assume to be separable in the cost function. Quantity q is produced with constant marginal cost and independent of quality. To simplify exposition, the marginal cost of quantity is c. The costs of quality are convex in the amount of quality provided: $\phi(T) = \gamma T^2/2$.

A monopolist maximizes profits given by

$$\Pi = (p(q) - c)q - \frac{\gamma}{2}T^2 = (\theta - q)qT - \frac{\gamma}{2}T^2 \tag{12.36}$$

A social planner maximizes total welfare, given by patients' welfare net of production costs:

$$SW = T \int_0^q (\theta - x)\, dx - \frac{\gamma}{2}T^2 - cq \tag{12.37}$$

Assume for the moment $c = 0$. The socially optimal values for quantity and quality are given by the solution to the following set of first-order conditions:

$$\frac{\partial SW}{\partial q} = T(\theta - q) = 0 \tag{12.38}$$

$$\frac{\partial SW}{\partial T} = \int_0^q (\theta - x)\, dx - \gamma T = 0 \tag{12.39}$$

Solving this set of first-order conditions yields:

$$q^s = \theta \tag{12.40}$$

$$T^s = \left(\theta q - \frac{1}{2}q^2\right)\frac{1}{\gamma} = \frac{\theta^2}{2\gamma} \tag{12.41}$$

The monopolist's first-order conditions for profit maximization are

$$\frac{\partial \Pi}{\partial q} = \theta - 2q = 0, \quad q^M = \frac{\theta}{2} < q^s \tag{12.42}$$

$$\frac{\partial \Pi}{\partial T} = (\theta - q)q - \gamma T = 0, \quad T^M = \frac{1}{\gamma}\frac{\theta^2}{4} < T^s \tag{12.43}$$

and the monopolist in equilibrium under-provides both quality and quantity.

Suppose that quantity (price) is regulated, and at the same value, whatever the decision maker (social planner/regulator or monopolist), the monopolist still offers lower quality than the social planner. The motive for this result lies in the fact that a social planner values all consumer surplus, while the monopolist values the marginal patient. An increase in quality increases benefits to all patients, whether they are intra-marginal or marginal. However, the monopolist only cares about the willingness to pay of the marginal patient for a quality increase.

A characteristic of health markets is the existence of health insurance protection, meaning that patients pay a fraction s of the cost of the service they demand. Consider $s > 0$, to avoid the need to impose a reservation price set by the national health service acting as a third-party payer.

Demand is now

$$sp = T(\theta - q) \tag{12.44}$$

although the monopolist receives p. Since the fraction $(1 - s)$ is paid by the government, the social planner's choice is the same as before. Take now the monopolist's problem:

$$\max_p \Pi^M = p\left(\theta - \frac{sp}{T}\right) - \gamma\frac{T^2}{2} = \frac{T(\theta - q)q}{s} - \gamma\frac{T^2}{2} \tag{12.45}$$

The corresponding first-order conditions are:

$$\frac{\partial \Pi^M}{\partial q} = \frac{T}{s}(\theta - 2q) = 0, \quad q = \frac{\theta}{2} < q^s \tag{12.46}$$

$$\frac{\partial \Pi^M}{\partial T} = \frac{(\theta - q)q}{s} - \gamma T = 0, \quad T = \frac{1}{2s}\frac{\theta^2}{\gamma} > T^s \tag{12.47}$$

The monopolist still sets a low quantity but quality will be larger or smaller than the socially optimal value. This occurs even with a quantity below the socially optimal level. Since patients pay only a fraction of the price, the market expands considerably. Too much quality emerges in this case due to a specific feature of health care demand, health insurance protection. Because patients are less price sensitive due to insurance, the monopolist uses more quality to increase demand.

12.3.2 Competition in quality

With competition between health care providers the arguments of the previous section holds. The model of Barros and Martinez-Giralt (2002), with both vertical differentiation (quality) and horizontal differentiation, yields basically the same result – too much quality is provided. This results from the system of patients' co-payments and the timing of decisions. That is, price and quality decisions being taken sequentially or simultaneously.

The natural interpretation for simultaneous or sequential decisions follows from easily reversible (low-cost) versus hardly reversible decisions (high-cost) decisions.

For example, primary care services, where investments in facilities are relatively small, and quality is highly related to time spent with the patient, can be an example of simultaneous decision making regarding price and quality.

In contrast, hospital services characterized by investment in wards, operating theaters and high-tech equipment, incur more costs when improving quality. It illustrates a situation of sequential decisions, with quality decisions being taken first for some period of time, observed by all market participants, and then price decisions being taken. In addition, the way providers compete is conditional on the payment system that is set.

We consider here three different regimes: fixed reimbursement rate, in which the same co-insurance rate is applied whatever the provider selected by the patient; fixed co-payment, in which the same amount is reimbursed whatever the provider selected – the amount is defined by a co-insurance applied to a preferred provider; and a pure preferred provider system, in which the patient receives no reimbursement whenever it goes to the outside provider, and receives certain co-insurance if the preferred provider is selected.

A rationale for the existence of co-payments by patients was provided in the context of the insurance decision under moral hazard (either *ex-ante* or *ex-post*). The essential issue was how the individual demand for health care was influenced by different types of co-payments.

We now complement the view on co-payments by looking at how different rules for the co-payment influence the way providers compete against each other. The central aspect is the way a co-payment is defined when a patient decides to use a provider that is not in the set of preferential providers defined by the payer.

Three main options are available. In the first system, the patient has to pay the total price of health care if he or she chooses to go to a provider out of the set of preferential providers. This system corresponds to the choice of a private provider in countries where a national health service is in place. Choosing the public NHS provider is free of charge or may have a co-payment, typically small when compared with the full cost of the service. The NHS funding does not pay when pure private providers are selected by patients.

A second regime is when the co-payment is the same whatever the provider selected by the patient. Defining the co-payment by a co-insurance rate common to all providers, the patient pays a pre-defined fraction of the price set by the provider. This system describes the traditional reimbursement approach of insurance companies (before the ideas of managed care became widespread).

A third option we consider has the payer defining a co-payment based on a set of preferred providers and the same co-payment value being paid in case the patient chooses a different provider, outside of the set of preferred ones by the payer. The patient has freedom of choice and faces always the same co-payment value whatever provider he or she selects. This system describes the reference pricing approach popular in several countries to reimburse the cost of pharmaceutical products. Such rules can also be found in the French health care system.

The analysis of market interactions between providers becomes more complex when both price and quality decisions are present, and whether or not the preferred provider(s) can act as a strategic leader(s) in the market.

To illustrate the fundamental aspects of each of the three regimes, our analysis considers first the simplest case: all providers behave in an identical way and no quality choice exists (alternatively, quality is set by regulation, being outside the set of strategic instruments available to providers). This simple set-up can be extended in several directions, without changing the essential elements.[9]

To make the arguments more precise, we make use of a small stylized model. The model has two providers, named provider A and provider B. The health insurance system, be it public or private, has already defined that provider A is a preferential provider. It can be so because it is a public provider within a national health service or because the health insurance company or sickness fund has set up a network that includes it, but not provider B. As we focus on market interaction between providers, we leave out the issue of why and how provider A is defined to be the preferential provider. Both health care providers are profit maximizers. This is not essential to our arguments although it helps to illustrate the main points of the analysis.

Providers are not perfect substitutes in the eyes of the patients. Since quality has been set aside in the simplest model, differentiation across providers may result from location or some other preference motive. To describe this sort of (horizontal) differentiation, we take the standard approach of seeing providers as located at the endpoints of a road (or, more generally, at the endpoints of a line representing the differentiation characteristic, be it geographic or not). To simplify exposition, this road has one length and there are exactly 1,000 patients at each point of the road.

The location of patients in this road describes their preferences over the two providers. Those located close to provider A choose this provider, for equal prices, due to their preferences.

The distance of a patient to each provider gives a measure of utility loss for not having access to a provider with the preferred characteristics. At each moment in time, patients demand one unit of health care.

We introduce now the financial mechanisms in place. In particular, we have to describe how each provider is treated in terms of the payment system.

As provider A is the preferential one, we assume that insurance protection is such that patients pay only a fraction c of the price charged by provider A. However, if provider B is selected by the patient, the value paid out of pocket by the patient depends on the payment mechanism defined by the insurance system.

The three possibilities discussed above are:

– the same fraction $c > 0$ of price must be paid by the patient, with the insurance mechanism paying the remainder $(1 - c)$. In this case, both providers are actually treated in the same way.

- the patient has to pay the full price. This corresponds to a system in which the insurance arrangement only covers the preferential provider. Resorting to providers outside the network is done at full cost by patients.
- the patient receives the same monetary value, whether it chooses provider A or provider B. Each time one of the providers asks a price above this value, the patient has to pay the excess amount. This roughly corresponds to what the reference pricing system for pharmaceuticals has been in several countries.

The three cases have been defined in a way that differences occur only when provider B is selected. Providers have full decision power over their prices, and for simplicity, production costs are normalized to zero.

We now describe the choice of each patient guided by their utility of choosing one of the providers. The utility of one individual localized in point x of the road, when they select a provider i is given by:

$$V(A,x) = y - cp_A - tx \tag{12.48}$$

$$V(B,x) = y - p_B - t(1-x) + I \tag{12.49}$$

where y is the patient's income, tx is the (utility) cost of choosing provider A, located at point 0 of the road; $t(1-x)$ is the (utility) cost of choosing provider B, located at point 1 of the road; t is the utility cost per unit of distance, measured in monetary units; $p_i, i = A, B$ is the price charged by provider i; c is the co-insurance rate paid by patients when choosing provider A and, finally, I is the compensation paid by the insurance protection system when the non-preferential provider B is selected by the patient. Typically, $I < p_B$. For our three cases of interest,

$I = (1-c)p_B$, when both providers are treated in an identical way,

$I = 0$, when no payment is due if the patient goes outside the network of preferred providers,

$I = (1-c)p_A$, when the same amount that would be paid had the patient chosen provider A, is made available to patients when they choose provider B.

In a more compact way, we can write,

$$I = \alpha(1-c)p_A + \beta(1-c)p_B, \qquad \alpha \in \{0,1\}, \beta \in \{0,1\} \tag{12.50}$$

The first case has $\alpha = 0, \beta = 1$; the second has $\alpha = 0, \beta = 0$; and the third case has $\alpha = 1, \beta = 0$.

Demand faced by each provider is determined by the location of the patient indifferent to going to one or the other provider. All patients from point 0 of the road up to this indifferent patient go to provider A, while all patients located between the indifferent patient and endpoint 1 of the road go to provider B.

The location of the indifferent patient solves the condition

$$V(A,x) = V(B,x). \tag{12.51}$$

Given our utility specification, this condition defines the indifferent patient as

$$x = \frac{1}{2} + \frac{\kappa p_B - \mu p_A}{2t} \tag{12.52}$$

where $\mu = c + (1-c)\alpha, \kappa = 1 - \beta(1-c)$.

Demand faced by provider A is $x \times 1{,}000$, while demand face by provider B is $(1-x) \times 1{,}000$, where 1,000 is the number of patients.

After establishing the choice of provider by patients, we can now describe how providers set their prices. Profits of providers are, respectively,[10]

$$\Pi_A = 1{,}000 x p_A; \quad \Pi_B = 1{,}000(1-x)p_B \tag{12.53}$$

Profit maximization in the choice of prices, assuming Nash behavior of providers (that is, each takes the price of the other provider, as given), yields as equilibrium prices:

$$p_A^* = \frac{t}{\mu}, \quad p_B^* = \frac{t}{\kappa} \tag{12.54}$$

The total payment made by the insurance arrangement and patients is:

$$T = p_A^* + (1-x)p_B^* \tag{12.55}$$

The insurance arrangement implies a cost to the insurer given by

$$(1-c)p_A^* x + (1-x)I(p_B^*) \tag{12.56}$$

The following table describes equilibrium prices and total costs to the system.

		Price	Total costs
$(\alpha=0, \beta=1)$	fixed reimbursement	$p_A=t/c, \; p_B=t/c$	$1000 \times \dfrac{t}{c}$
$(\alpha=0, \beta=0)$	pure reimbursement	$p_A=t/c, \; p_B=t$	$1000 \times \dfrac{t}{2}\left(1+\dfrac{1}{c}\right)$
$(\alpha=1, \beta=0)$	reference pricing	$p_A=t, \; p_B=t$	$1000 \times t$

Since all patients demand (and receive) one unit of care, benefits to patients are the same whatever payment mechanism is selected. Thus, comparison across models is based on the total (monetary) costs imposed by each alternative.

From the above table it is easy to see that reference pricing has the lowest prices and total (monetary) costs, while the (traditional) fixed reimbursement rate has the highest prices and total (monetary) costs.

In terms of utility costs, both the fixed reimbursement regime and the reference pricing regime achieve a split of patients that minimizes the utility costs from not having the most preferred provider (the one that would be located at the same point as the patient).

Overall, the third case does seem to yield a higher benefit to patients. Intuitively, how does this result emerge? To explain how it comes about, it is simpler to start with the fixed reimbursement regime and its effects.

Under a fixed reimbursement regime, the patient pays a certain fraction of the price, no matter which health care provider it chooses. In turn, health care providers know that a €1 increase in price results in a price increase to the patient equal to the fraction of the price he or she pays. The cost of increasing prices, in terms of demand lost to other competing health care providers, is small. Accordingly, providers of health care will set, in equilibrium, higher prices when patients pay a smaller fraction of the price. This market incentive to set high prices justifies why the old reimbursement system performed poorly in terms of prices and costs.

One could try to argue that preferential lists of providers are a good way to set competition and obtain more favorable prices. However, if prices can be determined by health care providers, selecting a set of preferred providers actually creates an artificial market advantage to such providers. They can raise the price more easily than outside providers (those not included in the preferred set). Any price increase of a preferred provider is only borne partially by patients, while outside providers face a situation in which any price increase is borne completely by patients. Therefore, preferred providers will tend to set higher prices than outside providers. Nonetheless, despite the asymmetry of market players induced by the creation of the set of preferred providers, there is more competition than in the traditional common rate of reimbursement to all providers.

Finally, we may consider a reference pricing system. The health insurer defines the reimbursement it pays to patients based on a preferential provider (or set of providers) but pays that same value to the patient irrespective of the provider chosen by the patient.

Although apparently similar, this last system is quite distinct from the previous one. The preferred provider does not have a strategic advantage as previously. When the preferred provider changes the price it charges, it is also influencing the reimbursement the patient receives in the alternative provider. By increasing his price, the provider increases the reimbursement the patient gets when it goes to the outsider provider, given the rules of reference pricing. Consequently, the preferred provider will lose more demand under reference pricing. The incentive of the preferred provider to increase prices is thus smaller. In equilibrium, prices under this regime will be lower than in either of the other two regimes.

Thus, the movement toward reference pricing is well rooted in economic principles, and should be a factor contributing to lower prices. In mixed markets, where both public and private providers compete, the health insurance arrangement can influence in an important way how providers compete. A good understanding of the economics of market interaction is thus important to ensure proper policy decisions are taken.

We are now in a position to discuss the implications for decisions under two different timings: simultaneous decisions of prices and qualities, or sequential decisions, with qualities being decided first, choices of quality being observed by all market participants and then prices being set. We identify the simultaneous decision model with primary care, as quality (say, time spent with the patient) can be easily adjusted. The sequential decision model corresponds more to hospital care (specialized care), including surgery rooms, hi-tech devices and imaging equipment which are usually long-term decisions.

Under simultaneous decisions, the following ranking of quality choices in equilibrium emerges, when two health care providers compete in the market:

$$T_A^{PP} > T_A^{FRR} > T_A^{FC} \tag{12.57}$$

$$T_B^{FRR} T_B^{FC} > T_B^{PP} \tag{12.58}$$

Provider A, denoted in subscript, is the preferred provider, leading to asymmetric choices of quality when the non-preferred provider, B, is excluded from health insurance coverage. Superscript PP refers to "preferred provider" system, in which going to the provider outside the network set by the third-party payer implies the patient paying the full price. Superscript FC refers to "fixed co-payment", in which the patient always receives the same value, whatever provider he or she selects. The value is defined as a fraction of the price of the preferred provider set by the third-party payer. Finally, superscript "FRR" refers to fixed reimbursement rate, in which the same percentage of the price is paid by the third-party payer, whatever provider the patient chooses for treatment.

The fixed reimbursement rate case leads to the highest investment in quality in the market. Under the fixed reimbursement rate regime, price competition is relaxed, allowing both providers to set high prices. Quality is the main way to attract patients and the high prices provide the marginal incentive to pay for the extra quality. Providers will invest heavily in quality.

The fixed co-payment contract has some interesting properties. It creates competition between health care providers. The relatively low prices that result force providers not to invest much in quality as the return on quality investment will be low.

Under sequential decisions (first qualities, then prices), the same ordering of qualities across co-payment regimes results. The important difference lies in the magnitude of investment. Sequential decisions lead to lower equilibrium levels of quality than do simultaneous decisions on price and qualities. Quality choices are influenced by the strategic incentive introduced by the sequential decision process.

The interplay of competition between health care providers and timing of decisions creates distinct incentives to quality investment. The following table, from Barros and Martinez-Giralt (2002), provides an overview of comparisons to the social optimum levels of quality investment.

		FRR	*FC*	*PP*
Simultaneous decisions	Prov. A	+	=	+
	Prov. B	+	=	−
Sequential decisions	Prov. A	+	−	+
	Prov. B	+	?	?

Under simultaneous decisions, the fixed co-payment system allows implementation of the first-best qualities. This no longer holds true under sequential decisions. These results also illustrate an additional moral hazard effect. Moral hazard in health care is usually associated with providing too much quantity due to the insurance protection at the moment of consumption.

The fixed reimbursement rate system leads to lower price sensitivity by patients. Health care providers are able to charge higher prices and use quality choice to attract patients. Moral hazard, given fixed total demand, appears through higher prices and higher (than socially optimal) quality.

Besides this moral hazard aspect, another issue can be present. Under the preferred provider system, choices of provider by patients are distorted relative to the first best. Patients bear a non-monetary cost associated with this distortion. Offering no payment for out-of-plan care may excessively harm the freedom to choose (showing up as welfare loss for those patients closest to the alternative provider). This adds to the moral hazard problem in quality choice.

The discussion so far assumed that quality is observed by patients and is incorporated in their decisions. Different issues arise when quality is not observed by patients. The interesting issues under unobservable quality of providers are more related to contracting by the third-party payer (health insurer) and are taken up in the next section.

12.3.3 Quality unobserved by patients

For certain health services, quality may not be easily observable by patients and/or payers. In such cases, health care providers may reduce quality in order to cut costs, leading to under-provision of quality. Thus, dealing with incentives for a correct balancing of cost-reducing and quality-enhancing efforts is a critical issue.

The payment system more appropriate to treat this issue involves a combination of prospective and cost reimbursement components. A simple model highlighting this trade-off is provided by Ma (1994). Consider a health care provider that can exert two types of effort: e_1, aimed at quality enhancing, and e_2 aimed at cost reduction. The cost of exerting effort is described by a convex cost function, $\phi(e_1 + e_2)$.

To simplify exposition, let quality $T = e_1$. The demand for the providers' services is characterized by $q = q(e_1)$. Prices are either regulated or irrelevant due to full coverage enjoyed by patients. Demand is increasing in quality but at a decreasing rate (meaning $q(e_1)$ is a concave function).

Let average cost of treatment be $c(e_2)$, decreasing in cost-reducing effort. The average cost of treating a patient is defined in expected terms and results from true cost resulting from a distribution $F(\tilde{c}, e_2)$, with density $f(\tilde{c}, e_2)$. Expected profit of the health care provider when it receives a prospective payment p per patient is:

$$\Pi = q(e_1)(p - c(e_2)) - \phi(e_1 + e_2), \quad c(e_2) = \int_0^{\hat{c}} (p - c) f(c, e_2) \, dc \tag{12.59}$$

The first-order conditions for the optimal choice of efforts by the health care provider are

$$q'(e_1)(p - c(e_2)) - \phi'(e_1 + e_2) = 0 \tag{12.60}$$

$$q(e_1)(-c'(e_2)) - \phi'(e_1 + e_2) = 0 \tag{12.61}$$

The value p can be set such that socially optimal efforts can be implemented.

The benefit from treatment under quality $T (= e_1)$ is $B(e_1)$, is assumed to be increasing and concave. Social welfare is defined as:

$$SW = b(e_1) - c(e_2)q(e_1) - \phi(e_1 + e_2) \tag{12.62}$$

The efficient effort levels are the solution to:

$$b'(e_1) - c(e_2)q'(e_1) - \phi'(e_1 + e_2) = 0 \tag{12.63}$$

$$-c'(e_2)q(e_1) - \phi'(e_1 + e_2) = 0 \tag{12.64}$$

Recalling the first-order conditions to the health care provider,

$$pq'(e_1) - c(e_2)q'(e_1) - \phi'(e_1 + e_2) = 0 \tag{12.65}$$

choosing $p = b'(e^*)/q'(e^*)$ the socially optimal efforts are implemented.

The prospective payment aligns directly the incentive for cost reduction, whatever the value of the payment. The relevant aspect is that the health care provider keeps all savings it obtains from cost-reducing effort, which is exactly the social value of these savings.

The exact value of the payment p can then be set in a way that induces the optimal level of effort/quality. Thus, even though quality levels cannot be included in a contract, as long as patients cannot be refused by the health care provider, a prospective payment adequately defined will achieve the first-best level of quality.

It remains to be seen whether the health care provider makes no loss. Ma (1994) shows this to be the case. This result is dependent on having a demand function independent of price, due to health insurance.

This reasoning holds true for providers that cannot refuse patients. When refusing high-cost patients, providers may increase profits. So, the payment mechanism must not have financial opportunities for dumping of patients. Of course, a large enough prospective payment would solve the issue, but it would be too costly. An alternative is a mixed payment system.

Profit to the health care provider is

$$\Pi = q(e_1)\left[\int_0^{c^*} (c^* - c)f(c, e_2)dc + \int_{c^*}^{\hat{c}} mf(c, e_2)dc\right] - \phi(e_1 + e_2) \tag{12.66}$$

The payment mechanism discussed does not allow for the possibility of refusal to serve some patients by the provider. To account for the possibility of dumping of patients, define now a payment system with the following characteristics (Ma 1998): If the health care provider has cost $c < c^*$, it receives c^*; if it has cost $c \geq c^*$, the provider receives $c + m$. For $c^* = \hat{c}$, the pure prospective payment results, while for $c^* = 0$, the cost reimbursement model emerges.

This payment system avoids dumping of patients, as the net revenue per patient is always non-negative by construction. The relevant question is whether instruments (c^*, m) of this payment system can be defined in a way that optimal efforts (and quality) can be implemented.

The first-order conditions in the choice if efforts are

$$\frac{\partial \Pi}{\partial e_1} = q'(e_1)\left[\int_0^{c^*} (c^* - c)f(c, e_2)dc + \int_{c^*}^{\hat{c}} mf(c, e_2)\,dc\right] - \phi'(e_1 + e_2) = 0$$

$$\frac{\partial \Pi}{\partial e_2} = q(e_1)\left[\int_0^{c^*} (c^* - c)\frac{\partial f}{\partial e_2}(c, e_2)\,dc + \int_{c^*}^{\hat{c}} m\frac{\partial f}{\partial e_2}(c, e_2)\,dc\right] - \phi'(e_1 + e_2) = 0$$

Since without dumping a prospective payment is socially optimal, under the possibility of dumping of patients by the provider, to implement the first-best choices of effort, it is enough to satisfy the same set of first-order conditions. That is, c^* and m must be such that

$$p = \int_0^{c^*} c^* f(c, e_2)\,dc + \int_{c^*}^{\hat{c}} (m + c)f(c, e_2)\,dc \tag{12.67}$$

$$0 = \int_0^{c^*} c^* \frac{\partial f}{\partial e_2}(c, e_2)\,dc' \int_{c^*}^{\hat{c}} (m + c)\frac{\partial f}{\partial e_2}(c, e_2)\,dc \tag{12.68}$$

Under certain technical conditions, this will be feasible, while under others it is not (see Ma 1998; Sharma 1998 for more details.)

12.4   Technology adoption and the medical arms' race

Over time, technology adoption has been identified as a major driver of the growth of health care costs. It is not surprising that it has come under close scrutiny. Several arguments have been put forward for excessive technology adoption to occur. One is the public pressure and physicians' desires to have a rapid transition from invention to use of new technologies. This pressure finds further support when patients are covered by health insurance protection.

Cost considerations become much less relevant at the moment of consumption (as patients are financially protected by health insurance and any future price increase is heavily discounted and shared with many others). On top of these arguments, competition between providers of care may also lead to excessive technology adoption.

The simplest way a technological arms' race can lead to overinvestment is linked to its role to guide demand. When patients are very responsive to observable technology, then providers competing in technology levels face a prisoners' dilemma situation. Overinvestment emerges naturally in that setting.

To illustrate, consider two providers, who differ in their adoption costs of the new technology. Provider 1 has cost c of adopting a new technology while provider 2 has cost $C > c$ of adopting the same technology. Patients pay p for a visit (or intervention by the health care provider), and there are N patients. Patients are assumed to be highly sensitive to the existence of technology: when both providers have the same technology level, consumers are split evenly; when one provider has a higher technology level, all patients go to the provider offering the highest quality of care.

The decisions by health care providers can be easily discussed in matrix form.

		Provider 2	
		$t = T$	$t = 0$
Provider 1	$t = T$	$Np/2 - c, Np/2 - C$	$Np - c, 0$
	$t = 0$	$0, Np - C$	$Np/2, Np/2$

For high costs of investment in the new technology, $C > c > p/2$, then no provider invests in the new technology. And for low costs of adoption, $c < C < Np/2$, then both providers want to invest in health care. Both could be better off by coordinating in not making the investment as demand would be the same, and costs would be saved.

In this explanation for the medical arms' race, the "excessive" investment in technology results from a coordination problem between competing firms. The crucial feature is why and how much demand is sensitive to technology investments.[11]

The usual next step is to state that investment in technology drives demand because it may work as a signal to the quality (skill) of the doctor, unknown to the patient.

Barros *et al.* (1999) suggest that overinvestment in technology may also result from signaling purposes. Providers of health care invest in technology as a way to send a credible signal about their true (unobservable) quality.

The essential feature for technology adoption to work as a signal on unobservable qualities of the doctor is that the cost of using more advanced technologies is less costly to higher quality doctors. Excessive technology adoption in this case will be done by higher quality doctors only and it will actually distinguish them in the eyes of patients by their technology choices.

But when the cost of technology adoption is sufficiently low and the cost of its use is essentially similar to all doctors, independent of their quality, then we should observe excessive technology adoption across the board, even if no information about quality of providers is revealed.

To formally present the argument, consider two types of medical doctors, high quality and low quality. Patients and health insurers do not know whether a particular doctor is high or low quality. Medical doctors may invest in one of two technology levels, high or low, $t \in \{0, T\}$, with $T > 0$ denoting the highest technology level. Quality of doctors means distinct costs of using the highest technology level. Let H denote the high-quality doctor and L denotes the other doctors. Let the intrinsic costs of using the technologies be described by

$$C^L(0) = C^H(0) = 0$$
$$C^L(T) = C > C^H(T) = c$$

When facing a doctor, each patient is unable to recognize whether he or she is of a high quality or a low quality without further information. By investing in technology, doctors may send a signal about their quality. Patients are willing to pay a higher amount to a high-quality doctor.

The question is then under which conditions is it likely to observe all doctors investing in the new technology, with no information being revealed, and under which conditions are we likely to observe only high-quality patients investing in technology, differentiating themselves from others and commanding a higher price.

Let π be the probability that a doctor is high quality. Let p^H and p^L be the values patients/payers are willing to pay to high- and low-quality doctors, respectively. Doctors have utility $U(p)$ from the value they receive, minus any cost of using technology that might result from their choices. Technically, the perfect Bayesian Nash equilibrium is to be found for the following game: first, nature selects the doctor that is matched with a patient; second, medical doctors decide how much to invest in technology; third, patients observe technology choices and update their views on the type of doctor they face. Fourth, patients (or payers acting as perfect agents for patients) set payments to doctors.

The case of uninformative investment in technology occurs for $t = T$ made by both types of doctors. When all doctors make this choice, patients (and payers) learn nothing from technology choices. Accordingly, since no information is gained, a wage $\bar{p} = \pi p^H + (1 - \pi)p^L$ is paid to all doctors. It is now crucial to know what patients infer if a doctor does not invest in technology. It can be shown that patients infer that (s)he must be a low-quality doctor.[12]

When $U(\bar{p}) - C > U(p^L)$, low-quality doctors want to invest in technology. So do high-quality doctors, as saving c ($< C$) by not investing only brings $p^L < \bar{p}$, as patients (and payers) will consider them as low-quality doctors.

The condition can be rewritten as:

$$U(\bar{p}) - U(p^L) > C \tag{12.69}$$

Thus, for C low, p^H high and/or π high, it is more likely to have "wasteful" (non-informative) investment in technology.

The other interesting situation is when technology investment is actually informative about doctors' intrinsic quality. If technology adopted is informative, then each doctor will receive a payment conditional on the investment in technology that he has done. Observing $t = T$ leads to payment p^H and $t = 0$ implies payment p^L.

For this situation to be an equilibrium, both types of doctors need to obtain higher surplus with their decisions, high-quality doctors investing in technology while low-quality doctors do not invest:

$$U(p^H) - c > U(p^L)$$
$$U(p^L) > U(p^H) - C$$

Rewriting

$$c < U(p^H) - U(p^L) < C \tag{12.70}$$

Notice that at this equilibrium, a low-quality doctor by investing in technology ($t = T$) would be taken to be a high-quality doctor and would receive wage p^H. On the other hand, where the high-quality doctor chooses not to invest in technology, patients (and payers) will take the doctor to be of low quality and a wage p^L will be paid.

Thus, when (a) wages offered to doctors of different skills are distinct but not too much; (b) high-quality doctors have low costs when investing in more technology; and (c) low-quality doctors have high costs when investing in technology, it is likely that investment in technology may work as a signal.

The two theories of medical arms' race for excessive technology adoption entail distinct policy implications. In the first case, the main problem relates to coordination of investment decisions. The second case has a different nature, related to information. Take a policy measure, like publication of "league tables" of health care providers. Under the prisoner's dilemma explanation for a medical arms' race, it will make demand more sensitive to technology differences across providers and it will exacerbate the problem.

In contrast, under the second explanation, based on informational asymmetries regarding providers, the publication of "league tables" renders useless investing in technology as a signal about quality. It should lead to a decrease in excessive investment in technology. The issue of a medical arms' race is not an exclusive to hi-tech procedures in health care. For example, general practitioners (GPs) may use high rates of prescription of pharmaceutical products to patients as a signal of their knowledge. The costs of overprescription are typically small for GPs. In the context of the model above, this characteristic should lead to overprescription, a form of excessive investment in technology. The creation of prescription guidelines increases the costs of overprescription to doctors. It may be sufficiently important to change their behavior to an equilibrium with lower prescription rates.

The empirical relevance of a medical arms' race has been documented in several works. It has focused on the relationship between competition and investment in technology, proxied by hospital costs or by hi-tech hospital services.[13]

13 Public and private provision

In this chapter we will argue that one consequence of the cost containment health sectors face is the increasing role of private provision in countries with national health services. This role appears in the market for provision of health care through the selection by insurers of preferred providers; the cooperation between public and private sector to build new facilities and share the provision and management responsibilities of clinical activities; and also in the time sharing of physicians between public and private practice.

13.1 Mixed markets

The notion of mixed markets has been traditionally applied to markets where both public (government-owned) and private firms compete against each other. This obviously occurs also in health sectors of countries where a national health service (NHS) exists.

However, in the health care sector, we have a particular feature that extends the scope of mixed markets. Even when the funding institution is private (say, a sickness fund or an insurance company), it is often the case that it defines sets of preferential providers. Not all providers are equal. Special relationships between the funding institution and the health care provider started in the context of managed care. The active role of funding institutions relative to health care providers is now a widespread phenomenon, making it non-exclusive to countries with a national health service.

The analysis of market equilibria when such particular relationships emerge, whether or not we are in the presence of a national health service, is what we take to be mixed markets in health care. The existence of a public provider competing with private providers is one important case, though not the only one of interest.

There are several relevant questions in this context: What is the best relationship between the third-party payer and the health care provider? What characteristics of the mechanism ruling the relationship are crucial? Does it require the existence of a public provider or is a properly defined relationship sufficient? To answer these questions, the analysis has to move from the one-to-one relationship of payer and provider to a market equilibrium context. On top of setting payment rules, the public payer (say, a national health service) may operate directly as the provider. Both quality and cost (price) are a concern.

Since the public payer (owning a provider) tends to be large relative to the market and has the coercive power of the government behind it, a reasonable description of market interaction is to have leadership by the public agency regarding decisions. As both quality and price decisions have to be made, two possibilities are of interest. In one case, the public provider decides quality and price levels, and the private provider decides afterwards. The public provider aims at maximizing social welfare. In the second case, quality decisions are more permanent. The public provider chooses its quality level, which is also observed by the private provider, who then decides on its own quality. After quality levels are set by both types of providers, prices are chosen simultaneously. As before, the public provider maximizes social welfare and the private provider maximizes own private profits.

The mixed-market equilibrium has been addressed by several authors in the literature. The focus has been on the impact of privatization waves, with or without subsidies being available after privatization,[1] on marginal cost difference.[2] Quality issues have been addressed by Delbono *et al.* (1996), showing that a public provider acting as a leader in quality choices will serve the upper segment of a vertically differentiated market.[3]

Unlike most of the previous literature on mixed markets, our concern is not on the role of cost effectiveness across public and private providers,[4] but rather on price and quality choices and whether ownership of a provider, together with the payment rule to private providers, is a sufficient set of instruments to achieve the socially optimal allocation.

To give a structure to discussion, we adopt a version of the model of Barros and Martinez-Giralt (2002). There are two providers in the market. Providers are located at the endpoints of the segment [0, 1]. This segment describes preferences of consumers over providers: without loss of generality, the provider located at 0 is owned by the payer (public provider) and is described by provider A. Provider B is located at 1 and is a private provider. Consumers are uniformly distributed along the line [0, 1], with density 1. That is, public ownership does not bring higher reputation or bias in consumers' preferences. Of course, price and quality decisions may well lead to asymmetric distribution of consumers across the public and the private provide. However, that will be the outcome of their choices, not a predetermined feature of the mixed market.

Let p_i be the price and T_i be the quality selected by provider i, $i = A, B$. The production cost of the health care good or service is normalized to zero in both providers.

The indirect utility $V(i, x)$, $i = A, B$ of a patient located at x and choosing provider i is given by

$$V(A, x) = Y + T_A - p_A - tx + I_A \tag{13.1}$$

$$V(B, x) = Y + T_B - p_B - t(1 - x) + I_B \tag{13.2}$$

where Y is income, $tx/t(1 - x)$ is the cost of going to provider A/B measured in monetary terms while I_i is the indemnity received by the patient when selecting provider i. The indemnity is defined as:

$$I_A = (1 - c_A^A)p_A \tag{13.3}$$

$$I_B = (1 - c_A^B)p_A + (1 - c_B^B)p_B \tag{13.4}$$

where $(1 - c_j^i)$ stands for how the price of provider j is taken into account in the reimbursement the patient receives from third-payer when going to provider i. The indemnity structure assumes that the patient pays a fraction c_A^A of the price of the public provider when treated there.

If the patient chooses the private provider, then the indemnity may be conditional on both the price asked by the private provider and how much the patient would receive if instead the public provider had been selected.

Demand faced by each provider is determined by the indifferent patient between going to provider A and provider B. Let x^* be the indifferent patient. Then, patients with $x < x^*$ choose to go to provider A while the others choose provider B.

The indifferent patient's location results from the solution to

$$V(A, x^*) = V(B, x^*) \tag{13.5}$$

and

$$x^* = \frac{1}{2} + \frac{T_A - T_B}{2t} + \frac{c_B^B p_B - c_A^A p_A - (1 - c_A^B) p_A}{2t} \tag{13.6}$$

The profits of each firm are

$$\Pi_A = p_A x - \phi(T_A), \quad \Pi_B = p_B(1 - x) - \phi(T_B) \tag{13.7}$$

and $\phi(T_i) = \theta T_i^2 / 2$, by assumption, stands for the cost function of quality level T_i of provider i.

Social welfare is defined as

$$W = \int_0^x (Y + T_A - t\tilde{x}) d\tilde{x} + \int_x^1 (Y + T_B - t(1 - \tilde{x})) d\tilde{x} - \phi(T_A) - \phi(T_B) \tag{13.8}$$

As mentioned above, we consider the case of all decisions of the public provider being taken first. Then, after observing the choices of the public firm, the private firm decides on its pricing and quality levels. As is standard, the model needs to be solved by backward induction.

Accordingly, we first characterize provider B's decisions. The best response functions of provider B are obtained from profit maximization and are given by:

$$\frac{\partial \Pi^B}{\partial p^B} = \frac{1}{2} + \frac{T_B - T_A}{2t} - \frac{2(1 - c_B^B) p_B - (c_A^A + 1 - c_A^B) p_A}{2t} = 0 \tag{13.9}$$

$$\frac{\partial \Pi^B}{\partial T^B} = \frac{p_B}{2t} - \theta T_B = 0 \tag{13.10}$$

Solving this system of equations, we obtain

$$T_B = \frac{T_A - t + (c_A^A - c_A^B) p_A}{1 - 4(1 - c_B^B) t\theta} \tag{13.11}$$

$$P_B = 2t\theta \frac{T_A - t + (c_A^A 1 - c_A^B) p_A}{1 - 4(1 - c_B^B) t\theta} \tag{13.12}$$

The public provider maximizes social welfare subject to three constraints: first, demand is determined by the location of the indifferent patient; second, the (optimal) choice of quality by provider B is anticipated by provider A, and third, the (optimal) choice of price by provider B is also anticipated by provider A. This implies, for example, that provider A anticipates that an increase in its quality dT_A, will be matched by a quality increase of

$$dT_B = \frac{1}{1 - 4(1 - c_B^B)t\theta} dT_A \tag{13.13}$$

by provider B. This anticipated reaction makes provider A recognize that its choices will influence provider B's choices.

Obtaining and solving the first-order conditions generates the following equilibrium values:

$$T_A = \frac{1 - 2(1 - c_B^B) + (1 - c_B^B)^2 t\theta}{\theta(1 - 2(1 - c_B^B) - (1 - c_B^B)^2 + 2(1 - c_B^B)^2 t\theta)} \tag{13.14}$$

$$P_A = \frac{(\theta t - 1)(2(1 - c_B^B)^2 t\theta + 1 - c_B^B - 1)}{(1 - c_A^A - (1 - c_A^B))(1 - 2(1 - c_B^B) - (1 - c_B^B)^2 + 2(1 - c_B^B)^2 t\theta)} \tag{13.15}$$

$$T_B = \frac{(1 - c_B^B)(t\theta - 1)}{(1 - 2(1 - c_B^B) - (1 - c_B^B)^2 + 2(1 - c_B^B)^2 t\theta)} \tag{13.16}$$

$$P_B = \frac{2t\theta(t\theta 1)(1 - c_B^B)}{(1 - 2(1 - c_B^B) - (1 - c_B^B)^2 + 2(1 - c_B^B)^2 t\theta)} \tag{13.17}$$

$$x = \frac{1 - 2(1 - c_B^B) + (c_B^B)^2 t\theta}{(1 - 2(1 - c_B^B) - (1 - c_B^B)^2 + 2(1 - c_B^B)^2 t\theta)} > \frac{1}{2} \tag{13.18}$$

Comparison with socially optimal values (Barros and Martinez-Giralt 2002, p. 128), shows that under a fixed co-payment or under the preferred provider rules, the optimal choice of qualities is achieved. A fixed co-payment regime means that the payer reimburses a patient going to provider B in the same amount it would pay if the patient had instead selected the public provider ($c_A^B = c_A^A$; $c_B^B = 0$). A preferred provider setting means that no reimbursement is made in case the patient chooses the private provider ($c_B^A = 0$, $c_B^B = 0$). Thus, a public provider with a first-mover advantage, together with the choice of the reimbursement rules, has a sufficient set of instruments to achieve the first best.

The leadership exerted by the public provider compensates for the distortions introduced by the strategic considerations of the sequential decisions. Leadership alone or public ownership without leadership do not allow achieving the socially optimal choices.

In addition, the fixed co-payment rule originates lower total payments than exclusion of the private provider from coverage by the payer.

The second way in which the public provider can exert leadership has sequential choices on quality, followed by simultaneous price decision by both providers. Under this timing of decisions, the optimal choices by both the public provider and the private provider will result in too much quality. The term "too much quality" means that both providers invest in more quality than it is socially optimal.

The higher quality of the public provider also implies a higher price by the public provider. These features of equilibrium are consistent with observation of national health services. They are usually seen as of higher quality than coexisting private sectors in the same country. They also seem to have higher costs (which corresponds to price in the model above) than the private sector.

Another type of mixed market arises when patients are not completely treated in the public sector, leading to waiting lists. The possibility of treatment in the private sector turns those markets into mixed markets in the sense that both public and private providers compete for the same patients. Given the specific nature of waiting lists, the economic issues associated with waiting lists are treated in the next chapter.

13.2 Public–Private Partnerships

13.2.1 Introduction

The term Public–Private Partnership (PPP) has entered the lexicon in health economics. The initial denomination in the UK, where it started, was Private Finance Initiative. Currently, there is no consensual and widely accepted definition of what constitutes a PPP. The more common definitions are based on characteristics of the relationship, such as contract duration (typically, long-term contracts are involved, often lasting 30 years), being projects traditionally executed by the public sector, or simply involving a contractual relationship between the public and the private sectors.

As a workable definition, a PPP is a long-term contract that a public entity awards to a private party for the construction and/or operation of an infra-structure often provided by the public sector.

The European Commission provides a broader definition of PPPs: "A public–private partnership (PPP) is a contractual agreement between the public and the private sectors, whereby the private operator commits to provide public services that have traditionally been supplied or financed by public institutions."[5]

We opt to focus on the basic economic features associated with the long-term contract.

The execution of large investment projects in the private sector implies several tasks: design of the project, financing, construction, and operation. The PPPs make a division of those tasks between the public and the private sector. Since several divisions may exist, the term Public–Private Partnership covers very different realities.

It may range from leaving to the private sector only the operation of the services (the fourth task), to have a PPP with all four tasks assigned to the private sector, or to have all but operations contracted with the private party. We can find examples of all these possibilities in different countries.

From an economic perspective, the key elements are the existence of a contract and the long-term relationship. The main economic issue is related to agency. If there were no agency issues in the contract set between the public and the private sector, the former would detail and set out clearly what had to be done, and the latter would just execute.

The analysis of Martimort and Pouyet (2008) shows that the nature of ownership, public or private, is not the crucial feature of a PPP that includes both design and construction and operation. The main (economic) motivation for a PPP lies in the economies of scope resulting from a better design leading to lower marginal costs of operation.

The creation of PPP is not free from criticism. Some claim it increases the potential for capture of public sector decision makers by private sector agents.

PPPs are often used in the health sector, and in other sectors, to bring to execution projects that traditionally were completely carried out in the public sector. There are two main motivations for governments (and public authorities) to pursue PPPs: (a) Acknowledging the current governments budget constraints, making it difficult if not impossible to carry out large investment projects, PPPs allow the investment being done now against a stream of future payments; (b) The expectation that the private sector will be more efficient in carrying out those tasks than the public sector.

Both motives do demand a careful discussion and appraisal. PPPs as a financial instrument to transform a large payment today into a flow of future payments only makes sense in a context in which issuing public debt is more costly than issuing private debt. The private party involved in the PPP has to raise funds in the private capital market. The cost of raising funds in capital markets must then be compared to the cost of public debt. Usually, interest rate spreads in public debt are lower than those of private debt due to the greater ability of governments to diversify risks. Thus, except in very particular circumstances, public debt is a better way to transform a large investment into a flow of future payments.

The implication of this argument is straightforward. The gains associated with a PPP cannot result alone from the financial aspects of the project. There is the need for other sources of gains of the PPP that make it of value to the public sector.

As argued above, the financial transformation of a lump-sum investment to a stream of payments cannot be the main reason for a PPP, leaving us with the efficiency motive.

The presumption about efficiency gains from PPPs results from existing evidence on public sector cost overruns and significant delays in concluding the projects being significantly higher than in the public sector.

13.2.2   *Value for money and the public sector comparator*

There are two important concepts related to PPPs: value for money and the public sector comparator. There is value for money in a PPP when the service provided is obtained with the lower possible cost given the volume and quality of service specified by the buyer of the service (the public sector).

The public sector comparator is basically the reservation price set in the process of selection of the private partner. It requires the cost value proposed by the private sector to carry on the project to be below what the cost would be of doing it within the public sector. There is some discussion on whether the reference point should be the average cost in the public sector, including its inefficiencies, or whether it should be the efficient value that could be commanded by the public sector (even if it is often actually unable to reach such an efficiency level).

13.2.3   *PPP and risk transfer*

One of the main issues in PPP contracting is risk transfer. A PPP usually involves a risk transfer from the public sector to the private sector. The risk transfer is an important tool of the PPP, not an objective in itself. This has become an area of confusion regarding PPPs. The transfer of risk emerges in this context as an instrument to attain the goal of more efficiency. The risk transfer cannot be an objective due to a simple reason: the private side requires payment for bearing risk. Since the public sector usually has better diversification opportunities than private parties, the amount required by the private sector to bear a certain level of risk is higher than the amount the public sector is willing to pay. Therefore, other motives must exist for the risk transfer to be part of the optimal PPP contract. The main motive is the moral hazard in the construction phase, which is better controlled by the private sector yielding gains that can be used for public sector savings and remuneration of the risk borne by the private party. The risk transfer only matters to the extent that it creates adequate incentives for the private party to be efficient (in terms of costs and of time to finish the project). We illustrate the point with a stylized model.

Let the cost of the project be $c(e) = \bar{c} - e - \varepsilon$, where e is an effort to lower construction costs and time, and ε is a random term, with zero mean, distribution function $F(\cdot)$ and density function $f(\cdot)$. The contractor has cost $\phi(e)$ of doing effort, with $\phi'(e) > 0$, $\phi''(e) > 0$, $\phi(0) = 0$. The public sector cannot commit to stopping the project. Therefore, it pays the required cost. In our terminology, it is a cost reimbursement model. This is the easiest way to generate excessive costs. More elaborated settings to originate cost overruns can also be used to illustrate the argument.

The public sector is risk neutral, due to the diversification possibilities. The private firm is risk averse, and maximizes expected utility of profits net of utility cost of doing effort:

$$V = \int U(p - c(e)) f(\varepsilon) \, d\varepsilon - \phi(e) \tag{13.19}$$

where U is a concave utility function and p is the price received under the contract with the public sector.

Take efficiency effort as given, for the moment, $e = \underline{e}$. When the public sector develops the project directly, no effort exists, or it is set at its minimum level, which we normalize to zero ($\underline{e} = 0$). Thus, the expected cost of the project is $\bar{c}$.

This is the maximum value the public sector is willing to pay for a private builder to develop the project. The minimum price the private party is willing to take, for the same effort $e = 0$, to realize the project is defined by:

$$\int U(p - \bar{c} + \varepsilon) f(\varepsilon) \, d\varepsilon \geq U(0) \tag{13.20}$$

Since U is a concave function, for $p = \bar{c}$,

$$\int U(\varepsilon) f(\varepsilon) \, d\varepsilon < U(0) \tag{13.21}$$

and the private entity is not willing to carry out the project at the maximum price the public sector is willing to pay.

Note that by paying a fixed price p to the private entity, the public sector transfers all the risk to the private sector. This simple model shows that a risk transfer *per se* cannot be used as a rationale for a PPP. As long as the private entity is more risk averse than the public sector, then for a risk transfer to be accepted by the private party, the public sector must pay more than it costs for it to build the project. Thus, the risk transfer cannot be an objective for the PPP. Other motivations must be found.

A first possible motivation comes from the public sector budget constraint. In this case, a project of cost $\bar{c}$ has a shadow cost $\bar{c}(1 + \lambda)$, and the shadow price λ of public funds under an active budget constraint provides a margin to remunerate the risk borne by the private sector in a PPP. Under the PPP, the price will be paid in the future, and the shadow cost λ does not exist.[6]

The other motivation is the mitigation of moral hazard in the efficiency effort. Consider now the situation of a private party being able to set efficiency effort according to its best interests. The PPP can have one of two forms (to illustrate the point in a more clearer way):

– either a price p is paid, independent of costs actually realized in the project; or,
– a cost-plus rule, $p(c) = (1 + m)c$, is used.

Take first the cost-plus rule. In this case there is no risk transfer to the private party, as all costs incurred are paid by the public sector plus a margin. The private sector even has an interest in the high-cost realizations, as the absolute remunerations are higher in such cost realizations. The efficiency effort selected by the private party will be the lowest possible. This can be easily seen from its optimization problem:

$$\max_e V = \int U(mc(e)) f(\varepsilon) d\varepsilon - \phi(e) \tag{13.22}$$

and the marginal incentive to do effort is:

$$-\int U'(m(\bar{c} - e - \varepsilon)) f(\varepsilon) d\varepsilon - \phi'(e) < 0 \tag{13.23}$$

The other payment mechanism transfers risk to the private party, as a fixed price is set, p_0. The objective function of the private provider is

$$V = \int U(p_0 - c) f(\varepsilon) d\varepsilon - \phi(e) \tag{13.24}$$

The first-order condition for maximization of the objective function on the effort level e is:

$$\int U'(p_0 - c) f(\varepsilon) d\varepsilon = \phi'(e) \tag{13.25}$$

Let e^* be the optimal level of effort exerted by private party. Its expected utility, in equilibrium, is:

$$V(e^*; \bar{c}) = \int U(p_0 - \bar{c} + e^* + \varepsilon) f(\varepsilon) d\varepsilon - \phi(e^*) \tag{13.26}$$

Let $p_0 = \bar{c}$, the expected cost to the public sector (equal to the expected cost under zero effort). Then, whenever $V(e^*; \bar{c}) > U(0)$ there is enough room to set $p_0 < \bar{c}$ such that the inequality still holds, and both private and public partners benefit from the PPP.

From this example, it should be clear that inducing effort is crucial, and the role of risk transfer is to provide incentives for the private party to exert efficiency effort to contain costs. The price paid by the public sector splits the efficiency gains between the two sides of the relationship.

Related to the risk transfer, there are several good discussions of the principles that should guide it. Oudot (2005) suggests two intuitive principles: each risk should be borne by the party that has the better ability to manage it, everything else constant, and should be borne by the party that has the least cost of taking it, everything else constant. The problem of defining who bears the risk arises when some party has a better ability to manage the risk but the other has a lower cost of bearing it. The PPP may also allow for the use of different incentive schemes. Under public construction and operation, it may be more difficult to use more powerful payment systems in terms of incentives, like prospective payments (which is actually one way to transfer risk to the private party). A PPP has an interest to the public sector also to the extent it allows the public sector to use incentives for efficiency that would be hard to otherwise implement.

13.2.4 Aspects of PPP design

To sum up, the argument about the role of risk transfer can be easily understood. The government can better diversify the risk than private entities. When a private party takes risk it also requires some return from assuming such risk. The wider diversification possibilities of the government usually imply that the value the government is willing to pay to transfer a risk is smaller than the value the private sector wants to receive to take up the risk. This difference in valuations of risk implies that some other source of gains from a PPP must be present so that risk transfers associated with the PPP contract can be mutually beneficial. The financial aspects alone are not sufficient for setting up a PPP by which investments today are transformed into a future flow of payments.

The crucial element is then the cost savings accruing from the more efficient private partner. These savings remunerate the risk taken by the private party and still entail less total overall costs to the public sector.

The transfer of risk as an instrument is based on incentive theory. The exact costs and time to complete the project are usually uncertain in the initial moment. A better control and monitoring is likely to reduce costs overruns and time delays in completing the project. Private monitoring seems to have proven, over the years, to be superior to public control with regard to these two aspects.

The PPP is based on a contract that in its simplest version may simply specify a fixed price to be paid by the public sector to the private contractor. This fixed price means that all savings from the control and monitoring of the project are to be owned by the private party. Consequently, the private party has incentive to keep costs low and time delays within control. Anticipating this high effort by the private party, the public sector will set a price below the cost that it would incur in the case where the project is carried out under traditional procurement and public monitoring and control. The public sector when setting a fixed price is making a transfer of all construction risk to the private partner, which is essential for the private partner to have the incentive to do the project efficiently. Suppose that instead the public partner announces that it will cover all and every cost borne by the private partner, thus avoiding any risk transfer to the private partner. The latter will then have no incentive whatsoever to keep costs down or delays under control.

It is worth stressing once again that risk transfers within PPP contracts are a tool and not an objective.

Optimal contract theory provides several guiding principles for the definition of risk sharing in PPP contracts. There are several types of risk, which may demand different treatment within the contract. For example, the most common risks are demand risk, construction cost risk, delay, interest rate risk, etc.

A first principle is that the private party should bear the risks which it has a greater ability to manage. The higher ability to manage the risk should be read in a broad sense, including the impact that decisions of the private party have for the value of the project. A second principle is that the contract should only care about risks that influence the economic value of the PPP.

13.2.5 PPPs involving management of clinical activities

The use of PPP in the health sector has become relatively widespread. Two general structures in the design of PPP seem to emerge. One consists of bundling investment and service provision into a single contract. The other contemplates two different contracts for the investment and for the provision of the service (operation of facilities, clinical management in the case of health care providers). A good source on PPPs in the health care sector is DLA Piper (2009), where a systematic review of PPPs in Europe, Canada, and Australia is carried out. We find a large number of countries using PPPs in health care, where some include in the PPP construction and management of clinical activities (for example, Spain, Portugal, and Italy), others have essentially construction-only PPPs (for example, France, Germany, Canada), and some have both types (Spain and Italy). The international experience shows that countries with a national health service funded through general taxation use PPPs more intensively, as they substitute for immediate public investment. From DLA Piper, we see that the UK, Italy, Spain, and Portugal rank high in intensity of PPPs and all of these countries have a national health service.

Barros and Martinez-Giralt (2009) address the question of how to set contracts within the second type of design, with both construction and management of clinical activities included in the PPP. A PPP of this type usually has two contracts, one with the institution in charge of the construction and maintenance of the hospital, the other with the entity in charge of clinical activities. Also, one of these parties will be responsible for the subcontracting of the soft facilities, thus yielding two variations of the contracting set-up, according to which contract includes the latter. We use the term soft facilities to describe the infrastructural support services, such as laundry, catering, security, parking, waste management, etc.

A crucial feature in this type of PPP for new hospitals is the inclusion of clinical activities management under a separate contract. When building the hospital (investment in infrastructures) is part of the PPP, the first-best allocation is always reached except when hard and soft facilities are bundled together in the contract. However, where restrictions are given by budget constraints we attain the first-best allocation when the externality arising from the investment in infrastructure affects only the level of quality of the software facilities, and not the cost of providing clinical services.

A particular point of discussion when two contracts are employed is where to include management of activities that could be, in principle, awarded to either of the two contracts. That is, should soft facilities provision be included in the same contract as clinical activities management, or put together with the infrastructures? From an economic point of view, two conflicting views can be presented. On the one hand, clinical activities management is probably in a better position to monitor quality of soft facilities provision. On the other hand, functional integration with hard facilities and heavy equipment may allow for less costly operation and better coordination. Since typical soft facilities activities (such as laundry, food catering, cleaning, security, and waste disposal) are contracted out, the question of which contract they should be allocated to can be seen as which party (clinical activities management or hard facilities management) entails smaller distortions in subcontracting such soft facilities provision. The answer to this question needs to weigh the nature of the contract that is established between the public party and each entity, as well as the type of contract that is used to ensure provision of soft facilities.

In the absence of cost externalities, a PPP procedure where soft facilities are subcontracted by the clinical services management is able to implement the first-best solution, but whenever provision of soft facilities is subcontracted by the hard facilities provider the first-best solution is not reachable.

The basic trade-off unveiled is between a better monitoring role performed by clinical activities management over the quality of soft facilities provision and the internalization of infrastructure investments impact on the costs of providing clinical services and on the costs of providing quality in soft facilities output. This latter aspect reflects the belief that a well-thought out hospital design facilitates clinical activities and lowers the cost of providing quality in non-medical services (the so-called soft facilities).

The analysis also has the implication that whenever the tender process for award of the PPP describes in detail the infrastructure investment to be made, the exact design about soft facilities becomes much less relevant for the efficiency of the contract. Since setting the details of the hospital profile is a lengthy process and, at the same time, decreases the potential for innovative actions and ideas by the private party, one may think that alleviating the process will contribute to a better PPP outcome. Our results point out that, in such a case, the exact design of the contract in regard to which entity soft facilities are related to becomes more relevant.

The definition of the PPP procedure, which entails two contracts plus a subcontract (for soft facilities quality), is not neutral from the social welfare viewpoint. Under the more general setting there is no easy trade-off between taking advantage of better monitoring (including soft facilities subcontracting in the responsibilities of clinical activities management) and internalizing cost externalities (including soft facilities contracting in the responsibilities of the infrastructures company). The first option is the right approach to implement the first-best whenever there are no cost externalities from infrastructure investment on the cost of clinical services. Otherwise, neither of the two options achieves the first-best allocation of resources.

13.2.6   *Contract renegotiation*

A second major issue with PPP in the health sector, especially those that include management of clinical activities, is renegotiation of activity levels and of technology used. The very nature of the health care sector makes any PPP contract involving clinical activities an incomplete contract.

The PPP does not end when the contract between the public and the private partner is signed. Long-term contracts of this sort are incomplete contracts by nature, that is, not all future contingencies can be predicted in the contract. Future technological innovations are likely to trigger contract renegotiations. There is currently no specific theory guidance on the issue.

Generally speaking, private partners have a clear advantage in future renegotiations – the cost to the public partner of closing or taking in hand the management of the project is sufficiently high to make it vulnerable to the negotiation demands by the private partner. The alternative is, of course, the public sector to take over the public partner activities in case demands from the latter become too costly to the public sector. In addition, the regularity at the international level is that renegotiations are more likely to be initiated by the public sector and only after a few years into the contract.[7]

Of course, if renegotiation creates future problems, one may think that would be enough to contractually eliminate the possibility of renegotiations. This solution is usually undesirable or unfeasible. In the first place, there is no commitment device for the government not to renegotiate. Second, in an environment with uncertainty about future conditions, making renegotiations impossible or too difficult loses flexibility to take advantage of new information and knowledge that arrive over time.

The possibility of renegotiation implies the need for the contract to specify the conditions under which renegotiation will take place. The contract should specify in a clear way which events may trigger renegotiation and whether both parties have the possibility of demanding renegotiation of contract, and how often.

13.3   Moonlighting

One important issue in countries where public provision exists is that a significant fraction of overall care is provided through moonlighting, or dual practice. This means that physicians (and perhaps other health professionals, such as nurses) hold a job both in the public and in the private sector. The dual practice of physicians is often discussed, given the ability doctors have of influencing their activity in one of the sectors with decisions in the activity of the other. For example, by shirking in the public sector, physicians may free up time to work in the private sector. Or by seeing patients in the private sector, physicians may refer them to the public sector. Thus, it is often claimed that restrictions to dual practice should exist, or that, at the very least, remuneration systems should take it into account. There are various motives identified in the literature for the existence of moonlighting, and several effects have been pointed out. We look here at the economic impact of dual practice, with an emphasis on whether or not, from a policy perspective, a ban on moonlighting should exist.

The starting point for moonlighting in this approach is the work by Holmstrom and Milgrom (1991). A worker holding multiple job positions means a lower cost of attracting a worker when the main job does not require exclusivity. But it also means that more effort is directed to the actions that are easily monitored or that are used in the payment mechanism.

Moonlighting has been formally addressed by Biglaiser and Ma (2007). They show that moonlighting can generally be welfare improving. The basic rationale for this result can be given in a simplified version of the model of Biglaiser and Ma (2007).

The population can have its health care needs satisfied by either a public or private provider. Quality of care is chosen by physicians, according to the time and effort they spend with patients. Biglaiser and Ma (2007) assume that monitoring of physicians' decisions regarding quality of care is more effective in the private sector than in the public sector. Our simplified version of their model takes this assumption to its extreme and assumes that no auditing of quality exists in the public sector, while perfect monitoring is present in the private sector.

Patients' benefits from one unit of health care of quality T is vT, where v is a random variable with support $[\underline{v}, \bar{v}]$, density function $f(\cdot)$ and probability distribution $F(\cdot)$. There are two types of patients demanding health care, poor and rich. Poor patients can only choose the public system, and rich patients may elect to receive care in the private sector at a price p.

There are two types of physicians, dedicated physicians and moonlighters. The dedicated physicians work only in the public sector and attach a higher value to patients' benefits from treatment. Physicians freely choose the quality levels of care provided to patients in the public sector. The payoff to a physician in the public sector is:

$$U = w - c(T) + \beta vT \tag{13.27}$$

where w is the (fixed) wage payment received, $c(T)$ is the cost of providing quality T and β reflects the weight given by the physician to patients' benefits. A high value for β reflects altruistic doctors, while a low β characterizes moonlighters.

There are N patients in need of treatment, half of which are poor. There are $D/2$ moonlighters and $D/2$ dedicated physicians.

The timing of decisions runs in the following sequence. In the first stage, the regulator sets the payment rules and decides whether or not to have a ban on moonlighting. A ban means that public sector doctors are not allowed to work in the private sector. In a second stage, patients are matched to physicians. Dedicated physicians choose the quality level they provide to each patient. Moonlighters may either treat the patient in the public sector, and choose the associated quality level, or refer the patient to their private practice. When matched to a patient, a physician learns how much the patient benefits from treatment, v. The price in the private sector is determined by a Nash bargaining procedure between patients and physicians.

Under the ban on moonlighting, for a payment unrelated to the quality of care T (which is not monitored), the moonlighter physician sets T to the lowest possible value, while the dedicated doctors set a quality level strictly above the minimum, by assumption. That is, we assume that

$$\beta^M v - c'(0) < 0 \tag{13.28}$$

where superscript M denotes moonlighters and the minimum quality level is normalized to zero, and

$$\beta^D v - c'(T) = 0 \tag{13.29}$$

where superscript D stands for dedicated doctors. The moonlighter skimps on quality, while the dedicated doctor provides more quality.

Consider the removal of the ban on moonlighting.[8] It now matters whether a moonlighting doctor is matched to a poor or a rich patient. When a moonlighter doctor receives a poor patient, the lowest quality level is provided as the poor patient cannot afford to pay price p and be treated in the private sector. Thus, poor patients are not affected by the existence of moonlighting.

The removal of the ban on moonlighting only makes a difference to rich patients who are matched to moonlighting doctors. Since they enter a bargaining process with physicians over the price, neither side has full bargaining power, the disagreement payoffs are those associated with the equilibrium with the moonlighting ban. That is, zero price and lowest quality provision by the moonlighting doctor, and benefits of $v \times 0$ to the patient. Then, it becomes clear that allowing moonlighting means that it only occurs when it is mutually beneficial to rich patients and doctors. Quality provided by the moonlighter will exceed the one he or she chooses in the public sector. Total welfare will be larger under moonlighting due to this effect as all other doctors and patients are unaffected by the moonlighting.[9]

The gain from moonlighting arises because quality of care can be monitored in the private sector, and a price p can be set for a high-quality level of care. Since quality choices are patient specific and no externality across patients exists, the argument for welfare improving moonlighting also survives the introduction of asymmetric information.

To have negative welfare effects from removal of the moonlighting ban it is sufficient to have a common resource constraint to both private and public activity at the physician level (say, effort time, or hours of work). Whenever the resource constraint is binding on the physician in the public sector in the absence of moonlighting, allowing moonlighting diverts scarce resources to the private sector. A reduction in the effort time or hours of work in the public sector needs to occur so that a moonlighting doctor can treat patients in private practice.

Another externality may result from the way dedicated doctors are affected by the activity of moonlighters. If dedicated doctors become dissatisfied with their relative position to moonlighter doctors, and decide to become moonlighters as well, the quality provided in the public sector drops. Overall, this may be a strong enough effect to lead to a global welfare reduction (rich patients opting for the private sector are better off anyway). This externality also creates a role for price regulation in the private sector. A price ceiling will discourage dedicated doctors from becoming moonlighters, as it limits the gains from exerting private practice.

Gonzalez and Macho-Stadler (2011) address the choice of regulation of dual practice (moonlighting) by a health authority managing a public sector. While Biglaiser and Ma (2007) focus on altruism as the source of differences across physicians, Gonzalez and Macho-Stadler (2011) consider different levels of ability by physicians. Their analysis crosses two different ways to account for the level of ability by the physician with three options for regulation (banning work in private sector to public sector physicians, incentive contracts in the public sector and limits to moonlighting).

In accordance with previous results, banning moonlighting totally is harmful to the public sector. Allowing moonlighting activities reduces the payments required by high ability doctors to work in the public sector. Banning moonlighting when the private sector is sufficiently attractive to doctors creates a discrete choice problem to doctors (to stay or to leave). The decision to leave the public sector is a possibility that harms public sector patients.

In their model, Gonzalez and Macho-Stadler (2011) have passive patients, an extreme version of physicians' agency. The impact of physicians on health may or may not be sensitive to doctors' skill level. The first alternative is taken as an approximation to the situation of developing countries while the second is identified with developed countries, as in the latter case, technology is a more important determinant of health care provision.

The reputation motive for moonlighting, which states that by working in the public sector physicians earn a reputation that extends to their private practice, leads to over-investment in quality in the public sector (Gonzalez 2004).

Delfgaauw (2007) addresses the role of heterogeneity in altruism across doctors. The coexistence of public and private provision is beneficial to patients as long as patients are not diverted from public facilities to private practices.

In a different vein, Brekke and Sorgard (2007) focus on the role of time constraints on physicians. This implies that allowing moonlighting reduces the public sector input. Globally, lower health care output results. Banning moonlighting may then be optimal when private sector competition is weak and public and private provision are close substitutes.

14 Bargaining

A common characteristic of managed care and national health systems is the presence of independent institutions that negotiate the reimbursement of health care provision. This chapter develops in detail the economic rationale and policy relevance of the analysis of explicit bargaining processes in health care provision. After an introduction to the basic features of bargaining theory, it moves on to an analysis of bargaining between third-party payers and providers. The main feature is that the outcome of the negotiation in terms of the reimbursement rules has an impact on the competition among providers and on the design of the health insurance contract.

Recent developments in health care financing include independent institutions that negotiate (bargain) the prices with the financing institutions. This is true with respect to health maintenance organizations (HMOs), managed care in general, but also in national health systems (NHSs) where decentralization and the split between provision and financing is implemented.

In this scenario, negotiation over contractual terms, including prices as one major element, becomes a relevant issue in the analysis of performance of health care systems. It is only recently that bargaining theory has entered in the analysis of the health care sector. The recognition of the strategic interaction among agents in the health care sector (patients, providers, and third-party payers) came with the application of models borrowed from the Industrial Organization tradition since the 1970s. It was in the early 1990s when a step forward was taken with the eruption of the models of bargaining. In many situations the health care sector has the structure of a bilateral monopoly/oligopoly. In this context, bargaining becomes the natural way to approach the interactions among agents.

This chapter develops in detail the economic rationale and policy relevance of the analysis of explicit bargaining processes in health care provision. A non-technical presentation of these intuitions is found in Barros and Martinez-Giralt (2006). The next section provides an introduction to the basic features of bargaining theory to help give those readers unfamiliar with this literature a better understanding of the arguments that will follow in the rest of the chapter.

14.1 A primer in bargaining theory

Bargaining is a resource allocation mechanism suitable in situations where the market mechanism does not operate. We have already referred to it in Chapter 4 when describing the bilateral monopoly and bilateral oligopoly market structures. These are instances capturing the essence of bargaining: an interaction involving negotiation on a variety of issues. Generally speaking such interaction may arise in economic, social, and political scenarios. Firms and unions negotiate to set wages; firms negotiate the terms of a merger or an acquisition; political parties negotiate the terms to form a coalition, married couples negotiate over the distribution of the domestic tasks. A stimulating non-technical introduction to bargaining theory is found in Muthoo (2000). More formal and attractive presentations of the basic bargaining theory are Osborne and Rubinstein (1990), or Binmore *et al.* (1986a). We will refer here to economic interactions. We leave it to the reader to translate the arguments into other scenarios.

DEFINITION 14.1 (BARGAINING). A bargaining situation arises when two or more economic agents can mutually benefit from trading, have conflicting interests over the terms of trade, and no agent can impose an agreement on another.

Following Muthoo (2000), "[e]ach player would like to reach some agreement rather than to disagree and not reach any agreement, but each player would also like to reach an agreement that is as favourable to her as possible" (p. 147). We want to identify first the main elements determining the outcome of a bargaining procedure and the bargaining power of the parties involved in the negotiation.[1]

14.1.1 The elements of a bargaining situation

Consider the situation of the management of a firm negotiating the yearly wage increase of their employees with the representatives of the unions. Both parties have conflicting interests because the unions aim at obtaining the highest possible wage while the management tries to concede the least possible wage increase. If there were no costs in the negotiation, it would be clear that each party would insist on its proposal and the negotiation would never end. However, both parties prefer to reach a quick agreement than get involved in lengthy negotiations because both parties face costs along the way. Therefore, one important element in the negotiation is its length, or in the technical jargon, the *delay to reach an agreement*. This delay in turn, depends on three other (related) elements of the negotiation: the *impatience* of the parties to reach an agreement, their *bargaining power*, and the *risk of a negotiation breakdown*.

Time is valuable to the negotiating parties because the value of €1 today is higher than the value of one euro tomorrow, given the interest rate that it yields. We capture the value of time by introducing a *discount rate*. Also, the initial situation of the parties at the moment of initiating the negotiation confers different levels of impatience to reach an agreement. A long-term unemployed individual is more impatient to accept a job offer than one recently unemployed. The financial capacity of the union to support its affiliates during a strike determines its capacity to lengthen the negotiation. This level of impatience in turn translates into bargaining power. Bargaining power is the ability of one party to influence the other in reaching an agreement. Hence, the more patient a party is (relative to the other party), the greater its bargaining power, and thus the higher the possibility of reaching an agreement more favorable to its interests.

It is often observed in negotiations that at some point, one of the parties leaves the negotiating table and the negotiation breaks down. Such a decision may arise from very different motivations: boredom, fatigue, the interference of a third party, etc. Regardless of the reason, a negotiation breakdown is possibly the worst outcome. Remember that both parties started negotiating because there were gains to trade (i.e. a surplus to share), and the issue was how to divide them. Therefore, a negotiation breakdown means that the two parties face an absolute loss. This explains why in real-life negotiations the parties often resume talks after a breakdown. Each party is endowed with some degree of *risk aversion to breakdown*. In turn, this implies that the higher the risk aversion of one party relative to the other, the lower its bargaining power and the lower the share of the surplus to be split between them.

Other elements determining the outcome of a negotiation procedure are the presence of outside options, the capacity of commitment, and the structure of information.

Sometimes it occurs that a negotiation fails because one party abandons the negotiating table to take up an opportunity somewhere else. The presence of this external opportunity to one or both parties (for instance the appearance of an alternative job offer in a wage negotiation) is termed an *outside option* of the party. Usually, the decision of a party to take its outside option is not accidental but strategic. The question is then how outside options affect the outcome of a negotiation procedure according to when and who may opt out. Having an outside option does not necessarily increase the party's bargaining power. The so-called *outside option principle* states that a player's outside option will increase the bargaining power of the agent if and only if the outside option is sufficiently attractive; if it is not attractive enough, then it will have no effect on the bargaining outcome. When one negotiator has an outside option, it may be used strategically as a threat in an attempt to gain bargaining power. However, the other party should only take into account those threats that are credible, that is threats that if the occasion arises will be implemented.

Commitment refers to actions taken by the negotiating parties prior to the negotiation that limit the negotiation possibilities. These actions are strategically chosen to favor the party's bargaining position. The first informal examination of this issue dates back to Schelling (1960) who illustrates the idea with the following example: prior to wage negotiations union representatives make statements to the members of the union where the ability and capacity of their representatives would be at stake if some minimal objectives were not achieved. Then, once at the negotiating table, these representatives make clear to the management that they cannot accept any offer below that predetermined objective even if they would like to because they no longer control the members and their own situation in the union would be threatened. Naturally, the commitment might be revoked but at a certain cost. Therefore, engaging in a commitment enhances the agent's bargaining power when the cost of backing down is sufficiently large.

Last but not least, we point out the possibility of bargaining situations where one party has information on something relevant that is ignored by the other party. For example, in a negotiation to set the price of a second-hand car, the seller has information on the quality of the car that the buyer does not know. This is an example of bargaining with *asymmetric information*. Typically, asymmetric information yields inefficient bargaining outcomes that materialize in costly delayed agreements.

14.1.2 *Equilibrium concepts*

There are two big families of bargaining models: *axiomatic bargaining* and *strategic bargaining* models. The former depart from a set of desirable properties about the outcome of the bargaining process and identify rules guaranteeing that outcome. In contrast the latter treats the bargaining process as a game and identifies the strategies to reach a certain equilibrium solution. The strategic approach originates in Rubinstein (1982) when he proposes a model of bargaining with alternating offers where negotiators made their offers and replies alternately over time in the course of the negotiation. The natural equilibrium candidate in this set-up is the subgame perfect equilibrium when information is complete or the sequential equilibrium under incomplete information. Both are refinements of the

Nash equilibrium concept. A rigorous analysis of these models is found in Osborne and Rubinstein (1990, ch. 3).

Section 14.1.3 presents the main features of Rubinstein's model and its equilibrium properties. The axiomatic bargaining approach originates in Nash (1950, 1953), who proposed what now is known as the Nash bargaining solution in a set-up where the negotiators make simultaneous offers. Section 14.1.4 presents Nash's proposal and its equilibrium properties. Although the two approaches appear to be very different, they turn out to be complementary in the sense that under some conditions in the setting up of the negotiation protocols, both approaches yield the same solution (see Binmore *et al.* 1986b, and Osborne and Rubinstein 1990, ch. 4.).

14.1.3   *Rubinstein's model of bargaining*

Rubinstein (1982) sets up the following problem:

> I will consider the following bargaining situation: two players have to reach an agreement on the partition of a pie of size 1. Each has to make in turn, a proposal as to how it should be divided. After one party has made such an offer, the other must decide either to accept it or to reject it and continue with the bargaining.
>
> (p. 98)

When one party accepts an offer, bargaining ends and the accepted split is implemented.

To complete the description of this model, it should be noted that (i) every offer made by any of the negotiators is independent of the previous offers, in the sense that the history of offers does not bind the present offer of the corresponding agent; (ii) players have preferences over the share of the pie they would like to obtain *and* the moment when to obtain it; (iii) each player has complete information about the preference of the other; (iv) the two negotiating parties may only differ in preferences and the (arbitrary) selection of the party starting the negotiation, and (v) unless an agreement is reached after the first proposal, delay imposes a cost on the negotiators in the form of a discount factor of future earnings relative to present earnings.

Sutton (1986) remarks that this modeling of the negotiation game allows a clear-cut identification of the effects of the sequence of moves and of the negotiators' preferences (summarized in the discount factors) in the characterization of the solution of the bargaining problem. Also, he provides three interpretations to the sequence of moves. A first interpretation regards the delay between successive moves as the agent's "speed of response" (see Martinez-Giralt and Ponsatí 1995); also it may represent the capacity of commitment of a party to propose an alternative split; finally the more natural interpretation would be to look at the sequence of moves "as stylized representations of bargaining processes, within which, by suitably altering the move structure, we may be able to represent certain differences between one bargaining environment and another" (p. 712).

Let two negotiators n_1 and n_2 where the subindex identifies the agent making the first offer, negotiate over how to divide a pie of unit size. Let δ_1 and δ_2 be their corresponding discount factors, where we assume $\delta_i \in (0, 1)$ so that both parties have an incentive to reach an agreement because the cake shrinks as time goes by. Let finally denote by x the share of the pie that negotiator n_1 receives if an agreement is reached. A strategy for a negotiator n_i in period t is a pair (x, t), where $0 \leq x \leq 1$ and the pair (x, t) is interpreted as "n_1 receives x and 2 receives $1 - x$ at time t". Figure 14.1 illustrates the sequence of infinite subgames $G_1, G_2, G_3 \dots$ of Rubinstein's bargaining game.

G₁

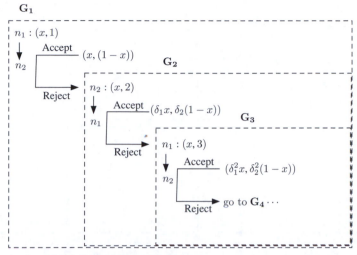

Figure 14.1 Rubinstein's bargaining game.

This game has many Nash equilibria but a unique subgame perfect equilibrium[2] where the payoffs depend on the relative impatience (discount rates) of the players, and on who moves first. In particular, the equilibrium payoffs are,

$$x = \frac{1 - \delta_2}{1 - \delta_1 \delta_2} \quad \text{and} \quad (1 - x) = \frac{\delta_2(1 - \delta_1)}{1 - \delta_1 \delta_2}. \tag{14.1}$$

One important characteristic of this equilibrium is that it is reached without delay. That is, in $t = 1$ negotiator n_1 proposes the split (14.1) and negotiator n_2 accepts. This is a consequence of the assumption of perfect information. Intuitively, both players know the preferences of the two players. Also, discounting makes the size of the pie shrink with delay. Therefore, n_1 can behave *as if* it would be player n_2 and compute n_2's best reply to any proposal. Accordingly, to maximize utility, n_1 proposes a split that is acceptable to n_2 when the size of the pie is maximum; that is, at the very beginning of the bargaining situation.

A particular case where $\delta_1 = \delta_2$ is of interest because the solution of the Rubinstein model coincides with the Nash bargaining solution (see below).

Several extensions deal with the (arbitrary) first mover advantage, the introduction of outside options for one or both negotiators, discount factors dependent of time, introducing asymmetric information, or considering more than two negotiators. A brief description of these extensions is found in Sutton (1986).

14.1.4 Nash's "demand game"

Nash (1953) proposed a two-person bargaining problem where both agents *simultaneously* submit proposals on how to divide a pie of size 1 between them. If the proposals are compatible, they are implemented. Otherwise, both get nothing. This is usually called the *disagreement point* or the *status quo point*.

Given the preferences of the two negotiators over the pie, Nash proposed four axioms that characterize the properties to be expected from the outcome of the bargaining process. A full description of these axioms can be found in Osborne and Rubinstein (1990, ch. 2). Here

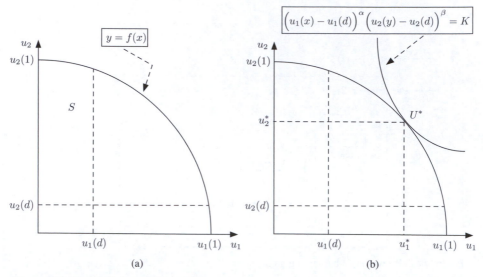

Figure 14.2 The Nash bargaining solution.

we highlight two of them: symmetry and Pareto optimality. Symmetry conveys the idea of anonymity, that is the outcome should treat the players equally. In more technical jargon, the utility space and the disagreement point are symmetric. Pareto optimality conveys the notion of efficiency. This means that we want to avoid situations where the agents make compatible claims that do not exhaust the pie. In other words, the axiom restricts the solution to points on the Pareto frontier of the utility space. Figure 14.2(a) illustrates the utility space (*S*). It contains all the pairs of utilities associated with all pairs of feasible claims. Points in the interior of *S* correspond to claims that do not exhaust the pie; $u_i(d)$ represents the corresponding utility values of the agents in case of disagreement, and $y = f(x)$ represents the Pareto frontier, that is the utility pairs associated with claims that exhaust the pie.

Note that reaching an agreement creates surplus for both agents because $u_i^* > u_i(d)$, $i = 1, 2$. Note also that both agents are tempted to raise their claims to get the highest share of that surplus, but at the same time they also must restrain their claims to avoid making incompatible claims. The problem arises because the two agents must decide their claims simultaneously, that is in ignorance of the claim of the other agent. Nash represented this dilemma in terms of a joint maximization of the surplus for any given distribution of bargaining power of the negotiators. Formally, let (x, y) represent the claims of individuals 1 and 2 respectively, and let (α, β) represent their respective bargaining powers. Then, the Nash bargaining solution allocation[3] is characterized by the solution of the following problem:

$$\max_{x,y} (u_1(x) - u_1(d))^\alpha (u_2(y) - u_2(d))^\beta \quad \text{s.t. } y = f(x)$$

Figure 14.2(b) represents the Nash bargaining solution.

14.2 Bargaining in health care markets

Most economic analyses of contract design in health care in fact assume that the party that makes the first move, typically the payer, makes a take-it-or-leave-it offer to the provider. We take here a broader view where the relationship between third-party payers and providers stem as the outcome of a three-stage game. In a first stage, the third-party payer (be it a NHS or private insurance company) offers health insurance contracts to consumers. Such contracts specify the insurance premium, the providers the individuals have access to when ill, and the associated co-payments. In a second stage, each insurance company defines the set of selected providers to which the individuals that have contracted a health insurance have access to when ill. Finally, in the third stage of the game, providers compete in prices and qualities in the market. The competitive process among providers is influenced by the selection decision of providers by the insurance companies to provide health care services to their population of insured individuals. This order of moves is the more natural one for health systems where the third-party payer has a very strong commitment to provide health care in case of need or when third-party payers and providers are able to renegotiate terms and conditions after insurance contracts have been signed with consumers.[4]

We tackle the third stage of the game in Barros and Martinez-Giralt (2002). There, we study the competitive effects on providers from different reimbursement rules. They translate into being included or excluded in the list of selected providers by an insurer, which, in turn, will have an impact on their decisions regarding quality and price. Also, we assume that all our providers are always active in the market. Generally, patients have to bear part of the cost of the treatment provided by an in-plan care provider. If, instead he or she visits an out-of-plan care provider, he or she pays the full price and obtains the indemnity from the insurer specified in the insurance contract.

We consider three basic alternatives to the indemnity associated with the out-of-plan provider. The first simply does not provide coverage for choices outside the preferred provider set. This covers a pure public system of health provision, such as the Spanish one, where a patient visiting a private provider (instead of a public one) has to bear the full cost of the treatment. The second alternative defines an indemnity equal to what the patient would have obtained should they have visited a preferred provider. This alternative tries to capture the idea of indemnity based on a reference price. It shares some features of the French system. It also shares some important features of the pharmaceutical sector. Finally, the third alternative is equivalent to the scenario where the insurer has selected both providers. This uses some features of the German system where together with the public providers there is a fringe of private providers regulated through bilateral agreements.

The type of questions we address refer to the characteristics of the market allocations according to the type of insurance contract offered by the insurer and to different assumptions about the timing of the decisions on prices and qualities taken by the providers.

We identify providers making simultaneous decisions on prices and qualities as an approach to the primary care sector, and sequential decisions (first qualities then prices) as an approach to the specialized health care sector. Our main conclusion is that enforcing the fixed co-payment rule on the primary health care sector is enough to make providers choose the optimal (welfare maximizing) prices and qualities. By contrast, in the specialized health care sector we need to consider a regulated (public) provider to reach the first-best solution in prices and qualities and implement either the fixed co-payment or the fixed reimbursement rules.

Next, we turn to the implications of our analysis for the health system organization. All governments in European Union member states have looked at ways to contain health expenditures. Direct and indirect controls over health care providers have been imposed in some countries where co-payments play an important role. In several countries we find controls on prices (pharmaceuticals, per-day treatment in hospitals), while in others no such controls exist. Co-payment changes have been frequent in European countries, mostly limited to the value of the co-payment while maintaining its structure (fixed reimbursement rates).[5] Moreover, co-payments are designed with insurance coverage in mind (typically, they have an upper limit). No role as a market mechanism underlies the choice of the structure and the value of co-payments. Thus, according to our analysis, the relative unsuccessful episodes of cost containment through co-payments are not totally surprising. The structure of the co-payment has been kept constant, while our results highlight the fact that changing its structure would have a greater impact.

The market most closely related to our setting is the pharmaceutical market. Reference prices, present in several countries, are much in the spirit of our approach.[6] Under a reference price system, a single price is set by the insurer (government or other institution) for a group of similar products. Any excess above the reference price has to be paid by the patient. Companies have freedom to set their prices in those countries that have adopted reference price systems. One objective behind the adoption of a reference price system has been to foster competition in the market. Several countries use this system (New Zealand, Germany, the Netherlands, Denmark, Sweden, and Italy). Providers (pharmaceutical companies) have argued against the reference price system on the basis that it distorts clinical decision making and limits freedom of choice. Our analysis shows that in this respect a fixed co-payment system performs as well as a fixed reimbursement rate system, and adds the advantage of tougher price competition among providers. It also reveals that exclusion of some providers from the reimbursement system (the pure preferred provider case) does induce distortions in the decision to visit a provider, which can be seen as limitations on the freedom of choice.

Although the pharmaceutical market is a very good application of our analysis (see Pecorino, 2002), we do believe it can be applied in a fruitful way to other providers. For example, visits to general practitioners in some countries (e.g. Ireland, France, Portugal, Sweden) are associated with co-payments, aimed at demand control. As long as GPs retain some control over the prices they charge, namely in private practice, we suggest that fixed reimbursement rate regimes should be changed to fixed co-payment systems. Also, Ellis and McGuire (1990) model the physician–patient relationship as a bargaining tool over the intensity of treatment to derive the consumer welfare maximizing combination of patient's insurance and provider reimbursement.

14.2.1 Negotiation between payers and providers

We focus here on models of explicit bargaining between two parties, which we call the *payer* and the *provider*. This corresponds to the second-stage of the overall game described earlier. On theoretical grounds, simple bargaining models can have their results transposed in a straightforward way: higher bargaining power and higher alternative-option values from providers originate higher prices. Therefore, a first empirical question comes to mind: how strong as negotiators are providers? Or, to put it another way, financing institutions/payers are usually large relative to providers although the latter can have a natural exclusive "catchment area" (in geographic terms or medical specialty). Then, what is the effect on prices from moving to an explicit bargaining situation? This is a relevant question but it is certainly not the only one. The special setting of health care markets brings to attention the optimal design of the negotiation procedure. In particular, timing and format of negotiations between payers/financing institutions and health care providers may lead to distinct outcomes.

The basic model of bargaining has a single third-party payer bargaining with a single provider over the division of a given surplus. Whenever the total surplus is constant, the greater the bargaining power, the greater the share of surplus captured. This simple model does not allow for outside options. When they are present, these outside option values also drive the outcome of the bargaining process. In particular, the higher the outside value of the third-party payer (the provider), the lower (the higher) the equilibrium price will be.[7]

The next logical step is in our view to use the bargaining model to discuss the particular institutional arrangement for bargaining in health care. In particular, two sorts of choices seem relevant to consider. On the one hand, we have the choice between the bargaining game and the use of "any willing provider" (AWP) clauses. The other one is whether it is preferable to negotiate with each provider on a one-to-one basis, or to do it with an association of providers. Both institutional arrangements can be found in practice.

The AWP approach has been debated mainly in the United States, where the enactment of "any willing provider" laws by some states has been taken to the Supreme Court, and has been upheld by a recent decision.[8] The AWP contracts are frequently used by governments and, to some extent, by private health plans or insurance companies. Simon (1997) studies both the characteristics of the states that have enacted AWP laws and their effect on managed care penetration rates and provider participation. Also, Ohsfeldt *et al.* (1998) explore the growth of AWP laws applicable to managed care firms and the determinants of their enactment.

These laws require managed care organizations to announce contractual conditions to providers (prices, quality, etc.). A provider that accepts such conditions can enroll in the network of the managed care organization. However, in some European countries we can find the use of AWP dispositions. Empirical work on the implications of the "any willing provider" laws by Carroll and Ambroise (2002), Glazer and McGuire (1993), Morrisey and Oshfeldt (2004), and Vita (2001) have been complemented by the novel theoretical treatment of Barros and Martinez-Giralt (2008) that is described in the next section.

14.2.2 *AWP vs. negotiation*

Barros and Martinez-Giralt (2008) address the question of how a third-party payer (e.g. an insurer) decides what providers to contract with. Two different mechanisms are studied and their properties compared. A first mechanism consists of the third-party payer setting up a bargaining procedure with both providers. The second mechanism is the "any willing provider" where the third-party payer announces a contract and every provider freely decides whether or not to sign it. The main finding is that the decision of the third-party payer depends on the surplus to be shared. When it is relatively high the third-party payer prefers the any willing provider system. When, on the contrary, the surplus is relatively low, the third-party payer will select a negotiated solution. The analysis of "any willing provider" clauses and its comparison with pure bargaining situations suggests that depending on the underlying context, namely, surplus to be shared, either one can lead to lower prices. This imposes further demands on empirical work related to impact of such laws. It also raises econometric issues: countries, states or third-party payers may introduce them because they fulfill the conditions to get lower prices that way. This endogeneity issue has not, to our knowledge, yet been tackled in empirical work.

To be precise, let us consider a population of consumers with a potential health problem. Each member of the population has a given probability of being sick. The expected mass of consumers demanding health care is uniformly distributed on a space of characteristics. The identifying characteristics of the consumer are independent of the probability of occurrence of the illness episode. In terms of insurance choice models, this adds a background risk to the demand for insurance, thereby reinforcing the demand for insurance (Eeckhoudt and Kimball 1992). The population we study is made up of patients and it is conceivably a subset of all people insured. The individual characteristics represent the differences providers have in consumers' eyes. They can be objective, like geographic distance, or subjective, such as personal taste for one provider over the other.[9] Whenever a patient cannot patronize his or her best-preferred provider, he or she suffers a loss in utility (or under the geographical interpretation, has to bear a transport cost). We assume the patients' utility loss increases at a constant rate t with the distance to his or her preferred provider. We also assume that consumers are subject to compulsory health insurance.

A consumer when signing the insurance contract does not know beforehand the position they will have in the characteristics space when sick. This implies that when both providers are successful in reaching an agreement, consumers can patronize either of them only bearing the disutility cost. In case of disagreement with one provider, consumers have the choice of patronizing the in-plan provider at zero cost or the out-of-plan provider at full cost. If no provider reaches an agreement with the insurer, it gives back the premia to consumers and providers compete on prices in a Hotelling-type market.

The insurance contract defines a premium to be paid by consumers, which is taken as given at the moment of contracting with providers. When selecting providers, the third-party payer (in line with the complete three-stage game described above) has already collected the insurance premia/contributions from consumers. Thus, total revenues of the insurance company are exogenously given at the stage in which negotiation between the third-party payer and the providers of health care takes place.

The conflict between the two sides of the bargaining process appears because the insurer's cost represents the providers' revenues. Naturally, the outcome of the negotiation hinges on the parameters of the bargaining problem. These are the distribution of bargaining power among the players and the so-called *status-quo*, or the fallback values, that is, the outcome that would arise should the negotiation fail. We assume that providers do not collude and that negotiations are carried simultaneously with the two providers who decide their actions in a non-cooperative way. In contrast with the existing literature, it is worth noting that in our setting, fallback values in one negotiation depend on the outcome of the other negotiation. This happens because providers after each negotiation compete in the market. Thus, the outcome of each negotiation is conditional on the expected price of the other provider. We force expectations to hold in equilibrium.

AWP contracts

"Any willing provider" contracts have the third-party payer announcing a price p, and leaving to the (symmetric) providers the option or not of joining the agreement. The providers are assumed to be equal in all the relevant dimensions but location in the space of characteristics and (possibly) prices. In a world of two providers (A, B), the set of possible decisions defines four different sub-games in prices, which in turn define previous-stage profits for providers. When *both providers choose to join the agreement*, each receives the price announced by the third-party payer and demand is split in half (a consequence of the uniform distribution of consumers in the space of characteristics and of symmetric location of the health care providers). In the other polar case of *both providers choosing not to join the agreement*, the market game is back to the (Hotelling) price game. The last possible case has *one provider joining the agreement* and accepting to receive the announced price, while the other stays out and sets its price freely. Providers are not allowed to balance bill patients. Thus, someone

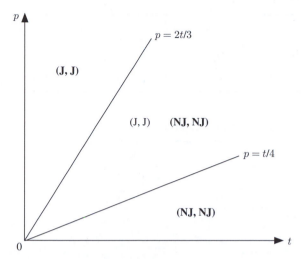

Figure 14.3 AWP equilibrium regimes.

visiting the provider that accepted the AWP contract pays nothing but if visiting the other, independent, provider pays its full price. Figure 14.3 represent the equilibrium configurations that may arise in the game for any given price p. We find three regions. For prices above $p = 2/3t$, both providers decide to join the AWP contract. This is the (J,J)-region. When the third-party payer announces a price below $p = 1/4t$ no provider decides to join and we obtain the (NJ,NJ)-region. Finally, for intermediate price levels both equilibria may arise. Using Pareto dominance (from the providers' viewpoint) as a selection criterion, it turns out that the (NJ,NJ) equilibrium dominates. Hence, the equilibrium where both providers join the agreement occurs above the high threshold only. Note that no asymmetric pattern of the type can be sustained in equilibrium.

The question left is now the optimal price that the third-party payer announces. The criterion is the minimization of total health expenditure. Third-party payer profits are defined by the premia collected R net of the reimbursement to providers and of a penalty F. This penalty captures the point that an insurer giving access to a smaller set of options in health care provision faces a cost to it (for example reputation, value of variety and freedom of choice to consumers, or money returned to insured people, despite the costs of real resources incurred anyway). Given the initial assumption of full insurance, all expenses will be paid, irrespective of the provider chosen by each particular consumer. The optimal price is the lowest price allowing for both providers accepting it. This is $p/t = 2/3$. This optimal price is also lower than the cost per unit of distance of not having a provider located in the preferred point of the space of characteristics, t, which guarantees that the third-party payer prefers to announce AWP contracts instead of allowing free competition between the parties (and having to reimburse consumers from the care they would seek in a pure private market equilibrium). Note that the payer needs to announce a fee sufficiently high to induce the participation of at least one provider. But in equilibrium with both providers participating, the fee is lower than what the take-it-or-leave-it offer would have been. In other words, the payer is willing to give away some monopoly (bargaining) power in order to induce an equilibrium with providers' participation, thus, softening the (full) bargaining power that a too-rigid payer would reflect in committing to a high fee. Table 14.1 summarizes the results.

Table 14.1 AWP equilibrium magnitudes

	A, B in	A in, B out	A, B out
Prices (p_A, p_B)	$t/4, t/4$	$t/4, t/2$	t, t
Demands (D_A, D_B)	$1/2, 1/2$	$3/4, 1/4$	$1/2, 1/2$
Profits (Π_A, Π_B, $\widehat{\Pi}$)	$t/8, t/8, R - t/4$	$3t/16, t/8, R - F - 3t/16$	$t/2, t/2, 0$

Table 14.2 Providers' profits alternatives

$i \setminus j$	Success	Fail
Success	Π_i, Π_j	$\widetilde{\Pi}_i, \overline{\Pi}_j$
Fail	$\overline{\Pi}_i, \widetilde{\Pi}_j$	$\underline{\Pi}_i, \underline{\Pi}_j$

Bargaining

Consider a situation where the third-party payer carries out negotiations *simultaneously* but *independently* with the providers. The distribution of bargaining power between the third-party payer and the providers is exogenously given. Note that this situation does not correspond with a process where after failing to close a deal with one provider, the third-party payer addresses the second one. In our scenario, the provider when accepting or rejecting a deal *does not know* the outcome of the other parallel negotiation process. Three scenarios may appear. Providers successfully close the negotiation with the third-party payer, none does, or only one is successful. When a negotiation fails, the third-party payer faces a penalty as before.

We use the Nash bargaining solution as an equilibrium concept. In our set up, as two negotiation processes are carried out simultaneously, the computation of expectations of the rival's behavior is more involved. In the standard Nash equilibrium approach, the expectation is that the rival's equilibrium price is held constant. However in our framework, since the outcome of the other negotiation depends also on decisions taken by the third-party payer, we require that expectations in equilibrium be correct. If, say, negotiation between the third-party payer and provider A fails, the third-party payer anticipates that its negotiation with provider B will result in a different price. That is, we assume that both parties, provider B and the third-party payer are aware that the negotiation with provider A failed. In other words, we are imposing rational expectations in the sense that price expectations of the parties involved in one negotiation about the outcome of the other negotiation must be equal to the equilibrium outcome. Our approach is in line with the analysis of parallel bargaining by Chae and Heidhues (1999, 2004).

Let $\widehat{\Pi}$ denote the third-party payer's surplus; Π_i are profits to provider i when both negotiations are successful; $\widetilde{\Pi}_i$ are profits to provider i when its negotiation succeeds while j's does not, $\overline{\Pi}_i$ are profits to provider i when its negotiation fails while j's is successful. Finally, $\underline{\Pi}_i$ are profits to provider i when both negotiations fail. Table 14.2 summarizes these alternative profit configurations.

Profits obtained by the third-party payer when negotiations are successful with both providers are given by the difference between the (exogenous) premia collected from the insured and the payment to providers in accordance with the terms of the respective negotiations, this is $R - \Pi_A - \Pi_B$. When only one provider (i) reaches an agreement, the revenues to the third-party payer are given by the difference between its revenues (the premia collected) and the sum of the payment to that provider and the penalty. Formally, $R - \widetilde{\Pi}_i - F$. Finally, if no negotiation succeeds, the third-party payer obtains zero revenues (as no insurance is contracted). In this latter case the market game is just a Hotelling price game between providers with fixed locations in the space of characteristics relevant to consumers. The symmetry of the solution implies equal demand to each provider so that in equilibrium, prices are $p_i = t$, and profits are $\underline{\Pi}_i = t/2$, $i = A, B$.

TWO SUCCESSFUL NEGOTIATIONS

Let us characterize first the conditions to be satisfied such that both negotiations are successful. As we assume full insurance, equilibrium with both providers accepting exists, given the symmetry between providers, when the same price prevails for both. Hence, providers will share the market evenly and their profits will be given by half of the respective equilibrium price since total demand is normalized to the unit, $\Pi_i = p_i/2$.

Two simultaneous bargaining problems have to be solved. As we use the Nash bargaining as a solution concept, the difference between the net revenues and the fallback values for the agents involved in the negotiation are the crucial elements. Formally, the negotiation with provider i is described by the following problem,

$$\max_{p_i}[(R - \Pi_i - \Pi_j) - (R - F - \widetilde{\Pi}_j)]^{\delta}(\Pi_i - \overline{\Pi}_i)^{(1-\delta)},$$

where p_i denotes the fee for provider i. Note that although R cancels from the Nash maximand, the solution still depends on R because R determines the solution when there is only one successful negotiation which is the disagreement point for the bargain with two successful negotiations. And R affects the outcome when there is one successful bargain because it does not form part of the payoff when there is no bargain at all.

The fallback level of the third-party payer is defined by the profits it obtains under the agreement with the other provider, net of the penalty associated with a smaller set of providers than the maximum possible, $R - F - \widetilde{\Pi}_j$.

The fallback for provider i is given by the profits available when the rival provider succeeds in its negotiation, $\overline{\Pi}_i$. These are the profits when provider i is out of plan, so that those patients patronizing it have to bear the full price of treatment, while its rival is an in-plan provider. This implies that the location of the consumer indifferent to either provider is given by $x(p_i) = \frac{1}{2} - \frac{p_i}{2t}$ and provider i's profits are given by $\overline{\Pi}_i(p_i) = p_i x(p_i)$. Thus, the maximizing price is $p_i = \frac{t}{2}$, and profits $\overline{\Pi}_i = t/8$.

Solving the first-order conditions, we obtain the (symmetric) prices:

$$p^a = \frac{2(1-\delta)}{2-\delta}\left[\frac{\delta t}{2} + (1-\delta)R + \delta F\right] + \frac{\delta t}{4(2-\delta)}$$

These (positive) prices are equilibrium prices if two additional consistency conditions are met: (i) no provider wants to leave the agreement, or $\Pi(p^a) = p^a/2 \geq \overline{\Pi}_i = t/8$, and (ii) the third-party payer obtains non-negative revenues, $R \geq p^a$.

ONE SUCCESSFUL NEGOTIATION ONLY

A similar reasoning will lead us to conclude that we cannot have equilibrium with only one provider successfully terminating the negotiation with the third-party payer. In other words, under explicit bargaining procedures with identical providers it cannot be the case of only one successful negotiation. Again, in our framework, the symmetry of players does result in a symmetric equilibrium. This is the case because the disadvantage in terms of demand from being left out is higher than the advantage of being a price-setter. The formal argument goes as follows. Assume that provider i accepts the deal while provider j rejects it. The negotiation process between the third-party payer and provider i is described by,

$$\max_{p_i}(R - \widetilde{\Pi}_i - F)^\delta (\widetilde{\Pi}_i - \underline{\Pi}_i)^{1-\delta}.$$

The solution of this problem is given by,

$$p_i = \frac{4}{3}\left(\frac{\delta t}{2} + (1 - \delta)(R - F)\right); \quad p_j = \frac{t}{2};$$

$$\widetilde{\Pi}_i = \frac{\delta t}{2} + (1 - \delta)(R - F); \quad \overline{\Pi}_j = \frac{t}{8}; \quad \text{and,}$$

$$\widehat{\Pi} = \delta\left(R - F - \frac{t}{2}\right).$$

The pair (p_i, p_j) will constitute an equilibrium price pair if (i) providers' prices and third-party revenues are non-negative and (ii) provider i does not want to quit the agreement (i.e. $\widetilde{\Pi}_i \geq \underline{\Pi}_i$) and provider j does not want to join it (i.e. $\overline{\Pi}_j \geq \Pi_j$).

Third-party revenues are non-negative if $R - F \geq t/2$. This condition is also sufficient to ensure that $p_i \geq 0$ and that provider i does not have incentives to leave the agreement. Provider j does not want to join if $R \leq t/4$. However, the latter condition is not compatible with the former, so that we cannot have an equilibrium with only one provider successfully terminating the negotiation with the third-party payer. Table 14.3 summarizes the results where the first element in each box refers to provider A, the second to provider B, and in the case of profits, the third item corresponds to the third-party payer profits.

Summarizing, under an explicit bargaining procedure with identical providers it cannot be the case that only one negotiation is successful. Moreover, it is not clear that the equilibrium price is smaller than the one prevailing in the stand-alone market (that is, without insurance to consumers). The condition for a higher price under bargaining relative to the stand-alone case is $\widetilde{R} \geq t/2$, which is compatible with the conditions for existence of a bargaining equilibrium. Finally, it is straightforward to see that an increase in the bargaining power of the third-party payer (measured by a higher δ) means a lower price, as one intuitively expects. The symmetry assumptions allow us to extend the outcome of the model to an arbitrary number of providers

Table 14.3 Bargaining equilibrium magnitudes

	A, B success	A success, B fail	A, B fail
Prices	p^a, p^a	$\frac{4}{3}\left(\frac{\delta}{t} + (1 - \delta)(R - F)\right), t/2$	t, t
Demand	$1/2, 1/2$	$3/4, 1/4$	$1/2, 1/2$
Profits	$p^a/2, p^a/2, R - p^a$	$\frac{\delta}{t} + (1 - \delta)(R - F), \frac{t}{8}, \delta\left(R - F - \frac{t}{2}\right)$	$t/2, t/2, 0$

in the sense that in equilibrium either all providers join the agreement with the third-party payer, or none accepts the proposal of the third-party payer.

A side issue that we do not consider in our analysis is the source of bargaining power of the agents. We assume it exogenously given. Wu (2009) examines precisely this question. After documenting the success of managed care in slowing the rate of growth in health care spending she focuses on the price discounting argument as its main driver. Managed care price discounting stems from a selective contracting mechanism. Managed care forms a provider network of providers and channels patients based on cost, quality and different incentive schemes. In this way, managed care obtains discounts from the promise of patient volume to its network of providers (and with the threat of exclusion to those providers not willing to grant favorable enough prices). Wu proceeds to test the size of the health plans and the demand elasticity measured by patient channeling within the provider network as key determinants for discounts. Her findings are as follows:

> first, size is important in the study markets. Large plans are generally able to obtain lower prices. This finding is consistent with the conventional wisdom on size effect. Second, demand elasticity may be even more important in determining discounts. More importantly, the elasticity effect can modify the conventional size effect. Therefore, the final discount a health plan attains depends on the interaction between its size and its ability to channel patients within the provider network.

The preferred negotiation format

The comparison between the bargaining mechanism and an "any willing provider" contract is only relevant when the price is above the threshold that leads to the use of "any willing provider" contracts by the third-party payer (that is, for $p \geq 2/3t$). Prices also need to satisfy conditions (i), and (ii) above. To carry out the comparison we need to introduce an additional assumption. Either we take the perspective of the third-party payer or of the providers. We have decided to consider the third-party payer's viewpoint. More generally, we could envisage an additional previous stage where providers and the third-party payer decide the negotiation format. Given that providers' revenues equal third-party payer expenses, this yields a battle-of-the-sexes type of situation. Typically, these games have multiplicity of equilibria. In this framework, our approach boils down to using the third-party payer viewpoint as an equilibrium selection mechanism. We find this more reasonable than the alternative approach because under AWP the third-party payer is the agent that makes the commitment.

From the point of view of the third-party payer, the simultaneous bargaining procedure is better than "any willing provider" if

$$\widehat{\Pi}_{SB} - \widehat{\Pi}_{AWP} = p - \left(\frac{\delta t}{4(2 - \delta)} + \widetilde{R} \frac{2(1 - \delta)}{2 - \delta} \right) > 0.$$

This condition defines a line, as shown in Figure 14.4, which allows for a simple description of the basic economic intuition which runs as follows. If net revenue ($\widetilde{R}$) is small, there is not much surplus to bargain for. Hence, prices will be below the price required in the AWP case to generate the acceptance outcome. The reverse occurs for high $\widetilde{R}$. Since the bargaining process transfers surplus to providers, the "any willing provider" contract is equivalent to a

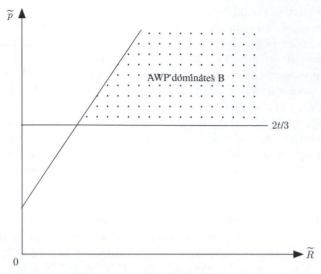

Figure 14.4 Optimal negotiation procedure.

"tough" bargaining position. The commitment to a price is more valuable when the aggregate surplus to share (R) is large.

A final clarifying comment is in order here. We have seen that under bargaining, given the symmetry of the model, both providers accept the same price. Why is it the case that under AWP announcing that price is not an equilibrium? Actually, under AWP we found that for any $p \geq t/4$ both providers join. Also, we have shown that there are two equilibria: where both providers join and where no provider joins. Artificially (since the Pareto criterion does not select among the two equilibria), we are forcing $p > 2t/3$ to eliminate the equilibrium where no provider joins as it cannot be an equilibrium of the full three-stage game. In other words, we are imposing a conservative behavior on the third-party payer in the sense that we are not allowing it to announce a price $p \in (t/4, 2t/3)$ so that no provider would decide to accept.

14.3   The institutional setting

We have seen the impact of different pricing policies reflecting different distributions of bargaining power on the outcome of the negotiation between payers and providers. Siciliani and Stanciole (2008) broaden the scope of the negotiation between a payer (say, the health authority) and a provider (e.g. a hospital) to consider prices (p) and/or activity (y) in three institutional settings. The so-called *activity-bargaining model* considers that, in a first stage, the purchaser sets the price, and that next, the level of activity is bargained between purchaser and provider. Alternatively, the *price-bargaining model* is also a two-stage set-up where first the price is bargained between payer and provider, and then the provider decides the level of activity. Finally, the third alternative considers the simultaneous bargaining of price and activity in what the authors label *efficient bargaining*. Table 14.4 summarizes these alternative regimes.

14.3.1   The model

Consider a payer and a provider of health care services. Let y denote the number of patients treated, p the price the provider receives per patient, $C(y)$, $C' > 0$, $C'' > 0$ the cost of treating

Table 14.4 The institutional settings

Efficient Bargaining	Activity Bargaining		Price Bargaining	
	Stage 1	Stage 2	Stage 1	Stage 2
Barg on (p, y)	Payer sets p	Barg on y	Barg on p	Hosp sets y

y patients, and $B(y)$, $B' > 0$, $B'' \leq 0$ the patients' benefits. The utility of the provider is defined as $U(p, y) = py - C(y)$, and the utility of the payer is $V(p, y) = B(y) - py$. The bargaining power of the payer is $\gamma \in [0, 1]$. Finally, $\bar{U}$ and $\bar{V}$ represent the outside options of the provider and payer respectively. The Nash bargaining solution characterizes the optimal solution of the bargaining games. Also, the multistage settings are solved by backward induction.

Activity bargaining

We start by solving the stage-2 negotiation game. For any given price p, the negotiation determines the level of activity y solving the following problem,

$$\max_y [B(y) - py - \bar{V}]^{\gamma} [py - C(y) - \bar{U}]^{(1-\gamma)}$$

The solution of this problem[10] is an activity level $y^a(p)$ satisfying

$$\frac{\gamma}{\tilde{V}}(B' - p) = \frac{1 - \gamma}{\tilde{U}}(C' - p) \tag{14.2}$$

where $\tilde{V} \equiv V - \bar{V}$ and $\tilde{U} \equiv U - \bar{U}$. That is, the optimal level of activity balances a weighted measure of the net marginal benefit of activity of the payer and of the net marginal cost of activity of the provider. Note that for prices high enough or low enough that the expressions in brackets in (14.2) have the same sign, the optimal activity y^a is an intermediate level between the desired levels of activity of payer and provider. The optimal level of activity is increasing (decreasing) in the payer's bargaining power and in the price for sufficiently low (high) prices.

Next, we compute the optimal level of price (stage 1 of the full game). This price is determined by the payer solving the following problem,

$$\max_p B(y^a(p)) - py^a(p).$$

Accordingly, the optimal price p^a arises as the solution of the first order condition,

$$B'(y)y'(p) = y + py'(p).$$

Price bargaining

In this setting the parties determine first the price as the outcome of a negotiation, and in a second stage the provider identifies its optimal level of activity. As before, using a backward induction argument, we start solving the stage 2 of the overall game.

In the second stage, the provider for any price p determines its utility maximizing level of activity solving the following problem.

$$\max_{y} py - C(y),$$

so that the optimal level of activity $y^P(p)$ arises as the solution of $p = C'(y)$. This level of activity is increasing in the price.

In the first stage of the game both agents (payer and provider) negotiate the optimal price. It is characterized by the solution of the following problem,

$$\max_{p}[B(y^P(p)) - py^P(p) - \bar{V}]^{\gamma}[py^P(p) - C(y^P(p)) - \bar{U}]^{(1-\gamma)}.$$

The optimal price p^P solves

$$\frac{\gamma}{\tilde{V}}B'(y)y'(p) + \frac{1-\gamma}{\tilde{U}}y = \frac{\gamma}{\tilde{V}}(y + py'(p)).$$

Accordingly, the optimal price balances the payer's marginal benefit of a higher price including the marginal benefit of higher activity and the provider's marginal benefit of a higher surplus with the payer's marginal cost of a higher price and the overall transfer to the provider.

Note that when $\gamma = 1$, i.e. the payer holds all the bargaining power, the optimal price is the solution of $B'(y)y'(p) = y + py'(p)$, while when the provider has all the bargaining power ($\gamma = 0$), the optimal price is the highest price compatible with the payer obtaining non-negative utility. These are the bounds of the optimal price for any distribution of bargaining power between payer and provider.

Efficient bargaining

The last setting contemplates both parties negotiating simultaneously on the price and the level of activity. Therefore, the problem to solve is,

$$\max_{p,y}[B(y) - py - \bar{V}]^{\gamma}[py - C(y) - \bar{U}]^{(1-\gamma)}.$$

From the set of first order conditions it follows that the optimal level of activity y^e is given by the solution of $B'(y) = C'(y)$, and the optimal price is given by

$$p^e = (1 - \gamma)\frac{B(y^e) - \bar{V}}{y^e} + \gamma\frac{C(y^e) + \bar{U}}{y^e}.$$

In other words, the optimal level of activity results from maximizing the joint surplus $U + V = B(y) - C(y)$ (and in this sense it is efficient), while the optimal price p^e is a weighted average of average patients' benefits and average cost of the provider.

Note that when the payer holds all the bargaining power ($\gamma = 1$) the optimal price is simply $p^e = (C(y^e) + \bar{U})/y^e$, i.e., the price equals the average cost as the payer extracts all the surplus from the provider. In the opposite extreme case where the provider has all the bargaining power ($\gamma = 0$), the optimal price is $p^e = (B(y^e) - \bar{V})/y^e$, i.e., the price equals the average benefit as the provider extracts all the surplus from the payer.

Comparison

To ease the comparison across the three regimes, Siciliani and Stanciole (2008) propose to consider the following assumption on the functional forms:

(a)   the benefit function is given by $B(y) = ay - \frac{b}{2}y^2$, showing decreasing marginal benefits;
(b)   the cost function is quadratic $C(y) = \frac{c}{2}y^2$;
(c)   the outside options are normalized to zero: $\bar{U} = \bar{V} = 0$.

The comparison between price bargaining and efficient bargaining is straightforward and summarized in the following proposition:

PROPOSITION 14.1   *If $\gamma > \frac{b}{b+c}$, then (a) $p^p > p^e$, (b) $y^e > y^p$, (c) $U^p > U^e$, (d) $V^e > V^p$.*

That is, if the bargaining power of the purchaser is above a certain threshold, efficient bargaining yields higher activity and lower prices than price bargaining. In turn, this induces higher purchaser's utility under efficient bargaining than under price bargaining while the provider is worse off in the former than in the latter. If the bargaining power of the purchaser is sufficiently low, all the results are reversed.

Note that the threshold is increasing in b (the degree of concavity) and decreasing in c (the degree of convexity). Then, when the purchaser has low bargaining power having more instruments to negotiate is counterproductive. This reflects the fact that the weaker party in a negotiation tries to negotiate along the least possible dimensions because it has little to gain from the negotiation, while the stronger party has the opposite interests. Accordingly, internalizing the scenario will likely yield problems of existence of equilibrium. From a policy viewpoint, however, the health authority has a degree of freedom to encourage purchasers to negotiate on price and activity simultaneously, or on price only. It is an empirical question to estimate the bargaining power of the purchaser and the provider in the health care markets.

The solution of the activity bargaining is complex and does not allow to derive manageable expression for price and activity. The comparisons thus rely on numerical simulations.

> Overall the numerical simulations suggest that in activity bargaining prices are lowest, the purchaser's utility is highest and the provider's utility is lowest. Activity is lower than in efficient bargaining. It is lower than in price bargaining when the bargaining power of the purchaser is below a certain threshold, which is between 0.7 and 0.95 in our simulations.
>
> Siciliani and Stanciole (2008, p. 21)

Summarizing the impact of bargaining power on activity, it follows that higher bargaining power reduces activity under price bargaining, increases activity under activity bargaining and has no effect on activity under efficient bargaining. Again, these are clear predictions from a policy perspective. Empirical work is necessary to test these predictions. Finally, extending the model to encompass quality and cost containment effort yields qualitatively similar results to those reported.

14.4   Bargaining within a national health service

In public systems, it is often the case that the national health service (NHS) contracts with private providers the provision of health care services. A popular contractual form is the setting of a fee for service. Despite a general trend towards different contractual forms in some countries, and for certain services provided, this approach is still dominant as Mossialos and Le Grand (1999, pp. 17–19) show in their review of payment systems for health care providers in the European Union.

Typically, the value of the fee is set in a negotiation procedure between the NHS and either an association representing providers or some providers individually. An interesting economic question here is whether the NHS would do better negotiating with an association instead of selecting the largest companies as preferential partners and then apply the the same price to all providers. This question also extends beyond the NHS framework. Presently (May 2010), in the US there is an attempt by Democrats in the State Senate and Assembly to pass a bill entitled "Health Care Providers Collective Negotiations Act", that would allow health care providers to bargain collectively with health care plans. The issue is controversial because proponents of the Act argue that it would benefit consumers because the collective negotiation of the conditions of health plans would reduce the imbalance of power between the market dominant plans and providers. However, opponents argue that collective negotiation would only result in higher prices and lower quality levels associated with their increased bargaining power against health care plans.

The general literature on bargaining, mostly with applications to the labor market, provides some rationale for providers to join forces and to negotiate as a single entity vis-à-vis the third-party payer. The direct application of most bargaining theory to health care settings faces a difficulty. This is the existence of market interaction among providers. Therefore, the value of one negotiation often is to be conditional on the outcome of some other (simultaneous) negotiation(s). Firm–unions' bargaining issues have similarities, allowing for useful analogies to health care settings. For example, Davidson (1988) considers unionized oligopolistic industries where wages can be negotiated at the firm level or at the industry level. In the former case, workers of each firm are represented by independent and separate unions, while in the latter case there is a single union representing all workers in the industry. This multipayer set-up is also used by Gal-Or (1997) to study the way third-party payers select providers to contract with. She considers two differentiated providers and finds that when consumers' valuation of accessing a full set of providers is small (large) relative to the degree of differentiation between payers, both payers choose to contract with only one of the two providers. In this way private insurers, by signing exclusive contracts with a subset of providers, secure more favorable terms in the negotiation. Petrakis and Vlassis (2000) provide a model of endogenous determination of the firm–union bargaining. According to the relative bargaining power of the unions, they choose to negotiate over wages only or over wages and employment as well. Chae and Heidues (2004) point out that when studying negotiations within and across groups, it is essential to define the preferences of the group. Their analysis provides a theoretical foundation for treating groups as single decision makers and generalizes the Nash bargaining model. Cai (2004) studies the bargaining structure of a game of complete information where a player bargains sequentially with a number of passive players to implement a project. It turns out that in equilibrium, the probability of the project getting implemented decreases with the number of passive players and their bargaining power. Finally, Stole and Zwiebel (1996a, b) and Wolinsky (2000) examine the effects of union bargaining on employment and other organizational design issues. This line of research is also related to other work, namely by Horn and Wolinsky (1988) and Inderst and Wey (2003). They show that as each supplier acts on the incremental surplus, under decreasing surplus function, doubling the incremental surplus is smaller than the entire surplus, which provides an incentive for providers to join forces and gain bargaining power in input markets.

At first sight, negotiating with the largest companies, which are also more efficient in production, may lead to lower prices. These firms can accommodate lower prices due to lower production costs. Negotiating with an association would mean that the interests of smaller, inefficient, companies would be considered, driving prices up. It is important to keep in mind that professional associations may act as devices to disclose information (mostly aggregate) for its members, but not as collusive devices. This view, however, ignores the fact that the more efficient companies may be tougher negotiators, and thus obtain a better (higher) price, which is extended afterwards to all other companies.

The question is then under which circumstances the third-party payer itself prefers to bargain with an association.[11] It turns out that it depends on the change in the outside option value for providers. Barros and Martinez-Giralt (2005a) show that by negotiating with an association, the third-party payer dilutes the outside option value of the more efficient providers. The more efficient providers are the ones that have more to gain from a bilateral bargaining process. The change in their bargaining power, measured by the outside option value, can more than compensate the willingness to take up lower prices due to higher efficiency. Remember that the bargaining strength comes from the fallback value (outside option) in case of failure in negotiations. For instance, assuming that patients will be treated, even if at the cost of direct payments, the more efficient companies will have relatively higher profits. Thus, they will be more demanding in negotiations than a sectoral association, because the latter takes into account the relatively low profits of the less efficient companies. Consequently, the association is willing to concede a less favorable surplus division in order to avoid failure of negotiations. In other words, the negotiation with the more efficient firms may benefit all providers and lead to higher expenditure by the NHS. If, alternatively, we assume that these providers in the case of negotiation failure will not treat patients, then the reinforcement of bargaining power of providers associated with the negotiation procedure including only the more efficient ones does not exist. There remains only the first effect: more efficient firms are more willing to take lower prices. In this case, the NHS benefits from negotiating with the more efficient providers only, instead negotiating with a sectoral association.

From a different perspective, the Medicare Modernization Act of 2003 expanded Medicare allowing private insurers to negotiate drug prices and rebates with retail pharmacies and drug manufacturers, rather than having Medicare negotiate a single price on behalf of all beneficiaries (Medicare Part D). Lakdawalla and Yin (2009) explore whether greater concentration among private insurers allows them to obtain lower prices for their members. In this case an increase in market power by the insurers may benefit consumers because private insurers have the capacity to limit the access of their members to pharmacies and drugs and thus extract some of the surplus from pharmacies and drug manufacturers and transfer it to their members. The empirical estimation shows that insurers that experience larger enrollment increases due to Part D implementation also had larger decreases in the prices paid to pharmacies. Also, they find that this effect spills over the population of non-Part D commercial enrollees. This external effect would not arise should the government negotiate drug prices for all Medicare beneficiaries.

14.4.1 *The formal analysis*

We consider a setting where a third-party payer, say, a national health service (NHS), has to negotiate prices of health care services with providers. We assume that there are two providers A and B, and that provider A is more cost efficient. In particular, provider B has a production cost $c > 0$ per patient treated whereas provider A's marginal cost is normalized to zero. Price negotiation can be carried out under two different regimes. In the first one, the providers join a sectoral or professional association. The association negotiates the price with the NHS. In the second regime, the NHS negotiates the price with the more efficient provider and extends the agreed price to the contract involving the other provider.

Alternatively, we could assume that the NHS negotiates with provider B and applies the resulting price to provider A. Nevertheless, this alternative seems to be quite difficult to implement, especially if the less efficient provider is also the smaller one in the market. In addition, if the inefficiency is large enough, an excessively high price may result anyway. Thus, considering that the NHS has the option, negotiating with the more efficient/largest providers seems the more reasonable choice.

The negotiation outcome is described by the Nash bargaining solution. In the case of failure to reach an agreement, both providers compete in prices à la Hotelling as in the previous section.

We assume that both providers are equally weighted in the objective function of the association, and that even in the presence of an association, providers do not collude. This is reasonable as competition rules explicitly forbid such role for sectoral associations. Nonetheless, if we allow for collusion, in the case of negotiation failure, prices will be equal to the reservation price of patients (or an even higher amount if there is a reimbursement rule by the third payer). Since out-of-pocket payments put patients at financial risk, there is room to negotiate prices above this collusive level. The major difference to our analysis is that, under collusion, breakdown of negotiations does not introduce product market asymmetries across providers. The third-party payer would be indifferent to negotiating with an association or with a subset of providers, extending afterwards the settled price to all providers. Note that if some providers can be excluded, we fall in the analysis of Section 14.2.2.

Consumers are insured and face a co-payment rate s. This assumption is innocuous for the analysis. Actually, all the qualitative results hold for any value $s \in (0, 1)$. Note that $s = 1$ implies no insurance to patients, which would be contradictory with the role of the third-party payer.

The NHS has a budget M from which it must pay providers. Having free funds is positively valued by the NHS as it allows for its productive application elsewhere in the health sector. The gain to the NHS from the negotiation is given by the difference in the net surplus under negotiation and in the case of failure. We denote by R such value net of the fallback value. In our simple model, given the assumption that a positive level of insurance coverage is always guaranteed to patients, it will be the payment to be made by the NHS to ensure provision in the private market plus the value, in monetary terms, of the extra insurance level provided to patients (a co-payment s). To be precise, we consider a situation where a NHS is financed by contributions from the population, either through the tax system or earmarked contributions. Utility of consumers is given by a utility function $U(\cdot)$ with positive marginal utility and risk aversion. Let Y be income and $T(Y)$ be the financial contribution to the health system.

In the case of negotiation failure, and insurance coverage with co-payment s, the expected utility is

$$EU_1 = qU(Y - T(Y) - t) + (1 - q)U(Y - T(Y)),$$

where q is the probability of being sick and t/s the private market equilibrium price if patients have to pay a fraction s of the price ($s \times t/s$ is then total copayment by patients).

If negotiations succeed, the patient receives full insurance and has expected utility given by $EU_2 = U(Y - T(Y))$

The objective function of the National Health Service is given by

$$W = M - p + \lambda EU,$$

where EU denotes expected utility of patients, M the financial value available, and $\lambda \in (0, 1)$ reflects the weight of consumers' utility on the objective function of the NHS. The financial value M can be seen as resulting from the patients' contributions $M = \int_Y h(Y)T(Y)dY$ where h is the density function of income distribution in the population. Both p and EU determine the fallback value for the NHS, $\overline{W}$:

$$\overline{W} = M - (1 - s)\frac{t}{s} + \lambda EU_1.$$

Then,

$$W - \overline{W} = \lambda q[U(Y - T(Y)) - U(Y - T(Y) - t)] + (1 - s)\frac{t}{s} - p = I + (1 - s)\frac{t}{s} - p,$$

where I represents the insurance value to patients. Finally, we define

$$R = I + (1 - s)\frac{t}{s}.$$

Denote by $\Pi_i, i = A, B$ the profits of each provider and by $\overline{\Pi}_i; i = A, B$ their profits in the case of negotiation failure.

Let us first characterize the equilibrium in a private market without a third-party payer. In a similar fashion as in Section 14.2.2, the indifferent patient is given by

$$x(p_A, p_B) = \frac{s(p_B - p_A)}{2t} + \frac{1}{2}.$$

Profits are defined by,

$$\overline{\Pi}_A = p_A x(p_A, p_B), \quad \text{and} \quad \overline{\Pi}_B = (p_B - c)(1 - x(p_A, p_B)).$$

First-order conditions yield,

$$p_A(p_B) = \frac{t}{2s} + \frac{p_B}{2}, \quad \text{and} \quad p_B(p_A) = \frac{t + cs}{2s} + \frac{p_A}{2}.$$

Solving for prices we obtain,

$$p_A = \frac{3t + cs}{3s}, \quad \text{and} \quad p_B = \frac{3t + 2cs}{3s}.$$

Substituting those prices in the expression of the indifferent patient we obtain the equilibrium profits,

$$\overline{\Pi}_A = \frac{(3t + cs)^2}{18ts}, \quad \text{and} \quad \overline{\Pi}_B = \frac{(3t - cs)^2}{18ts}. \tag{14.3}$$

These profits define the fallback values for the providers in case of negotiation failure. It may be the case that the NHS does not have precise knowledge on firms' marginal costs. Nevertheless, appealing to data like market shares, the facilities provided by the different providers, cash-flow, etc., the NHS may infer the relative position of providers in terms of efficiency. We stylize this situation by assuming that the firms' costs are known by the NHS.

When the NHS negotiates with the sectoral/professional association, the equilibrium solves the following program:

$$\max_p \Omega = (R - p)^\delta \left(p - \frac{c}{2} - \frac{(cs + 3t)^2}{18ts} - \frac{(3t - cs)^2}{18ts} \right)^{1-\delta},$$

where now $R \equiv (1 - s)(xp_A + (1 - x)p_B) + I$, and x is the indifferent consumer between providers A and B. It is given by $x = s(p_B - p_A)/(2t) + (1/2)$, and p_A and p_B are the private market prices of providers A and B respectively. Solving the first-order condition yields the equilibrium price:

$$p^+ = (1 - \delta)R + \delta \left(\frac{c}{2} + \frac{(cs + 3t)^2}{18ts} + \frac{(3t - cs)^2}{18ts} \right).$$

Equilibrium profits are given by,

$$\Pi_A = p^+/2; \quad \Pi_B = (p^+ - c)/2.$$

Finally, consider the negotiation with the more efficient provider. The price determined by the negotiation applies to both providers. We assume the third-party payer wants to have all providers active. The program to be solved is:

$$\max_p \ \Omega' = (R - p)^\delta \left(\frac{p}{2} - \frac{(3t + cs)^2}{18ts} \right)^{1-\delta}$$

$$\text{s.t.} \quad \frac{1}{2}(p - c) \geq 0. \tag{14.4}$$

Let us first consider the problem without the constraint of non-negative profits for provider B. Following this, we will show that provider B has strictly positive profits as well.

The first-order condition leads, after manipulation, to the following equilibrium price:

$$p' = (1 - \delta)R + \delta \frac{(cs + 3t)^2}{9ts}.$$

We know from the bargaining process that the equilibrium price must be such that

$$p > \frac{(3t + cs)^2}{9ts}.$$

Thus, if

$$\frac{(3t + cs)^2}{9ts} - c > 0$$

holds, then provider B makes strictly positive profits. This condition can be rewritten as:

$$c^2 s^2 + 3t(3t - cs) > 0. \tag{14.5}$$

In the private-market equilibrium, prices must cover costs. Thus, from (14.3), we require $3t - cs > 0$. Hence, condition (14.5) always holds and the non-negative profit constraint in problem (14.4) is not binding in equilibrium.

It is straightforward to see that,

$$p' - p^+ = c\delta/6 > 0.$$

Thus, the price is lower when the NHS negotiates with an association. Since a uniform price is set in both cases, demand is evenly split between the two providers, and both earn higher profits if the NHS negotiates with the more efficient one.

The result hinges on the tougher position taken by the more efficient provider. Since it is relatively more efficient it has less to lose in the event of negotiation failure. This drives the price up, and more than compensates the downward effect of lower costs of production.

To conclude the analysis, we show that even if condition $3t - cs > 0$ does not hold, the qualitative features of the equilibrium are the same. Hence, suppose that $3t - cs < 0$. This means that $p_B < c$ in the private market. That is, if negotiations between providers and the third-party payer break down, the private market outcome results in the least-efficient provider being driven out of the market. Assuming that the reservation price is high enough, the remaining provider serves the entire market at price $p = c - t/s$. Even the most distant patient prefers the more efficient provider.[12] Profits of the more efficient provider are, in this case, $\Pi = c - t/s$, as it gets all demand. This price is higher than the one under duopoly for the more efficient provider $(c - t/s > (3t + cs)/3s$ under $cs > 3t)$. Then, we have $\overline{\Pi}_A = c - t/s$.

The third-party payer negotiating only with the more efficient provider solves:

$$\max_p \ \Omega = (R - p)^\delta \left(\frac{1}{2}p - c + t/s\right)^{1-\delta}$$

$$\text{s.t.} \ \ p \geq c.$$

The constraint ensures that the second provider is active in the market. Let us ignore for the moment the constraint. The associated first-order condition is,

$$-\delta\left(\frac{1}{2}p - c + t/s\right) + (1 - \delta)\frac{1}{2}(R - p) = 0.$$

The equilibrium price is, therefore,

$$p^* = (1 - \delta)R + 2\delta(c - t/s).$$

For this to be a well-defined equilibrium, one has to have $R - p^* > 0$, which originates the condition $R > 2(c - t/s)$. Computation of $p^* - c$ yields,

$$p^* - c = (1 - \delta)R + 2\delta(c - t/s) - c > 2(1 - \delta)(c - t/s) + 2\delta(c - t/s) - c$$

$$= (cs - 2t)/s > 0,$$

where the inequalities follow from the above conditions.

Consider now the negotiation with an association:

$$\max_{p} \quad \Omega = (R - p)^{\delta} \left(p - \frac{1}{2}c - c + t/s \right)^{1-\delta}$$

s.t. $\quad p \geq c.$

The first-order condition is,

$$-\delta \left(p - \frac{3}{2}c + t/s \right) + (1 - \delta)(R - p) = 0.$$

From it, we obtain the equilibrium price:

$$p' = (1 - \delta)R + \delta \left(\frac{3}{2}c - \frac{t}{s} \right).$$

This equilibrium is well defined if $R - p' > 0$ or $R > (3/2)c - t/s$.

Comparing the prices under both regimes, we have:

$$p^* - p' = \frac{\delta}{2s}(cs - 2t) > 0.$$

Thus, as before the equilibrium price is higher in the case of negotiating only with the more efficient providers. Again, it is straightforward to check that all providers make strictly positive profits:

$$p' - c = (1 - \delta)R + \delta \left(\frac{3}{2}c - \frac{t}{s} \right) - c > \frac{3}{2}c - \frac{t}{s} - c = \frac{cs - 2t}{2s} > 0,$$

since $cs > 3t$.

The policy implication of the analysis is that the NHS should avoid negotiating with the largest providers, if they are significantly more efficient and have a valuable outside option in the private market (a possibility in case of chronic conditions and lack of capacity in the public system). Instead, it should promote negotiations over prices with an association representative of all providers' interests. According to our findings, all providers benefit from partial negotiation with the efficient firms. So, the association will not take over price negotiations without pressure from the NHS for that to happen. The analysis reassesses the role of professional associations in price determination processes, at least in some health care markets.

In the Portuguese dialysis sector, the NHS negotiates prices for each dialysis session with the two largest providers. The price settled in this agreement is then applied to all companies. Surprisingly enough, the smaller companies have not been claiming a role in the price-determination process. Given that it is reasonable to assume that the largest providers are the more efficient ones, being subsidiaries of vertically integrated multinationals, our model presents an explanation for the current satisfaction of all firms with the status quo. All firms benefit from the tougher position of the largest firms, compared to what would be the stance of an association including all providers. Thus, it seems that these providers are able to force the terms of the negotiation on the NHS.

Naturally, the existence of negotiations between the payer and professional associations in health care is not specific to Portugal or to dialysis. We found it in Belgium for determination of hospital fees, of specialized ambulatory care and dental care, for example (Crainich and Closon 1999). Also in Germany, France and Austria, negotiations took place between payers and representatives of providers of ambulatory care. In Germany, the negotiation takes place between sickness funds and physicians' associations (Busse and Howorth 1999); in France, there were the conventions between Assurance-Maladie and private doctors' unions (Lancry and Sandier 1999); and in Austria, between the regional chambers of doctors and the social insurance funds (Engelbert 1999).

A caveat on the structure of the negotiation is in order. We have assumed that only one negotiation is carried out. This implies that there is no room for price discrimination. Alternatively, one could think of a sequential bargaining procedure. In such a case, the NHS would first negotiate with one provider and then with the other. We provide some intuition for two alternative scenarios. Negotiating with the most efficient provider is better when after failing in the bargaining with the more efficient provider, the third-party payer negotiates with the less efficient provider and excludes the former from coverage. Also, if the negotiated price with the less efficient provider is extended to the more efficient provider, then again it is more advantageous for the third-party payer to negotiate with the more efficient provider only rather than engage in sequential negotiations. In the analysis we also rule these situations out because price discrimination on the fee per session is typically seen as undesirable and usually faces strong opposition by providers. Also, conducting sequential negotiations adds considerably to transaction costs. The settlement of prices may take several months and involves the use of real resources by both parties. Taking these two elements together, we find it reasonable to assume that only one negotiation takes place and the resulting price applies to all providers.

14.5 Ways to enhance bargaining power

A feature present in countries with a NHS is the coexistence of a public and a private sector. Often, the public payer contracts with private providers while holding idle capacity. This phenomenon has usually been interpreted in terms of inefficiency from the management of public facilities. Reviews along these lines in different countries are from Busse and Howorth (1999), Crainich and Closon (1999), Engelbert (1999), and Lancry and Sandier (1999).

Barros and Martinez-Giralt (2005b) present a different rationale for the existence of such idle capacity: the public sector may opt to have idle capacity as a way to gain bargaining power vis-à-vis the private provider, under the assumption of a more efficient private than the public sector. The analysis borrows extensively from the model in Section 14.4.

Consider a setting where a third-party payer, say, a national health service (NHS), has to negotiate prices of health care services with (two) providers. The NHS has a budget from which it must pay providers. The NHS positively values free funds as it allows for its productive application elsewhere in the health sector. The gain to the NHS from the negotiation is given by the difference in the net surplus under negotiation and in the case of failure. As a positive level of insurance coverage is always guaranteed to patients, that gain net of the fallback value will be the payment to be made by the NHS to ensure provision in the private market plus the value, in monetary terms, of the extra insurance level provided to patients (a co-payment). Health care providers organize themselves as an association. The association negotiates the contractual conditions (price) with the NHS representative. The price agreed by the association with the NHS is common to all members of the association. The negotiation outcome is described by the Nash bargaining solution. In the case of failure to reach an agreement, both providers compete à la Hotelling in the market.

The model develops in two stages. In the first stage the NHS decides its capacity; in the second stage price bargaining between the NHS and the association of providers occurs. The model is solved as usual, by backward induction.

The net surplus for the agents (providers and the NHS) is given by the difference between the surplus or profits earned from treating patients at the agreed price and the corresponding surplus or profits at the free market equilibrium price (in case of negotiation failure). Also, if negotiations fail, the fallback value for the NHS is defined as the budget left after reimbursing those patients exceeding the public sector capacity and paying the cost of the capacity installed.

Assume the marginal cost of treatment in the private sector is normalized to zero, and let $\mu > 0$ be the marginal cost of treatment in the public sector. Thus, μ also represents the difference in efficiency between private and public practice. In the absence of capacity constraints and equal efficiency in public and private facilities, only public sector treatment would be provided by the third-party payer. Accordingly, a necessary condition for the public sector to contract with the private providers is that it is less efficient.

Let M denote the budget of the NHS, κ be the capacity installed and m the capacity used, $m < \kappa$. The cost of capacity building is $\phi(\kappa)$, increasing and convex in κ. We consider a population of patients with size 1. Whenever $\kappa > m$ in equilibrium, we say that the public sector is not capacity constrained.

The net surplus for the providers is given by the difference of serving $(1 - m)$ patients at the agreed price p and serving $(1 - \kappa)$ at the free private market equilibrium price. On the third-party payer side, the surplus from the agreement is given by

$$M - p(1 - m) - \mu m \tag{14.6}$$

as m patients are treated in the public sector at cost μ and the remaining are treated in the private sector at price p.

14.5.1   *Price negotiation*

If negotiations fail, the fallback value of the third-party payer is:

$$M - \tilde{p}(1 - \kappa)(1 - s) - \kappa\mu \tag{14.7}$$

where $\tilde{p}$ is the price paid by the patients that exceed public sector capacity, of which the third-party payer reimburses a fraction $1 - s$. Thus, the price from the second-stage bargaining problem solves

$$\max_{p} \Omega = (\mu\kappa + (1 - \kappa)(1 - s)\tilde{p} - m\mu - (1 - m)p)^{\delta}$$

$$\times ((1 - m)p - (1 - \kappa)\tilde{p})^{1-\delta} \tag{14.8}$$

Note that the bargaining procedure, in this particular case, divides between the providers and the third-party payer the cost savings from producing in the private sector, $(\kappa - m)\mu$, minus the cost-shifting to patients in case of negotiations failure, $s(1 - \kappa)\tilde{p}$.

We must require that each player has a positive gain from engaging in the negotiation. This requirement implies $\mu(k-m)-(1-\kappa)s\tilde{p}>0$.

Solving for the equilibrium price yields:

$$p=(1-\delta)\frac{\kappa-m}{1-m}\mu+\frac{1-\kappa}{1-m}\tilde{p}(1-(1-\delta)s) \tag{14.9}$$

The value of $\tilde{p}$ is given by the private market equilibrium when patients pay a fraction s of the price. Thus, $\tilde{p}=t/s$. Note that as we are assuming symmetric providers, this is the price that results when assuming $c=0$ in the computation of (14.3).

14.5.2 Building capacity

We now consider the first stage, the capacity installed and its utilization. These decisions take into account the continuation of the game, and how the negotiated price will be affected by them.

The objective function of the third-party payer is the surplus generated, taking into account the game continuation:

$$S=M-m\mu-(1-m)p(\kappa,m)-\phi(\kappa)$$

where p is the equilibrium price of the negotiation stage, and therefore depends on both κ and m. It turns out that,

$$\frac{\partial S}{\partial m}=-\mu\delta<0$$

Hence, the optimal capacity utilization is in this case, zero. On the other hand,

$$\frac{\partial S}{\partial k}=[\delta\tilde{p}-(1-\delta)(\mu-\tilde{p}(1-s))]-\phi'(\kappa)$$

Whenever the term in square brackets is positive, there will be a positive equilibrium value for capacity, which will be kept idle. The only reason to build capacity here is the strategic effect associated with the negotiation stage. Increasing κ reduces the fallback value of the providers, valued at the margin by $\tilde{p}$. This helps in obtaining a lower price in the negotiation stage. On the other hand, it may reduce or increase the fallback value of the third-party payer, as it depends on whether using the extra capacity costs more than using the private market. That is, if $\mu>(1-s)\tilde{p}$, the third-party payer would prefer to buy in the private market.[13] Each of these marginal changes in the fallback values resulting from capacity decisions are weighted by the bargaining power of each side. Of course, if the cost difference between public and private treatment is sufficiently high, the optimal capacity may well be zero in the public sector, and there will be a capacity constraint. However, the important point is that the public sector may choose to have slack capacity as a way to improve its negotiation terms. Naturally, this only has value if there is some gain from using the private sector vis-à-vis public facilities.

The argument is akin to the Dixit-Spence (Dixit 1979, 1980; Spence 1977, 1979) excessive capacity result, where a firm builds extra capacity as a commitment to be aggressive in the market. The idle capacity works as a commitment to extract more surplus from more efficient private providers that negotiate prices with the public payer. Therefore, empirical assessments of the role of idle capacity in the public sector must take into account whether negotiations with the private sector exist.

Besides NHS countries, the development of managed care health insurance in the United States has also induced the formation of strategic alliances between hospitals and physicians. There are two theoretical arguments supporting this phenomenon. On the one hand, the transaction cost economies hypothesis supports those alliances as a way to obtain efficiency gains allowing lower prices being offered to managed care plans. On the other hand, the bargaining market power theory rationalizes the hospital–physician relationship as an attempt to improve the bargaining position against managed care plans and thus increase prices (see Gal-Or 1999a, b). Which theory better explains the phenomenon is an empirical issue taken up by Cuellar and Gertler (2006). Using panel data from Arizona, Florida and Wisconsin for 1994–1998, they estimate the impact of integration on hospital performance to find "strong support for the market power explanations and little support for the transaction cost economies explanations of hospital–physician integration" (p. 2).

14.6 Empirical evidence

Even though explicit negotiations exist in countries with NHSs (such as the UK and Canada) and with private insurance-oriented systems (such as the United States), a crucial difference can be identified. In NHSs, negotiations often take place between third-party payers (the government or health plans) and professional associations (such as medical associations). This sets the negotiation in terms of bilateral monopoly. On the other hand, health maintenance organizations, such as the ones that emerged in the United States, use negotiations with providers in a competitive setting. The third-party payer uses the outside option it has, looking for an alternative provider, to put pressure upon providers and obtain lower prices. Different contributions comparing the UK and US health systems are from Quam and Smith (2005) on the differences in insurance systems; Ham (2005) on differences in values and politics; Starfield (2005) on organizational differences; and Feachem and Sekri (2005) on integrated health care.

There is a recent line of literature looking at the empirical impact of negotiation (bargaining) processes between providers and insurers/third-party payers of health care. The first empirical issue addressed in the literature is whether or not managed care organizations are able to obtain advantageous conditions through bargaining. The debate has one side claiming that lower costs associated with managed care are the outcome of quality degradation. The other side claims that lower costs are due to the ability of managed care organizations to obtain lower prices from providers. The existing empirical evidence favors the last interpretation over the former, as reported in Cutler *et al.* (2000), Ho (2004), Maude-Griffin *et al.* (2001), Melnick *et al.* (1992), and Sieg (2000) among others.

Also, in the National Health Service in the UK changes in bargaining power seem to have produced visible effects. One of the main policy experiments in the UK, the fundholding GPs (present in the system until 1999 when concern over risk selection issues led to their elimination), implied an important shift of bargaining power towards GPs, especially those that were fundholders. The empirical research looking at hospital discrimination (favoritism of patients associated with fundholders) can also be used to address the impact of bargaining power shifts. According to Propper *et al.* (2002), the fundholding GPs were able to obtain lower waiting times for their patients. The ability of GP fundholders to channel money is a reinforcement of their bargaining position vis-à-vis hospitals, and prompted better conditions for the patients of GP fundholders. Thus, understanding "time" as a sort of price in a health system where monetary prices are administratively fixed, the increased bargaining power of GPs, created by the different institutional arrangement (fundholding), has lowered the price/time paid (as a side note, concerns over risk selection issues led to the elimination of the fundholding system to be substituted by primary care groups).

Since lower prices seem to have been obtained by payers when moving the interaction between third-party payers and providers to an explicit bargaining process, a second empirical question arises: the source of the bargaining power of insurers and providers. Theory suggests that size and the existence of outside options do increase a side's bargaining strength. The studies on the sources of bargaining power in health care can be divided into two camps: one looking at bargaining power of third-party payers; the other one detailing the bargaining power of providers, usually hospitals. On the latter line of empirical research, Brooks *et al.* (1997, 1998) and Town and Vistnes (2001) look at hospital competition, and ownership type, as sources of bargaining power. Their findings conform well to what we should expect (and explore below in terms of theoretical background): competition between hospitals to attract health plans and patients reduce their bargaining power, and lower prices are observed. Moreover, the increased HMO penetration over time was associated with a decrease in hospitals' bargaining power.

With respect to third-party payers, the evidence from existing studies suggests that availability of alternatives is a more significant source of bargaining power than size alone. Availability of alternatives enables health care third-party payers to channel patients to different providers. Studies by Ellison and Snyder (2001), Pauly (1998), Sorensen (2003) and Staten *et al.* (1988) give empirical support to this view. Pauly (1998) noted that size did not preclude small-managed care organizations from obtaining significant discounts from hospitals. Sorensen (2003) takes a step further and finds that the ability of third-party payers to direct patients to designated providers has a greater impact than size.

It should also be apparent that some of the theoretical testable predictions are yet to be taken to the data. Nevertheless, the empirical papers reviewed above can be interpreted in the framework of the basic model of bargaining, as they attempt to identify the sources of the third-party payer bargaining power, or of the provider, or the impact of increasing the value of the outside option, or decreasing the value of profits should negotiations fail. The theoretical works by Gal-Or (1997, 1999a, b), Barros and Martinez-Giralt (2005a, b, 2008), Milliou *et al.* (2003) and Fingleton and Raith (2005) elaborate on this model. The particular market structures assumed to contextualize the simple theoretical bargaining process allow discussing different aspects. These are the impact (i) of product differentiation across providers and (ii) of mergers of providers in the outside values. Gal-Or (1999b) and Milliou *et al.* (2003) discuss the role of vertical mergers between hospitals and physician practices in increasing the bargaining power of the latter vis-à-vis third-party payers. In Gal-Or (1997, 1999a), Barros and Martinez-Giralt (2005a, b, 2008) and Fingleton and Raith (2005), the value lies in the way the bargaining process is organized.

15 Waiting lists

The existence of waiting lists is a concern in countries with a national health service and public provision of health care. Our discussion starts with a basic model of waiting lists, showing how pure random elements in demand and supply, namely arrival to the system and treatment times, generate waiting lists and waiting times. Next, we consider the role of waiting times as a market equilibrium device. Finally, we briefly report on evidence about waiting list management schemes and policy interventions aimed at mitigating the issue.

The existence of waiting lists is a common phenomenon in several countries, namely those with a national health service and public provision of health care. Waiting lists are usually subject to a hot policy debate. It is not surprising that several theories exist about their role, and empirical analysis has also been growing in recent years.

The international dimension of waiting lists was revealed by the work of Hurst and Siciliani (2003) at OECD, though since their analysis no update on international comparisons of waiting lists and waiting times has been published.

The discussion of waiting lists, its rationale and eventual solutions has both a theoretical and an empirical side. We start by reviewing basic concepts about waiting lists and their effects and then move to a brief discussion on the empirical evidence.

At the more basic level, waiting lists can be seen as a result of random activity. Since demand for medical services arrives at uncertain moments, this would be enough to generate waiting lists unless treatment capacity far exceeds demand levels. Adding uncertainty on treatment times has the same ability to increase waiting lists and waiting times. This rather mechanical view does not account, by definition, for behavior of economic agents. Considering behavior of several agents was the next logical step in the analysis of waiting lists.

The first issue addressed in the literature was the role of waiting time as a variable to bring demand and supply into equilibrium. Then, the strategic use of waiting lists became a topic for research.

As waiting times and waiting lists rank high in public discussions, it is of no surprise that several policies have been used by different governments across countries to tackle the issue. Evaluation of such policies has also come under scrutiny by researchers and policy makers at large.

Our discussion starts with the presentation of the basic model of waiting lists, showing how pure random elements in demand and supply, namely arrival to the system and treatment times, generate waiting lists and waiting times. Under a very simple framework, we highlight that waiting lists and waiting times will be generally present under a management of the health system that is concerned with the costs of idle resources.

Next, assuming that demand does depend on waiting times, we consider the role of waiting times as a market equilibrium device.

The strategic use of waiting lists can be done by different agents, pursuing their own objectives, either public or private. We will look at three distinct issues. The first is how the public sector may want to maintain a certain waiting time as a way to divert some demand to the private sector.

A common discussion about the interaction between the private and the public sector with regard to waiting lists and waiting times is the claim that the private sector aims at cherry picking the easiest cases from the waiting list, thus exerting a negative impact upon the public sector mix. This claim is not necessarily true once we recognize that patients are not passive agents and do make a choice of whether or not to switch from the public sector waiting list to private sector treatment.

Most analysis of waiting lists take the providers as a black box. However, often the public sector is also involved in doing extra activity, paid separately, to help cut waiting lists and reduce waiting times. In this case, perverse incentives within the public sector may easily arise.

Finally, we briefly report on evidence about waiting list management schemes and policy interventions aimed at mitigating the issue.

15.1   The mechanics of waiting lists

In a rather mechanical way, we may see waiting lists as the result of a mismatch between the time of arrivals of new patients to be treated and the time of treatment, both of them being random variables. Whenever the time of arrival of patients for treatment is random and/or the time to treat the patient is random, the health system will face a trade-off between idle resources and waiting lists. A couple of very simple examples illustrate. Consider first the case of a provider, say, a primary health care facility, which schedules patients to be seen every half-hour. Suppose that a general practitioner can see, and treat, a patient in 15 minutes if it is a simple case or in 45 minutes if the patient has a more complex clinical condition. Suppose further that each type of patient has equal probability of occurrence. It is easy to see that average treatment time equals the time between arrivals of patients. Still, a waiting list will develop. Let's see how. Suppose the clinician only sees four patients (to simplify explanation). If the four patients are all low complexity patients, each is received by the physician at the scheduled time. No waiting time or waiting list exists. However, the physician will be idle half of the time.

Suppose now that all four patients have complex conditions. Then, the first patient has no wait, the second patient waits 15 minutes, the third 30 minutes and the fourth 45 minutes. A waiting list develops and the physician has no idle time.

Next take alternating cases, with the low complexity patient being scheduled first. Then the second patient has no wait but the third will wait 15 minutes. The physician will be idle for 15 minutes after treating the first patient.

In alternating complex cases with the more complex case showing up in the first patient, it is the case that the second and fourth patients will wait 15 minutes.

From these simple examples, it becomes clear that the simple stochastic nature of random treatment times generates waiting lists and waiting time to patients and idle time to the physician.

Of course, one or the other can be easily avoided, but at the cost of increasing the non-target variable. By setting an interval of 45 minutes between patients, there will be no waiting list or waiting time. The drawback is the creation of significant idle time of a scarce resource (in this example, the GP). If having no idle resources is the major concern, then scheduling all patients to appear in the first moment the GP starts to see patients ensures that he or she has no idle time. The drawback is that patients will face long waiting times, and a waiting list will be present.

The example discussed illustrates the basic trade-off faced: waiting time of patients vs. the cost of resources to provide treatment.

To this mechanical view, economic theory has added behavioral elements: people will demand more or less health care according to waiting times (making arrivals to the system for treatment to not be purely random); providers can organize or be paid in ways that lead to decisions that change treatment times. Governments may set rules or make available resources in strategic ways, to use waiting time as a device to discipline demand. These elements will considerably enrich the analysis.

Although the example was cast in terms of visits to GPs, the same reasoning can be applied to elective surgery.

More formally, let W be the total waiting time of a patient in the system, including waiting time before treatment and treatment time. Let W_q be the average waiting time for treatment, it is the time spent in the list. Let l be the average time between arrival of patients. Let m be the average treatment time. Let L_q be the average number of patients in the waiting list and L_s be the average number of patients under treatment. Assume the underlying stochastic processes to follow an exponential distribution. In a stationary state it can be shown that:

$$L_q = \frac{l^2}{m(m-l)} \tag{15.1}$$

Define $r = l/m$, then

$$L_q = \frac{r^2}{1-r}, \quad L_s = r, \quad L_q = W_q l \tag{15.2}$$

and

$$W_q = \frac{l}{m(m-l)} \tag{15.3}$$

The reason for this result is simple to explain. Suppose a patient enters the system. When he leaves, after treatment, there will be in the system on average L patients. Under a first-come-first-served system, only patients that arrive after the patient are waiting for treatment. If a patient takes a time W within the system, and l is the number of new patients per unit of time, the number of arrivals to the system from entry to exit of our patient is lW. So, $L = lW$. For the system to be stationary, it is required $l < m$ ($r < 1$). Otherwise, the waiting list will be growing without bounds. Under this condition, the system will be idle a fraction $1 - l/m$ of the time.

Suppose a social planner cares both about patients' waiting time and waste of resources (measured by idle time). The utility function of the social planner is by assumption:

$$SW = W_q^{-\alpha_1}\left(1 - \frac{l}{m}\right)^{-\alpha_2} = \left(\frac{l}{m(m-l)}\right)^{-\alpha_1}\left(1 - \frac{l}{m}\right)^{-\alpha_2} \tag{15.4}$$

where $\alpha_1 > 0$ and $\alpha_2 > 0$ denote the weights given to waiting time and idle time, respectively. The social planner has a choice over m, as it can commit more or less resources to treatment. The optimal choice of m is given by

$$m = \frac{\alpha_1 + \alpha_2}{2\alpha_2} l \tag{15.5}$$

Two implications follow from this optimal choice. First, for the system to be stationary, $m > l$ and $\alpha_2 < \alpha_1$, that is, the importance of idle resources must be smaller than the importance of patients' waiting time. Otherwise, waiting lists and waiting times will be always growing. Second, if over time more importance is attached to patients' waiting times, more capacity m will be built in the health system and more often there will be idle times in the system. Bringing waiting times to zero usually entails too much capacity and too much idle time. This trade-off means that waiting times and waiting lists are a way to manage the waste in the system derived from randomness of arrivals of patients and treatment times. This feature explains why objectives set for waiting times in several countries are defined in terms of non-zero times, and using the concept of admissible waiting time (that is, waiting time without significant or irreversible deterioration of the health of the patient), conditional on clinical conditions (say, waiting times for cancer interventions tend to be much smaller than for ophthalmology interventions).

15.2 Waiting time as an equilibrium device

As described earlier, demand and supply must be equal in equilibrium. The usual instrument to achieve such equilibrium is the price. Sometimes, there is no explicit monetary price and other variables must reconcile demand and supply. In the context of waiting lists, waiting time is one such variable.

Demand is usually taken to be related to waiting times – the higher the waiting time, the lower demand is. This characteristic of demand can be obtained in simple models. Consider, for example, the modeling approach of Martin and Smith (1999), representative of the early literature on waiting lists.[1]

A patient has utility A from treatment. If treatment is delayed for t periods, the patient discounts it at a rate g. The valuation of being treated t periods in the future is Ae^{-gt}. The discount rate g includes value of time, loss of earnings, lower quality of life, pain and suffering, etc. Patients may differ on g and on A.

The patient has a cost c of looking for care. If the patient is treated in the private sector, it has to pay a price p and is treated immediately.

Assuming that the patient always goes for treatment,[2] the demand directed at the public sector is given by all patients who have

$$A \le \frac{p}{1 - e^{-gt}} \tag{15.6}$$

To simplify explanation, assume that V is uniformly distributed in $[\underline{A}, \bar{A}]$. Then, demand for the public sector is

$$D_{pub} = \frac{p}{1 - e^{-gt}} - \underline{A} \tag{15.7}$$

From it, an increase in the waiting time t leads to lower demand for the public sector, while a higher price in private care leads to a higher demand. An increase in g, the cost of waiting, leads to lower demand for public care.

The supply side needs to model the availability of resources to tackle the waiting list within a general framework of resources constraint. To simplify exposition we assume a timeless view, in the sense that queue size is equal to demand and future waiting times are equal to current waiting times.

Waiting times are a function of resources devoted and the existing demand (queue), $t = f(S, D_{pub})$, where S are resources devoted to treatment. This "production function" of waiting times has $\partial f/\partial S < 0$ and $\partial f/\partial D_{pub} > 0$.

Utility of managers of health care providers is derived from waiting times (negatively) and resources devoted other clinical activities, N (besides the one giving origin to the waiting list):

$$\Pi = \Pi(t, N) \tag{15.8}$$

This objective function has $\partial \Pi/\partial t < 0$ and $\partial \Pi/\partial N > 0$. Resources are limited, and the managers face a budget constraint

$$B = S + N \tag{15.9}$$

The choice problem of the managers can be written as:

$$\max_{S} \Pi(f(S, D_{pub}), B - S) \tag{15.10}$$

and demand is taken as given by the manager. The relationship $f(\cdot)$ can be written as

$$t = \frac{\lambda D_{pub}}{S} \tag{15.11}$$

where S is expressed in beds and λ is the number of bed days per patient. Assuming a particular functional form for the utility function of the manager:

$$\max_{S} \Pi = \left(\lambda \frac{D_{pub}}{S}\right)^{-\alpha_1} (B - S)^{\alpha_2} \tag{15.12}$$

The optimal choice of S is

$$S = \frac{\alpha_1 B}{\alpha_1 + \alpha_2 \dfrac{1}{\lambda D_{pub}}} \tag{15.13}$$

An increase in demand leads more resources being devoted to service patients. Still in equilibrium, an increase in demand leads to an increase in waiting time:

$$t = \frac{\lambda D_{pub}}{S} = \frac{\lambda D_{pub}}{\dfrac{\alpha_1 B}{\alpha_1 + \alpha_2 \dfrac{1}{\lambda D_{pub}}}} = \frac{\lambda D_{pub}}{B} - \frac{\alpha_2}{\alpha_1 B} \tag{15.14}$$

Conditions (15.7) and (15.14) determine the equilibrium value of the queue and of the waiting time. The comparative statics on the exogenous parameters show that increases in g lead to both higher waiting times and higher waiting lists. An increase in p, the price of treatment in the private sector, has the same qualitative effect – increases both waiting times and waiting lists, as more people opt to stay in the public sector. Less obvious is the impact of an increase in the budget available to the managers. Increasing the budget allows for an increase of resources devoted to the waiting list activity, which decreases waiting time, which in turn creates further demand. It turns out that the latter effect dominates, implying a decrease in waiting times and an increase in the waiting list following, in equilibrium, from a higher budget being made available to the managers of health care providers.

15.3   Selecting from a waiting list

Most analysis assume that patients become passive after they enter the waiting list. Such an assumption is unwarranted when discussing the interplay of public and private sectors and in particular the claim that the private sector chooses to treat the mildest cases from the waiting list. This is not necessarily true in equilibrium. The basic trade-off faced by patients in waiting lists is between cheaper treatment and longer waiting time in the public sector and paying a higher monetary price in the private sector for immediate treatment. Whenever the costs of treatment are increasing due to the severity of the clinical case and payment in the private sector is independent of case severity, then it is clear that private sector institutions or doctors have a clear incentive in inviting the mildest cases from the public waiting list to be treated in the private sector. However, we need to take into account whether or not patients want to take the opportunity to be treated in the private sector. Assuming that patients with higher severity have a higher willingness to pay for a reduction in waiting time, it follows that mild-condition patients may actually be willing to wait for the free treatment in the public sector. Thus, in equilibrium we may have milder-condition patients being invited for treatment in the private sector with the least severe of them opting to stay in the public sector waiting list. The severity mix of private sector may then be higher or lower than in the public sector.

To formalize this intuition we present a simplified version of the model of Barros and Olivella (2005). The patient has the choice of being treated for free in the public system but having a waiting time t or going to the private sector, paying a price p and being treated immediately. Let the utility of a patient be given by

$$U = A - t\theta \tag{15.15}$$

where A is a basic utility level in the absence of sickness, t is waiting time in the public sector and θ is the severity of illness.

Patients with low severity will choose to stay in the public system. There will be a critical severity level θ^c such that all patients with severity above it will opt for the private sector for treatment. This critical level solves the indifference condition for patients:

$$A - p = A - t\theta^c \tag{15.16}$$

Physicians may propose that patients be treated in the private sector at price p, but higher severity patients have a higher treatment cost. Let $\theta^{\max}$ be the highest severity that doctors are willing to treat in the private sector, let θ^h the severity level that leads physicians to advise intervention (and inclusion of a patient in the waiting list) and let 1 the (normalized) highest severity. Patients are uniformly distributed over severity levels.

We take waiting time in the public system to be

$$t = \theta^c - \theta^h + 1 - \theta^{\max} \tag{15.17}$$

(that is, treatment time equals the number of patients that remain in the public waiting list).

The conditions (15.16) and (15.17) define the equilibrium values of θ^c and t. Note that the critical severity that leads patients to prefer the private sector depends on waiting time, but waiting time depends on many people stay in the public waiting list, which is determined by how many of them decide to go to the private sector.

However, we still have to account for the choice of $\theta^{\max}$ by physicians. The number of patients moving from the public waiting list to the private sector depends on whether physicians offer them the treatment, and the decision of physicians to which patients to offer that opportunity depends on how patients at the margin react. For example, increasing slightly the severity of patients that physicians are willing to treat on the private sector means a decrease on the public sector waiting list. This reduction in the public sector waiting list increases the threshold above which low severity patients decide to take up the offer of private treatment. Thus, physicians gain more severe patients to treat and lose less severe patients (who decide to stay on the waiting list as waiting time reduces).

Consider the cost of treatment of a patient of severity θ in the private sector to be

$$c = a\theta \tag{15.18}$$

The objective function of physicians in the private sector is:

$$V = p(\theta^{\max} - \theta^c) - \int_{\theta^c}^{\theta^{\max}} a\theta \, d\theta = p(\theta^{\max} - \theta^c) - \frac{1}{2}a((\theta^{\max})^2 - (\theta^c)^2) \tag{15.19}$$

From maximization of this utility function on $\theta^{\max}$ we obtain the following condition:

$$(p - a\theta^{\max})(2\theta^c - \theta^h + 1 - \theta^{\max}) = (p - a\theta^c)\theta^c \tag{15.20}$$

Conditions (15.16) and (15.17), the following summary condition results

$$p = \theta^c(\theta^c - \theta^h + 1 - \theta^{\max}) \tag{15.21}$$

Then, the equations (15.20) and (15.21) define the equilibrium of the system.

In equilibrium, both low severity patients (the ones between θ^h and θ^c) and very severe patients (above $\theta^{\max}$) remain in the public waiting list, the first ones by choice over the private option as they have a relatively low cost from waiting, the second ones from lack of option, as physicians are not willing to take them in private practice. The private sector serves the patients in the range θ^c to $\theta^{\max}$. Without further knowledge about the actual values of the relevant parameters and distribution of patients over severity levels, we cannot establish whether the severity mix in the public sector is smaller or larger than in the private sector.

15.4 The perverse incentives of waiting lists

The literature on waiting lists has treated the public sector provider in a very simple way. Still, in some countries the supply-side response to waiting list-oriented policies must actually come from the public sector providers. As some of the policies involve extra payments for additional treatments aimed at reducing the waiting times and the waiting list, this may produce unexpected results as the same agents are involved in producing both current and additional activity. The most obvious effect would be current activity to be reduced for two reasons. First, diverting resources to perform additional activity would harm current duties. Second, by reducing the current activity level, waiting lists increase, providing further justification for the added funding. On the reverse side, we may have that additional activity can only be done if some efficiency gains are generated, and these will be common to all activities, thus benefiting current production as well.

To model this situation, the physicians are the crucial decision makers. Consider a representative physician maximizing his/her utility, which depends on patients treated and payment received. The physician also bears the costs of ensuring efficiency in the organization. Physicians carry out two activities: regular activity in the public sector, and extra activity aimed at reducing waiting lists. The extra activity is paid on a case basis, while the regular activity is paid under a salary contract. Patients treated in regular activity are more valued by doctors.

Let the utility of physicians be given by

$$U = U_1(dq_1, q_2) + U_2(w + pq_2) - (q_1 + q_2)c \qquad (15.22)$$

where the first term U_1 is utility from treating patients, with d measuring the relative value of regular activity, U_2 is the utility from consumption resulting from total revenues, made up of salary w and price p per case of extra activity, and the third term is the cost of provision of capacity $K = q_1 + q_2$ with constant marginal cost c.

The first-order conditions for utility maximization yield:

$$\frac{\partial U_1}{\partial q_1} d - c = 0 \qquad (15.23)$$

$$\frac{\partial U_1}{\partial q_2} - \frac{\partial U_2}{\partial w} p - c = 0 \qquad (15.24)$$

In this simple setting, increasing the payment p for extra activity raises both activity levels as long as $\partial^2 U_1 / \partial q_1 \partial q_2 > 0$. The direct effect of increasing the price p is to increase the level of activity q_2, which in turn, under the stated assumption on utility, increases marginal utility of regular activity q_1, leading to an increase in this one as well. In this case, a situation of crowd-in exists.

The assumption of constant marginal costs is also important here. If marginal costs of each activity are increasing in the level of production of the other activity, then in equilibrium, if this effect is sufficiently strong, an increase in price p could decrease the activity level q_1, to save on the cost's side.[3] In this case, a partial crowding-out exists. Regular activity is reduced to make way for the extra activity to take place, but overall activity increases.

The discussion so far assumed the ability of the physicians to increase total capacity. Whenever total capacity is fixed, full crowding-out will result from paying for extra activity. Reduction of regular activity fuels further demand for extra activity.

We can cast the analysis within a framework similar, but simpler, to that of Martin and Smith (1999). Take the demand side of waiting list to be simply determined by total waiting time:

$$D = D(t) \qquad (15.25)$$

Since the extra activity is paid by the public sector anyway, we can safely ignore its impact on the demand for treatment through other channels but the waiting time.

Assume waiting time is defined by:

$$t = \frac{D(t) - q_1 - q_2}{e} \tag{15.26}$$

where e is efficiency effort done by managers in the public sector. The public sector has a target time $\bar{t}$ and contracts out at price p the activity level q_2 such that the target is achieved. Then, quantity q_2 is determined by

$$q_2 = D(\bar{t}) - q_1 - e\bar{t} \tag{15.27}$$

The utility of the public sector managers is the same as above, just adding the cost of exerting effort. Since waiting time is set at a target value it does not matter for our analysis whether managers care about it or not. The public sector managers solve the following problem:

$$\max_{q_1, e} U = U_1(dq_1 + q_2) + U_2(w + p(D(\bar{t}) - q_1 - e\bar{t})) - cq_1 - cq_2 - \phi(e) \tag{15.28}$$

The set of first-order conditions reveals that $e = 0$, that is, there are no incentives for efficiency. The motive is clear. A less efficient provider leads to higher waiting times, which require the public sector to contract out more extra activity, paid at price p. This can be easily seen from

$$\frac{\partial U}{\partial e} = -\frac{\partial U_2}{\partial e} - \phi'(e) < 0 \tag{15.29}$$

The other first-order condition sets

$$\frac{\partial U_1}{\partial q_1} d + \frac{\partial U_2}{\partial w}(-p) = 0 \tag{15.30}$$

Under the (reasonable) assumption of

$$\frac{\partial U_2}{\partial w} + pq_2 \frac{\partial^2 U_2}{\partial w^2} > 0$$

then an increase in price p induces a reduction in q_1, and the crowding-out effect is present even if waiting times are targeted by the public sector.

15.5 Policy interventions aimed at waiting lists

Probably the most common approach to reducing waiting times has been more resources being made available by the public sector. As discussed above, more resources may lead to a reduction in waiting times, but an increase in waiting lists may actually occur, as the lower waiting times trigger further demand. Moreover, whenever the extra resources are available on a temporary time limit, only a temporary reduction in waiting times is to be expected.

A second possibility is paying for more activity. If the activity-based payments is restricted to the extra activity to reduce waiting lists, then crowding-out phenomena may occur.

An interesting approach to deal with long waiting times was adopted in England. As in other countries reference times were set for maximum acceptable waiting times. Unlike other countries penalties to managers were set if the objectives were not met. In particular, managers could be fired for failing to achieve enough progress. This system has been termed "targets and terror" and addressed empirically by Propper *et al.* (2008). Using a difference-in-differences approach, they find that such a policy induced a significant reduction in the number of patients waiting, with a more pronounced effect at longer waits.

Other options for action are demand containment measures and introduction of choice to patients. With regard to the last, the effects resulting from more choice to the patients seem to be fairly modest. On the first option, it involves, at least, two types of approaches. One is based on using other forms of rationing and prioritization of patients. The second approach consists of different ways to manage the waiting list, for example with a centralized management system, that pools opportunities for intervention from several hospitals with an overall demand for treatment. This approach not only benefits from "risk diversification", it also reduces the incentive for strategic behavior by any particular health care provider (as the increase in actions induced in the waiting list may actually benefit another health care provider in the system). The empirical evidence regarding these options is still scant.

16 Referrals, gatekeeping, and levels of care

This chapter looks at the degree of vertical integration of primary care and acute care providers. Primary care activities have three main roles: treatment provided, referrals to hospitals, and prevention activities. These three activities are interdependent and efficiency efforts and incentives at the primary care level influence performance in all of them. In turn, this interdependence generates an externality on hospitals in terms of their effort to increase efficiency. This externality may lead to sub-optimal decisions from a social perspective, which may or may not be solved with appropriate payment mechanisms.

An important problem in the provision of health care is related to vertical integration of primary care and acute care providers. The role of primary care physicians as gatekeepers to the health system is widely recognized.

According to most policy views, primary care providers should be the first point of contact of the patient within the health system. Upon this first contact, the primary care physician should guide the patient inside the health system: ordering tests, prescribing medication, referring to specialists, receiving the patient back from hospital discharge, etc. One main decision in this role is that of referral. The primary care physician has to decide whether the patient should be treated by him/her or referred to a specialist or hospital care. In this decision, the physician may or may not take into account the impact of his or her decisions on other agents in the system, depending on the institutional framework. Thus, there is the potential here for existence of an externality, leading to sub-optimal decisions from a social point of view.

Of course, primary care physicians have other decisions to take. They should also be proactive in health promotion (prevention activities), for example, or organize their activity in an efficient way.

Despite their conceptual role being usually clearly defined within the health system, empirical evidence shows that reality is still far from that ideal situation, namely in relation to the referral decision.

This fact has motivated several experiments with different institutional frameworks, namely in countries with national health services in place, to further improve their decisions to the benefit of the population's health, while helping to reduce costs. Two important examples are England and Norway. A series of reforms of primary care activities took place in England over the past 20 years, ranging from budget-holders physicians to primary care trusts, involving a long series of indicators to control, to measure and to pay their activity. In Norway, several reforms have changed the way primary care physicians are paid, and lists of patients are formed.

16.1   The referral externality

From the point of view of the health system, primary care activities have three main roles: treatment of patients, referrals to hospitals, and prevention activities. These three activities are interdependent and efficiency efforts and incentives at the primary care level influence performance in all of them.

The level and quality of referrals from primary care to the hospital is also influenced, to some extent, by how much the hospital invests in a relationship with primary care, though arguably with less impact than primary care efforts. The hospital also exerts efficiency effort to increase its efficiency. This last efficiency effort is conditional on the number and type of patients that arrive at the hospital. Thus, payment systems at primary care level may indirectly affect hospital incentives for efficiency.

In economic terms, there is an externality across levels of health care, which may or may not be solved with appropriate payment mechanisms. Alternatively, functional integration (vertical integration across levels of health care) may also be an option.

As we describe below, using the simple setting of Barros and Martinez-Giralt (2003), both options are feasible to achieve the first-best allocation of resources as long as payment mechanisms are adequately defined. The same framework also identifies the expected effects from vertical integration, which will be highly dependent on the payment system set for hospitals and primary care.

To discuss the relevant issues, we consider two economic agents, the "hospital" and "primary care units". The hospital decides on its efficiency effort, while taking passively all patients that demand its services, including the ones referred by the primary care unit.

The primary care unit takes two main decisions: prevention effort, that reduces the probability of a person becoming a patient, and efficiency effort, that determines what types of patients can be successfully treated at primary care level (thus, determining referrals to the hospital).

To simplify explanation, we ignore health insurance decisions and assume that all members of the population are fully insured. The population is composed of N identical individuals, with probability $p(e_1)$ of becoming sick, where e_1 is the prevention effort exerted by the primary care unit. The probability of sickness is decreasing in effort ($p'(e_1) < 0$) at a decreasing rate ($p''(e_1) > 0$).

An individual that becomes sick suffers a health loss $L = \bar{L} + \eta$, where η reflects illness severity and $\bar{L}$ is the minimum health loss from sickness. The utility loss η can be recovered by treatment. Illness severity in each case is withdrawn from a probability distribution $F(\eta)$ with support $[\underline{\eta}, \overline{\eta}]$, $\eta \geq 0$.

When severity is low, treatment does not require sophisticated technology, while when high η treatment requires significant medical specialization and resources. The primary care unit defines a referral rule $\hat{\eta}$ such that all patients with $\eta \leq \hat{\eta}$ are treated at the primary care facilities, while patients with $\eta > \hat{\eta}$ are referred to the hospital. The referral threshold $\hat{\eta}$ depends positively on the effort e_2 made by the primary care unit. We assume $\hat{\eta}'(e_2) > 0$ and $\hat{\eta}''(e_2) < 0$. The primary care unit has therefore two decision efforts, e_1 and e_2, which have costs associated, which we take to be increasing at increasing rates (that is, denoting by $\phi_i(e_i)$ the cost of effort e_i, $\phi_i'(e_i) > 0$, $\phi_i''(e_i) > 0$.)

Treating a patient at primary care level has a diagnosis cost of v, which holds for all patients, whether they are referred to the hospital or treated at primary care facilities. The cost of treatment of a patient with severity η is $\tilde{c}(\eta)$, with positive and increasing marginal costs ($\tilde{c}'(\eta) > 0$, $\tilde{c}''(\eta) > 0$). The average cost of a patient treated in primary care is:

$$c(e_2) = \int_{\underline{\eta}}^{\hat{\eta}(e_2)} \tilde{c}(\eta) \, dF(\eta) \qquad (16.1)$$

Let W be the revenues to the primary care unit. The payment rule for primary care can be (potentially) defined over the number of people visiting the primary care unit, $Np(e_1)$, the average cost of treatment in primary care, $c(e_2)$, population covered, N, and the number of people treated at the primary care unit, $Np(e_1)F(\hat{\eta})(e_2)$.

For simplicity, we use the reduced form $W(e_1, e_2)$ for revenues. Later on, some further structure will be defined. The payment schedule has the following properties $\partial W/\partial e_1 < 0$, $\partial W/\partial e_2 > 0$ and $\partial^2 W/\partial e_{ii} < 0, i = 1, 2$.

Take now the hospital. It cannot influence demand. The only decision is about efficiency effort, e_3, that lowers treatment costs at the hospital. Let $\phi(e_3)$ be the cost of efficiency effort, again assuming positive and increasing marginal costs of effort ($\phi_3'(e_3) > 0$, $\phi_3''(e_3) > 0$). Let $K(e_3; e_2)$ be the per patient cost of treatment at the hospital, defined by:

$$K(e_3; e_2) = \int_{\hat{\eta}(e_2)}^{\bar{\eta}} h(\eta, e_3) f(\eta) \, d\eta \qquad (16.2)$$

where h is the cost of treating a patient of severity η when choosing an effort level e_3, with $\partial K/\partial e_3 < 0$ and $\partial^2 K/\partial e_3^2 < 0$.

The revenues of the hospital are generally described by $R(e_1, e_2, e_3)$, as the payment rule to the hospital may depend on the average cost per patient treated, $K(e_3; e_2)$, and on the total number of patients treated within the hospital, $Np(e_1)(1 - F(\hat{\eta}(e_2)))$.

Even without solving explicitly the equilibrium choices (see next section on this), inspection of objective functions reveal that effort e_2 affects the number of patients the hospital receives, which in turn influences the incentives for efficiency effort at the hospital level. But when deciding e_2, the primary care unit ignores the fact that it changes the incentives at the hospital level. This will lead to overall sub-optimal decisions from the social point of view.

The main arguments exposed are applicable to other settings, which are more general in one direction, but less general in others. Garcia-Mariñoso and Jelovac (2003) consider a case of referral decisions from a general practitioner to a specialist. In their model, the GP is less expensive than a specialist but it may not be able to treat the patient. There is a trade-off between a cheaper treatment, which may be incomplete and leading to waiting costs to the patient, or a sure but expensive treatment. The GP may find the clinical condition of the patient, which provides enough knowledge on whether or not a specialist is sufficient for successful treatment.

Their interest is on the payment mechanism to GPs and its incentive properties. Nonetheless, more or less referral activity under that trade-off also generates the same questions regarding the referral externality.

16.2 Vertical integration vs. market mechanism

One fundamental issue is the referral externality from primary care physicians to acute care providers, hospitals in particular. In simple terms, the primary care physician may not take into account the impact of his or her referral decisions upon hospital costs and decisions.

We discuss this externality in a more detailed way, looking at several decisions that are potentially affected: efficiency effort by primary care physicians, prevention effort exerted in primary care, and efficiency effort by hospitals. Moreover, the exact impact of this externality does depend on the way all providers of care are paid. The institutional framework may amplify or solve the externality, according to the payment rules that are set up.

The main problems raised by the externality are simple to identify. Whenever primary care physicians can refer patients to other providers at no cost to them, they will refer too much, which leads them to provide under-effort for both efficiency and prevention activities.

The analysis of the optimal payment system involves first the characterization of the socially optimal levels of the three efforts. Taking b to denote benefits from treatment, the social welfare function is defined by:

$$V = bN - Np(e_1)L - Np(e_1)c(e_2) - vNp(e_1) + Np(e_1)h(e_2, e_3)$$
$$- \phi_1(e_1) - \phi_2(e_2) - \phi_3(e_3) \tag{16.3}$$

where the first term is total benefit from treatment, which is independent of place of treatment, the second term is the utility loss of being sick, which occurs with probability $p(e_1)$, the third term is expected cost of treatment at primary care, given the referral policy, the fourth term is the cost to have the initial visit of a patient to the primary care facility, the fifth term is the expected cost of treating a patient in the hospital, given the referral policy at primary care, and the last three terms collect the costs associated with each type of effort.

The set of first-order conditions for social welfare maximization leads to marginal benefit equal to marginal cost of each type of effort.

Marginal benefit of prevention effort is the expected cost savings resulting from avoiding sickness episodes, and the associated first-order condition is:

$$-Np'(e_1)(c(e_2) + v + h(e_2, e_3) + L) = \phi'(e_1) \tag{16.4}$$

The marginal benefit from primary care efficiency effort is given by the reduction in treatment costs, taking also into account the change in the referral pattern. The associated first-order condition is:

$$-Np(e_1)(c'(e_2) + h_1(e_2, e_3)) = \phi'(e_2) \tag{16.5}$$

The marginal benefit of efficiency effort at the hospital is the reduction of expected treatment costs. The associated first-order condition is:

$$-Np(e_1)h_2(e_2, e_3) = \phi'(e_3) \tag{16.6}$$

For concreteness, let's now define the payment rule to primary care and to hospitals. Take first an extended capitation payment rule to primary care:

$$W = b_1N + b_2p(e_1)N + b_3Np(e_1)F(\hat{\eta}(e_2)) \tag{16.7}$$

where b_1 is a pure capitation value, for each person, under the responsibility of the primary care institution, b_2 is a payment per patient that visits the primary care facility and b_3 is the payment for each patient treated completely at the primary care facility.

The hospital is paid according to a mixed system:

$$R = \alpha + \beta N p(e_1) h(e_2, e_3) \tag{16.8}$$

where α is a prospective component while β is the cost sharing component and $Np(e_1)h(e_2, e_3)$ is the expected cost.

Determining the first best payment rules can be done by looking at which parameters lead to individual decisions of hospitals and primary care centres coinciding with social optimum values.

The objective function of the primary care center (superscript "P") is:

$$\Pi^P = W - Np(e_1)(c'(e_2) + v) - \phi_1(e_1) - \phi_2(e_2) \tag{16.9}$$

The objective function of the hospital (superscript "H") is given by

$$\Pi^H = R - \phi_3(e_3) - Np(e_1)h(e_2, e_3) \tag{16.10}$$

The primary care center chooses prevention effort (e_1) and efficiency effort (e_2) to maximize its objective function. The hospital selects the efficiency effort e_3 to maximize Π^H.

Taking into account the above definitions for the payment rules, and considering first the situation where primary care centers and hospitals are managed separately, the corresponding first-order conditions for private optimal decisions are:

$$Nb_2 p'(e_1) + b_3 Np'(e_1)F(\hat{\eta}(e_2)) - Np'(e_1)(c(e_2) + v) - \phi'(e_1) = 0$$
$$b_3 Np(e_1)F'\hat{\eta}'(e_2) - Np(e_1)c'(e_2) - \phi'(e_2) = 0$$
$$\beta Np(e_1)h_2 - h_2 Np(e_1) - \phi'(e_3) = 0$$

Straightforward comparison with the conditions determining the socially optimal solution results in the following requirements:

$$b_2 + b_3 F = -h(e_2, e_3) - L \tag{16.11}$$
$$b_3 F'\hat{\eta}'(e_2) = -h_1(e_2, e_3) \tag{16.12}$$

And the solution for (b_2, b_3) in this system of two equations provides the optimal values for the payment system.

A simpler characterization can be obtained if we further enlarge the payment rule, allowing the primary care centre to pay a value for referrals done, a fraction b_4 of the expected hospital cost $h(e_2, e_3)$. The payment rule becomes:

$$W = b_1 N + b_2 p(e_1)N + b_3 Np(e_1)F(\hat{\eta}(e_2)) + b_4 h(e_2, e_3) \tag{16.13}$$

Under this payment rule, and comparing once again the first-order conditions of the individual maximization problem of the primary care provider and the first-order condition of the social planner, to achieve the first-best allocation:

$$b_2 = -(h(e_2, e_3) + L) \tag{16.14}$$

$$b_3 = 0 \tag{16.15}$$

$$b_4 = 1 \tag{16.16}$$

Thus, under independent management, the first-best allocation of resources can be achieved with a capitation value b_1 that allows non-negative profits to the primary care centre, to which a value is deducted based on the number of patients treated, calibrated to reflect the (expected) costs to patients and to hospitals. The penalty associated with patients' costs corrects the prevention incentives, while the penalty for hospital costs corrects prevention and referrals (controlled by efficiency effort) to avoid future hospital episodes. Hospitals are to be paid prospectively ($\alpha > 0$, $\beta = 0$).

Under joint management, the health care provider maximizes $\Pi^H + \Pi^P$ and therefore internalizes the costs of referrals. Thus, the payment system only needs to correct for the prevention externality. Using the same approach, it is straightforward to establish that the parameter values for the payment functions that implement the first-best solution are:

$$b_2 = -L, \quad b_3 = 0, \quad b_4 = 0, \quad \beta = 0, \quad \alpha > 0, \quad b_1 > 0 \tag{16.17}$$

Using an adequate definition of payment rules, the first-best allocation of resources is achieved under both independent and joint management. This is not surprising given the full information context of the model.

The same model is used by Barros and Martinez-Giralt (2003) to discuss the impact of moving from independent to joint management under payment rules that are observed (and which do not match the socially optimal ones described above).

The analysis shows the relevance of the referral externality. For example, under capitation payment to primary care and prospective budget to the hospital, prevention efforts increase when moving from an independent to an integrated management system. The reason is simple. Under the capitation system, the primary care center under independent management does not take into account in referral decisions the cost it imposes upon hospitals. Thus, both prevention and efficiency efforts at primary care level are low. However, it suffices to have a fee-for-service payment structure in primary care to have ambiguous effects associated with vertical integration. Moving from independent management to joint management internalizes the referral externality, which induces at impact an increase in both efficiency and prevention efforts at primary care level. But an increase in prevention under fee-for-service decreases payments to primary care, which undermines the initial incentives to increase prevention effort.

Incentives for hospital efficiency also change, which in the integrated regime will interact with the other efforts. Depending on the margin resulting from the fee-for-service integration leads to ambiguous results regarding prevention level, referral rate and hospital average costs.

The referral externality has, therefore, important implications to definition of payment mechanisms. Functional integration and payment systems are substitutes but we seldom witness the latter being used in health systems to compensate the referral externality. The exception was the UK system of GP fund holders, in which GPs had to pay for care they prescribed to their patients (see Dusheiko *et al.* 2007). In a more limited sense, the management of pharmaceutical budgets by German GPs also follows the same economic principles. The existence of a referral externality also raises the rationality of using a gatekeeping system in the access to health care, a topic taken up in the next section.

16.3   Gatekeeping

The absence of gatekeeping means the patient can go directly to the specialist or choose the GP. The only instrument available to economic authorities is the set of co-payments of each type of provider. The co-payment for seeing a specialist may be conditional on having a referral from a GP, to induce a price-guided unofficial gatekeeping.

Health systems vary considerably in their organization. Each country has its particularities. One characteristic that has been identified in country-wise comparisons that seems to help contain health expenditure growth is presence of gatekeeping system. Simply stated, the gatekeeping system consists of requiring patients to see a general practitioner, who would either treat the patient or define which provider (specialist, hospital treatment) the patient must see next. Still, some countries or health insurance schemes do allow for an easier access to specialists than others.

The economics literature has addressed the advantages and disadvantages of gatekeeping. Two particular characteristics of gatekeeping have been highlighted. First, gatekeeping shares features with vertical integration in other sectors. Analysis of the effects of this vertical integration is an approach to understanding the effects of gatekeeping.

The other characteristic is that gatekeeping brings more knowledge (the diagnosis by the GP) to the decision process, but it may delay treatment to some patients. The decision under uncertainty and the value of information gathering, and its implications for payment systems to physicians, is the other approach increasing our knowledge about the implications of gatekeeping systems.

The GP incentives play an important role, so it is worth describing in some detail the context of the GP decision process. When a GP sees a patient, he or she learns private information about the patient and receives (or collects) further information, which is more accurate than the initial information the patient holds. The GP may choose to treat the patient. If treatment fails, the patient must be sent to the hospital for treatment. The payment system will influence the intensity of referrals, and different regimes can be considered (including capitation and cost reimbursement).

In the health system without gatekeeping, the decision to see a specialist is based only on the information the patient has. In a system with gatekeeping, the decision to see a specialist is based on both the information of the patient and the information received (and processed) by the physician.

In Brekke *et al.* (2007), the gatekeeper has mainly an informational role. It informs patients about their conditions and the available options. The comparison of regimes is between a mandatory rule making patients go to the GP before having access to a hospital and the absence of that rule. Patients may want to see a GP before going to a hospital, even when it is not mandatory. Hospitals are differentiated at the eyes of the consumer and choose the quality of their services.

The main point Brekke *et al.* (2007) make relates to the social optimality of a strict gatekeeping system. The authors point out that more informed patients create more competition across hospitals. Since quality is the main instrument to attract patients, more information on the side of the patients leads to more quality. In fact, it may lead to too much quality from a social point of view. This increased competition in quality may or may not improve welfare. The excessive quality results in equilibrium as prices are exogenously set and investing in quality is the main way for hospitals to attract patients. The costs of quality can be larger than the benefits of extra information to patients from gatekeeping, a case more likely to occur when the patient already has highly accurate information about his or her health care needs.

This (apparently) ambiguous view on the imposition of gatekeeping as a rule in the health system is conditional on the set of exogenously given prices. Second-best price regulation leads to dominance in social welfare terms of the gatekeeping system. The incentive of hospitals to choose too much quality is curbed down by lower regulated prices. This opens the door to reap the information benefits from the gatekeeping system without inducing too much investment in quality.

When the cost of a specialist's time and the cost of waiting to patients are high, the referral from a GP has more value and a gatekeeping system dominates. The payment system to the GP must involve a bonus when the patient is treated in primary care or, what is essentially the same, that GPs pay some value when they refer patients to specialists. It should contain a payment independent of providing treatment and some bonus for patients that do not require treatment to create an incentive for prevention effort. Although in a different setting, these results coincide and extend to different information settings the Barros and Martinez-Giralt (2003) implications for payment structure.

A related issue is that GPs face pressure from patients to over-refer. It means that the payment system has to be strong enough to compensate such pressure for over-referral. The pressure from patients is larger under a gatekeeping system. Without gatekeeping, patients with a strong high-severity belief go directly to the specialist and the pressure to over-refer is smaller. As such, there is room for less powerful incentives.

Garcia-Mariñoso and Jelovac (2003) take a passive view of patients. However, patients have information and expectations about their condition and benefits from treatment. Patients can also exert pressure with GPs to obtain a referral to a specialist. The design of the payment system, on the one hand, and the choice of gatekeeping vs. a non-gatekeeping regime can also be dependent on patients' actions.

The other type of strategic interaction is competition between GPs. Karlsson (2007) takes up this issue and the impact of competition between GPs regarding their quality choices. Patients have an active role in searching. Quality is a credence good. GPs have different abilities, leading to quality variation. Patients then search for the best treatment. The main finding in Karlsson (2007) is that capitation payments under gatekeeping may not provide adequate incentives, due to the active role of patients.

In Gonzalez (2010), the assumption that a GP cannot treat high severity patients is retained. The main trade-off addressed is between accuracy of information possessed by the patient and the cost of incentives to the GP. These two elements interact in a non-trivial way. When the patient's information is highly accurate, it is best to ignore the contribution of the GP and save the cost of incentives to GPs, as the additional gain from the GP's diagnosis is small. Of course, if the information of the patient is not accurate, then ignoring it is optimal, and focus is on incentives to GPs to produce the diagnosis. Thus, out of the extremes (highly informative or highly uninformative signals to the patient about his health condition), using a gatekeeping system is optimal.

The use of economic incentives of the type discussed can be found, as an approximation, in the fundholding scheme introduced in the UK in 2005. GP fundholders were allocated a budget from which they would purchase some specialist services for their patients (see Dusheiko *et al.* 2007 and Malcomson 2004 for a description and an assessment).

17 Pharmaceutical market

The pharmaceutical market is a fundamental element of the health care sector. This chapter reviews the main elements driving its decision making: R&D investment, patents, the introduction of new drugs both from the perspective to carry out phase IV trials, and in terms of the acceptance of those new products for reimbursement by third-party payers. Then, we turn our attention to regulatory issues aimed at enhancing price competition in the health care market and to contain the public pharmaceutical cost. Among the most popular regulatory policy measures we find the promotion of generic drugs and the implementation of reference prices. Finally, the retail pharmacy market is briefly discussed, namely the rationale for entry restrictions.

17.1 R&D and patents

The pharmaceutical market has rate of innovation as one of its main characteristics. Every year new products are introduced in the market. The pace of innovation results from large investments, in a long and uncertain R&D process. At every stage of the innovation process, there are products that do not survive to the next phase.

The direct R&D costs are just one part of the economic cost involved. Since directing funds to R&D of new pharmaceutical products means that the same funds cannot be invested elsewhere, the economic cost of R&D has to include the opportunity cost associated with it. The opportunity cost of not investing in alternative applications of funds depends also on the time before investment produces any returns.

DiMasi *et al.* (2003) compute this opportunity cost taking as reference an average lapse of time between the start of the clinical trials and introduction into the market of a new product, of about seven and half years.

Finally, estimates must be adjusted to compensate for the fact that not all products reach the market. The few successes must compensate for the hazards of many that fail.

The overall estimate by DiMasi *et al.* (2003) puts the R&D cost of a new product in the range of 800 Million USD (at 2000 prices).[1] Updating according to the inflation rate, it reaches about 1,000 million USD. This is most likely an under-estimate, as historically R&D costs have grown faster than the general inflation rate.

The above figures show that researching new products is a lengthy and costly process, with lots of uncertainty about obtaining a return on the investment made and to compensate for the risk. For innovation to exist, some form of appropriation of (part of) its value must exist for the innovator.

So, the product resulting from the innovation effort is difficult to imitate, the owner of the innovation has a unique resource and may be able to recover the investment made at the start. On the other hand, when imitation is easy to perform, some other mechanism must be devised to provide incentives for companies to invest in R&D.

In the case of pharmaceutical products, the general expertise of companies in the market and the information disclosed in the process of bringing the product to the market make imitation likely, in the absence of explicit protection mechanisms.

Patent protection, granting a legal monopoly to sales of the new pharmaceutical product, comes about as a way to give companies a means to recover their investment. The legal monopoly given by the patient has a predetermined time period. At the end of it, imitation becomes possible. We observe it in the so-called generics market.

Patents are a fundamental aspect in the innovation process for new pharmaceutical products. In the absence of a mechanism of appropriation of innovation value, firms competing against each other would find refraining from investing in R&D to be a dominant strategy, and no new products would appear.

Even though patents dominate as a way to ensure there is a return to R&D, it is not a perfect system. On the one hand, the private incentive for innovation (given by the monopoly profits enjoyed during the patent period) is smaller than the social value generated. On the other hand, the monopoly market structure implied by the patent leads to monopoly pricing, which results in higher prices than it is socially optimal *after* the innovation has been achieved.

17.2   Market access

Once R&D activities have been concluded successfully, the next challenge is to introduce the new pharmaceutical product in the market. The existence of third-party payers, associated with health insurance protection, creates new issues for market access. Not only the new pharmaceutical product has to demonstrate safety, quality and efficacy, it must also be accepted for reimbursement by third-party payers. Otherwise, the new pharmaceutical product is at a huge disadvantage in competition against reimbursed pharmaceutical products.

It has become common to third-party payers to require proof on both therapeutic value added, and economic advantage associated with the new pharmaceutical product.

Economic advantage has acquired a very precise meaning – to pass an economic evaluation standard. This has become known as a fourth hurdle to market access by new pharmaceutical products.

These economic evaluation hurdles are assessed, and decisions produced by, usually, specific institutions. The most well known of the institutions is the NICE – National Institute for Health and Clinical Excellence in the United Kingdom. The same approach is being followed in many countries.

Under the label of economic evaluation it is possible to find several variations in the analysis. Another often used term for economic evaluation is cost-effectiveness, used in a rather general sense.

The more common variations of economic evaluation are cost minimization, cost-effectiveness (in narrow sense), cost-utility and cost–benefit analysis.

The purpose of economic evaluation is to determine if a new pharmaceutical product has a clear advantage over existing alternatives. Of course, having more benefits for fewer or equal costs ensures dominance of the new pharmaceutical product. However, the more common case is that a new pharmaceutical product has both higher costs and higher benefits. It implies that some comparison of added benefits against extra costs needs to be done.

Whenever all relevant alternatives lead to exactly the same benefits, then the comparison is much easier to perform – it is enough to look at costs and choose the alternative with lower costs for the same benefit. This is the cost minimization.

When benefits cannot be assumed to be equal across all options, but a single effect of interest can be computed, cost-effectiveness analysis can be performed. The typical indicator is cost per unit of benefit. The implicit assumption is that benefits are worthwhile, even if not easily measurable in a monetary scale.

Cost-effectiveness analysis measures the benefit impact of alternative courses of action in a single (physical) measure that makes sense within the scope of the problem.

Still, this approach has its own limitations. As is easy to recognize, health has many dimensions. Thus, multiple benefits may result from health care interventions. These different dimensions can be aggregated to a single indicator, and then the cost of point gain in that indicator assessed.

The most used model of cost utility takes QALY – quality adjusted life years as the index for utility. As discussed previously, the QALY is a useful concept but also open to criticism.[2]

The institutions in charge of assessing economic evaluation studies for new pharmaceutical products have enacted methodological guidelines and refused in several instances to include the new product in the list of drugs reimbursed by the third-party payer.

The widespread use of this fourth hurdle has made access to market by new products harder. In turn, faced with more demanding thresholds for inclusion in the list of reimbursed pharmaceuticals, pharmaceutical companies look for different approaches to gain access to the market. These new approaches, such as the so-called risk-sharing agreements, are still emerging. We should see economic analysis detailing their advantages and disadvantages in the near future.

17.3   International reference pricing

International reference pricing, also known as external referencing, is a system to define prices in which the price is set based on the prices of similar (or comparable) products in reference countries. The definition of the reference countries is part of the system. Some countries take the average price of the set of reference countries, while others take the minimum price. This has become a widespread system in Europe.

The existing international referencing establishes a set of complex interrelations across countries. Table 17.1 gives an overview of international referencing in Europe. In the left column, we have the country using international referencing to set pharmaceutical prices, with countries used for reference in line. An empty column means that country does not use international referencing.

The use of international referencing is done by each country in an unilateral way. This provides incentives to launch earlier in higher-price markets and to delay launch of new products in lower-price markets. The existing price controls on new pharmaceutical products appear to have a significant and negative impact on their introduction in national markets by pharmaceutical companies (Danzon *et al.* 2005; Danzon and Epstein 2008; Heuer *et al.* 2007). Launch delay is usually defined as the difference in months between the launch in a particular market and its first global launch. Approval of new pharmaceutical products is done, in the European Union, by the European Medicines Evaluation Agency (EMEA), which allows for a centralized authorization process to introduce a new drug in the market. However, inclusion in positive lists for reimbursement has to be done on a country-by-country basis. The EMEA also allows for a mutual recognition procedure. Under this procedure, companies start the

Table 17.1 International reference pricing

	AT	BE	DK	FI	FR	DE	EL	IE	IT	NL	PT	ES	SE	UK
Austria (AT)								X						
Belgium (BE)								X		X		X		
Denmark (DK)								X						
Finland (FI)								X						
France (FR)								X		X	X	X		
Germany (DE)					X			X		X				
Greece (EL)											X			
Ireland (IE)														
Italy (IT)					X						X	X		
Netherlands (NL)								X						
Portugal (PT)														
Spain (ES)					X			X		X				
Sweden (SE)														
United Kingdom (UK)					X			X				X		
European Union (EU)	X	X		X			X		X					
Norway				X										
Iceland				X										

authorization procedure in one country and ask for mutual recognition in other countries. Danzon *et al.* (2005) report launch delays associated with new chemical entities (NCEs) in several OECD countries. There is substantial variation in launch delays in Europe, despite the existence of a centralized authorization procedure through EMEA at the European Union level. The overall finding is that lower prices lead to both a lower number of products introduced in the market and longer delays. This may suggest a negative effect from international referencing as a way to determine prices. The delays, according to Danzon *et al.* (2005) and Danzon and Epstein (2008), are due to price regulation and pharmaceutical companies strategies.

International reference pricing has direct and indirect implications for the pharmaceutical market of each country. The direct effect is the introduction of a cap on prices, based on the prices of the reference countries instead of cost-based prices. This is usually the aim of health authorities when adopting the system.

The indirect effects result from adjustment of pharmaceutical companies. In particular, to avoid the impact of low prices, either as reference to other countries or as resulting from concerns about parallel trade within the European Union Single Market, companies delay launch of new products in some markets.

The recent work by Garcia-Mariñoso *et al.* (2011) addresses the role of international price referencing in the context of a bargaining between third-party payers (in particular, health authorities or a national health service) and the pharmaceutical company. The important point is that external referencing affects the bargaining game in a non-trivial way.

The strategic effect of international reference pricing is twofold. By committing to international price referencing, a country avoids negotiating with the pharmaceutical company. Therefore, a company adopts it when it is a weaker negotiator. In turn, a country's negotiation power is lower the higher the co-payments in its payment system and the smaller its size. The second strategic effect shows up in the negotiation of the pharmaceutical company with other countries. The pharmaceutical company has more to lose if the negotiations with the reference country break down, as in this case the product is delisted in both countries. There is an international externality introduced by international reference pricing. Its role depends on whether or not the denial of reimbursement leads to absence from the market or just selling the product at full price to patients. In the latter case, the externality for international reference pricing is more relevant than in the former.

The following simplified model illustrates the forces at play. Let v_i, $i = H, F$ be the value of pharmaceutical product to the health authority in country i. There is no production cost of the drug. R&D is a sunk cost. The pharmaceutical company intends to sell the product in both countries. It negotiates the price in each country with the respective health authority. The negotiation is described by the (generalized) Nash bargaining solution.

In the bargaining process, if there is no agreement on the price to set, two options exist: either the product is not sold, and the pharmaceutical company receives zero profits, or the product is marketed without reimbursement. In the latter case, value to patients is $\underline{v}_i < v_i$, while in the former there is no value to the patients.

International reference pricing means that a country adopts the price resulting in the bargaining taking place in the other country (the reference country).

To simplify explanation, we assume that patients always receive one unit of the drug, whatever the price agreed. Thus, price p_i stands for both price and profits of the pharmaceutical company. If the pharmaceutical company markets the product without reimbursement, it has profits $\underline{p}_i$.

The bargaining problem under independent negotiations is described by (assuming the new product is introduced in the market even if it has no reimbursement):

$$\max_{p_i} \Omega_i = (v_i - \underline{v}_i)^{\delta}(p_i - \underline{p}_i)^{1-\delta} \tag{17.1}$$

The price resulting from this maximization problem is:

$$p_i = \delta \, \underline{p}_i + (1 - \delta)(v_i - \underline{v}_i) \tag{17.2}$$

When country H adopts international reference pricing, there is only the negotiation in the reference country, F. If negotiations break down, the new pharmaceutical product will not be elected for reimbursement in both countries. The negotiation in country F is now:

$$\Omega_F = (v_F - p - \underline{v}_F)^{\delta}(2p - \underline{p}_H - \underline{p}_F)^{1-\delta} \tag{17.3}$$

Notice the change of the payoff to the pharmaceutical company, as the negotiation in the reference country determines sales (and profits) in both countries.

The equilibrium price is now

$$p = \delta \frac{\underline{p}_F + \underline{p}_H}{2} + (1 - \delta)(v_F - \underline{v}_F) \tag{17.4}$$

International reference pricing occurs for

$$2(1 - \delta)(v_H - \underline{v}_H - (v_F - \underline{v}_F)) > \delta(\underline{p}_F - \underline{p}_H) \tag{17.5}$$

If countries are of similar size, and $\underline{p}_H > \underline{p}_F$, then external reference pricing is more likely to be chosen. If reservation prices are similar across countries then the country with higher difference $(v_i - \underline{v}_i)$ wants to set reference pricing.[3]

17.4   Making sense of phase IV trials

The so-called phase IV of clinical trials provides a good example of application of economic analysis. Phase IV consists of the realization of post-approval clinical trials, when the drug is already introduced in the market. Currently, phase IV clinical trials are not mandatory and it may not be clear why pharmaceutical companies would voluntarily engage in such tests. Only consumers would gain from that information, according to conventional wisdom.

However, this view does miss a crucial point. It ignores that pricing strategies of pharmaceutical companies do differ according to the information available to consumers.

Suppose a certain product already present in the market faces competition by a new drug. The new product can be of higher or lower quality than the existing drug. Assume that, on average, the quality of the new drug is similar to the quality of the existing pharmaceutical product. From the point of view of consumers, the quality being similar leaves to the price the role of decision factor for consumption. Thus, price competition among pharmaceutical firms will be fierce and prices will tend to be low.

A clinical trial, in this context, brings further information about the new product. If perfectly informative clinical trials allow consumers to know whether the new product is of higher or of lower quality than the existing one. Whatever the outcome of the clinical trial, both firms will benefit from the new information. The clinical trial generates information that creates differentiation between the two products from the consumers' point of view. The quality difference among products revealed by the phase IV clinical trial allows the higher quality product to set a higher price, and forces the lower quality product to set a price lower than the price selected by the pharmaceutical company with the high quality price. Nonetheless, price competition among firms will be smaller – a price reduction does not capture all demand for the high quality product. Both firms, in equilibrium, will choose higher prices, and enjoy higher profits, than when no quality difference was perceived by consumers. The high quality product is bought by those consumers who value relatively more quality, while the lower quality pharmaceutical drug is consumed by those that are more price sensitive.

The argument is developed formally in Gronqvist and Lundin (2009), who also report background information on pharmaceutical companies conducting clinical trials and revealing results, which sometimes gives a quality advantage to their product, while other times does not.

17.5   Generics substitutions

An issue that has gained relevance is the substitution of branded pharmaceuticals at the retail pharmacy level. Different options have been adopted across countries, including no substitution being possible, doctors required to explicitly allow for substitution and pharmacists being able to substitute for generics when the patient asks it. A more extreme situation occurs when the third-party payer requires substitution to be performed.

The incentives of pharmacies to substitute generics for branded pharmaceuticals depend on the relative remuneration they receive. Brekke *et al.* (2010) point out that in a model of vertical product differentiation, a lower price of branded pharmaceutical product has two opposite effects. On the one hand, it lowers the margin to the pharmacist from the branded drug. This is likely to produce more substitution. On the other hand, a lower price for the branded drug lowers its cost to the patient, who then is more reluctant to switch from the branded product to the generic alternative (as long as it faces a co-payment in pharmaceutical consumption). These two forces can be illustrated with a simple model of vertical product differentiation. Let v be the health gain to the patient (measured in monetary terms) from consumption of the branded product. A generic product is seen as of lower value to consumers and it is valued as θv, $\theta < 1$.

Utility from treatment varies across patients, in the range $[\underline{v}, \bar{v}]$, under a uniform distribution of valuations. Notice that all patients value the branded drug more than the generic product. Patients pay a co-payment s_b and s_g for the branded product and the generic, respectively. Patients with a high valuation for the treatment will choose the branded product, while patients with low valuation opt for the generic. The demand for the branded drug includes all patients with valuation above a threshold $\hat{v}$, with all the remaining patients taking the generic product. The threshold value $\hat{v}$ is determined by

$$\hat{v} - s_b = \theta \hat{v} - s_g \tag{17.6}$$

or

$$\hat{v} = \frac{s_b - s_g}{1 - \theta} \tag{17.7}$$

Retail pharmacies are the other economic agent. They face wholesale prices $w_b > w_g$, which are exogenously determined. A retail pharmacy may also devote effort to convince patients of the value of generics. This effort, e, increases valuation $\theta(e)$, $\theta'(e) > 0$, but at a decreasing rate, $\theta''(e) < 0$. Exerting this effort has cost $\phi(e)$ for the pharmacy. Prices to patients are regulated. The problem faced by the retail pharmacy is to choose the effort level that maximizes its profit:

$$\max_e D_b(p_b - w_b) + D_g(p_g - w_g) - \phi(e) \tag{17.8}$$

where

$$D_g = \frac{\hat{v} - \underline{v}}{\bar{v} - \underline{v}}, \qquad D_b = \frac{\bar{v} - \hat{v}}{\bar{v} - \underline{v}}, \qquad \hat{v} = \frac{s_b - s_g}{1 - \theta(e)} \tag{17.9}$$

The pharmacy incentives for generic substitution are given by

$$\frac{\partial \Pi}{\partial e} = \frac{(p_g - w_g - (p_b - w_b))(s_b - s_g)\theta'(e)}{(\bar{v} - \underline{v})(1 - \theta(e))^2} - \phi'(e) \tag{17.10}$$

For this incentive to be positive, $p_g - w_g > p_b - w_b$ and $s_b > s_g$. Let $p_g = (1 + m)w_g$, $p_b = (1 + m)w_b$, then the first condition becomes $w_g < w_b$.

Under $w_g < w_b$, there is no incentive of pharmacists to induce consumption of generics. Generic substitution is totally patient driven, which requires patients to face a higher co-payment in the branded pharmaceutical than in the generic. This illustrates that generic substitution levels are driven by both patients' decisions and retail pharmacy actions. The use of price systems to induce generic substitution must have two features: offer a higher remuneration to the pharmacy when selling the generic product, and patients facing a higher co-payment when buying a branded product.

17.6 Domestic reference pricing

Economic analysis can contribute in several ways to our understanding of how the pharmaceutical market operates. Take the definition of how reimbursements systems are defined. Traditionally, insurance protection schemes asked patients to pay a percentage of the full price of the pharmaceutical process. Currently, the adoption of reference pricing systems has become popular.

In these systems, patients are asked to pay the difference between the price set by the pharmaceutical company and a reference price (which can be administratively set or defined by a rule).

The interesting question from the economic point of view is why one system should be preferred over the other. Under the traditional system of reimbursement, the patient pays only a fraction of the price, and the insurer, public or private, covers the remaining. The less is the percentage paid by the patient, the more he or she is protected in the event of sickness. However, it also means that patients are less price sensitive. Pharmaceutical companies facing a less price sensitive demand will set higher prices. If patients pay 20 percent of the drug price, then a €10 price increase results in an extra payment by patients of €2. Market equilibrium involves relatively high prices.

The reference pricing system, on the other hand, gives full insurance to patients when the price set by the pharmaceutical company is below the reference price and no insurance protection in the value above the reference price is given. The reference pricing system introduces a higher sensitivity to price by patients without reducing their insurance coverage. The higher price sensitivity of demand stimulates price competition among pharmaceutical companies, resulting in lower prices. Taking the example above, a €10 increase in the price of a pharmaceutical product is fully paid by patients if the initial price was already equal or above the reference price.

The differences between the traditional reimbursement model and the reference pricing system can be illustrated with a simple model.

Let p_i be the price set by pharmaceutical company i. There are only two companies in the market, A and B. We normalize production costs to zero to simplify the analysis. Patients have preferences over the two alternative drugs. Some patients have better results (higher utility) with one, while others prefer the alternative drug. Preferences are represented by a line segment of length one. Denote $V(i, x), i = A, B$, the utility that a patient located in point x of the preferences line obtains when buying the pharmaceutical product produced by pharmaceutical company i:

$$V(A, x) = Y - p_A - tx + I_A \tag{17.11}$$

$$V(B, x) = Y - p_B - t(1 - x) + I_B \tag{17.12}$$

where Y is income, tx ($t(1 - x)$) is the cost of choosing provider A (provider B), measured in monetary units, and I_i is the compensation received when choosing provider i.

The traditional reimbursement system is given by $I_i = (1 - c)p_i$, meaning the patient pays a fraction c of the pharmaceutical cost. The reference pricing system implies $I_i = p_r$, where p_r is the reference price. Let's assume that both firms set $p_i \geq p_r$.[4]

The traditional reimbursement rules lead to equilibrium prices given by

$$p_A = p_B = t/c \tag{17.13}$$

while the reference pricing system originates equilibrium prices equal to:

$$p_A = p_B = t < t/c \tag{17.14}$$

Since pharmaceutical prices are identical, in both equilibria, demand is evenly split between the two pharmaceutical products. Total costs are higher under the traditional reimbursement system, as discussed above, since the patient is less price sensitive in this case.

Another common policy is the definition of positive lists of pharmaceutical products to be reimbursed. Included drugs benefit from a reimbursement rate $(1 - c)$, patients paying the remaining fraction c. Excluded drugs receive no reimbursement, patients have to pay the full price.

If the pharmaceutical company has freedom to set prices, even when its product is included in the positive list, then this "list" system leads to lower cost than the traditional reimbursement system but entails a higher cost than the reference pricing system. This holds true even if the price of the pharmaceutical product of a preferred provider is used to set the reference price.

Using the same notation of the model above, the "list" system is represented by

$$I_A = (1 - c)p_A, \quad I_B = 0 \tag{17.15}$$

when pharmaceutical product B is excluded from the list of reimbursed drugs and the drugs included in the list have a reimbursement rate of $(1 - c)$ of the price.

Under the reference pricing system where the reference price is determined as the price of provider A times a reimbursement rate $1 - c$,

$$I_A = (1 - c)p_A, \quad I_B = (1 - c)p_A \tag{17.16}$$

The resulting equilibrium prices and total payments to pharmaceutical companies are described in the next table.

Systems	Prices	Total payments
Reference pricing system	$p_A = p_B = t$	t
"List" system	$p_a = t/c, \ p_B = t$	$\dfrac{t}{2}\left(1 + \dfrac{1}{c}\right)$

Again, the reference pricing system works better. The "list" system, although better than the traditional reimbursement system, does not provide low prices as the reference pricing system. The main reason for it is the advantage that it confers to drugs that are included in the list vis-à-vis excluded drugs. The included drugs can have higher prices than excluded drugs because patients only pay a fraction of the price.

The reference pricing system with a preferred provider (the reimbursement to provider A sets the reference price to provider B) yields the same outcome as the pure reference pricing system described initially. This holds true despite the way the reference price is set. The crucial element is that at the margin the consumer faces the full price increase resulting from pharmaceutical firms' strategies.

17.7 The generics paradox

Introduction of generic competition has been associated with a price increase of the original branded drug, and not a decrease, as one might expect from increased competition. This effect has been termed the "generic competition paradox". Following entry by more competitors, the traditional expectation from economic theory is a decrease in prices, as more competition develops in the market.

The evidence initially gathered by Frank and Salkever (1997) and later on by Regan (2008), among others, pointed to a different sort of effects. Theory has been reconciled with the available evidence through the recognition of the role of heterogeneous patients in the market. Some patients are highly sensitive to price of pharmaceuticals, while others have low sensitivity to price differentials between branded drugs and generic products.

The branded product manufacturer during the patent period serves the full market. Its pricing strategy covers both price-sensitive and price-insensitive patients. This changes when generic entry occurs. The original branded drug product faced with strong competition may prefer to serve only the price insensitive patients, increasing the price of the branded drug. Upon entry of generics, the profits of the branded drug producer decrease considerably even if its price increases. Prices in generic products will converge to marginal cost of production as more competitors enter the market. The above argument can be illustrated with a very extreme and quite simple model.

Suppose that two groups of patients are present in the market for a given pharmaceutical product: price sensitive and price insensitive patients. The price-sensitive patients see no difference between a generic product and the original branded pharmaceutical product. These patients buy from the cheapest source. The price-insensitive patients do not buy generic products. There are n_1 price-sensitive patients and n_2 price-insensitive patients.

All patients have a reservation price v from the drug and all buy at most one unit of the pharmaceutical product. Marginal cost of production of the drug is c, irrespective of being a generic producer or the originator of the branded drug.

During the patent period, the originator faces no competition. It charges the monopoly price $p^m = v$. It serves the full market obtaining monopoly profits:

$$\Pi_O^m = (v - c)(n_1 + n_2) \tag{17.17}$$

where subscript O stands for the originator producer.

Allowing entry of generic producers, the entrants have an incentive to price aggressively. Under our assumptions, as patients buy from the cheapest source, price of generic producers equals marginal cost of production, $p_g = c$. The originator may follow the price cuts of generic producers, in which case they make zero economic profits. However, the existence of price-insensitive patients offers the originator a different pricing strategy, which is not available to generic producers.

By keeping $p_0 = v$, it makes profits

$$\Pi_0^p = (v - c)n_2 > 0 \tag{17.18}$$

Thus, concentrating sales in a fraction of the market that is price insensitive is better for the originator.

Let's account now for the price increase after entry by the generic producers. We introduce heterogeneity across groups of patients: Let $v_1 < v_2$ be the reservation prices of price-sensitive and price-insensitive patients, respectively. Under the patent period,

$$\Pi_O^M = (v_1 - c)(n_1 + n_2) > (v_2 - c)n_2 \tag{17.19}$$

as long as $v_2 - v_1$ is not very large. Then, after entry by generics producers,

$$p_O = v_2 > v_1 \tag{17.20}$$

and entry triggers a price increase by the branded drug producer. It is straightforward to extend the argument to less extreme demand functions. In addition, it is possible to generate different demand elasticities appealing to distinct health insurance coverage (Kong 2009).

17.8 Retail pharmacy

The sale of pharmaceutical products sold only under prescription by a physician is usually heavily regulated. Unlike other retail activities, many countries have strict controls over who can sell pharmaceutical products and under what conditions. Entry regulations and restrictions (like ownership restricted to pharmacists) are frequent.

The economic modeling approach has been used to study this particular market. Competition between retail pharmacies is often done at the level of services provided, as prices to patients and margins are often regulated. The geographic dimension of competition assumes an important role.

The model by Waterson (1993) has become a reference point for the analysis of the retail pharmacy market. It assumes n identical pharmacies, except for location. Each pharmacy serves patients within a radius r from its location. Demand is assumed to be price inelastic (either due to insurance or the absolute need for the drug). The main difference to the standard models of Hotelling (1929) and Salop (1979) is to consider that consumers are distributed in a two-dimension space. Pharmacies' location is described as the center of a circle. All patients inside the circle go to the pharmacy at the center.

Assuming regulated prices, distance to the pharmacy is the main criterion of choice to consumers. The circles of influence of each pharmacy adjust to the level of competition so to preserve the property that all patients inside the circle go to the pharmacy at the center. This assumption, which works as a generalization of the more standard models of geographic competition of Hotelling and Salop, implies that patients in the space not covered by any circle are discarded. Waterson (1993) consider this error of approximation to be lower than when using the Hotelling or the Salop model.

Pharmacies are symmetric so that all have the same radius r. Total demand faced by a pharmacy is:

$$Q = \int_0^r 2\pi x N q \, dx = \pi r N q \tag{17.21}$$

where N is the size of population, q is the per capita consumption of pharmaceutical products, π is the standard mathematical number pi, and r is the ray. We normalize $N = 1$ without loss of generality.

If price is regulated, pharmacies must have some other decision variable to compete, besides location. It may be the level of service to the patient, like opening hours, absence of queues inside the pharmacy, etc. We opt to present our discussion using price as the relevant competition variable, but the analysis can be easily adjusted to take another competition variable as relevant instead of price. We look at the impact of price liberalization in retail pharmacy.

Let p^r be the regulated price. Price regulation implies that patients face the same price whatever location they choose to go, so the equilibrium indifferent consumer between two pharmacies is located at $u/2$ where u is the distance between two pharmacies.

Under free entry but price regulation pharmacies will enter until economic profits are zero:

$$\Pi_i = (p^r - c)Q_i - F = 0 \tag{17.22}$$

where Q_i is demand faced by pharmacy i and F is the fixed cost of operating a pharmacy. Ignoring integer problems, in a surface A there can be n circles, where

$$n = \frac{A}{\pi r^2} \tag{17.23}$$

Substituting in the profit equation, using demand definition (17.21),

$$\Pi = (p^r - c)q\frac{A}{n} - F = 0 \tag{17.24}$$

from which the equilibrium number of pharmacies is:

$$n^r = \frac{Aq(p^r - c)}{F} \tag{17.25}$$

Let's now take a price liberalization. Pharmacies can freely choose the prices charged to patients. Each pharmacy faces neighbors with price $\bar{p}$. In each ray of length u, the indifferent patient between pharmacy i and its competitor is given by

$$x = \frac{u}{2} + \frac{\bar{p} - p_i}{2t} \tag{17.26}$$

Total demand faced is

$$Q_i = \pi x^2 q \tag{17.27}$$

The problem of price choice is

$$\max_{\{p_i\}}(p_i - c)\left(\frac{u}{2} + \frac{\bar{p} - p_i}{2t}\right)\pi q - F \tag{17.28}$$

Obtaining the first-order condition and using the property that in equilibrium $p_i = \bar{p} = p^*$,

$$\left(\frac{u}{2}\right)^2 + (p^* - c)\left(-\frac{u}{2t}\right) = 0 \tag{17.29}$$

from which

$$p^* = c + \frac{ut}{2} = c + rt \tag{17.30}$$

Equilibrium profits are

$$\Pi = tr^3\pi q - F \tag{17.31}$$

so,

$$r = \left(\frac{F}{t\pi q}\right)^{1/3} \tag{17.32}$$

and

$$n^f = A q^{1/3} t^{2/3} F^{-2/3} \pi^{-1/3} \tag{17.33}$$

The next step is to evaluate the optimal number of pharmacies. Total patients' welfare is

$$SW = Aq(v - tx - p) \tag{17.34}$$

The zero-profit condition for the firm implies

$$p = c + \frac{Fn}{Aq} \tag{17.35}$$

Substituting in SW:

$$Aq(v - c) - (Aqtx + nF) \tag{17.36}$$

For n_S circles, total costs that depend on the number of pharmacies are given by

$$\Omega = n_S \int_0^r (2tx) q x \pi \, dx + n_S F \tag{17.37}$$

The social problem is to minimize patients' transport costs and pharmacies' fixed costs, as patients' benefits net of production costs are fixed and prices are just a transfer within society.

The first-order condition of the social planner is

$$\frac{\partial \Omega}{\partial n_S} = -\frac{1}{2} n^{-3/2} q \frac{2}{3} \pi^{-1/2} A^{3/2} + F = 0 \tag{17.38}$$

The socially optimal number of pharmacies, n^S, is:

$$n^S = \left(\frac{1}{3}\right)^{2/3} F^{-2/3} q^{2/3} \pi^{-2/3} t^{2/3} A = \left(\frac{1}{3}\right)^{2/3} n^f \tag{17.39}$$

and it follows $n^S < n^f$.

Under free entry and no price regulation, we observe too much entry from a social point of view. The reason for excessive entry lies in the business-stealing effect – a new pharmacy gets its business mostly from existing pharmacies. The private incentive to entry (the profit the new pharmacy expects to make) exceeds the social benefit of one more pharmacy (which cancels out the profit transfer between pharmacies).

Free entry with a well-set regulated price achieves the first best number of pharmacies, the price being defined by

$$p^r = c + \frac{Fn^S}{qA} \tag{17.40}$$

The alternative is obviously to set entry regulation to avoid excessive entry. Several countries have entry regulations based on distance between pharmacies and number of population covered by the pharmacy. This route becomes more attractive than price regulation, as prices of pharmaceutical products at retail level are usually regulated taking into account the demands from the pharmaceutical industry to have a "fair" return on the development of new products and the interest of patients' and of the third-party payer in not paying too much. Thus, regulation of entry by pharmacies is not usually a concern when setting pharmaceutical prices. Moreover, price decisions are taken on a product-by-product basis, and our analysis above should see p as a general price index for the bundle of products sold by a pharmacy.

To sum up, one main result from the literature (Waterson 1993; Jansson 1999) is that excessive entry may result from free entry. Nuscheller (2003) shows, allowing for horizontal and vertical differentiation, that excessive entry is still to be expected and it does not require that in equilibrium demand for quality is distorted. Curiously enough, most European Union countries have in place restrictions on the opening of new pharmacies.[5] Economic theory does lend support to limitations to free entry, as it would lead to too many pharmacies in the market.

Notes

2 Demand

1 We will abuse notation because q_i will denote both good i and the quantity of good i. However, the context will avoid any misinterpretation.
2 We should note that non-transitive relations among alternatives appear very often in other domains. Particularly, games like rock-paper-scissors, the cycle rock beating scissors, scissors beating paper, and paper beating rock, prevent a single strategy dominating the gameplay. Many combat or strategy-based video games contain this type of cycle in their strategies.
3 Illuminating readings on the solution of programming problems is Arrow and Enthoven (1961) and on optimization in general, Intriligator (1971).
4 Technically, this requires a strictly quasi-concave utility function, and in turn, a set of fairly restricting conditions on preferences.
5 See Section 2.2.6 for the definition of income elasticity.
6 This is an unfortunate choice of lexicon because it leaves an ambiguity when referring to normal goods with respect to changes in income or to the price of the good. The context of the argument should be clear enough to solve the ambiguity.

3 Supply

1 The mathematically-inclined reader can easily confirm that the second-order condition for a maximum is also satisfied as long as marginal cost is non-decreasing.

4 Markets

1 On the definition of a market see CPB (2000).
2 Monopsony and oligopsony are the "symmetric" market structures to monopoly and oligopoly, and the same arguments apply. Bilateral monopoly and bilateral oligopoly are structures where the allocation of resources is determined through a negotiation procedure. On this, the reader is referred to Chapter 14.
3 Note that this is not the only mechanism that can operate in a market. Other mechanisms often found are auctions, rationing, or restricted prices.

5 Regulation

1 This line of thought has also received contributions from Becker, Peltzman and Posner, among others.
2 The interested reader will find surveys in Joskow (2007), Joskow and Rose (1989) and Braeutigam (1989).
3 The rate of return is defined in terms of gross profits, this is the ratio of revenue minus variable (labor) costs to capital.
4 This condition is known as the Samuelson condition.
5 An illuminating presentation is found in Koopmans (1957).

6 See Macho-Stadler and Perez-Castrillo (2001), ch. 4.2 and Mas-Colell *et al.* (1995) ch. 14C.
7 On contract design see Chapter 11.

6 Mergers and acquisitions

1 Volume 37(4), December 2010.
2 Volume 58(4), December 2010.
3 See http://www.dutchnews.nl/news/archives/2009/12/hospital_mergers_boost_prices.php.
4 The Merger Regulation contains the main rules for the assessment of concentrations, whereas the Implementing Regulation concerns procedural issues. See http://ec.europa.eu/competition/mergers/legislation/legislation.html.
5 Karrer-Rueedi (1997) studies the forces leading to vertical and horizontal merger in the drug industry.

7 For-profit and nonprofit organizations

1 Some recent general appraisals of nonprofit organizations are Anheier (2005) and Holland and Ritvo (2008).
2 Other elements, such as the health state of the population in the catchment area of the hospital and the feeling of security in case of a potential illness episode, may play a role in the decision of capacity of the hospital. However, we concentrate our analysis on the medical services aspect of the hospital.

8 Essential concepts in health economics

1 Formal definitions of mortality, life expectancy, and hazard rate can be found in Jack (1999, pp. 9–14).
2 See Phelps (1999) for a more detailed description.
3 A public good in contrast with a private good must satisfy two properties. (i) the marginal cost of introducing an additional consumer is zero; (ii) the cost of excluding an individual from consuming the good (or service) is infinite. A (public) park or the public transport are examples of public goods.
4 Translated from the original in Spanish.
5 Translated from the original in Catalan.
6 This section is based on Artells (1994, pp. 19–28).

9 Demand for health and health care

1 On the disparities among reported estimates of VSL, see Doucouliagos *et al.* (2011).
2 Grossman's model is set in discrete time. A continuous-time version of the model can be found in Wagstaff (1986b) and Zweifel *et al.* (2009, pp. 79–83).
3 This is the increase in the amount of healthy time caused by a unit increase of the stock of health. Note that it is measured as time saved from illness. Accordingly, $W_t G_t$ gives the increase in income in $t + 1$.
4 See Grossman (1972a, pp. 235–240) or Grossman (2000, pp. 369–371) for the formal derivation of this argument.
5 If all probabilities and transition probabilities remain constant over time the sequence of states follows a Markov process.

10 Insurance

1 Here we offer solely the definitions of and elaborate on the concepts as needed for the arguments that follow. More extensive treatments of these concepts and extensions can be found in Mas-Colell *et al.* (1995).

11 Contracts and asymmetric information

1 We follow closely Barros (2009, ch. 11.3).
2 Assume $x^* > \tilde{x}$. Then, concavity of $B(\cdot)$ implies that $B'(x^*) < B'(\tilde{x})$. In turn, from (11.1) and (11.8) it follows that $U'(y - x^*) < U'(y - p\tilde{x})$. Again, the concavity of $U(\cdot)$ yields $y - x^* > y - p\tilde{x}$ or $p\tilde{x} > x^*$. Summarizing we have obtained that $p\tilde{x} > x^* > \tilde{x}$ that is a contradiction.
3 Any alternative tie-breaking rule would lead us to consider a contract ε below $\widetilde{C}_L$ thus avoiding the indifference between both contracts.
4 We follow closely Barros (2009, ch. 11.5).

12 Competition in health care markets

1 See Laffont and Tirole (1993).
2 The "quantity" q can be seen as a composite good of the several hospital activities.
3 This utility function for providers was used in Ellis and McGuire (1986).
4 It is easy to verify that under our assumptions, the second-order conditions for a maximum holds.
5 It can be easily verified that the second-order condition for a maximum is also satisfied.
6 A more general formulation is presented in Barros (2003).
7 Formally, $\bar{p} = \int_{p \in \Omega_i} p \, dp / \int_{p \in \Omega_i} dp$. See Barros (2003, p. 1027) for further details and discussion.
8 In contrast, under horizontal differentiation, same patients prefer one product, while other patients prefer another. Patients do rank products but the rankings are different across patients.
9 See Barros and Martinez-Giralt (2002) for extensions considering quality choices and heterogeneous patients in severity levels.
10 Remember the assumption of zero costs for simplification.
11 According to different values for the parameters, other equilibria, namely with only provider investing, or with none investing, may emerge.
12 The argument requires the application of the Intuitive Criterion.
13 See, for example, Robinson and Luft (1985, 1987), Dranove *et al.* (1992) and James (2002).

13 Public and private provision

1 White (1996).
2 George and Lay Manna (1996).
3 Surveys of the general literature can be found in Nett (1993) and de Fraja and Delbono (1990).
4 See Cremer, Marchand and Thisse (1989), Pal (1998), Majumdar and Pal (1998), Matsumura (2003) among others.
5 DG Internal Policies of the Union – Directorate A – Economic and Scientific Policy, Public and Private Partnerships, Models and Trends in the European Union (IP/A/IMCO/SC/2005-161).
6 We may see p as the net present value of future payments and abuse notation using U to denote lifetime utility.
7 Guasch (2004), Guasch *et al.* (2007, 2008).
8 Biglaiser and Ma (2007) consider an auditing game. The auditing game allows for payments conditional on the audited value of quality and to have more than the minimum quality level provided by the moonlighting doctors. Still, the underlying motive for welfare improvement from existence of moonlighting is the same as in the simpler version of the model.
9 The argument holds true in the presence of an auditing game in which the moonlighters in the public sector report a quality q and are audited about it.

14 Bargaining

1 It is implicitly assumed that all parties involved in the negotiation are equally skilled, have well-defined preferences over the potential outcomes of the negotiation, and are rational.
2 A detailed (and readable) proof of Rubinstein result is found in Binmore (1992).
3 This game has a continuum of Nash equilibria, namely all the efficient allocations can be supported as Nash equilibria. The Nash bargaining solution allocation is just one of them. Nash modified the game introducing some uncertainty on the agents' payoffs. The beauty of this modification is that in the limit as uncertainty vanishes, the only Nash equilibrium allocation left is precisely the Nash bargaining solution.

4 Of course, it may be the case that in certain circumstances a different timing assumption is needed. For example, there are States in the US where insurers have to show evidence that providers are willing to accept the insurance plan within a given geographic region prior to marketing the plan. If there is no renegotiation of prices after consumers sign insurance contracts, a different timeline of decisions would result. We see our timing assumptions as describing most situations though.

5 See Mossialos and Le Grand (1999) for an overview of recent experiments in cost containment in European countries.

6 See Bloor *et al.* (1996) for a short review of reference prices and Mossialos and Le Grand (1999) for a more detailed discussion.

7 A useful illustration supporting this solution and other alternatives can be found in Clark (1995) and Cuadras-Morato *et al.* (2001).

8 See http://www.supremecourt.gov/oral_arguments/argument_transcripts/00-1471.pdf.

9 We assume away quality differences across providers. For quality issues in the provision of health care in the context of vertical differentiation models see, for example, Jofre-Bonet (2000) and the references therein.

10 The interested reader will find the computational details in Siciliani and Stanciole (2008).

11 A different but related line of research proposed by Jelovac (2002) studies the financing of pharmaceutical products in a national health system where negotiations between the public financing agency and pharmaceutical laboratories are affected by the conditions on the demand side. In particular, by the level of co-payments. Also Wright (2004) contributes to this discussion, focusing on the Australian regulation system for drug introduction, and the price bargaining process for new drugs.

12 To be rigorous, $p = c - t/s - \varepsilon$, where ε is the smallest unit available to denominate prices.

13 We assume that it is credible that in case of negotiations failure, the public sector will use all its capacity. If this was not the case, the only equilibrium price would be the private market equilibrium price.

15 Waiting lists

1 For a more recent account of developments in the waiting list literature, see Iversen and Siciliani (2011).

2 Martin and Smith (1999) do consider a more general setting in which patients may not be treated.

3 These implications can be derived from comparative statics exercises on the first-order conditions above.

17 Pharmaceutical market

1 They base their estimates on an analysis of 68 products, and allowing explicitly for the probability of reaching the next stage.

2 For a more in-depth analysis of economic evaluation methods, see Drummond *et al.* (2005).

3 Of course, providing a more detailed structure allows for a richer set of implications. See Garcia-Mariñoso *et al.* (2011).

4 For $p_i < p_r$, there is no extra demand for either product as patients face a zero price, pharmaceutical companies would not set voluntarily a price below the reference price.

5 See the OBIG Report 2006.

References

Abbey, D.C. (2009) *Healthcare Payment Systems. An Introduction*, London, CRC Press.

Abellán, J.M., Pinto, J.L., Méndez, I. and Badía, X. (2004) "A test of the predictive validity of non-linear QALY models using time trade-off utilities," Department of Economics and Business, Universitat Pompeu Fabra, Economics Working Paper 741.

Ablasser-Neuhuber, A. and Plank, R. (2010) "Vertical agreements and EU competition law," *Global Competition Review*, The European Antitrust Review, Article 44, available at: http://www.glbalcompetitionreview.com/reviews/28/sections/98/chapters/1091/vertical-agreements/.

Akerlof, G. (1970) "The market for 'lemons': quality uncertainty and the market mechanism," *Quarterly Journal of Economics*, **84**: 488–500.

American Academy of Actuaries (2009) "Risk classification in the voluntary individual health insurance market," *Issue Brief*, March, available at http://www.actuary.org/pdf/health/risk_mar09.pdf.

Anheier, H.K. (2005) *Nonprofit Organizations: Theory, Management, Policy*, New York, Routledge.

Arrow, K.J. (1951) "Alternative approaches to the theory of choice in risk-taking situations," *Econometrica*, **19**: 404–437.

— (1963) "Uncertainty and the welfare economics of medical care," *American Economic Review*, **53**: 941–973.

— (1965) "The theory of risk aversion," in *Aspects of the Theory of Risk Bearing*, Helsinki, Y. Jahnssonin Saatio: Chapter 2; reprinted in *Essays in the Theory of Risk Bearing* (1971), Amsterdam, North Holland, pp. 90–109.

— and Enthoven, A.C. (1961) "Quasi-concave programming," *Econometrica* **29**(4): 779–800.

Artells Herrero, J.J. (1994) "Características del sector sanitario en los países industrializados," in Cuervo, J.I. Varela, J. and Belenes, R. (eds.) *Gestión de Hospitales. Nuevos Instrumentos y Tendencias*, Barcelona, Ediciones Vicens Vives S.A., pp. 1–35.

Averch, H. and Johnson, L.J. (1962) "Behaviour of firms under regulatory constraints," *American Economic Review*, **52**(5): 1052–1069.

Barr, N. (1989) "Social insurance as an efficiency device," *Journal of Public Policy*, **9**: 59–82.

Barros, P.P. (2003) "Cream-skimming, incentives for efficiency and payment system," *Journal of Health Economics*, **22**(3): 419–443.

—, (2009) *Economia da Saúde. Conceitos e comportamentos*, Coimbra, Edições Almedina.

— and Martinez-Giralt, X. (2002) "Public and Private Provision of Health Care," *Journal of Economics & Management Strategy*, **11**(1): 109–113.

— and Martinez-Giralt, X. (2003) "Preventive health care and payment systems," *Topics in Economic Analysis & Policy*, **3**: 10.

— and Martinez-Giralt, X. (2005a) "Negotiation advantages of professional associations in health care," *International Journal of Health Care Finance and Economics*, **5**: 1–14.

— and Martinez-Giralt, X. (2005b) "Bargaining and idle public sector capacity in health care," *Economics Bulletin*, **9**: 1–8.

— and Martinez-Giralt, X. (2006) "Models of Negotiation and Bargaining in Health Care," in *The Elgar Companion to Health Economics*, Jones, A.M. (ed.) Cheltenham, Edward Elgar, pp. 233–241.

— and Martinez-Giralt, X. (2008) "Selecting health care providers: 'any willing provider' vs. negotiation," *European Journal of Political Economy*, **24**: 402–414.

— and Martinez-Giralt, X. (2009) "Contractual design and PPPs for hospitals. Lessons for the Portuguese model," *The European Journal of Health Economics*, **10**(4): 437–453.

— and Olivella, P. (2005) "Waiting lists and patient selection," *Journal of Economics & Management Strategy*, **14**(3): 623–646.

—, Pinto, C.G. and Machado, A. (1999) "A signalling theory of excessive technological adoption," *Health Care Management Science*, **2**(2): 117–123.

—, Garcia, B., Jelovac, I., Martinez-Giralt, X. and Olivella, P. (2006) *Competition in Health Provision and Insurance*, Madrid, Fundación BBVA.

Becker, G.S., Philipson, T. J. and Soares, R. R. (2005) "The quantity and quality of life and the evolution of world inequality," *American Economic Review*, **95**(1): 277–291.

Belli, P. (2001) "How adverse selection affects the health insurance market," Policy research working paper 2574, World Bank, Development Research Group.

Bergman, M.A., Coate, M.B., Jakobson, M. and Ulrick, S.W. (2010) "Comparing merger policies in the European Union and the United States," *Review of Industrial Organization*, **36**: 305–331.

Biglaiser, G. and Ma, A. (2007) "Moonlighting: Public Service and Private Practice," *The RAND Journal of Economics* Winter: 1113–1133.

Binmore, K.G. (1992) *Fun and Games: A Text on Game Theory*, Lexington, MA, D.C. Heath.

—, Rubinstein, A. and Wolinsky, A. (1986a) "Non-cooperative models of bargaining," in Aumann, R.J. and Hart, S. (eds.) *Handbook of Game Theory with Economic Applications*, Amsterdam, North-Holland.

—, Rubinstein, A. and Wolinsky, A. (1986b) "The Nash Bargaining solution in economic modelling," *RAND Journal of Economics*, **17**: 176–188.

Bleichrodt, H. and Quiggin, J. (1999) "QALYs and consumer demand for health care," *Journal of Health Economics*, **18**: 681–708.

Bloor, K., Maynard, A. and Freemantle, N. (1996) "Lessons from international experience in controlling pharmaceutical expenditure III: regulating industry," *British Medical Journal*, **313**: 33–35.

Boulding, K.W. (1948) *Economic Analysis*, New York, Harper.

Braeutigam, R.R. (1989) "Optimal policies for natural monopolies," in Schmalensee, R. and Willig, R.D. *Handbook of Industrial Economics*, Volume 2, Amsterdam, North-Holland, Chapter 23.

Brekke, K.R. and Sorgard, L. (2007) "Public vs. private health care in a National Health Service," *Health Economics*, **16**(6): 579–601.

Brekke, K.R.R., Nuscheler, K.R.R. and Straume, O.R. (2007) "Gatekeeping in health care," *Journal of Health Economics*, **26**(1): 149–170.

—, Grasdak, A., Holmas, T. (2009) "Regulation and pricing of pharmaceuticals: reference pricing or price-cap regulation?." *European Economic Review*, 53: 170–185.

—, Siciliani, L. and Straume, O.R. (2011) "Quality competition with profit constraints: Do non-profit firms provide higher quality than for-profit firms?," CEPR Discussion Paper No. 8284.

Brooks, J.M., Dor, A. and Wong, H.S. (1997) "Hospital–insurer bargaining: an empirical investigation of appendectomy pricing," *Journal of Health Economics*, **16**: 417–434.

—, Dor, A. and Wong, H.S. (1998) "The impact of physician payments on hospital–insurer bargaining in the U.S.," in Chinitz, D. and Cohen, J. (eds.) *Governments and Health Care Systems*, London, John Wiley & Sons.

Brousselle, A., Denis, J.-L. and Langley, A. (1999) "What do we know about hospital mergers? A selected annotated bibliography," Resource document, Canadian Health Services Research Foundation.

Bumgardner, L. (2005) "Antitrust law in the European Union. The law is changing – but to what effect?," *Graziadio Business Report*, **8**, available at http://gbr.pepperdine.edu/053/euantitrust.html

Burns, L.R. and Pauly, M.V. (2002) "Integrated delivery networks: a detour on the road to integrated health care?," *Health Affairs*, **21**: 128–143.

Busse, R. and Howorth, C. (1999) "Cost containment in Germany: twenty years' experience," in Mossialos, E. and Le Grand, J. (eds.) *Health Care and Cost Containment in the European Union*, Ashgate, pp. 303–339.

Cabral, L.M.B. (2000) *Introduction to Industrial Organization*, London, MIT Press.

Cai, H. (2004) "Uncertainty and commitment in multilateral bargaining," unpublished paper available at http://www.econ.ucla.edu/people/papers/Cai/Cai259.pdf.

Calem, P.S., Dor, A. and Rizzo, J.A. (1999) "The welfare effects of mergers in the hospital industry," *Journal of Economics and Business*, **51**: 197–213.

Calsamiglia, X. (1994) "En defensa de l'estat del benestar, contra els seus entusiastes," in López Casasnovas, G. (ed.) *Anàlisi Econòmica de la Sanitat*, Barcelona, Departament de Sanitat i Seguretat Social, Generalitat de Catalunya.

Capps, C.S., Dranove, D., Greenstein, S. and Satterthwaite, M. (2002) "Antitrust policy and hospital mergers: recommendations for a new approach," *Antitrust Bulletin*, **47**: 677–714.

Carroll, A. and Ambrose, J. (2002) "Any willing provider laws: their financial effect on HMOs," *Journal of Health, Politics, Policy and Law*, **27**: 927–945.

Castaneda, M.A. and Falaschetti, D. (2008) "Does a hospital's profit status affect its operational scope?," *Review of Industrial Organization*, **33**: 129–159.

Caves, R.E. (1989) "Mergers, takeovers, and economic efficiency. Foresight vs. hindsight," *International Journal of Industrial Organization*, **7**: 151–174.

Chaé, S. and Heidhues, P. (2004) "A group bargaining solution," *Mathematical Social Sciences*, **48**: 37–53.

— and Heidhues, P. (1999) "Bargaining power of a coalition in parallel bargaining: advantage of multiple cable system operators." Unpublished paper, Department of Economics, Rice University.

Chamberlin, E. (1933) *The Theory of Monopolistic Competition*, Cambridge, Mass., Harvard University Press.

Chen, Y. (2001) "On vertical mergers and their competitive effects," *RAND Journal of Economics*, **32**: 667–685.

Church, J. (2009a) "Vertical mergers," in Collins, W.D. (ed.) *Issues in Competition Law and Policy*, Volume 2, Chapter 61, Chicago, American Bar Association, Section of Antitrust Law, pp. 1455–1501.

— (2009b) "Conglomerate mergers," in Collins, W.D. (ed.) *Issues in Competition Law and Policy*, Volume 2, Chapter 62, Chicago, American Bar Association, Section of Antitrust Law, pp. 1503–1552.

Ciliberto, F. and Dranove, D. (2006) "The effect of physician–hospital affiliations on hospital prices in California," *Journal of Health Economics*, **25**: 29–38.

Clark, D. (1995) "Priority setting in health care: an axiomatic bargaining approach," *Journal of Health Economics*, **14**: 345–360.

Cochrane, J.H. (1995) "Time-consistent health insurance," *Journal of Political Economy*, **103**: 445–473.

Collins, W.D. (ed.) (2009) *Issues in Competition Law and Policy*, Chicago, American Bar Association, Section of Antitrust Law.

Connelly, L.B. (2002) "Welfarist and non-welfarist conceptions of 'health promotion'," Discussion Papers in Economics, Finance and International Competitiveness, 104, Queensland University of Technology.

— (2004) "Economics and health promotion," *European Journal of Health Economics*, **5**: 236–242.

Conway, K.S. and Kutinova, A. (2006) "Maternal health: does prenatal care make a difference," *Health Economics*, **15**: 461–488.

CPB (2000) "Publishers caught in the web? Strategies, performance and public policy. General framework," Working Paper, No. 119, CPB Netherlands Bureau for Economic Policy Analysis, The Hague.

Crainich, D. and Closon, M.-C. (1999) "Cost containment and health care reform," in Mossialos, E. and Le Grand, J. (eds.) *Health care and cost containment in the European Union*, Ashgate, pp. 219–266.

Cremer, H., Marchand, M. and Thisse, J.-F. (1989) "The public firm as an instrument for regulating an oligopolistic market," *Oxford Economic Papers*, **41**: 283–301.

Cropper, M.L. (1977) "Health, investment in health and occupational choice," *Journal of Political Economy*, **85**: 1273–1294.

Cuadras-Morato, X., Pinto-Prades, J.L. and Abellan-Perpiñan, J.M. (2001) "Equity considerations in health care: the relevance of claims," *Health Economics*, **10**: 187–205.

Cuellar, A.E. and Gertler, P.J. (2006) "Strategic integration of hospitals and physicians," *Journal of Health Economics*, **25**: 1–28.

Culyer, A.J. (2005) *The Dictionary of Health Economics*, Cheltenham, Edward Elgar, pp. 1–10.

— and Newhouse, J.P. (2000) "Introduction: the state and scope of health economics," in Culyer, A.J. and Newhouse, J.P. (eds.) *Handbook of Health Economics* (Volume 1A), Amsterdam, North-Holland.

Cutler, D. and Zeckhauser, R. (2000) "The anatomy of health insurance", in Culyer, A.J. and Newhouse, J.P. (eds.) *Handbook of Health Economics*, Amsterdam, North-Holland, Chapter 11: 584–585.

—, McClellan, M. and Newhouse, J.P. (2000) "How does managed care do it?," *RAND Journal of Economics*, **31**: 526–548.

d'Aspremont, C., Gabszewicz, J.J. and Thisse, J.F. (1979) "On Hotelling's 'Stability in competition'," *Econometrica*, **47**: 1045–1050.

Dafny, L. (2005) "How do hospitals respond to price changes?," *American Economic Review* **95**(5): 1525–1547.

— (2009) "Estimation and identification of merger effects: an application to hospital mergers," *Journal of Law and Economics*, **52**: 523–550.

Danzon, P. and Epstein, A. (2008) "Effects of regulation on drug launch and pricing in interdependent markets," NBER Working Papers 14041.

Danzon, P., Wang, R. and Wang, L. (2005) "The impact of price regulation on the launch delay of new drugs-evidence from twenty-five major markets in the 1990s," *Health Economics*, **14**(3): 269–292.

Daughety, A. (1990) "Beneficial concentration," *American Economic Review*, **80**: 1231–1237.

David, G. (2009) "The convergence between for-profit and nonprofit hospitals in the United States," *International Journal of Health Care Finance and Economics*, **9**: 403–428.

Davidson, C. (1988) "Multiunit bargaining in oligopolistic industries," *Journal of Labor Economics*, **6**: 397–422.

—, and Deneckere, R. (1984) "Horizontal mergers and collusive behavior," *International Journal of Industrial Organization*, **2**: 117–132.

de Fraja, G. and Delbono, F. (1990) "Game theoretic models of mixed oligopoly," *Journal of Economic Surveys*, **4**(1): 1–17.

Debreu, G. (1959) *Theory of Value: An Axiomatic Analysis of Economic Equilibrium*, London, Wiley.

Delbono, F., Denicolo, V.A. and Scarpa, C. (1996) "Quality choice in a vertically differentiated mixed duopoly," *Economic Notes*, **25**: 33–46.

Delfgaauw, J. (2007) "Dedicated doctors: public and private provision of health care with altruistic physicians," Tinbergen Institute DP 07-010.

Deneckere, R. and Davidson, C. (1985) "Incentives to form coalitions with Bertrand competition," *The RAND Journal of Economics*, **16**: 473–486.

Deneffe, D. and Mason, R.T. (2002) "What do not-for-profit hospitals maximize?," *International Journal of Industrial Organization*, **20**: 461–492.

DePamphilis, D.M. (2008) *Mergers, Acquisitions, and Other Restructuring Activities*, New York, Academic Press.

DiMasi, J., Hansen, R. and Grabowski, H. (2003) "The price of innovation: new estimates of drug development costs," *Journal of Health Economics*, **22**(2): 151–185.

Dixit, A.K. (1979) "A model of duopoly suggesting a theory of entry barriers," *Bell Journal of Economics*, **10**: 10–20.

— (1980) "The role of investment in entry deterrence," *Economic Journal*, **90**: 95–106.

— and Stiglitz, J.E. (1977) "Monopolistic competition and optimum product diversity," *American Economic Review*, **67**: 297–308.

DLA Piper (2009) *European PPP Report 2009*. Available at: http://www.dlapiper.com

Dobson, P.W. and Waterson, M. (1996) "Vertical restraints and competition policy," Research Paper 12, Office of Fair Trading, London.

Doucouliagos, H., Stanley, T.D. and Giles, M. (2011) "Are estimates of the value of statistical life exaggerated?," SWP 2011/2, Faculty of Business and Law, Deakin University.

Dowie, J. (1975) "The portfolio approach to health behavior," *Social Science and Medicine*, **9**: 619–631.

Dranove, D. (1988) "Pricing by non-profit institutions. The case of hospital cost-shifting," *Journal of Health Economics*, **7**: 47–57.

Dranove, D., Shanley, M. and Simon, C. (1992) "Is hospital competition wasteful?," *RAND Journal of Economics*, **23**(2): 247–262.

Drummond, M.F., Sculpher, Mark J. and Torrance, Mark J. (2005). *Methods for the Economic Evaluation of Health Care Programmes*, Oxford, Oxford University Press.

Dulleck, U., Kerschbamer, R. and Sutter, M. (2009) "The economics of credence goods: on the role of liability, verifiability, reputation and competition," Working Papers in Economics and Statistics, University of Innsbruck.

Dusheiko, M., Gravelle, H., Yu, N. and Campbell, S. (2007) "The impact of budgets for gatekeeping physicians on patient satisfaction: evidence from fundholding," *Journal of Health Economics*, **26**: 742–762.

Eeckhoudt, L. and Kimball, M. (1992) "Background risk, prudence and the demand for insurance," in Dionne, G. (ed.) *Contributions to Insurance Economics*, Huebner International Series on Risk, Insurance and Economic Security, London, Kluwer Academic, pp. 239–254.

Eggleston, K. (2000) "Risk selection and optimal health insurance-provider payment systems," *Journal of Risk and Insurance*, **67**: 173–196.

Ellis, R.P. (2008) "Risk adjustment in health care markets: concepts and applications," in Lu, M. and Jonsson E. (eds.) *Financing Health Care: New Ideas for a Changing Society*, Weinheim, Wiley-VCH Verlag GmbH & Co. KGaA, pp. 177–222.

— and McGuire, T. (1990) "Optimal payment systems for health services," *Journal of Health Economics*, **9**: 375–396.

Ellis, R.P. and McGuire, T.G. (1986) "Provider behaviour under prospective reimbursement. Cost sharing and supply," *Journal of Health Economics*, **5**: 129–151.

Ellison, S.F. and Snyder, C.M. (2001) "Countervailing power in wholesale pharmaceuticals," MIT Working Paper.

Ehrlich, I. and Becker, G.S. (1972) "Market insurance, self-insurance, and self-protection," *Journal of Political Economy*, **80**: 623–648.

Engelbert, T. (1999) "Expenditure and cost control in Austria," in Mossialos, E. and Le Grand, J. (eds.) *Health Care and Cost Containment in the European Union*, Ashgate, pp. 605–633.

European Commission (2003) *The Health Status of the European Union. Narrowing the Health Gap*, Health and consumer protection program, Luxemburg.

Evans, R. (1974) "Supplier-induced demand: some empirical evidence and implications," in *The Economics of Health and Medical Care*, Perlman, M. (ed.), Macmillan, New York, pp. 162–173.

Farrell, J. and Shapiro, C. (1990) "Horizontal mergers: an equilibrium analysis," *American Economic Review*, **80**, 107–126.

— and Shapiro, C. (1991) "Horizontal mergers: reply," *American Economic Review*, **81**, 1007–1011.

— and Shapiro, C. (2010) "Antitrust evaluation of horizontal mergers: an economic alternative to market definition," *The B.E. Journal of Theoretical Economics. Policies and Perspectives*, **10**: 9.

Fauli-Oller, R. (1997) "On merger profitability in a Cournot setting," *Economics Letters*, **54**: 75–79.

Feachem, R.G.A. and Sekri, N.K. (2005) "Moving towards true integration," *British Medical Journal*, **330**: 787–788.

Federal Trade Commission and Department of Justice (2004) "Improving health care: a dose of competition," report, Federal Trade Commission and Department of Justice, Washington, D.C.

Feldstein, P.J. (2002) *Health Care Economics*, New York, Delmar Publishers.

Fingleton, J. and Raith, M. (2005) "Career concerns of bargainers," *Journal of Law, Economics, and Organization*, **21**: 179–204.

Folland, S., Goodman, A.C. and Stano, M. (2009) *The Economics of Health and Health Care*, Boston, Prentice Hall.

Frank, R.G. and Salkever, D.S. (1997) "Generic entry and the pricing of pharmaceuticals," *Journal of Economics and Management Strategy*, **6**: 75–90.

Fuchs, V.R. (1993) *The Future of Health Policy*, Cambridge, Mass., Harvard University Press.

Gabszewicz, J.J. and Thisse, J.F. (1979) "Price competition, quality and income disparities," *Journal of Economic Theory*, **20**: 340–359.

— and Thisse, J.F. (1980) "Entry (and exit) in a differentiated industry," *Journal of Economic Theory*, **22**: 327–338.

— and Thisse, J.F. (1982) "Product differentiation with income disparities. An illustrative model," *The Journal of Industrial Economics*, **31**: 115–129.

— and Thisse, J.F. (1986a) "Spatial competition and the location of firms," in *Location Theory*, in Lesourne, J. and Sonnenschein, H. (eds.) *Fundamentals of Pure and Applied Economics*, Chur, Harwood Academic Publishers.

— and Thisse, J.F. (1986b) "On the nature of competition with differentiated products," *The Economic Journal*, **96**: 160–172.

Gal-Or, E. (1997) "Exclusionary equilibria in health care markets," *Journal of Economics & Management Strategy*, **6**: 5–43.

— (1999a) "Mergers and exclusionary practices in health care markets," *Journal of Economics & Management Strategy*, **8**: 315–350.

— (1999b) "The profitability of vertical mergers between hospitals and physician practices," *Journal of Health Economics*, **18**: 623–654.

Garcia-Mariñoso, B. and Jelovac, I. (2003) "GPs' payment contracts and their referral practice," *Journal of Health Economics*, **22**(4): 617–635.

— Jelovac, I. and Olivella, P. (2011). "External referencing and pharmaceutical price negotiation," *Health Economics*, **30**: 737–755.

Gaynor, M. (2006) "Is vertical integration anticompetitive? Definitely maybe (but that's not final)," *Journal of Health Economics*, **25**: 175–180.

— (2006) "What do we know about competition and quality in health care markets?," NBER Working Paper No. 12301.

— and Vogt, W.B. (2003) "Competition among hospitals," *RAND Journal of Economics*, **34**: 764–785.

George, K. and La Manna, M. (1996) "Mixed duopoly, inefficiency, and public ownership," *Review of Industrial Organization* **11**: 853–860.

Getzen, T.E. (1997) *Health Economics. Fundamentals and Flow of Funds*, New York, John Wiley & Sons.

Glazer, J. and McGuire, T.G. (1993) "Should physicians be permitted to 'balance bill' patients?" *Journal of Health Economics*, **11**: 239–258.

— and McGuire, T.G. (2006) "Optimal Risk Adjustment," in Jones, A. (ed.) *The Elgar Companion to Health Economics*, Cheltenham, Edward Elgar, pp. 279–285.

Gonzalez, P. (2004) "Should physicians' dual practice be limited? an incentive approach," *Health Economics*, **13**: 505–524.

Gonzalez, P. and Macho-Stadler, I. (2011) "A theoretical approach to dual practice regulations in the health sector," Working Papers 11.01, Universidad Pablo de Olavide, Department of Economics.

Greaney, T.L. and Boozang, K.M. (2005) "Mission, margin, and trust in the nonprofit health care enterprise," *Yale Journal of Health Policy, Law, and Ethics*, **5**: 1–87.

Groff, J.E., Lien, D. and Su, J. (2007) "Measuring efficiency gains from hospital mergers," *Research in Healthcare Financial Management*, January 1.

Gronqvist, E. and Lundin, D. (2009) "Incentives for clinical trials," *Economics of Innovation and New Technology* **18**(5): 513–531.

Grossman, M. (1972a) "On the concept of health capital and the demand for health," *Journal of Political Economy*, **80**: 223–255.

— (1972b) *The Demand for Health: A Theoretical and Empirical Investigation*, New York, NBER.

— (2000) "The human capital model," in Culyer, A.J. and Newhouse, J.P. (eds.) *Handbook of Health Economics* (Volume 1A), Amsterdam, North-Holland, pp. 347–408.

— (2004) "The demand for health, 30 years later: a very personal retrospective and prospective reflection," *Journal of Health Economics*, **23**: 629–636.

Guasch, J. (2004) "Granting and renegotiating infra-structure concessions – doing it right,' WBI Development Studies, World Bank Institute, Washington, D.C.

—, Laffont, J.-J., and Straub, S. (2007) "Concessions of infra-structure in Latin America: government-led renegotiations,' *Journal of Applied Econometrics* **22**: 1267–1294.

—, Laffont, J.-J. and Straub, S. (2008) "Renegotiation of concession contracts in Latin America – evidence from the water and transport sectors," *International Journal of Industrial Organization*, **26**: 421–442.

Haas-Wilson, D. and Gaynor, M. (1998) "Increasing consolidation in healthcare markets: what are the antitrust policy implications?," *Health Services Research*, **33**: 1403–1419.

Hallfors, D., Cho, H., Sanchez, V., Khatapoush, S., Kim, H. M. and Bauer, D. (2006) "Efficacy vs. effectiveness trial results of an indicated model substance abuse program: implications for public health," *American Journal of Public Health*, **96**: 2254–2259.

Ham, C. (2005) "Money can't buy you satisfaction," *British Medical Journal*, **330**: 597–599.

Hansmann, H.B. (1980) "The role of the nonprofit enterprise," *Yale Law Review Journal*, **39**: 835–901.

— (1996) *The Ownership of Enterprise*, Cambridge, Belknap Press of Harvard University Press.

Harrison, T.D. (2006) "Hospital mergers: who merges with whom," *Applied Economics*, **38**: 637–647.

— and Lybecker, K.M. (2005) "The effect of the nonprofit motive on hospital competitive behavior," *Contributions to Economic Analysis and Policy*, **4**, Article 3.

Hart, O. and Tirole, J. (1990) "Vertical integration and market foreclosure," *Brookings Papers on Economic Activity. Microeconomics*, 205–286.

Helwege, A. (1996) "Preventive versus curative medicine: a policy exercise for the classroom," *Journal of Economic Education*, **27**: 59–71.

Hennessy, D.A. (2000) "Cournot oligopoly conditions under which any horizontal merger is profitable," *Review of Industrial Organization*, **17**: 277–284.

— (2008) "Prevention and cure efforts both substitutes and complement," *Health Economics*, **17**: 503–511.

Heuer, A., Mejer, M. and Neuhaus, J. (2007) "The national regulation of pharmaceutical markets and the timing of new drug launches in Europe," Kiel Institute for the World Economy, Working Paper No. 437.

Ho, K. (2004) "Selective contracting in the medical care market: explaining the observed equilibria," Harvard University, unpublished paper.

— and Hamilton, B.H. (2000) "Hospital mergers and acquisitions: does market consolidation harm patients?," *Journal of Health Economics*, **19**: 767–791.

Holland, T.P. and Ritvo, R.A. (2008) *Nonprofit Organizations: Principles and Practices*, New York, Columbia University Press.

Holmstrom, B. and Milgrom, P. (1991) "Multitask principal–agent analysis, incentive contracts, asset ownership and job design," *Journal of Law, Economics and Organization*, **7**: 24–52.

Horn, H. and Wolinsky, A. (1988) "Worker substitutability and patterns of unionization," *Economic Journal*, **98**: 484–497.

Horwitz, J.R. and Nichols, A. (2009) "Hospital ownership and medical services: market mix, spillover effects, and nonprofit objectives," *Journal of Health Economics*, **28**: 924–937.

Hotelling, H. (1929) "Stability in competition," *Economic Journal*, **39**: 41–57.

Huckman, R.S. (2006) "Hospital integration and vertical consolidation: an analysis of acquisitions in New York State," *Journal of Health Economics*, **25**: 58–80.

Hurst, J. and Siciliani, L. (2003) "Explaining waiting times variations for elective surgery across OECD countries," OECD Health Working Papers 7.

Hutchens, R. and Pettit, J. (2009) *Deal or No Deal? Outcomes from a Decade of Healthcare M&A*, New York, Booz & Company.

Iizuka, T. (2007) "Experts' agency problems: evidence from the prescription drug market in Japan," *RAND Journal of Economics*, **38**: 844–862.

Inderst, R. and Wey, C. (2003) "Market structure, bargaining, and technological choice," *RAND Journal of Economics*, **34**: 1–19.

Intriligator, M.D. (1971) *Mathematical Optimization and Economic Theory*, Englewood Cliffs, N.J., Prentice-Hall.

Iversen, T. and Siciliani, L (2011) "Non-price rationing and waiting times," in Glied, S. and Smith, P. (eds), *The Oxford Handbook of Health Economics*, Oxford University Press, pp. 649–670.

Jack, W. (1999) *Principles of Health Economics for Developing Countries*, Washington D.C., The World Bank.

James, P. (2002) "Is the medical arms race still present in today's managed care environment?," NYU working paper EC-02-09.

Jamison, M.A. and Berg, S.V. (2008) *Annotated Reading List for a Body of Knowledge on Infrastructure Regulation*, World Bank. Available at http://www.regulationbodyofknowledge.org/documents/bok/bok_narrative.pdf

Jansson, E. (1999) "Libre competencia frente a regulación en la distribución minorista de medicamentos," *Revista de Economía Aplicada*, **19**: 85–112.

Jegers, M., Kesteloot, K., De Graeve, D. and W. Gilles (2002) "A typology for provider payment systems in health care," *Health Policy*, **60**: 255–273.

Jehle, G.A. and Reny, P.J. (2001) *Advanced Microeconomic Theory*, Boston, Mass., Addison-Wesley.

Jelovac, I. (2002) "On the relationship between the negotiated prices of pharmaceuticals and the patients' co-payment," CREPP WP 2002/04, Universit de Lige.

Jofre-Bonet, M. (2000) "Health care: private and/or public provision," *European Journal of Political Economy*, **16**: 469–489.

Joskow, P.L. (2007) "Regulation of natural monopolies," in Polinsky, A.M. and Shavell, S. (eds.) *Handbook of Law and Economics*, Volume 2, Amsterdam, North-Holland, Chapter 16.

— and N.K. Rose, N.K. (1989) "The effects of economic regulation," in Schmalensee, R. and Willig, R.D. (eds.) *Handbook of Industrial Economics*, Volume 2, Amsterdam, North-Holland, Chapter 25.

Kamien, M. and Zang, I. (1990) "The limits of monopolization through acquisition," *Quarterly Journal of Economics*, **105**: 465–499.

— and Zang, I. (1991) "Competitively cost advantageous mergers and monopolization," *Games and Economic Behavior*, **3**: 323–338.

— and Zang, I. (1993) "Monopolization by sequential acquisition," *Journal of Law, Economics & Organization*, **9**: 205–229.

Karlsson, M. (2007) "Quality incentives for GPs in a regulated market," *Journal of Health Economics*, **26**(4): 699–720.

Karrer-Rueedi, E. (1997) "Adaptation to change: vertical and horizontal integration in the drug industry," *European Management Journal*, **15**: 461–469.

Keiding, H. (*c.* 2000) *Lecture notes on health economics*, Unpublished paper, available at http://www.econ.ku.dk/lpo/sund.htm

Kennedy, S. (2004) "The relationship between education and health in Australia and Canada," Social and Economic Dimensions of an Aging Population Research Papers, McMaster University.

Kong, Y. (2009) "Competition between brand-name and generics – analysis on pricing of brand-name pharmaceutical," *Health Economics*, **18**(5): 591–606.

Koopmans, T.C. (1957) *Three Essays on the State of Economic Science*, New York, McGraw-Hill.

Kreps, D. M. (1990) *A Course in Microeconomic Theory*, New York, Harvester Wheatsheaf.

Krishnan, R.A. and Krishnan, H. (2003) "Effects of hospital mergers and acquisitions on prices," *Journal of Business Research*, **56**: 647–656.

Kristin Madison, J.D. (2007) "Hospital mergers in an era of quality improvement," *Houston Journal of Health Law & Policy*, **7**: 265–304.

Kuhn, M. and Siciliani, L. (2008) "Upcoding and optimal auditing in health care (or the economics of DRG creep)," CEPR Discussion Papers 6689.

Kverndokk, S. (2000) "Why do people demand health," University of Oslo, HERO Working Paper 2000:5.

Kwoka, J. and Pollit, M. (2010) "Do mergers improve efficiency? Evidence from restructuring the US electric power sector," *International Journal of Industrial Organization*, **28**: 645–656.

Laffont, J.J. and Tirole, J. (1993) *A Theory of Incentives in Procurement and Regulation*, Cambridge, Mass., MIT Press.

Lakdawalla, D. and Philipson, T. (2006) "The nonprofit sector and industry performance," *Journal of Public Economics*, **90**: 1681–1698.

—, and W. Yin (2009) "Insurer bargaining and negotiated drug prices in Medicare Part D," NBER Working Paper No. 15330, September.

Lancry, P.-J. and Sandier, S. (1999) "Twenty years of cures for the French health care system," in Mossialos, E. and Le Grand, J. (eds.) *Health Care and Cost Containment in the European Union*, Ashgate, pp. 443–478.

Leibenluft, R.F. (2007) "Antitrust enforcement and hospital mergers: a closer look," Bureau of Competition, Federal Trade Commission. Presented at the "First Friday Forum" of the Alliance for Health Grand Rapids, Michigan.

Leibenstein, H. (1969) "Organizational and frictional equilibria, X-efficiency and the role of innovation," *Quarterly Journal of Economics*, **83**: 600–623.

— (1973) "Competition and X-efficiency," *Journal of Political Economy*, **81**: 765–777.

Leibowitz, A.A. (2004) "The demand for health and health concerns after 30 years," *Journal of Health Economics*, **23**: 663–671.

Ma, C.A. (1994) "Health care payment systems: cost and quality incentives," *Journal of Economics and Management Strategy*, **3**(1): 93–112.

Ma, C.A. (1998) "Health care payment systems: cost and quality incentives – reply," *Journal of Economics and Management Strategy*, **3**(1): 139–142.

Ma, Ch-T. and Burguess, Jr., J.F. (1993) "Quality competition, welfare, and regulation," *Journal of Economics*, **58**: 153–173.

Macho-Stadler, I. and Pérez-Castrillo, D. (2001) *An Introduction to the Economics of Information. Incentives and contracts*, Oxford, Oxford University Press.

Malani, A. and David, G. (2008) "Does nonprofit status signal quality?," *Journal of Legal Studies*, **37**: 551–576.

Malcomson, J. (2004) "Health Service Gatekeepers," *RAND Journal of Economics*, **35**(2): 401–421.

Martimort, D. and Pouyet, J. (2008) "To build or not to build: normative and positive theories of public – private partnerships," *International Journal of Industrial Organization*, **26**(2): 393–411.

Martin, S. (2002) *Advanced Industrial Organization*, Oxford, Blackwell.

Martin, S. and Smith, P.C. (1999) "Rationing by waiting lists: an empirical investigation," *Journal of Public Economics*, **71**, 141–164.

Martinez-Giralt, X. and Ponsatí, C. (1995) "Bargaining at variable rhythms," *Revista Española de Economía*, **12**: 133–139.

Mas-Colell, A., Whinston, M.D. and Green, J. (1995) *Microeconomic Theory*, New York, Oxford University Press.

Matsumura, T. (2003) "Endogenous role in mixed markets: a two-production-period model," *Southern Economic Journal*, **70**: 403–413.

McCarthy, T. and Thomas, S. (2003) "Geographic market issues in hospital mergers," in American Bar Association (ed.) *Health Care Mergers and Acquisitions Handbook*, American Bar Association. Section of Antitrust Law, Chicago, Chapter 3.

McGuire, A. (2000) "Physician agency," in Culyer, A.J. and Newhouse, J.P. (eds.) *Handbook of Health Economics*, Amsterdam, North-Holland, Chapter 9: 461–536.

McGuire, A., Henderson, J. and Mooney, G. (1999) *The Economics of Health Care*, London, Routledge.

McKie, J.W. (1985) "Market definition and the SIC approach," in Fisher, F. (ed.) *Antitrust and Regulation*, Boston, Mass., MIT Press, pp. 85–100.

Maude-Griffin, R., Feldman, R. and Wholey, D. (2001) "A Nash bargaining model of the HMO premium cycle," unpublished paper.

Melichar, L. (2009) "The effect of reimbursement on medical decision making: do physicians alter treatment in response to a managed care incentive?," *Journal of Health Economics*, **28**: 902–907.

Melnick, G.A., Zwanziger, J., Bamezai, A. and Pattison, R. (1992) "The effects of market structure and bargaining position on hospital prices," *Journal of Health Economics*, **11**: 217–233.

Milliou, C., Petrakis, E. and Vettas, N. (2003) "Endogenous contracts under bargaining in competing vertical chains," CEPR Discussion Paper 3976.

Morris, S., Devlin, N. and Parkin, D. (2007) *Economic Analysis in Health Care*, Chichester, West Sussex, John Wiley & Sons.

Morrisey, L. and Ohsfeldt, R.L. (2004) "Do 'any willing provider' and 'freedom to choose' laws affect HMO market share?," *Inquiry*, **40**: 362–374.

Mossialos, E. and Le Grand, J. (1999) "Cost containment in the EU: an overview," in Mossialos, E. and Le Grand, J. (eds.) *Health care and cost containment in the European Union*, Ashgate, pp. 1–12.

Motta, M. (2004) *Competition Policy: Theory and Practice*, Cambridge, Cambridge University Press.

Mueller, D.C. (1989) "Mergers: Causes, effects and policies," *International Journal of Industrial Organization*, **7**: 1–10.

Mujumdar, D.S. and Pal, D. (1998) "Effects of indirect taxation in a mixed oligopoly," *Economics Letters*, **58**: 199–204.

Musgrave, R.A. (1959) *The Theory of Public Finance*, New York, McGraw-Hill.

Muthoo, A. (2000) "A non-technical introduction to bargaining theory," *World Economics*, **1**: 145–166.

Muurinen, J.M. (1982) "Demand for health: a generalized Grossman model," *Journal of Health Economics*, **1**: 5–28.

Narciso, S. (2004) Essays on Policies for the Health Care Sector: The Relationship between Agents and their Incentives, thesis, Universidade Nova de Lisboa.

Nash, J. (1950) "The bargaining problem," *Econometrica*, **18**: 155–162.

— (1953) "Two-person cooperative games," *Econometrica*, **21**: 128–140.

Needleman, J. (2001) "The role of nonprofits in health care," *Journal of Health Politics, Policy and Law*, **26**: 1113–1130.

Nelson, P. (1970) "Information and consumer behavior," *Journal of Political Economy*, **78**(2): 311–329.

Nett, L. (1993) "Mixed oligopoly with homogeneous goods," *Annals of Public and Cooperative Economics*, **64**: 367–393.

Newhouse, J.P. (1970) "Toward a theory of nonprofit institutions: an economic model of a hospital," *American Economic Review*, **60**: 64–74.

Nuscheler, R. (2003) "Physician reimbursement, time consistency, and the quality of care," *Journal of Institutional and Theoretical Economics*, **159**: 302–322.

OBIG Report (2006) "Surveying, assessing and analyzing the pharmaceutical sector in the 25 EU member states," report commissioned by the DG Competition Commission, Office for Official Publications.

OECD (2003) *The Non-profit Sector in a Changing Economy*, Paris, OECD.

— (2009) *Health at a Glance 2009*, Paris, OECD. Available at www.oecd-ilibrary.org/social-issues-migration-health/health-at-a-glance-2009_health_glance-2009-en

— (2010) *Health Data 2010*, Paris, OECD. Available at www.ecosante.org/oecd.htm

Ohsfeldt, R.L., Morrisey, M.A., Nelson, L. and Johnson, V. (1998) "The spread of state any willing provider laws," *Health Services Research*, **33**: 1537–1562.

Olivella, P. and Vera-Hernandez, M. (2006) "Testing for adverse selection into private medical insurance," IFS Working Papers W06/02, Institute for Fiscal Studies.

Ordover, J.A., Saloner, G. and Salop, S.C. (1990) "Equilibrium vertical foreclosure," *American Economic Review*, **80**: 127–142.

Ortún Rubio, V. (1990) *La Economía en Sanidad y Medicina: Instrumentos y Limitaciones*, Barcelona, La Llar del Llibre.

Osborne, M.J. and Rubinstein, A. (1990) *Bargaining and Markets*, San Diego, Academic Press.

Oudot, J.-M. (2005) "Risk-allocation: theoretical and empirical evidences. Application to Public–Private Partnerships in the defence sector," mimeo.

Pal, D. (1998) "Endogenous timing in a mixed oligopoly," *Economics Letters*, **61**: 181–185.

Paolucci, F., Schut, E., Beck, K., Gress, S., Van De Voorde, C. and Zmora, I. (2007) "Supplementary health insurance as a tool for risk-selection in mandatory basic health insurance markets," *Health Economics, Policy and Law*, **2**: 173–192.

Pauly, M.V. (1987) "Nonprofit hospitals in medical markets," *American Economic Review*, **77**: 257–282.

— (1998) "Managed care, market power and monopsony," *Health Services Research*, **33**: 1439–1440.

— and Redisch, M. (1973) "The not-for-profit hospital as a physicians' cooperative," *American Economic Review*, **63**: 87–99.

— and Satterthwaite, M.A. (1981) "The pricing of primary care physicians' services: a test of the role of consumer information," *Bell Journal of Economics*, **12**: 488–506.

Pecorino, P. (2002) "Should the US allow prescription drug reimports from Canada?," *Journal of Health Economics*, **21**: 699–708.

Pepall, L., Richards, D. J., and Norman, G. (2005) *Industrial Organization: Contemporary Theory and Practice*. South-Western, Mason, OH.

Petrakis, E. and Vlassis, M. (2000) "Endogenous scope of bargaining in a union–oligopoly model: when will firms and unions bargain over employment," *Labour Economics*, **7**: 261–281.

Phelps, Ch.E. (1973) *Demand for Health Insurance: A Theoretical and Empirical Investigation*, Santa Monica, RAND Corporation.

— (2009) *Health Economics*, New York, Addison-Wesley.

Phlips, L. and Thisse, J.F. (1982) "Spatial competition and the theory of differentiated markets: an introduction," *The Journal of Industrial Economics*, **31**: 1–9.

Pindyck, R.S. (1985) "The measurement of monopoly power in dynamic markets," *Journal of Law and Economics*, **28**: 193–222.

Place, M.D. (2007) "The importance of not for profit health care," paper presented at the 13th Annual Conference on Catholic Sponsorship, Center for Catholic Health Care and Sponsorship, Loyola University, Chicago.

Pratt, J. W. (1964) "Risk aversion in the small and in the large," *Econometrica*, **32**: 122–136.

Propper, C., Croxson, B. and Shearer, A. (2002) "Waiting times for hospital admissions: the impact of GP fundholding," *Journal of Health Economics*, **21**: 227–252.

Propper, C., Sutton, M., Whitnall, C. and Windmeijer, F. (2008) "Did targets and terror reduce waiting times in England for hospital care?' *The B.E. Journal of Economic Analysis & Policy*, **8**(2): 5.

Quam, L. and Smith, R. (2005) "What can the UK and US systems learn from each other," *British Medical Journal*, **330**: 530–533.

Regan, T. (2008). "Generic entry, price competition, and market segmentation in the prescription drug market," *International Journal of Industrial Organization*, **26**: 930–948.

Reinhardt, U.E. (1985) "The theory of physician-induced demand – reflections after a decade," *Journal of Health Economics*, **4**: 187–193.

Rey, P. and Tirole, J. (2007) "A primer on foreclosure," in Armstrong, M. and Porter, R. (eds.) *Handbook of Industrial Organization*, Volume 3, Amsterdam, Elsevier, Chapter 33: 2145–2220.

Ringel, J.S., Hosek, S. D., Vollaard, B. A. and Mahnovski, S. (2005) *The Elasticity of Demand for Health Care. A Review of the Literature and its Application to the Military Health System*, RAND Corporation, Santa Monica, CA.

Robinson, J.C. and Luft, H.S. (1985) "The impact of hospital market structure on patient volume, average length of stay, and the cost of care," *Journal of Health Economics*, **4**(4): 333–355.

— and Luft, H.S. (1987) "Competition and the cost of hospital care, 1972–1985," *Journal of the American Medical Association*, **257**(23): 3241–3245.

Roemer, M.I. (1961) "Bed supply and hospital utilization: a national experiment," *Hospitals*, J.A.H.A., **35**: 988–993.

Rose-Ackerman, S. (1996) "Altruism, nonprofits, and economic theory," *Journal of Economic Literature*, **34**: 701–728.

Rothschild, M. and Stiglitz, J.E. (1976) "Equilibrium in competitive insurance markets: an essay on the economics of imperfect information," *Quarterly Journal of Economics*, **90**: 629–649.

Royalty, A.B. and Solomon, N. (1999) "Health plan choice: price elasticities in a managed competition setting," *Journal of Human Resources*, **34**(1): 41.

Rubinstein, A. (1982) "Perfect equilibrium in a bargaining model," *Econometrica*, **50**: 97–109.

Sackett, D.L. and Torrance, G.W. (1982) "The utility of different health states as perceived by the general public," *Journal of Chronic Disease*, **31**: 697–704.

Salant, S., Switzer, S. and Reynolds, R. (1983) "Loses from horizontal merger: the effects of an exogenous change in industry structure on Cournot-Nash equilibrium," *The Quarterly Journal of Economics*, **98**: 186–199.

Salop, S.C. (1979) "Monopolistic competition with outside goods," *Bell Journal of Economics*, **10**: 141–156.

— (1987) "Symposium on mergers and antitrust," *Journal of Economic Perspectives*, **1**: 3–12.

— and Scheffman, D.T. (1987) "Cost-raising strategies," *Journal of Industrial Economics*, **36**: 19–34.

Satterthwaite, M.A. (1979) "Consumer information, equilibrium industry price, and the number of sellers," *Bell Journal of Economics*, **10**: 483–502.

Schelling, T.C. (1960) *The Strategy of Conflict*, Cambridge, Mass., Harvard University Press.

Schleifer, A. (1985) "A theory of yardstick competition," *RAND Journal of Economics*, **16**(3): 319–327.

Schlesinger, M. and Gray, B.H. (2006a) "Nonprofit organizations and health care: some paradoxes of persistent scrutiny," in Powell, W.W. and Steinberg, R. (eds.) *The Nonprofit Sector: A Research Handbook*, New Haven CT, Yale University Press, Chapter 16, pp. 378–414.

— and Gray, B.H. (2006b) 'How nonprofits matter in American medicine, and what to do about it," *Health Affairs*, **25**: 287–303.

Schneider, U., Volker, U. and Wille, E. (2008) "Risk adjustment systems in health insurance markets in the US, Germany, Netherlands and Switzerland," CESifo DICE Report 3/2008.

Shain, M. and Roemer, M.I. (1959) "Hospital costs relate to the supply of beds," *Modern Hospital*, **4**: 71–73.

Shaked, A. and Sutton, J. (1982) "Relaxing price competition through product differentiation," *Review of Economic Studies*, **49**: 3–14.

— and Sutton, J. (1983) "Natural oligopolies," *Econometrica*, **51**: 1469–1484.

— and Sutton, J. (1984) "Natural oligopolies and international trade," in Kierzkowski, H. (ed.) *Monopolistic Competition and International Trade*, Oxford, Oxford University Press, pp. 34–50.

Sharma, R.L. (1998) "Health care payment systems: cost and quality incentives – comment," *Journal of Economics and Management Strategy*, **7**(1): 127–137.

Shen, Y. and Ellis, R.P. (2002) "How profitable is risk selection? A comparison of four risk adjustment models," *Health Economics*, **11**: 165–174.

Siciliani, L. and Stanciole, A. (2008) "Bargaining and the provision of health services," Discussion Paper 08/28, Department of Economics, University of York.

Sieg, H. (2000) "Estimating a bargaining model with asymmetric information: evidence from medical malpractice disputes," *Journal of Political Economy*, **108**: 1006–1021.

Simon, C.J. (1997) "Economic implications of 'any willing provider' legislation," unpublished working paper, University of Illinois-Chicago.

Singh, A. and Vives, X. (1984) "Price and quantity competition in a differentiated duopoly," *RAND Journal of Economics*," **15**: 546–554.

Sloan, F.A. (1998) "Commercialism in nonprofit hospitals," in Weisbrod, B.A. (ed.) *To Profit or Not to Profit: The Commercial Transformation of the Nonprofit Sector*, New York, Cambridge University Press, pp. 151–168.

— (2000) "Not-for-profit ownership and hospital behavior," in Culyer, A.J. and Newhouse, J.P. (eds.) *Handbook of Health Economics*, Amsterdam, North-Holland, Chapter 21, pp. 1141–1174.

— and Hall, M.A. (2002) "Market failures and the evolution of state regulation on managed care," *Law and Contemporary Problems*, **65**: 169–206.

— Picone, G.A., Taylor Jr., D.H. and Choue, S.-Y. (2001) "Hospital ownership and cost and quality of care: is there a dimes worth of difference?," *Journal of Health Economics*, **20**: 1–21.

— and Steinwald, B. (1980) *Insurance, Regulation, and Hospital Costs*, Lexington (MA), Lexington Books.

Sorensen, A.T. (2003) "Insurer–hospital bargaining: negotiated discounts in post-deregulation Connecticut," *The Journal of Industrial Economics*, **51**: 469–490.

Spang, H.R., Bazzoli, G.J. and Arnould, R.J. (2001) "Hospital mergers and savings for consumers: exploring new evidence comparing merging hospitals with their nonmerging market rivals can yield a more accurate assessment of mergers effects," *Health Affairs*, **20**: 150–158.

Spence, M. (1973) "Job market signaling," *Quarterly Journal of Economics*, **87**: 355–374.

— (1977) "Entry, capacity, investment, and oligopolistic pricing," *Bell Journal of Economics*, **8**: 534–544.

— (1979) "Investment strategy and growth in a new market," *Bell Journal of Economics*, **10**: 1–19.

Starfield, B. (2005) "Why is the grass greener?," *British Medical Journal*, **330**: 727–729.

Staten, M., Umbeck, J. and Dunkelberg, W. (1988) "Market share/market power revisited: a new test for an old theory," *Journal of Health Economics*, **7**: 73–83.

Stigler, G.J. (1950) "Monopoly and oligopoly by merger," *American Economic Review*, **40**: 23–34.

— (1971) "The theory of economic regulation," *Bell Journal of Economics*, **2**(1): 3–21.

Stole, L.A. and Zwiebel, J. (1996a) "Intrafirm bargaining under nonbinding contracts," *Review of Economic Studies*, **63**: 375–410.

— and Zwiebel, J. (1996b) "Organizational design and technology choice under intra-firm bargaining," *American Economic Review*, **86**: 195–222.

Straub, T. (2007) *Reasons for Frequent Failure in Mergers and Acquisitions. A Comprehensive Analysis*, Wiesbaden, DUV Deutscher Universitäts-Verlag, GWV Fachverlage GmbH.

Sutton, J. (1986) "Non-cooperative bargaining theory: an introduction," *Review of Economic Studies*, **53**: 709–724.

Thurner, P.W., and Kotzian, P. (2001) "Comparative health care systems: outline for an empirical application of new institutional economics approaches." Paper delivered to the European Consortium for Political Research meeting April 2001, Grenoble. Available at: http://www.mzes.uni-mannheim.de/publications/papers/comparativehcs.pdf

Torrance, G.W. (1986) "Measurement of health state utilities for economic appraisal. A review," *Journal of Health Economics*, **5**: 1–30.

Town, R. and Vistnes, G. (2001) "Hospital competition in HMO networks," *Journal of Health Economics*, **20**: 733–53.

—, Wholey, D., Feldman, R. and Burns, L.R. (2006) "The welfare consequences of hospital mergers," NBER Working Paper No. 12244.

Van de ven, Wynand P.M.M., and Ellis, R.P. (2000) "Risk adjustment in competitive health plan markets," in Culyer, A.J. and Newhouse, J.P. (eds.) *Handbook of Health Economics*, Elsevier, Amsterdam, Volume 1, Chapter 14: 755–845.

Vickers, J. and Waterson, M. (1991) "Vertical relationships: an introduction," *The Journal of Industrial Economics*, **39**: 445–450.

Vita, M.G. (2001) "Regulatory restrictions on selective contracting: an empirical analysis of 'any willing provider' regulations," *Journal of Health Economics*, **20**: 951–966.

Vogt, W.B. (2009) "Hospital market consolidation: trends and consequences," *Expert Voices*, November, NIHCM Foundation.

Wagstaff, A. (1986a) "The demand for health: a simplified Grossman model," *Bulletin of Economic Research*, **38**: 93–95.

—— (1986b) "The demand for health: some new empirical evidence, *Journal of Health Economics*, **5**: 195–233.

Waldman, D.E. and Jensen, E.J. (2007) *Industrial Organization. Theory and Practice*, Boston, Addison-Wesley.

Waterson, M. (1993) "Retail pharmacy in Melbourne: actual and optimal densities," *The Journal of Industrial Economics*, **11**(4): 403–419.

Weinstein, M.C. and Stason, W.B. (1977) "Foundations of cost-effectiveness analysis for health and medical practices," *New England Journal of Medicine*, **296**: 716–721.

Weisbrod, B.A. (1994) *The Nonprofit Economy*, Cambridge, Mass., Harvard University Press.

Werden, G.J. (1991) "Horizontal mergers: comment," *American Economic Review*, **81**, 1002–1006.

White, M.D. (1996) "Mixed oligopoly, privatization and subsidization," *Economics Letters*, **53**: 189–195.

Wicks, E.K., Meyer, J.A. and Carlyn, M. (1998) "Assessing the early impact of hospital mergers. An analysis of the St. Louis and Philadelphia markets," Economic and Social Research Institute.

Williamson, O.E. (1968) "Economies as an antitrust defense: The welfare tradeoffs," *American Economic Review*, **58**: 18–36.

Wolf, A.K. (2009) "The new EC guidelines on non-horizontal mergers," *The Columbia Journal of European Law Online*, **15**: 55–58.

Wolinsky, A. (1993) "Competition in a market for informed experts' services," *RAND Journal of Economics*, **24**: 380–398.

—— (2000) "A theory of the firm with non-binding employment contracts," *Econometrica*, **68**: 875–910.

Wright, D.J. (2004) "The drug bargaining game: pharmaceutical regulation in Australia," *Journal of Health Economics*, **23**: 785–813.

Wu, V.Y. (2009) "Managed care's price bargaining with hospitals," *Journal of Health Economics*, **28**: 350–360.

Zeckhauser, R.J. and Shepard, D.S. (1976) "Where now for saving lives?," *Law and Contemporary Problems*, **40**: 5–45.

Zhu, S. (2006) "Converge? Diverge? A comparison of horizontal merger laws in the United States and European Union," *World Competition*, **29**: 635–651.

Zimmerman, H. (2009) "Review of the literature on hospital mergers: impact of hospital mergers on access to affordable health care, access to care for underserved populations, balanced health care system, and market share." Report prepared for the RI Department of Health.

Zweifel, P. and Breyer, F. (1997) *Health Economics*, Oxford, Oxford University Press.

—— and Manning, W.G. (2000) "Moral hazard and consumer incentives in health care," in Culyer, A.J. and J.P. Newhouse (eds.) *Handbook of Health Economics*, Amsterdam, North-Holland, Chapter 8: pp. 409–459.

——, Breyer, F. and Kifmann, M. (2009) *Health Economics*, Heidelberg, Springer-Verlag.

Index